impressum

Träger des internationalen literaturfestivals berlin
Peter-Weiss-Stiftung für Kunst und Politik e.V.

Herausgeber
Ulrich Schreiber
Jana Thiele

Redaktion
Jana Thiele

Biographien
Dagmar Seidel und siehe Anhang

Fotorechte
Virginia Maiorino, Christoph Janke

Lektorat
Hanno Depner
Beatrice Fassbender
Miriam Gabriela Möllers

Übersetzung der Biographien ins Englische
Chloe Aridjis
Chantal Benjamin
Heddi Feilhauer
Kathleen Noreisch

Korrektorat
Bettina Baer
Tom Bantock
Simon Garnett
Reinald Gußmann

Gestaltung
Veruschka Goetz mit Caroline Götzger
veruschka götz typographers berlin

Satz
Caroline Götzger

Titelgestaltung
Veruschka Goetz
Titelzitat unter Verwendung des 101. Sonetts
von William Shakespeare

Verlag
Vorwerk 8
www.vorwerk8.de

Druck
Druckhaus Köthen

Papier
100g/m² Alster

Bindung
Leipziger Großbuchbinderei

ISBN 3-930916-67-3

inhaltsverzeichnis
content

literaturen der welt | 010

kaleidoskop | 076

internationale kinder- und jugendliteratur | 146

vorwort
Ulrich Schreiber

Liebe Leserinnen und Leser,

mit dem Ihnen vorliegenden Katalog möchten wir die eingeladenen Autorinnen und Autoren des 4. internationalen literaturfestivals berlin vorstellen. Dieser Katalog, der zeitgleich mit dem vierten Band der Berliner Anthologie erscheint, zeichnet sich durch ausführliche Biographien aus, er enthält Bibliographien und Fotos der Autoren. Das Motto des diesjährigen Katalogs ist »Make answer, Muse!«: inspiriert von Shakespeares Sonett 101, in dem er die ungnädige Muse anruft. Individuelle Antworten waren gefragt und sind in Fülle und Vielfalt eingetroffen. Die Autoren schrieben Texte, Dialogszenen und Gedichte, skizzierten, fotografierten und gaben Auskunft über ihre ganz persönlichen Lockmittel für verschüchterte und zornige Musen. So ist nicht nur ein aktuelles Nachschlagewerk der Weltliteratur entstanden, das viele Autoren erstmals in Deutschland vorstellt, sondern in aufwendiger Gestaltung auch eine Dokumentation, wie dem gefürchteten writer's bloc zu begegnen ist.

Programmarchitektur und Vielfalt des Festivals knüpfen an die Gestaltung der Vorjahre an. Elf international hochangesehene Autoren und Persönlichkeiten des literarischen Lebens konnten wiederum als Juroren für das Programm »Literaturen der Welt« gewonnen werden. Neben den drei neuen Juroren Mario Vargas Llosa (Peru), Iris Radisch (Deutschland) und Philip Jeyaretnam (Singapur) sind dies Alberto Manguel (Kanada/Frankreich), Abdelwahab Meddeb (Tunesien/Frankreich), Martin Mooij (Niederlande), Ilma Rakusa (Schweiz), Veronique Tadjo (Elfenbeinküste/Südafrika), Shashi Tharoor (Indien/USA), Eliot Weinberger (USA) und Yvonne Vera (Simbabwe).

Der »Berliner Blick« auf die Literaturen des In- und Auslandes wird im Programm »Kaleidoskop« aufscheinen. Auf das Programm »Internationale Kinder- und Jugendliteratur« dürfen sich wiederum alle jüngeren Leser freuen. In der Sparte »Reflections«, dem Programm für den literarischen und politischen Diskurs, werden Gespräche über Literaturen in nahen und fernen Ländern stattfinden und über die Zukunft der UNO, die Grenzen Europas und das Feuilleton im arabischen Raum diskutiert. Das Rahmenprogramm bringt, schon obligatorisch, einen Poetry-Slam, zudem HipHop, Lesungen in Gefängnissen und Veranstaltungen mit polnischen und italienischen Autoren, die in Berlin wohnhaft sind. Auch die Programme »Scritture Giovani«, das Programm der Gäste des DAAD in Berlin, das Filmprogramm sowie die Sparte »Erinnerung, sprich« werden wie in den Vorjahren zum Esprit des Festivals beitragen.

Wir haben vielen Institutionen zu danken – zuallererst dem Hauptstadtkulturfonds, der uns auch in den beiden Folgejahren unterstützen wird und so das Festival überhaupt möglich machte. Wir danken dem Auswärtigen Amt, der Friedrich-Ebert-Stiftung, der Robert-Bosch-Stiftung und der Heinrich-Böll-Stiftung sowie den vielen Sponsoren – allen voran DER SPIEGEL sowie den Firmen MIM, Škoda, argonauten, der Dresdner Bank sowie illy café. Wiederum gelang es, Botschaften, ausländische Kulturinstitute und Hotels zu gewinnen, denen wir herzlich für die Unterstützung bei den Flügen und Übernachtungen danken. Markus Hayn und Tobias Willemeit danken wir für die Art Direction, Veruschka Götz für die Gestaltung dieses Bandes, Matthias Lilienthal für die freundschaftliche Kooperation mit dem Theater Hebbel am Ufer.

Besonders möchte ich mich bei Joachim Sartorius bedanken. Er hat sich auch im Vorfeld der positiven Entscheidung des Bundes deutlich vernehmbar für eine weitere Finanzierung des Festivals unter dem Dach der Berliner Festspiele ausgesprochen – und dies mit uns durchsetzen können. Zudem danken wir Hermann Beil, Frank Berberich und Arnulf Conradi für ihre andauernde Treue zu unserer noch jungen Institution. Nicht auszudenken, wenn sie gerade in den kritischsten Phasen der letzten Jahre nicht ihr Wort für uns eingelegt hätten!

Ich wünsche allen Besuchern des Festivals bei der Erkundung neuer Seelen- und Naturlandschaften, beim Studieren ungewohnter Haltungen und Erfahren unerhörter Geschichten wunderbare Stunden und Tage.

Ulrich Schreiber

foreword
Ulrich Schreiber

Dear Readers,

We would like to present the invited writers of the fourth international literature festival berlin with this catalogue which appears at the same time as the fourth volume of the Berlin Anthology and features detailed biographies as well as bibliographies and photographs of our authors. The motto of this year's catalogue is »Make answer, Muse!«, inspired by Shakespeare's Sonnet 101, in which he appeals to the ungracious muse. Individual replies were requested, and these arrived in abundance and diversity. The authors wrote texts, scenes in dialogue and poems, they sketched and photographed, and thus offered information about their highly personal bait for trapping their intimidated or wrathful muses. A current reference book of world literature has resulted, introducing many writers for the first time in Germany and also providing a documentation, in elaborate design, of how the dreaded writer's bloc is to be confronted.

The programme's structure and the diversity of the festival follow the design of former years. Eleven prestigious writers and personalities from literary life become in turn jurors for the Literatures of the World programme. In addition to three new jurors, Mario Vargas Llosa (Peru), Iris Radisch (Germany) and Philip Jeyaretnam (Singapore), the jury consists of Alberto Manguel (Canada/France), Abdelwahab Meddeb (Tunisia/France), Martin Mooij (Netherlands), Ilma Rakusa (Switzerland), Veronique Tadjo (Ivory Coast/South Africa), Shashi Tharoor (India/USA), Eliot Weinberger (USA) and Yvonne Vera (Zimbabwe).

The »Berlin View« on national and international literatures will appear in the programme »Kaleidoscope«. Young readers meanwhile are catered for with the programme »International Children and Youth Literature«. In the category »Reflections«, the programme for literary and political discourse, talks on the literature of lands far and near will be held, including the future of the United Nations, the borders of Europe, and the cultural section within the Arab world will be discussed. The Fringe Programme presents a Poetry Slam, HipHop, readings in prisons and events with Polish and Italian authors who reside in Berlin. The programmes »Scritture Giovani«, the programme of DAAD guests in Berlin, the Film Programme as well as the category »Speak, Memory« will as in previous years contribute to the spirit of the festival.

We have many institutions to thank – first and foremost the capital's cultural funding, which will support us over the next two years as well, and have made the festival possible. We thank the Federal Foreign Office, the Friedrich-Ebert-Stiftung, the Robert-Bosch-Stiftung and the Heinrich-Böll-Stiftung as well as many sponsors – at the fore, DER SPIEGEL as well as the companies MIM, Škoda, argonauten, Dresdner Bank, illy café and Elisabetta Foradori for her excellent wines. We have again received support from embassies, foreign cultural institutes and hotels, whom we sincerely thank for their assistance with flights and accommodation. We thank Markus Hayn and Tobias Willemeit for the art direction, Veruschka Götz for the layout of this volume, Matthias Lilienthal for the friendly cooperation with the Theater Hebbel am Ufer.

I would especially like to thank Joachim Sartorius. He was instrumental in bringing about the federal government's welcome decision to continue funding the festival under the auspices of the Berliner Festspiele. Furthermore, we thank Hermann Beil, Frank Berberich and Arnulf Conradi for their enduring faith in our institution. Imagine if they had not been there for us during the most critical phases of the past few years!

I would like to wish all the visitors to our festival wonderful days and hours as they explore new spiritual and natural landscapes, experience unusual approaches and undreamed of tales.

Ulrich Schreiber

literaturen der welt

philip jeyaretnam | singapur
k. s. maniam
alfian bin sa'at
duong thu huong

alberto manguel | kanada | frankreich
javier cercas
edgardo cozarinsky
hassan dawud

abdelwahab meddeb | tunesien | frankreich
alberto mussa
nabil naoum
bernard noël

martin mooij | niederlande
bernlef
adrian mitchell
hagar peeters

iris radisch | deutschland
david albahari
juri andruchowytsch
susanne riedel

ilma rakusa | schweiz
fuad rifka
jelena schwarz
jean-philippe toussaint

véronique tadjo | elfenbeinküste | südafrika
tanella boni
hamidou dia
zakes mda

shashi tharoor | indien
joseph olshan
alka saraogi
m. t. vasudevan nair

mario vargas llosa | peru
andrés barba
alonso cueto
álvaro enrigue

yvonne vera | simbabwe
chris abani
aritha van herk
leone ross

eliot weinberger | usa
taha muhammad ali
semezdin mehmedinović
aharon shabtai

chris abani
david albahari
taha muhammad ali
juri andruchowytsch
andrés barba
bernlef
tanella boni
javier cercas
edgardo cozarinsky
alonso cueto
hassan dawud
hamidou dia
duong thu huong
álvaro enrigue
aritha van herk
k. s. maniam
zakes mda
semezdin mehmedinović
adrian mitchell
alberto mussa
nabil naoum
bernard noël
joseph olshan
hagar peeters
susanne riedel
fuad rifka
alfian bin sa'at
alka saraogi
jelena schwarz
aharon shabtai
jean-philippe toussaint
m. t. vasudevan nair

chris abani

biography

Chris Abani was born in Afikpo, Nigeria. He published his first novel »Masters of the Board« (1985) at sixteen, for which he suffered severe political persecution. His other novel is »GraceLand« (2004), a coming of age story about a young Nigerian Elvis impersonator and his struggle against overwhelming odds. His poetry collections include »Kalakuta Republic« (2000), »Daphne's Lot« (2003) and »Dog Woman« (2004). He is the recipient of the 2001 PEN USA West Freedom-to-Write Award, the 2001 Prince Claus Award and a 2003 Lannan Literary Fellowship. He is a Middleton Fellow at the University of Southern California and is a Visiting Assistant Professor at the University of California Riverside.

Masters of the Board
Delta
Owerri, 1985
Sirocco
Delta
Owerri, 1987
Kalakuta Republic
Saqi
London, 2000
Daphne's Lot
Red Hen Press
Los Angeles, 2003
GraceLand
C. H. Beck
München, 2004
[Ü: Thomas Brückner]

Chris Abani wurde in Afikpo, Nigeria, geboren. Mit sechzehn Jahren veröffentlichte er seinen ersten Roman »Masters of the Board« (1985), in dessen Folge er schweren politischen Verfolgungen ausgesetzt war. Sein zweiter Roman »GraceLand« (2004; dt. »GraceLand«, 2004) erzählt die Geschichte eines jungen Elvis-Darstellers und seines Kampfes gegen die absurden Unwägbarkeiten des Alltags. Mit »Kalakuta Republic« (2000), »Daphne's Lot« (2003) und »Dog Woman« (2004) liegen drei Lyriksammlungen vor. 2001 wurde er mit dem PEN USA West Freedom-to-Write-Award sowie dem Prins Claus Prijs ausgezeichnet, 2003 erhielt er das Lannan Literary Fellowship. Chris Abani ist Middleton Fellow an der University of South California und Gastprofessor an der University of California Riverside.

david albahari

biography

David Albahari was born in Péc, former Yugoslavia, in 1948. He studied English language and literature in Belgrade. His first volume of short stories was published in 1973. »Opis smrti« was published in 1982, and this volume of short stories won that year's Ivo Andrić Award. Some of the stories in »Opis smrti« were included in »Words Are Something Else«, which was published in 1996. Albaharis novel »Mamac« (1996; engl. »Bait«, 2001) won the NIN Award in 1997 and the Balkanica Award in 1998. His works have been published in fourteen languages. The numerous books translated into Serbian by Albahari include Nabokov, Updike, and Shepard.
According to Albahari the I Ching has exerted an important influence on his life and his works which are based on very personal and family experiences. »If you understand what is going on inside the family, you will understand what is going on in the world. Patterns repeat themselves, only the scales are different.« Thus the reader approaches the historical reality implicatively through the protagonists' subjective impressions that are presented in the various layers of their individual memories and life experiences. A concise and experimental structure is prevalent in »Description of Death«; its grotesque effect is evoked by a partially expressive imagery when in one of the short stories a father is depicted walking on water or in another one some camp inmates go on hunger strike for corsetry. In spite of his endeavours, Albahari, Serbian of Jewish ancestry, could not avoid the politicisation of his life and works during the war in former Yugoslavia. Consequently in 1991, he agreed to chair the Federation of Jewish Communes of Yugoslavia and to help evacuate the Jewish population from Sarajevo. Two years later Albahari preferred the »rootlessness« of Canadian exile to the overpowering and more and more threatening political pressures in his home town Belgrade. From the distance abroad, however, the history of his native country has developed into a prominent theme. Based on his autobiographical emigrant experience, Albahari tells his mother's life story in »Bait«. While researching into Yugoslavian history for biographical details, the first-person narrator articulates his ambivalent feelings towards his memories, his identity and the sense of history in his new surroundings. The novel »Gec i Majer« (1998; Eng. »Gotz and Meyer«, 2004) describes the investigations into the deportation of Jewish people during World War II, tracing down two SS-officers guilty of murdering them. Albahari's alienating elements of speech prevent the reader from identifying with the protagonists, whereas the narrator cannot maintain a critical, unemotional attitude and is destroyed by the confrontation with the past. David Albahari lives in Calgary, Canada.

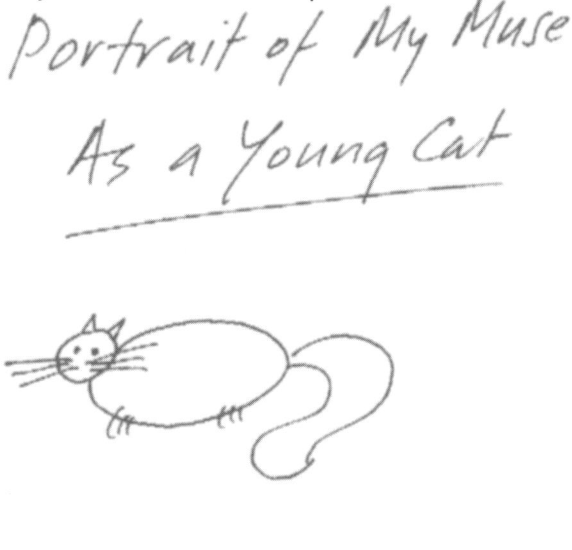

Beschreibung des Todes
Wieser
Klagenfurt, 1993
[Ü: Ivan Ivanji]
Tagelanger Schneefall
Zsolnay
Wien, 1997
[Ü: Mirjana und Klaus Wittmann]
Mutterland
Eichborn
Frankfurt am Main, 2002
[Ü: Mirjana und Klaus Wittmann]
Götz und Meyer
Eichborn
Frankfurt am Main, 2003
[Ü: Mirjana und Klaus Wittmann]

David Albahari wurde 1948 in Péc im ehemaligen Jugoslawien geboren. In Belgrad studierte er Englische Literatur und Sprache. Sein erster Band mit Kurzgeschichten erschien 1973. Sein Buch »Opis smrti« (1982; dt. »Beschreibung des Todes«, 1993) wurde 1982 mit dem Ivo Andrić-Preis ausgezeichnet, der Roman »Mamac« (1996; dt. »Mutterland«, 2002) erhielt 1997 den NIN-Preis und 1998 den Balkanica-Preis. Sein Werk wurde mittlerweile in vierzehn Sprachen übersetzt. Albahari wiederum übersetzte u. a. Nabokov, Updike und Shepard ins Serbische.

Albahari bezeichnet das I Ging als wichtigen Einfluss auf sein Leben und Schreiben, in dessen Mittelpunkt das Persönliche und die Familie stehen. »Wenn man versteht, was in einer Familie vor sich geht, versteht man auch, was in der Welt vor sich geht. Muster wiederholen sich, nur der Maßstab ändert sich.« In den vielschichtigen Erinnerungs- und Erlebnisebenen seiner Figuren konturieren sich die geschichtlichen Ereignisse. Subjektive Bilder erlauben die Annäherung an das Geschehen. Die Kurzgeschichten seines Erzählungsbandes »Beschreibung des Todes« sind in verdichteter, experimenteller Form gehalten. Häufig verwendet er dabei groteske Bilder: ein Vater läuft über das Wasser und Lagerinsassen treten in Hungerstreik, um Mieder tragen zu dürfen.

Trotz gegenteiliger Bemühungen konnte sich Albahari als jüdischer Serbe der Politisierung seines Lebens und seiner Arbeit im Krieg in Jugoslawien nicht entziehen. 1991 übernahm er das Amt des Vorsitzenden des Verbandes der jüdischen Gemeinden Jugoslawiens. In dieser Funktion war er maßgeblich an der Evakuierung der Juden Sarajevos beteiligt. Zwei Jahre später wählte er freiwillig die »Entwurzelung« des kanadischen Exils, um der »Zwangspolitisierung« zu entkommen, von der er sein Leben bestimmt sah. Aus der Ferne tritt jedoch die Geschichte seiner Heimat verstärkt in den Vordergrund seines Werkes. Ausgehend von seiner autobiographischen Situation als Auswanderer erzählt er in »Mutterland« die Lebensgeschichte seiner Mutter. Dabei setzt sich der Ich-Erzähler nicht nur mit ihrer Biographie vor dem Hintergrund der jugoslawischen Geschichte auseinander, sondern thematisiert zugleich seine Ambivalenzen gegenüber dem Umgang mit Erinnerung, Identität und Geschichte in seiner neuen Heimat. Der Roman »Gec i Majer« (1998; dt. »Götz und Meyer«, 2003) beschreibt die Suche nach im 2. Weltkrieg verschwundenen Juden. Sie führt den Erzähler auf die Spur zweier SS-Offiziere, die für deren Ermordung verantwortlich sind. Albahari verhindert durch verfremdende Elemente in seiner Sprache die Identifizierung des Lesers mit den Protagonisten. Für den Erzähler werden diese jedoch so real, dass er an der Vergangenheit zerbricht.
David Albahari lebt in Calgary, Kanada.

Like every cat—
She comes and leaves
Only when she wants it
So I just sit and wait—
Sometimes she doesn't care at all
Sometimes she adores me
And that explains why
Some of my stories are very short—
And why I believe in silence

taha muhammad ali

biography

Taha Muhammad Ali was born in Saffuriya, a village in Galilee, Palestine, in 1931. He attended primary school but was unable to continue his formal education since as a boy he had to support his family. During the Arab-Israeli War in 1948 his village suffered heavy bombardment and was eventually razed. His family was able to flee to Lebanon and a year later Taha Muhammad Ali returned to Israel, where he settled in Nazareth and opened a souvenir shop. At this same time he devoted himself to literature. He taught himself classical Arabic as well as English and began writing poetry. The first of his four volumes of poetry was published rather late, when he was fiftytwo. His first book of stories was published last year. »Never Mind: Twenty Poems and a Story« (2000) is available in English. A major Palestinian poet, Taha Muhammad Ali is esteemed primarily for his plainspoken and quietly sophisticated poetry. His poems mainly concern personal memories juxtaposed to political events. An important source of inspiration for his poetry and short stories is Saffuriya, his childhood village, a place inextricably bound to memories of life in that time and place.
Simple people stand at the centre of Taha Muhammad Ali's works. One of his most well-known poems is »Abd el-Hadi Fights a Superpower«, dating from 1973, where the eponymous protagonist is an ordinary man to whom the idea of revolt against injustice is remote. In »Post-Operative Complications Following the Extraction of Memory«, also written in 1973, the year of the Yom Kippur War, the speaker describes himself as »a camel fleeing the slaughterhouse«. His later poems are increasingly marked by longing, hope, and bittersweet reminiscence. Taha Muhammad Ali writes in a powerful style, using structures based on classical Arabic poetry. However he does not yield to embellishment in his diction, but tends towards simple words and images. He has appeared alongside Aharon Shabtai and his English translator Peter Cole in readings in Israel, the US, and Europe. The public were as much interested by the force of the poetry as by the courage of the poets to point in this way towards a possible coexistence in Israeli-Palestinian everyday life. Taha Muhammad Ali lives in Nazareth.

Al-Qasida ar-rabia wa-asar qasa'id u-hra
an-Nasira
as-Saut, 1983
Al-Barakah fi al-Quran al karim
Al-Iskandariyah
Dar Nashr
al-Thaqafah, 1990
Never Mind: Twenty Poems and a Story
Ibis Edition
Jerusalem, 2003
[Ü: Peter Cole, Yahya Hijazi, Gabriel Levin]

أجلس: وإذا استعصى على الوحي، أستذكر
مواضيع فكرت فيها ولم أكتبها بعد، أو بدأت في كتابتها
ولم أفرغ منها، فيكون ذلك كرائحة الطعام تفتح الشهية
إلى الزاد، والموضوع يكون هو الرائحة والوحي هو الطعام
وإذا أصرّ الوحي على عدم المجيء، أدع كل شيء
وأذهب لأنام!

Taha Muhammad Ali wurde 1931 in Saffuriya, einem Dorf in Galilea, Palästina, geboren. Er besuchte die Grundschule, konnte seine reguläre Ausbildung jedoch nicht fortsetzen, da er schon als Junge die Familie unterstützen musste. Im arabisch-israelischen Krieg 1948 wurde das Dorf stark bombardiert und schließlich dem Erdboden gleich gemacht. Seine Familie konnte in den Libanon fliehen. Taha Muhammad Ali kehrte ein Jahr später nach Israel zurück, wo er sich in Nazareth niederließ und einen Souvenirladen eröffnete. Seit dieser Zeit widmete er sich der Literatur. Er brachte sich selbst klassisches Arabisch und Englisch bei und begann Gedichte zu schreiben. Erst relativ spät, im Alter von zweiundfünfzig Jahren, veröffentlichte er den ersten von bisher vier Lyrikbänden. Im letzten Jahr erschien sein erster Erzählungsband. In englischer Übersetzung liegt »Never Mind: Twenty Poems and a Story« (2000) vor. Als einer der führenden palästinensischen Dichter wird Taha Muhammad Ali vor allem für seine offene und einfühlsam-differenzierte Poesie geschätzt. Seine Gedichte thematisieren persönliche Erinnerungen, die er wiederum in Beziehung zu politischen Ereignissen setzt. Wichtige Inspiration für seine Lyrik und Kurzgeschichten ist Saffuriya, das Dorf seiner Kindheit - ein Ort, mit dem Erinnerungen an das Leben damals verbunden sind.

Im Mittelpunkt seiner Arbeiten stehen meist einfache Menschen. Eines seiner bekanntesten Gedichte ist »Abd el-Hadi Fights a Superpower« aus dem Jahr 1973, dessen Titelheld ein einfacher Mensch ist, dem die Idee fern liegt, sich gegen Ungerechtigkeiten aufzulehnen. In »Post-operative Complications Following the Extraction of Memory«, das ebenfalls 1973 im Jahr des Yom-Kippur-Krieges entstand, bezeichnet sich das lyrische Ich als »ein Kamel, das die Schlachthäuser flieht«. Spätere Gedichte sind von Sehnsucht, Hoffnung und bittersüßen Reminiszenzen geprägt. Taha Muhammad Ali verwendet Formen, die auf der klassischen arabischen Dichtung basieren, ohne sich jedoch dem Ornament zu beugen. Stattdessen bevorzugt er einfache Worte und prägnante Bilder. In Israel, den USA und Europa trat er bei gemeinsamen Lesungen mit Aharon Shabtai und seinem englischen Übersetzer Peter Cole auf. Das Publikum war von der Kraft der Poesie ebenso begeistert wie vom Mut der Poeten, auf diese Art ein Zeichen für eine mögliche Koexistenz im israelisch-palästinensischen Alltag zu setzen. Taha Muhammad Ali lebt in Nazareth.

I sit down-and if the vision resists me, I call to mind
subjects I've thought of but haven't yet written about,
or things I started to write but didn't finish.
And that is like the smell of 'ful', Egyptian brown beans,
which makes me hungry. The subjects and things are the
smell, and the vision is the food.
And if the vision persists in its absence, I leave it all,
and go to sleep.

Ich setze mich hin - und sollte sich die Vision mir widersetzen,
rufe ich mir Themen ins Gedächtnis, über die ich schon einmal
nachgedacht, aber noch nicht geschrieben habe, oder Dinge, die
ich angefangen habe zu schreiben, aber nicht zu Ende brachte.
Und das ist wie der Geruch von 'ful', ägyptischen braunen
Bohnen, der mich hungrig macht. Die Themen und die
Dinge sind der Geruch, und die Vision ist das Essen.
Und sollte sich die Vision dann immer noch nicht einstellen,
lasse ich alles sein und gehe schlafen.

juri andruchowytsch

biography

Yuri Andrukhovych was born in 1960 in Ivano-Frankivsk, Ukraine, where he lives today. After studying journalism in Lviv he began his literary career with the publication of poems in literary magazines. In 1985, »Nebo i ploshtshi« (t: Heaven and squares) appeared, the first of his four volumes of poetry to date. His military service in the Red Army provided the inspiration for the script of his 1991 film »Oxygen Starvation«, as well as seven short stories published in 1989. Together with Viktor Neborak and Oleksandr Irvanets he founded »Bu-Ba-Bu« (Burlesque-Bluster-Buffonery) in 1985, a performance group that, especially at its peak between 1988 and 1992, had a lasting influence on the Ukrainian literary scene. Their performances of satirical, onomatopoeic, and carnivalesque experimental poetry expressed their objections to socialist realism. The same complex, grotesquely carnivalesque style is prevalent in his novels »Recreatsii« (1992; Engl. »Recreations«, 1998), »Moscoviada« (1993; t: The Moscoviad), and »Perverziia« (1996; Engl. »Perverzion«, 2002), making Yuri Andrukhovych one of the most controversial figures of present day Ukrainian literature. The main theme of the surrealistic satire »Recreatsii« concerns the sociopolitical situation of the Ukraine during the years directly preceding independence. »Moscoviada«, a swansong to the Soviet Union, is based on Andrukhovych's observations at the Gorki Institute while staying in Moscow from 1989 to 1991. A complex structure, an abundance of motifs, sub-plots and narrative elements, as well as a baroque love of playing with the language, are the hallmarks of »Perverziia«, a postmodern version of »Death in Venice«.

Andrukhovych's »literary activsm« has been motivated by the particular geographical and cultural situation of his native country: located at the EU's eastern border after Poland's entry, the Ukraine has remained »terra incognita« for most people in western Europe and the US. In 2003, Andrukhovych established the Polish-Ukrainian internet magazine »Potyah 76« (t: Train 76) which is of interest not least against the background of the two countries' Galician literary heritage. In a collection of essays on the Ukraine entitled »The Last Territory« (2003), written in the form of »fictitious regional studies«, he reflects upon this geographical »non-existence« in Europe. In the spring of 2004 he published another volume of essays, »My Europe«, the literary documentation of a journey with the Polish writer Andrzej Stasiuk. Yuri Andrukhovych has been awarded numerous national and international prizes including in 2001 the Herder Award of the Alfred Toepfer Foundation, which rewards cultural achievements in eastern Europe.

Spurensuche im Juli
Brodina
Reichelsheim, 1995
[Ü: Anna Halia Horbatsch]
Recreations
CIUS Press,
Toronto/Edmonton, 1998
[Ü: Marko Pavlyshyn]
Das letzte Territorium
Suhrkamp
Frankfurt am Main, 2003
[Ü: Alois Woldan]
Mein Europa
mit Andrzej Stasiuk
Suhrkamp
Frankfurt am Main, 2004
[Ü: Alois Woldan]

Juri Andruchowytsch wurde 1960 in Iwano-Frankiwsk, Ukraine, geboren, wo er auch heute lebt. Nach dem Journalistik-Studium in Lwiw begann 1982 seine literarische Karriere mit der Veröffentlichung von Gedichten in Literaturzeitschriften. »Nebo i ploschtschi« (Ü: Himmel und Plätze), der erste von bisher vier Gedichtbänden, erschien 1985. Der Militärdienst in der Roten Armee inspirierte ihn zu einem Drehbuch, das 1991 unter dem Titel »Oxygen Starvation« verfilmt wurde, sowie zu sieben Erzählungen, die 1989 publiziert wurden. Ebenfalls 1985 gründete er zusammen mit Viktor Neborak und Oleksander Irwanets die Performancegruppe »Bu-Ba-Bu« (Burlesk-Balagan-Buffonada), die insbesondere von 1988 bis 1992, auf dem Höhepunkt ihres Schaffens, nachhaltigen Einfluss auf die ukrainische Literaturszene nahm. Ihren Unmut gegenüber dem Sozialistischen Realismus äußerten sie performativ in satirischen, lautpoetischen und karnevalesken Gedicht-Experimenten. Auch in den Romanen »Rekreatsii« (1992, Ü: Feiertage), »Moscoviada« (1993, Ü: Moskowiade) und »Perverzija« (1996, Ü: Perversion), die Juri Andruchowytsch zum kontroversesten Autor der ukrainischen Gegenwartsliteratur machten, sind die stilistischen Vorlieben für das Vielschichtige und Grotesk-Karnevaleske unübersehbar. Die surreale Satire »Rekreatsii« thematisiert die gesellschaftliche und politische Situation der Ukraine unmittelbar vor der Unabhängigkeit. »Moscoviada« ist ein Abgesang auf die Sowjetunion und basiert auf Beobachtungen, die Andruchowytsch während seines Aufenthalts am Maxim Gorki Institut von 1989 bis 1991 in Moskau machte. »Perverzija«, eine postmoderne Variante von »Der Tod in Venedig«, zeichnet sich durch eine komplexe Struktur, eine Fülle von Motiven, Handlungssträngen, narrativen Elementen und eine barocke Lust an Sprachspielereien aus.
Beweggrund für Andruchowytschs »literarischen Aktivismus« ist die besondere geographische und kulturelle Situation seines Heimatlandes. Mit dem Beitritt Polens an die Außengrenze der EU gerückt, ist die Ukraine in Westeuropa und den USA noch immer weitgehend eine »terra incognita«. 2003 initiierte er »Potyah 76« (Ü: Zug 76), ein Internetmagazin in ukrainischer und polnischer Sprache, das nicht zuletzt vor dem Hintergrund des gemeinsamen galizischen Literaturerbes interessant ist. Die (Nicht-)Verortung der Ukraine in Europa reflektierte er in »Das letzte Territorium« (2003), einer Essaysammlung in Form einer »fiktiven Landeskunde«. Im Frühjahr 2004 erschien mit »Mein Europa« ein weiterer Essayband – die literarische Dokumentation einer gemeinsamen Reise mit dem polnischen Schriftsteller Andrzej Stasiuk. Juri Andruchowytsch wurde mit zahlreichen nationalen und internationalen Preisen gewürdigt, u. a. 2001 mit dem Herder-Preis der Alfred Toepfer Stiftung, einer Auszeichnung für kulturelle Leistungen in Osteuropa.

andrés barba

biography

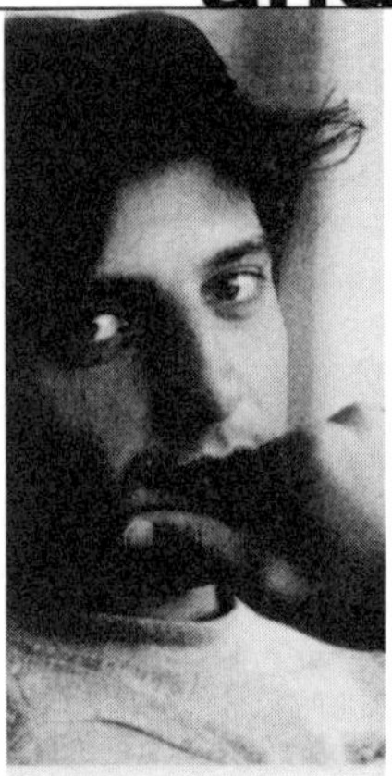

Andrés Barba was born in Madrid, Spain, in 1975. He obtained a degree in Spanish Philology, and then studied Philosophy. He went on to teach at Bowdoin College, in Maine, USA. Barba's writing first attracted attention with the publication of his novella, »El hueso que más duele« (1997; t. The bone that most hurts), which came out when the author had just turned twenty. It won the Ramón J. Sender prize for narrative. From the start critics praised his brutally honest tone, realist style and remarkable insight into human relationships. His second novel, »La hermana de Katia« (2001; t. Katia's sister), was a finalist for the XIX Premio Herralde de Novela 2001, and was very well received by the reading public as well as by the press. The novel tells the story of a fourteen year old girl who lives in a small flat in Madrid with her sister – who by night does striptease – and their prostitute mother. Although narrated in the third person, we are told of the girl's thoughts, fears, desires and sensations – and yet she remains anonymous, referred to simply as »Katia's sister«. Critics have praised the novel's astonishingly convincing portrayal of innocence. »La recta intención« (2002; t. The honest intention) was Barba's third book. It is comprised of four novellas in which the author deals with such themes as lack of communication, guilt, fear of getting close to others, fear of being rejected by one's beloved, an obsession with personal fortitude, and the inability to forgive. The tales have been called »authentic parables of modern times«. His most recent novel, »Ahora tocad música de baile« (2004; t. Now play a dance tune), tackles the theme of Alzheimer's, an illness which befalls the protagonist, Inés Fonseca. It is as much a domestic novel as a psychological exploration, and the story is told through three alternating voices and at four different stages of the illness. The narrative gaps serve as a way of mapping Inés's mental deterioration, which becomes more apparent and severe with each instalment. For this novel, Barba was praised for his sharp realism, reinforced by his refusal to be superficial or banal.

The young author currently teaches at the Universidad Complutense in Madrid and has represented Spain at several international conferences for young writers. He also contributes to various media. During the summer of 2004 he taught at a Creative Writing workshop in Madrid. His work has been translated, or is currently being translated, into English, French, German, Serbian, Dutch and Italian.

La recta intención
Anagrama
Barcelona, 2002
Katías Schwester
Kunstmann
München, 2003
[Ü: Sabine Giersberg]
Ahora tocad música de baile
Anagrama
Barcelona, 2004

Andrés Barba wurde 1975 in Madrid, Spanien, geboren. Nach einem Grundstudium der Spanischen Philologie absolvierte er ein Philosophiestudium und war anschließend als Dozent am Bowdoin College in Maine, USA, tätig. Erste Aufmerksamkeit errang der Autor mit Anfang zwanzig durch die Veröffentlichung seiner Erzählung »El hueso que más duele« (1997; Ü: Der Knochen, der am meisten weh tut), die den Ramón J. Sender-Preis gewann. Von Anfang an lobte die Kritik den brutal-ehrlichen Ton, den realistischen Stil und eine bemerkenswerte Einsicht in menschliche Beziehungen. Sein zweiter Band, »La hermana de Katia« (2001; dt. »Katias Schwester«, 2003), kam 2001 in die Finalrunde des XIX Premio Herralde de Novela und wurde von Presse und Leserschaft überaus positiv aufgenommen. Der Roman erzählt die Geschichte eines vierzehnjährigen Mädchens, das mit seiner Schwester, die nachts als Stripperin, und ihrer Mutter, die als Prostituierte arbeitet, in einer kleinen Wohnung in Madrid lebt. Obwohl in der dritten Person erzählt, erfährt man ihre Gedanken, Ängste, Sehnsüchte und Empfindungen – und dennoch bleibt sie eine Fremde ohne Namen, schlicht als »Katias Schwester« bezeichnet. Die Kritik hob die erstaunliche Überzeugungskraft dieses Porträts der Unschuld hervor. »La recta intención« (2002; Ü: Die ehrliche Absicht) ist Barbas drittes Buch. Es beinhaltet vier Erzählungen, in denen der Autor den Mangel an Kommunikation, Schuld, die Angst vor der Nähe anderer und vor der Zurückweisung durch geliebte Personen, Größenwahn und das Unvermögen zum Verzeihen thematisiert. Diese Geschichten wurden »authentische Parabeln der modernen Zeit« genannt. Barbas letzter Roman, »Ahora tocad música de baile« (2004; Ü: Jetzt spiel ein Tanzlied), nimmt das Problem Alzheimer auf; eine Krankheit, von der die Protagonistin Inés Fonseca befallen ist. Das Buch ist gleichermaßen Familienroman und psychologische Erkundung. Die Geschichte wird von drei alternierenden Stimmen und in vier verschiedenen Stadien der Krankheit erzählt. Die erzählerischen Leerstellen lassen Inés' zunehmenden mentalen Verfall immer deutlicher werden.

Barba bedient sich eines scharfen Realismus, der sich durch die Abwesenheit alles Oberflächlichen und Banalen auszeichnet. Der junge Schriftsteller lehrt derzeit an der Universidad Complutense in Madrid, vertrat Spanien auf einigen internationalen Konferenzen für junge Autoren und ist für verschiedene Medien tätig. Im Sommer 2004 gab er einen Workshop in Kreativem Schreiben in Madrid. Barbas Werke wurden bzw. werden derzeit ins Englische, Französische, Deutsche, Serbische, Niederländische und Italienische übersetzt.

I've asked the muse, but the muse doesn't answer...

bernlef

biography

Bernlef (formerly also J. Bernlef) was born Henrik Jan Marsman in 1937 in Sint Pancras, a village north of Alkmaar, in the Netherlands. After obtaining his high school diploma in 1955 he worked in a bookshop, until he was drafted. His first poems were published in a magazine under his real name until the late 1950's, when a reviewer mentioned a late author by the same name. Bernlef resided in Sweden several times between 1958 and 1960, where he started his writing career. Upon his return to the Netherlands in 1960 he published his first volume of poems »Kokkels« (t: Shells) and a collection of short stories »Stenen spoelen« (t: Stone rinsing). Five years later his first novel »Stukjes en beetjes« (t: Bits and pieces) followed. Since then he has written numerous poems and short stories as well as several essays, film scripts, plays, reviews, and a book on jazz. He has trans-lated into Dutch the Swedish authors Lars Gustafsson, Per Olof Sundman, and Tomas Tranströmer, as well as the American authors Elizabeth Bishop and Marianne Moore. Bernlef was awarded numerous prizes including the Constantijn-Huygens-Prijs for his complete works in 1984, and the renowned PC Hoft-Prijs for poetry in 1994. His theoretical as well as experimental investigations into language and text have exerted a decisive influence on Dutch literature. Declaring any existing text to be literature, the avant-garde magazine »Barbarber« became the platform for him and his co-founders Karl Schippers and Gerard Brands from 1958 to 1971. The group experimented with literary forms, drawing their inspirations from Dada as well as everday speech and ready-mades. In his position as editor of the literary magazine »Raster« between 1977 and 1987, Bernlef again focused his attention on the borderline between poetry and prose.
Both his poems and his prose keep challenging the question of how far subjective and objective experience, memory and its loss, observation and reception can be cast into language. Thus his bestknown novel »Hersenschimmen« (1984; engl. »Out of Mind«, 1988) conveys an Alzheimer patient's gradual decline in his powers of memory. Bernlef's factual, even detached style offers a precise insight into the process of losing coherence until the protagonist's disconnected perceptions can no longer be translated into words and end in total alienation. In his latest novel »Boy« (2000) he analyses observers' reactions to a deaf and dumb boy. Bernlef lives and works in Amsterdam.

Kokkels
Querido
Amsterdam,1960
Meeuwen
Querido
Amsterdam, 1975
Hirngespinste
Nagel & Kimche
Zürich, 1986
[Ü: Maria Csollány]
Publiek geheim
Querido
Amsterdam, 1987
Zwischen Eisbergen
Suhrkamp
Frankfurt am Main,1993
[Ü: Helga van Beuningen]
Achter de rug. Gedichten 1960-1990
Querido
Amsterdam, 1997
Aambeeld
Querido
Amsterdam, 1998
Boy
Querido
Amsterdam, 2000

Bernlef (früher auch: J. Bernlef) wurde 1937 als Hendrik Jan Marsman in Sint Pancras, einem Dorf nördlich von Alkmaar, Niederlande, geboren. Nach dem Abitur 1955 arbeitete er bis zur Einberufung zum Militärdienst in einer Buchhandlung. Die ersten Gedichte erschienen in den späten fünfziger Jahren in einer Zeitschrift unter seinem richtigen Namen, bis ein Rezensent Parallelen zu einem verstorbenen Lyriker gleichen Namens zog. Zwischen 1958 und 1960 hielt sich Bernlef wiederholt in Schweden auf, wo er ernsthaft mit dem Schreiben begann.
Zurück in den Niederlanden veröffentlichte er 1960 gleich zwei Titel: den ersten Gedichtband »Kokkels« (1960, Ü: Muscheln) sowie den Erzählband »Stenen spoelen« (Ü: Steine waschen). Sein erster Roman »Stukjes en beetjes« (Ü: Stückchen und Bisschen) kam 1965 heraus. Seither schrieb er zahlreiche weitere Gedichte und Erzählungen, einige Essays, Drehbücher und Theaterstücke sowie Kritiken und zwei Bücher über Jazz. Er übersetzte aus dem Schwedischen unter anderem Lars Gustafsson, Per Olof Sundman und Tomas Tranströmer sowie aus dem Amerikanischen Elizabeth Bishop und Marianne Moore. Er erhielt zahlreiche Auszeichnungen, darunter 1984 den Constantijn-Huygens-Prijs für sein Gesamtwerk und 1994 den renommierten PC Hooft-Prijs für Lyrik. Einfluss auf die niederländische Literatur nahm Bernlef auch durch die theoretisch-experimentelle Auseinandersetzung mit Sprache und Text. 1958 gründete er mit den Dichtern K. Schippers und G. Brands die Zeitschrift für Texte »Barbarber« (erschienen 1958 bis 1971), in der sie postulierten, jeder Text könne Literatur sein. In diesem Sinne widmeten sie sich literarischen Experimenten, inspiriert von Dada, Readymades und Alltagssprache. 1977 bis 1987 war Bernlef Redakteur der Literaturzeitschrift »Raster«, die sich mit dem Grenzbereich zwischen Lyrik und Prosa beschäftigte.
Bernlef interessiert in seinen Gedichten und seiner Prosa vor allem die Frage, inwieweit sich subjektives und objektives Erleben, Erinnern und Vergessen, Beobachtung und Wahrnehmung in Sprache fassen lässt. So auch in seinem bekanntesten Roman »Hersenschimmen« (1984; dt. »Hirngespinste«, 1986). Bernlef schildert distanziert durch seinen klaren, nüchternen Sprachstil die innere Erfahrungswelt eines Alzheimerkranken, den zunächst schleichenden, dann rapiden Verlust der Erinnerung und die daraus folgende Beziehungslosigkeit zur ehemals vertrauten Umgebung. Am Ende erreicht die Entfremdung ein Stadium, in dem sich sogar direkte Wahrnehmungen nicht mehr in Worte fassen lassen. In seinem Roman »Boy« (2000) analysiert er die Wahrnehmung eines taubstummen Jungen durch die Menschen seiner Umgebung. Bernlef lebt in Amsterdam.

Ich mache mir keine Sorgen.
Es gibt noch so viel anderes zu tun:
leben zum Beispiel.
Aber wenn es dann doch zu lange dauert, setze ich mich an Übersetzungen. Ein Übersetzer hat schon ein Gedicht vor sich. Die Übersetzungsarbeit bringt mich immer in eine gewisse Stimmung, um selbst wieder etwas zu probieren. Dies ist eine Methode, die viele Komponisten auch verwendet haben: Bearbeite eine bereits vorhandene Komposition, und neue Musik wird rasch folgen. Die Bearbeitung des Materials eines anderen wirkt wie ein Katalysator.
100% waterproof!

tanella boni

biography

Tanella Boni was born in Abidjan, Ivory Coast, in 1954. She studied Philosophy in French Toulouse and at the Sorbonne in Paris, where she received a doctorate in 1987. For twenty five years she has worked as Philosophy Professor at the University of Cocody in Abidjan, and since 1984 has published six volumes of poetry, two novels (1990; »Une vie de crabe« and 1995, »Les Baigneurs du Lac Rose«), as well as three children's books, among them »De l'autre côté du soleil« (1991). In addition to philosophical articles she regularly writes art and literary reviews for various magazines, among them »Africultures« and »Mots pluriels«. From 1991 to 1997 Boni was President of the Association of Writers of the Ivory Coast. Since her poetry debut (»Labyrinthe«) in 1984 she has – just like Véronique Tadjo – become the embodiment of a new generation of writers whose female voices contrast with the male dominance of Ivory Coast literature.

In »Labyrinthe« and her second volume of poetry, »Grains de sable« (1993), Tanella Boni focuses on the search for one's own path as poet. She chooses the labyrinth as an image for these painful initiation processes which are rife with solitude, sadness and doubt. Starting from the innermost point, the authorial »I« embarks on a search, gets lost along this or that dead-end street, and finally finds a way out. With commanding metaphors, Tanella Boni handles themes such as the relationship between the sexes in Africa, the burden of tradition, social grievances, as well as the intense desire for freedom and the free word. Succinct speech rhythms are characterised by word play and strengthening repetitions. As both poet and co-organiser of Abidjan's international poetry festival, Boni searches for ways to connect modern Francophone verse with the theatrical oral recitation forms of traditional poetry. In her latest volume of poetry, »Gorée île baobab« (2004), she tells the story of the island of Gorée, formerly the last stop on the slave trade before the crossing to North and South America, and today a place of remembrance for the African diaspora. In doing so she remembers the horror of Africa's early history. »Today, in an Africa eroded by war and all kinds of disease, it is essential that literary genres like poetry can play an important role.« Tanella Boni lives in Abidjan.

Labyrinthe
Akpagnon
Rée-sur-Seine, 1984

Une vie de crabe
Les nouvelles éd. Africaines
du Sénéngal (NEAS)
Dakar, 1990

Grains de sable
Éd. Le Bruit des Autres
Solignac, 1993

Il n'y a pas de Parole Heureuse
Éd. Le Bruit des Autres
Solignac, 1997

Les Baigneurs du Lac Rose
Serpents à Plumes
Paris, 2002

Tanella Boni wurde 1954 in Abidjan, Elfenbeinküste, geboren. Sie studierte Philosophie im französischen Toulouse und an der Sorbonne in Paris, wo sie 1987 promovierte. Sie arbeitet seit fünfundzwanzig Jahren als Philosophieprofessorin an der Universität Cocody in Abidjan. Seit 1984 veröffentlichte sie sechs Lyrikbände, die beiden Romane »Une vie de crabe« (1990; Ü: Ein Krabbenleben) und »Les Baigneurs du Lac Rose« (1995; Ü: Die Badenden des Lac Rose) sowie drei Kinderbücher, darunter »De l'autre côté du soleil« (1991; Ü: Die andere Seite der Sonne). Neben philosophischen Fachartikeln schreibt sie regelmäßig Literatur- und Kunstkritiken für verschiedene Magazine, unter anderem für »Africultures« und »Mots pluriels«. Von 1991 bis 1997 war sie Präsidentin des Schriftstellerverbandes der Elfenbeinküste. Seit sie 1984 ihr lyrisches Debüt »Labyrinthe« veröffentlichte, ist sie – ebenso wie Véronique Tadjo – zum Inbegriff einer neuen Generation von Schriftstellerinnen geworden, die der männlichen Dominanz in der Literatur der Elfenbeinküste ihre weiblichen Stimmen entgegensetzen.
In »Labyrinthe« und ihrem zweiten Gedichtband »Grains de sable« (1993; Ü: Sandkörner) thematisiert Tanella Boni die Suche nach dem eigenen Weg als Dichterin. Als Bild für diesen schmerzhaften Initiationsprozess, der geprägt ist von Einsamkeit, Trauer und Zweifeln, wählt sie das Labyrinth. Ausgehend vom Innersten begibt sich das lyrische Ich auf die Suche, verirrt sich unterwegs in dieser oder jener Sackgasse, um letztendlich doch einen Ausweg zu finden. Themen wie die Geschlechterverhältnisse in Afrika, die Last der Traditionen, soziale Missstände sowie den starken Wunsch nach Freiheit und dem freien Wort fasst Tanella Boni in eindrucksvolle Metaphern. Wortspiele und bekräftigende Wiederholungen bestimmen den prägnanten Sprachrhythmus. Als Dichterin und Mitorganisatorin des internationalen Festivals der Poesie in Abidjan versucht sie Wege zu finden, die moderne französischsprachige Lyrik mit den theatralen mündlichen Vortragsformen der traditionellen Poesie zu verbinden. In ihrem neuesten Lyrikband »Gorée île baobab« (2004; Ü: Gorée – Insel des Baobab) erzählt sie von der Insel Gorée, ehemals letzter Stop der Sklavenschiffe vor der Überfahrt nach Nord- und Südamerika und heute Erinnerungsort der afrikanischen Diaspora. Zugleich erinnert sie an die Greuel der jüngeren Geschichte Afrikas. »Im heutigen, von Krieg und all diesen Krankheiten zermürbten Afrika, ist es von essentieller Bedeutung, dass literarische Genres wie die Poesie eine wesentliche Rolle spielen können.« Tanella Boni lebt in Abidjan.

Answer Muse

"je ne te vois pas Muse
et je ne sais où tu es
j'ignore ta résidence
ton téléphone ton e-mail
voilà pourquoi je ne t'appelle
jamais je ne t'écris pas
et nous ne nous sommes
jamais rencontrées
je suis mon chemin
comme je l'entends"

javier cercas

biography

Javier Cercas was born in Ibahernando/Cáceres, Spain, in 1962. He lectured at the University of Illinois, USA, for two years in the 1980's, and has been a professor of Spanish Literature at the University of Gerona since 1989. He has published literary studies, translations and essays and has been a regular columnist for »El País«. In 1987, his first volume of short stories appeared »El móvil« (t: The motive), followed by his first novel »El inquilino« (1989; t: The tenant). Its protagonist is a professor of literature at an American university who has »a difficult relationship with reality«.
As a member of an academic microcosm bounded by conceitedness and competitiveness, Professor Mario Rota is confronted by his own fears after suffering a minor injury. His anxiety disorders are reinforced by the sudden appearance of Mr. Berkowickz, who not only moves into the adjacent apartment but, also takes over both the professors's classes and his girlfriend. The novel is an ironic variation on the traditional doppelganger motif, playfully depicting the concept of dual reality.
Javier Cercas' further novels are equally marked by irony, by the paradox of a seemingly ›realistic narration‹, and by references to the act of writing and to literature per se. He has published another novel, »El vientre della ballena« (1997; t: The belly of the whale), and a collection of short stories »Relatos reales« (2000; t: True tales). His most recent novel, »Soldados de Salamina« (2001; Eng. »Soldiers of Salamis«, 2004), became a resounding success and gained numerous awards including the Premio Salambó in 2002. An authentic event of the Spanish Civil War is presented in a self-reflective tone as the core of the book. The notorious episode recalls how Rafael Sánchez Mazas, chief ideologist and co-founder of the fascist Falange, escaped from a Republican firing squad only because the soldier tracking him down spared his life. The narrator, a journalist and unsuccessful writer, launches a search for that unknown soldier. He plunges himself into investigations, files and documents, talks to contemporary witnesses, and encounters obstacles – with surprising results. Above all, he is obsessed with writing »a truly authentic story« about it all. With his particular narrative strategy Cercas lets the reader participate in the making of the novel and, at the same time, reflects on the quest for truth versus forgery, documentary versus fiction. He comes to the conclusion that »literary truth is neither historical nor journalistic, it is a different kind of truth, more universal and more valuable; it is a moral, a poetic truth«. Javier Cercas lives in Gerona.

El vientre de la ballena
Tusquets Editores,
Barcelona, 1997
Una buena temporada
Editora Regional
de Extremadura
Merida, 1998
Relatos reales
El Acantilado
Barcelona, 2000
Soldaten von Salamis
Berlin Verlag
Berlin, 2002
[Ü: Willi Zurbrüggen]
El móvil
Tusquets Editores
Barcelona, 2003
Der Mieter
Wagenbach
Berlin, 2003
[Ü: Willi Zurbrüggen]

Javier Cercas wurde 1962 in Ibahernando/Cáceres, Spanien, geboren. In den achtziger Jahren war er zwei Jahre Dozent an der Universität Illinois, USA. Seit 1989 ist er Professor für Spanische Literatur an der Universität Gerona. Er veröffentlichte literaturwissenschaftliche Arbeiten, Übersetzungen und Essays und schreibt regelmäßig eine Kolumne für »El País«. 1987 kam sein erster Erzählungsband »El móvil« (Ü: Der Grund) heraus, zwei Jahre später folgte der erste Roman »El inquilino« (1989; dt. »Der Mieter«, 2003), in dessen Mittelpunkt ein Literaturprofessor steht, der »ein schwieriges Verhältnis zur Wirklichkeit« hat. Mario Rota sieht sich – ausgelöst durch eine kleine Verletzung – im eitlen, von Konkurrenz geprägten Mikrokosmos einer amerikanischen Universität mit seinen Ängsten konfrontiert. Denn plötzlich taucht Mr. Berkowickz auf, der zunächst in die Nachbarwohnung einzieht, dann Rotas Vorlesungen übernimmt und ihm schließlich die Freundin ausspannt. Javier Cercas variiert auf ironische Art das klassische Doppelgängermotiv und spielt mit der Idee einer zweiten Realität.

Ironie, das Paradoxon der ›wirklichen Erzählung‹ sowie selbstreferentielle Verweise auf das Schreiben und die Literatur an sich bestimmen auch seine weiteren Werke. Er veröffentlichte einen zweiten Roman, »El vientre de la ballena« (1997; Ü: Der Bauch des Wals), und den Erzählband »Relatos reales« (2000; Ü: Wirkliche Erzählungen), bevor 2001 sein jüngster Roman »Soldados de Salamina« (dt. »Soldaten von Salamis«, 2002) zu einem großen Erfolg wurde. Die selbstreflexive Geschichte über die Recherche einer historischen Begebenheit, die sich im Spanischen Bürgerkrieg zugetragen hat, erhielt zahlreiche Auszeichnungen, u. a. den Premio Salambó 2002. Ausgangspunkt ist die Anekdote, dass Rafael Sánchez Mazas, Mitbegründer und Chefideologe der faschistischen Falange, die Flucht vor einem regierungstreuen Erschießungskommando nur überlebte, weil ihn sein Verfolger laufen ließ. Der Erzähler, ein Journalist und erfolgloser Schriftsteller, begibt sich auf die Suche nach diesem unbekannten Soldaten. Er recherchiert, sichtet Dokumente, spricht mit Zeitzeugen, stößt auf Hindernisse und überraschende Erfolge – und ist darauf fixiert, über all das eine »Erzählung nach der Wirklichkeit« zu schreiben. Vermittels der narrativen Strategie, den Leser quasi an der Entstehung des Romans teilhaben zu lassen, reflektiert Cercas die Frage nach Wahrheit und Fälschung, Dokumentation und Fiktion. Er kommt zu dem Schluss: »Die literarische Wahrheit ist nicht die historische, auch nicht die journalistische Wahrheit: sie ist eine andere Art Wahrheit, universeller und wertvoller; sie ist eine moralische, poetische Wahrheit.«

Javier Cercas lebt in Gerona.

edgardo cozarinsky
biography

Edgardo Cozarinsky was born in Buenos Aires, Argentina, in 1939. He studied literature in Buenos Aires and founded the film magazine »Flashback«. During the 1960's and 70's he wrote reviews and film criticism as well as a number of essays, among them a study of Henry James entitled »El laberinto de la apariencia« (1964; t: The labyrinth of appearance). The volume »Borges y el cine«, a collection of rare film criticism that Borges composed between 1931 and 1945, with an accompanying essay by Cozarinsky, was published in 1970 (in Europe the book appeared under the title »Borges en/y/sobre el cine«; Engl. »Borges In/And/On Film«, 1988). In 1979 Cozarinsky was awarded the essay prize given by the newspaper »La Nación« for »El relato indefendible« (t: The indefensible report), an essay on gossip as narrative mode. In 1974 he left Argentina due to the dramatic political climate which arose after Juan Perón's death and he went into exile in Paris, where he has lived ever since.
Above all, Edgardo Cozarinsky is known for his extensive work in film. He shot his first experimental feature film in Argentina in 1970. His second feature film »Les apprentis sorciers« (1977; t: The sorcerer's apprentices) laid the cornerstone for his French film career. Over the following years he worked on film scripts, short films, feature films, TV productions and a series of semi-documentary portraits of artists, among them Jean Cocteau, Sarah Bernhardt, Italo Calvino, Van Gogh and Andrei Tarkovsky. One of his best-known films is »La guerre d'un seul homme« (1981; t: One man's war), about the German occupation of Paris, a montage of archival material drawn from French newsreels, and the diary entries of Ernst Jünger. Just as Cozarinsky's cinematic essays are both fiction and documentary, so his writing blurs the boundaries between essay and narrative. With »Vudú Urbano« (1985; Eng. »Urban Voodoo«, 1990) he embarked on a ›sentimental journey‹, from which he sent thirteen so-called ›postcards‹. In this case it concerns fictitious anecdotes meant to conjure up images in the reader's imagination. These are based on collective images and clichés, comparable to picture postcards. Cozarinsky wrote this book in English – in the language he calls foreigner's English – with the aim to make the original untraceable. The city, exile, and travels into the past are also central themes of the nine stories from »La novia de Odessa« (2001; Eng. »The Bride from Odessa«, 2004) as well as of the volume of essays »El pase del testigo« (2001; t: The witness' pass).

Borges en/y/sobre el cine
Fundamentos
Madrid, 1981
Vudú Urbano
Anagrama
Barcelona,1985
La novia de Odessa
Emecé
Buenos Aires, 2001
El pase del testigo
Editorial Sudamericana,
Buenos Aires, 2001
The Bride from Odessa
Farrar, Straus & Giroux
New York, 2004
[Ü: Nick Caistor]

Edgardo Cozarinsky wurde 1939 in Buenos Aires, Argentinien, geboren. Er studierte Literatur in Buenos Aires und gründete das Filmmagazin »Flashback«. In den sechziger und siebziger Jahren schrieb er Rezensionen und Filmkritiken sowie einige Essays, darunter »El laberinto de la apariencia« (1964; Ü: Das Labyrinth der Erscheinung) über Henry James. 1974 gab er den Band »Borges y el cine« heraus (in Europa erschienen als »Borges en/y/sobre el cine«; engl. »Borges In/And/On Film«, 1988), eine Sammlung von seltenen Filmkritiken, die Jorge Luis Borges zwischen 1931 und 1945 verfasst hatte, ergänzt durch einen begleitenden Essay von Cozarinsky. Für »El relato indefendible« (Ü: Der unhaltbare Bericht), einen Essay über den Tratsch als narrative Form, erhielt Cozarinsky 1979 den von der Tageszeitung »La Nación« vergebenen Essaypreis. 1974 verließ er wegen der dramatischen politischen Situation nach dem Tod Juan Peróns Argentinien und ging ins Exil nach Paris, wo er seither lebt.

Edgardo Cozarinsky ist vor allem für sein umfangreiches filmisches Werk bekannt. Seinen ersten experimentellen Spielfilm drehte er 1970 in Argentinien. 1977 begann er mit seinem zweiten Spielfilm »Les apprentis sorciers« (Ü: Die Zauberlehrlinge) sein Filmschaffen in Frankreich. In den folgenden Jahren arbeitete er an Drehbüchern, Kurzfilmen, Spielfilmen, Produktionen für das Fernsehen und an einer Reihe von semi-dokumentarischen Künstlerportraits, u. a. über Jean Cocteau, Sarah Bernhardt, Italo Calvino, Van Gogh und Andrej Tarkowskij. Einer seiner bekanntesten Filme ist »La guerre d'un seul homme« (1981; Ü: Der Krieg eines Einzelnen) über die deutsche Besatzung von Paris, eine Montage von Archivmaterial aus französischen Wochenschauen und Tagebucheintragungen Ernst Jüngers. Ebenso wie Cozarinskys filmische Essays zugleich Fiktion und Dokumentation sind, verwischt sich in seinem Schreiben die Grenze zwischen Essay und Erzählung. Mit »Vudú Urbano« (1985; Ü: Städtischer Voodoo) geht er auf eine ›sentimentale Reise‹, von der er dreizehn sogenannte ›Postkarten‹ sendet. Hierbei handelt es sich um fiktive Anekdoten, die in der Vorstellung des Lesers Bilder abrufen sollen, welche auf kollektiven Images bzw. Klischees basieren und mit Postkartenbildern vergleichbar sind. Cozarinsky schrieb dieses Buch auf Englisch – in der Sprache, die er foreigner's English nennt – in der Absicht, das Original unauffindbar zu machen. Von der Stadt, dem Exil und der Reise in die Vergangenheit erzählt er auch in den neun Erzählungen von »La novia de Odessa« (2001; Ü: Die Braut aus Odessa) sowie im Essayband »El pase del testigo« (2001; Ü: Der Pass des Zeugen).

alonso cueto

biography

Alonso Cueto was born in Lima, Peru, in 1954. He studied at the Universidad Católica de Perú, graduating in 1977. He lived in Madrid teaching English and travelled through Europe until 1979. In that year he went on to do a Master's and Ph.D. at the University of Texas in Austin, which he received in 1984. His doctoral thesis dealt with the subject of age and the city in the stories of the Uruguayan writer Juan Carlos Onetti. Cueto's first publication, a collection of short stories entitled »La batalla del pasado« (1983; t: Last year's battle), is said to have echoes of Henry James due to its focus on the lives of cosmopolitan Peruvian exiles in Europe and the United States. It has also been called one of the most important books in modern Peruvian literature.

Much of his work however focuses on the middle classes of Lima, whom he soon turned towards as the main source for his subject matter. His characters went from being nostalgic and contemplative to lively and quotidian, more in the tradition of Raymond Carver than that of Julio Ramón Ribeyro and Mario Vargas Llosa, whose works depicted the burgeoning middle class as both heroic and somewhat pathetic. Cueto emerges as more of a neo realist, searching for signs of simple humanity within the humdrum of daily life. He has said that the greatest aspiration for any writer is to give life to a character. He has also said, in another interview, that it is in the profound simplicity of Cervantes where he feels most at home – his own tone is often understated. Cueto has won several distinctions for his literary work, among them the Anna Seghers Prize for his oeuvre (Berlin 2000) and a grant from the John Simon Guggenheim Memorial Foundation (2002). His first novel, »El tigre blanco« (t: The white tiger), won the Premio Wiracocha in 1985. The jury consisted of Mario Vargas Llosa, Julio Ramón Ribeyro and Blanca Varela.

His most recent novel, »Grandes miradas« (2003; t: Big views), is set during the final months of President Fujimori's dictatorship, and tells the true story of a judge assassinated in the year 2000 for his refusal to succumb to corruption. Another character drawn from real life is Vladimiro Montesinos, former spy chief and Fujimori's closest advisor, said to have ordered the execution. In the novel, the murdered judge's girlfriend vows to avenge his death by killing Montesinos. The novel ends with the government's downfall, but not before many intrigues and unexpected twists have transpired.

Cueto is currently a columnist on the daily newspaper »Peru 21« as well as Professor of Journalism at the Peruvian University of Applied Sciences in Lima. He also conducts a programme of writing workshops at the Centro Cultural of the Universidad Católica de Perú.

El tigre blanco
Wiracocha-Diselpera
Lima, 1985

La batalla del pasado
Apoyo
Lima, 1996

Deseo de noche
Apoyo
Lima, 1997

Los vestidos de una dama
Peisa
Lima ,1998

Demonio del mediodía
Peisa
Lima ,1999

Cinco para las nueve y otro cuentos
Alfaguara
Lima, 2000

El otro amor de Diana Abril
Peisa
Lima, 2002

Grandes miradas
Peisa
Lima, 2003

Nunca he tenido problemas con la falta de inspiración pues vivo en un medio en el que las historias circulan con la naturalidad del aire. Lima es una sociedad oral en la que la gente se junta a conversar y en la que el chisme, esa variedad de la narrativa, es un acontecimiento excepcional. En las conversaciones, todavía se celebra la novedad de una historia, cierta o falsa, sobre un personaje conocido. Por otro lado, el encuentro de grupos sociales y étnicos distintos en el Perú es una fuente permanente de conflictos, es decir de historias. Lo mejor que le puede pasar a un escritor es vivir en un país como el Perú, en el que las diferencias sociales fabrican historias de aspiraciones y desencuentros entre sus gentes. La sociedad limeña es una industria incansable de relatos. Mi problema es que creo que me moriré sin contar todas las historias que me rodean.

Alonso Cueto wurde 1954 in Lima, Peru, geboren. Nach seinem Studium an der Universidad Católica de Perú, das er 1977 abschloss, lebte er als Englischlehrer in Madrid und reiste durch Europa. 1979 nahm er in Austin, Texas, ein Master- und Promotionsstudium auf. Er graduierte 1984 mit einer Dissertation über das Gesetz des Alters und die Stadt in den Kurzgeschichten des uruguayischen Autors Juan Carlos Onetti. Cuetos literarisches Debüt erschien 1983 unter dem Titel »La batalla del pasado« (Ü: Die Schlacht des vergangenen Jahres). Den darin vereinigten Erzählungen, die sich dem Leben peruanischer Exilanten in Europa und den Vereinigten Staaten widmen, wird wegen ihrer Thematik oft eine Nähe zu Henry James nachgesagt. Der Band wurde zudem mehrfach als eines der bedeutendsten Bücher moderner peruanischer Literatur bezeichnet.

Größtenteils jedoch steht die Mittelklasse Limas, die bald Cuetos wichtigste Inspirationsquelle wurde, im Zentrum seines Werkes. Seine Protagonisten wurden dabei immer weniger nostalgisch und nachdenklich, statt dessen lebhafter und alltäglicher, was sie der Tradition Raymond Carvers näher bringt als derjenigen von Julio Ramón Ribeyro und Mario Vargas Llosa, bei denen die bourgeoise Mittelklasse eher heroisch und anrührend erscheint. Cueto entwickelte sich zum Neorealisten, der sich inmitten des Stumpfsinns des täglichen Lebens auf die Suche nach der einfachen Menschlichkeit begibt. Die größte Sehnsucht eines Schriftstellers sei es, so Cueto, seine Figuren zum Leben zu erwecken. Seine literarische Heimat finde er am ehesten in der hintergründigen Einfachheit von Cervantes. Cueto erhielt mehrere Auszeichnungen, darunter den Anna-Seghers Preis für sein Gesamtwerk (2000) und ein Stipendium der John Simon Guggenheim Memorial Foundation (2002). Für seinen ersten Roman »El tigre blanco« (Ü: Der weiße Tiger) gewann er 1985 den Premio Wiracocha. Jurymitglieder waren Mario Vargas Llosa, Julio Ramón Ribeyro und Blanca Varela.

Sein jüngster Roman »Grandes miradas« (2003; Ü: Große Blicke) spielt in den letzten Monaten der Diktatur von Präsident Fujimori und erzählt die wahre Geschichte eines Richters, der 2000 einem Attentat zum Opfer fiel, nachdem er sich der Korruption verweigert hatte. Angeblich wurde die Ermordung von Vladimiro Montesinos, dem früheren Geheimdienstchef und engsten Berater Fujimoris, in Auftrag gegeben. Auch diese Figur wurde nach der Realität gezeichnet. Im Roman schwört die Freundin des getöteten Richters Rache und will Montesinos umbringen lassen. Nach vielen Intrigen und unerwarteten Wendungen endet das Buch mit dem Sturz der Regierung.

Alonso Cueto ist derzeit Kolumnist der Tageszeitung »Peru 21« und Professor für Journalistik an der Universität für Angewandte Wissenschaften in Lima. Außerdem leitet er ein Programm von Schreibwerkstätten am Kulturzentrum der Universidad Católica de Perú.

Da ich in einer Welt lebe, in der Geschichten mit der gleichen natürlichen Leichtigkeit kreisen wie Luft, hatte ich niemals Probleme mit einer ausbleibenden Inspiration. Lima ist eine mündliche Gesellschaft, in der Menschen zum Plaudern zusammenkommen und in der Klatsch, diese Variante der Prosa, eine unglaubliche Chance darstellt. Während eines Gesprächs freut man sich an der Neuheit einer Geschichte über einen bekannten Menschen – ganz gleich ob sie wahr oder erfunden ist. Auf der anderen Seite ist das Zusammenkommen verschiedener sozialer und ethnischer Gruppen in Peru eine ständige Quelle für Konflikte, das heißt auch: für Geschichten. Es kann einem Autor nichts Besseres passieren als in einem Land wie Peru zu leben, in dem soziale Differenzen Erzählungen von Hoffnungen und Missverständnissen zwischen den Menschen hervorbringen. Limas Gesellschaft ist eine niemals stillstehende Fabrik von Anekdoten. Mein Problem ist, dass ich glaube sterben zu müssen, bevor ich Zeit hatte, all diese mich umgebenden Geschichten zu erzählen.

hassan dawud

biography

Hassan Daoud was born in Beirut, Lebanon, in 1950. After studying Arabic Literature he worked in Beirut as a journalist during the civil war. From 1979 to 1988 he worked writer for the daily paper »Alsafir Daily«. After that, he was a correspondent for eleven years for the international Arab newspaper »Al-Hayat«, which is published in London. Daoud wrote about social themes, as well as book reviews, art and cultural criticism for the feature pages. At present he is the chief editor of »Nawafez«, the cultural supplement of the Beirut daily paper »Al-Mustaqbal Daily«. His commentary on political and cultural events in the Arab world appears in European newspapers as well, for example in the »Neue Zürcher Zeitung«. As writer, he has so far published two volumes of short stories and four novels. His first novel, »Binâyat Mathilde« (1983; Eng. »The House of Mathilde«, 1999), takes place in a Beirut apartment building during the civil war. At the centre of this social microcosm of Muslim and Christian tenants stands Mathilde, who has offered shelter to a nameless refugee in hiding. Hassan Daoud, who himself grew up in a house in which Muslims, Druzes and Christians, as well as immigrants from Russia and Armenia, all lived together, makes strikingly apparent the background for the disturbance in Lebanese society through the changes in the daily lives of the tenants. In his further novels too he limits events to a concretely defined space. Daoud frequently tells stories from the perspective of people living at the margins of society. In so doing, he renounces to the greatest possible extent descriptions of local features. Instead, he pens precise observations and subtle details in a trimmed-down language divested of psychological meaning.

In »Ayyâm zâ'ida« (1990; t: Added days), through the continuous monologue of an old man, in which the past and present, memories and dreams are blended into a flow of thought, he depicts the wilful struggle against a family which is indifferent towards him to the point of hostility, but also the futile battle against growing helplessness, physical decline and death. The protagonist of »Ghinâ' al-bitrîq« (1998; t: The song of the penguin), impaired by a physical abnormality, also lives distanced from his fellow men. He obsessively spies and eavesdrops on a young female neighbour. The novel was hailed as »The Best Book from Lebanon in 1998«. Hassan Daoud's most recent novel, »Makiage khafif lihazihi Allailah« (t: A mild makeup for tonight), appeared in 2003. Daoud lives in Beirut.

L'immeuble Mathilde
Actes Sud
Paris, 1998
[Ü: Youssef Seddik]
Der Gesang des Pinguins
Lenos
Basel, 2000
[Ü: Doris Kilias]
Des jours en trop
Actes Sud
Paris, 2001
[Ü: Edwige Lambert]
Tage zuviel
Lenos
Basel, 2002
[Ü: Hartmut Fähndrich]

Hassan Dawud wurde 1950 in Beirut, Libanon, geboren. Nach dem Studium der Arabischen Literatur arbeitete er während des Bürgerkriegs als Journalist in Beirut. Von 1979 bis 1988 war er freier Autor für das Feuilleton der Tageszeitung »Alsafir Daily«. Anschließend war er elf Jahre lang als Korrespondent der internationalen arabischen Zeitung »Al-Hayat« tätig, die in London herausgegeben wird. Er schrieb u. a. Artikel über gesellschaftliche Themen sowie Buchrezensionen, Kunst- und Kulturkritiken für das Feuilleton. Derzeit ist er Chefredakteur der Kulturbeilage »Nawafez« der Beiruter Tageszeitung »Al-Mustaqbal Daily«. Seine Kommentare zu politischen und kulturellen Ereignissen im arabischen Raum erscheinen auch in europäischen Zeitungen, etwa in der »Neuen Zürcher Zeitung«. Als Schriftsteller veröffentlichte er bisher zwei Bände mit Erzählungen und vier Romane.

1983 erschien sein erster Roman »Binâyat Mathilde« (1983; engl. »The House of Mathilde«, 1999), der in einem Beiruter Apartmenthaus während des Bürgerkriegs spielt. Im Zentrum dieses sozialen Mikrokosmos aus muslimischen und christlichen Mietern steht Mathilde, die einen namenlosen Flüchtling bei sich versteckt hält. Hassan Dawud, der selbst in einem Haus aufwuchs, in dem Muslime, Drusen und Christen sowie Einwanderer aus Russland und Armenien gemeinsam lebten, macht hier eindrucksvoll anhand der Veränderungen im Alltag der Mieter die Hintergründe für die Erschütterungen der libanesischen Gesellschaft sichtbar. Auch in seinen weiteren Romanen begrenzt er das Geschehen auf einen fest definierten Raum. Häufig erzählt er aus der Perspektive von Menschen, die am Rande der Gesellschaft stehen. Dabei verzichtet er weitestgehend auf die Einbindung des Geschehens in lokale Kontexte. Statt dessen fasst er präzise Beobachtungen und subtile Details in eine reduzierte Sprache, die frei von psychologischen Deutungen ist.

In »Ayyâm zâ'ida« (1990; dt. »Tage zuviel«, 2002) entfaltet sich im fortgesetzten Monolog eines alten Mannes, in dem sich Vergangenheit und Gegenwart, Erinnerungen und Träume zu einem Gedankenfluss vermischen, ein sturer Kampf gegen die Familie, die ihm gleichgültig bis ablehnend gegenübersteht, aber auch ein vergeblicher Kampf gegen zunehmende Hilflosigkeit, körperlichen Verfall und den Tod. Auch der Protagonist von »Ghinâ' al-bitrîq« (1998; dt. »Der Gesang des Pinguins«, 2000) lebt, beeinträchtigt durch eine körperliche Missbildung, ein Leben auf Distanz zu seinen Mitmenschen. Obsessiv beobachtet und belauscht er eine junge Nachbarin. Der Roman erhielt die Auszeichnung ›Bestes Buch des Libanon 1998‹. 2003 erschien Hassan Dawuds jüngster Roman »Makiage khafif lihazihi Allailah« (Ü: Ein zartes Make-Up für heute abend). Hassan Dawud lebt in Beirut.

hamidou dia

biography

Hamidou Dia was born in Saldé, a village in Senegal, in 1953. He studied Philosophy in Dakar and Paris. He obtained a doctorate in French Literature at the University of Laval in Canadian Québec, and wrote his thesis on the theme of languages, nationalities and identities in literature. For over twenty years he has taught Philosophy and Comparative Literature at the Universities of Connecticut, Laval and Dakar. He also worked as editor and literary critic for various publications, among them the Québec literary magazine »Etudes littéraires« and the journal »Nuit Blanche«. From 1997 to 2001 he was chief editor of »Présence Africaine«, a journal which since its founding in 1947 has shaped the postcolonial discourse of African intellectuals.

Already in the early 1980's Hamidou Dia was occupied with two heavyweights of black literature and the African opposition. In 1981 he published the biography of the Martinique author and theorist Frantz Fanon, who as a doctor became involved in the Algerian resistance against the French colonial power in the 1950's, and also the biography of the Franco-Senegalese poet David Diop, in whose work is reflected the hope for a liberated, independent Africa. Dia has published several books on African literature. »Introduction à la littérature négro-africaine« (t: Introduction to Black African literature) was published in 1983. He has also edited the anthologies »Poètes d'Afrique et des Antilles« (2002; t: Poets from Africa and the Antilles) and »Poésie africaine et engagement« (2002; t: African Poetry and commitment). He has also published essays on important writers of postcolonial literature, among them the Senegalese author Boubacar Boris Diop (1990) and the major Caribbean poet Aimé Césaire (2004). He is presently at work on a book on the poet Véronique Tadjo. His own literary work includes the novel »Les sanglots de l'espoir« (1987; t: Sobs of dispair), the novella »Le serment« (1987; t: The vow) as well as two volumes of poetry. In the first, »Koumbi Saleh ou Les pâturages du ciel« (1993; t: Koumbi Saleh or heavenly pastures), he commemorates his ancestors and Koumbi Saleh, the ruined, once splendid, trading centre for gold, salt, and slaves in the former kingdom of Ghana. Dia won the Prix Jasmin d'argent de la poésie francophone for his volume of poetry »Les remparts de la mémoire« (t: The ramparts of memory). Hamidou Dia lives in Dakar.

Les Sanglots de l'espoir
Les Nouvelles Éditions Africaines du Sénégal
Dakar, 1987

Le Serment
Actuel
Paris, 1987

Koumbi Saleh ou Les pâturages du ciel
Les Nouvelles Éditions Africaines du Sénégal
Dakar, 1993

Les Remparts de la memoire
Présence Africaine
Paris, 1999

Poètes d'Afrique et des Antilles
La Table Ronde
Paris, 2002

Poésie africaine et engagement
Acoria
Paris, 2003

Hamidou Dia wurde 1953 in Saldé, einem Dorf in Senegal, geboren. Er studierte Philosophie in Dakar und Paris. An der Universität Laval im kanadischen Québec erlangte er 1995 seinen Doktortitel in Französischer Literatur mit einer Arbeit über Sprachen, Nationalitäten und Identitäten in der Literatur. Seit mehr als zwanzig Jahren lehrt er Philosophie und Vergleichende Literaturwissenschaften an Universitäten in Connecticut, Laval und Dakar. Er arbeitete als Redakteur und Literaturkritiker für verschiedene Publikationen, darunter für das Québecer Literaturmagazin »Études littéraires« und die Zeitschrift »Nuit Blanche«. Von 1997 bis 2001 war er Chefredakteur von »Présence Africaine«, jener Zeitschrift, die seit ihrer Gründung 1947 den postkolonialen Diskurs der afrikanischen Intellektuellen entscheidend prägte.
Mit zwei großen Vertretern der schwarzen Literatur und des afrikanischen Widerstandes hatte sich Hamidou Dia schon zu Beginn der achtziger Jahre beschäftigt. 1981 veröffentlichte er die Biographien des Theoretikers und Schriftstellers Frantz Fanon aus Martinique, der sich in den fünfziger Jahren als Arzt im algerischen Widerstand gegen die französische Kolonialmacht engagierte, und des franko-senegalesischen Dichters David Diop, in dessen Werk sich die Hoffnung auf ein vom Kolonialismus befreites, unabhängiges Afrika widerspiegelt. Hamidou Dia publizierte mehrere Bücher über afrikanische Literatur. 1983 erschien z. B. »Introduction à la littérature négro-africaine« (1983; Ü: Einführung in die schwarz-afrikanische Literatur). Außerdem ist er Herausgeber der Anthologien »Poètes d'Afrique et des Antilles« (2002; Ü: Dichter aus Afrika und von den Antillen) und »Poésie africaine et engagement« (2002; Ü: Afrikanische Poesie und Engagement). Er veröffentlichte Essays über wichtige Autoren der postkolonialen Literatur, unter anderem über den senegalesischen Schriftsteller Boubacar Boris Diop (1990) und den großen karibischen Poeten Aimé Césaire (2004). Zur Zeit arbeitet er über die Dichterin Véronique Tadjo. Sein eigenes literarisches Werk umfasst den Roman »Les sanglots de l'espoir« (1987; Ü: Schluchzer der Hoffnung), die Novelle »Le serment« (1987; Ü: Der Schwur) sowie zwei Lyrikbände. Mit seinem ersten Gedichtband »Koumbi Saleh ou Les pâturages du ciel« (1993; Ü: Koumbi Saleh oder die Weiden des Himmels) erinnert er an die Vorfahren und an das zerstörte, ehemals glanzvolle Handelszentrum für Gold, Salz und Sklaven Koumbi Saleh im alten Königreich Ghana. Für den Gedichtband »Les remparts de la mémoire« (1999; Ü: Der Schutzwall der Erinnerung) wurde Hamidou Dia mit dem Prix Jasmin d'argent de la poésie francophone ausgezeichnet. Hamidou Dia lebt in Dakar.

duong thu huong

biography

Duong Thu Huong was born in the Thai Binh province of North Vietnam in 1947. She was involved in the war against the USA since her school days. For nearly ten years during the Vietnam war she supported herself as a singer and member of an artist's group for the entertainment of soldiers at the front (»Sing louder than the bombs«), chiefly at the border with South Vietnam, which was exposed to the heaviest bombings. After the end of the war in 1975, by dint of the capitulation of South Vietnam, she worked in the film studios of Hanoi. Four years later she became the first female correspondent during the war against China. It was this war above all that disillusioned her forever. Back in Hanoi she published many short stories which found a large readership, especially »Chuyen tinh ke'truóc lúc dong« (1981), a story about the unfortunate love between a singer and a soldier, whose recent divorce was called off by the intervention of the Communist Party. At the start of the 1980's she spoke out at official Party events and at congresses of the writers' organisation, as well as in interviews for various Party publications, criticising bureaucracy, corruption and »intellectual cowardice«. Her works were banned from publication as of 1982. Since 1985 she finds herself, as she herself has expressed it, »continually in a ›Third War‹ against the authorities and against a dictatorial regime«. For a short period of time the censorship of her books was repealed. During this time she published a children's book and the novel »Ben Kia Bo Ao Vong« (Eng. »Beyond Illusions«, 2003), both of which became bestsellers. A ban of her work was once more ordered as a result of certain passages in her third novel »Nhung Thien Duong Mu« (1993; Eng. »Paradise of the Blind«, 1994) about the horrors of land reform from 1953, and her work was pulled from circulation.

In 1990 she sent her manuscript of »Tieu thuyet vo de« (1997), in which she depicts the disillusionment of the soldier Quan in the face of the desolate situation of the land and the Party's greed for power, for publication in France and the USA. That same year she was barred from the Party and her documentary film on the inhuman living conditions in a camp for mentally ill war veterans was destroyed. In 1991 she was imprisoned with no right to trial, and was released after seven months thanks to international protests. In 1991 she was awarded the Prix Femina and the UNESCO Literature Prize. »My writing is a battle to convince others of the necessity of democracy and the upholding of human rights.« Duong Thu Huong lives in Hanoi.

Paradise of the Blind
Penguin
New York, 1994
[Ü: Nina McPherson,
Huy Duong Phan]
Histoire d'amour racontée avant l'aube
La Tour d'Aigues
Editions de l'aube, 1995
[Ü: Kim Lefèvre]
Roman ohne Namen
Unionsverlag
Zürich, 1997
[Ü: Ursula Lies]
Au-delà des illusions
Picquier
Arles, 2000
[Ü: Huy Duong Phan]
Memories of a Pure Spring
Picador
London, 2001
[Ü: Nina McPherson,
Huy Duong Phan]
Myosotis
Picquier
Arles, 2001
[Ü: Huy Duong Phan]

Duong Thu Huong wurde 1947 in der Provinz Thai Binh in Nordvietnam geboren. Seit ihrer Schulzeit engagierte sie sich für den Krieg gegen die USA. Nahezu zehn Jahre lang hielt sie sich im Vietnamkrieg als Sängerin und Mitglied einer Künstlergruppe zur Unterhaltung der Soldaten (»Lauter als die Bomben singen«) an der Front auf, hauptsächlich an der Grenze zu Südvietnam, die den schwersten Bombardements ausgesetzt war. Nach Beendigung des Krieges 1975 durch die Kapitulation Südvietnams arbeitete sie in den Filmstudios von Hanoi. Bereits vier Jahre später war sie die erste weibliche Kriegskorrespondentin im Krieg gegen China. Es war vor allem dieser Krieg, der sie nachhaltig desillusionierte. Zurück in Hanoi veröffentlichte sie mehrere Erzählungen, die eine große Leserschaft fanden, insbesondere »Chuyên tinh kê'truóc lúc rang dông« (1981; dt. »Liebesgeschichte, vor der Morgendämmerung erzählt«, 1992), eine Geschichte über die unglückliche Liebe zwischen einer Sängerin und einem Soldaten, dessen zuvor erfolgte Scheidung durch die Einmischung der Partei rückgängig gemacht wird. Zu Beginn der achtziger Jahre äußerte sie in Reden auf offiziellen Parteiveranstaltungen und Kongressen der Schriftstellervereinigung sowie in Interviews für verschiedene Parteipublikationen Kritik an Bürokratie, Korruption und ›intellektueller Feigheit‹. Nach 1982 erhielt sie Publikationsverbot. Seit 1985 befindet sie sich, wie sie es selbst formuliert, »fortwährend in einem ›dritten Krieg‹ gegen die Autoritäten und gegen ein diktatorisches Regime«. Kurzfristig wurde das Publikationsverbot aufgehoben. In dieser Zeit avancierten ein Kinderbuch und der Roman »Bên Kia Bo Ao Vong« (engl. »Beyond Illusions«, 2003) zu Bestsellern, das Verbot wurde jedoch neuerlich verhängt wegen der Passagen über die Schrecken der Landreform von 1953 in ihrem dritten Roman »Nhung Thien Duong Mu« (dt. »Bitterer Reis«, 1993) und ihre Werke aus dem Umlauf gezogen.
1990 schickte sie ihr Manuskript von »Tiêu thuyêt vô dê« (dt. »Roman ohne Namen«, 1997), in dem sie die Desillusionierung des Soldaten Quan angesichts der desolaten Situation im Land und der Machtgier der Partei schildert, zur Publikation nach Frankreich und in die USA. Im selben Jahr wurde sie aus der Partei ausgeschlossen und ihr Dokumentarfilm über die unmenschlichen Lebensbedingungen in einem Lager für psychisch kranke Kriegsveteranen zerstört. 1991 wurde sie ohne Gerichtsverfahren inhaftiert und erst nach sieben Monaten aufgrund von internationalen Protesten wieder freigelassen. Sie erhielt 1991 den Prix Femina und den UNESCO-Literaturpreis. »Mein Schreiben ist ein Kampf dafür, andere von der Notwendigkeit der Demokratie und dem Einhalten der Menschenrechte zu überzeugen.« Duong Thu Huong lebt in Hanoi.

álvaro enrigue

biography

Álvaro Enrigue was born in Mexico in 1969. Having studied communications at the Ibero-American University in Mexico City, he went on to take a Master's degree in Latin American Literature at the University of Maryland. He is currently working on his Ph.D., while teaching translation and Creative Writing at the same time. In addition, Enrigue has worked as part-time professor at the Ibero-American University in Mexico City, and he has acted as editor for various cultural journals. Since 1990 Enrigue has worked as a literary critic, writing for magazines both in Mexico and in Spain, such as »Letras Libres,« »Vuelta,« »Lateral« and »Insula«. His first novel: »La muerte de un instalador« (t: The death of a plumber) won the Joaquín Mortiz Award for a first novel in 1996. Enrigue has also published a collection of short stories: »Virtudes capitales« (1998; t: Capital virtues) and the novel: »El cementerio de sillas« (2002; t: The cemetery of chairs) which in 2003 was selected as the best novel by the Mexican literary magazine »Tempestad«.

Considered as one of a cast of rising young Mexican writers, Enrigue is especially recognised for his independent stance with regard to his contemporary Mexican writers under forty, many of whom banded together to form movements such as the »Crack« and »Boomerang« generations. Although Enrigue went to university with one of »Crack's« founder members, Ignacio Padilla, still he prefers to work unconstricted by the boundaries of a collective doctrine or program. Enrigue's work has been described as post-modern, whereas it might be more accurate to declare that he develops ancient themes in a contemporary way that avoids a specific geographical setting. »El cementerio de sillas,« for example, traces the family saga of a small group of »garamantes« – mythological beings who originated in Africa and fought the Cyclops – up to the tribulations of their descendents in the New World. Employing various narrative techniques – such as the diary form, omniscience, and polyphony – the novel embraces myriad themes ranging from African exodus to contemporary exile, and from individual salvation to the disintegration of ethnicity and identity. Critics have described the novel as a biting satire that merges contemporary events with the remote: legend with history, tragedy with comedy.

Enrigue has written numerous articles on literature which were broadcast in various radio programmes in Mexico; he also gave live broadcasts on literature for both adults and children, and co-hosted, with two other critics, the live programme »La conjura de necios« which dealt with literature and literary life. Álvaro Enrigue currently lives in Washington, D. C.

La muerte de un instalador
J. Mortiz
Mexiko, 1996

Virtudes capitales
J. Mortiz
Mexiko, 1998

El cementerio de sillas
Ediciones Lengua de Trapo
Madrid, 2002

Álvaro Enrigue wurde 1969 in Mexiko-Stadt geboren. Nach dem Studium der Kommunikationswissenschaften an der Ibero-Amerikanischen Universität in Mexiko-Stadt wechselte er zur Universität Maryland und schloss mit einem Master in lateinamerikanischer Literatur ab. Derzeit arbeitet er an seiner Dissertation und lehrt Übersetzung und Kreatives Schreiben. Zwischenzeitlich war er zudem Teilzeitprofessor an der Ibero-Amerikanischen Universität und Herausgeber verschiedener Kulturzeitschriften. Seit 1990 arbeitet Enrigue als Literaturkritiker und verfasste Artikel für spanische und mexikanische Magazine wie »Letras Libres«, »Vuelta«, »Lateral« und »Insula«. Sein Roman »La muerte de un instalador« (Ü: Der Tod eines Installateurs) gewann 1996 den Joaquín Mortiz Award als bester Erstlingsroman. Er veröffentlichte eine Sammlung von Kurzgeschichten, »Virtudes capitales« (1998; Ü: Wichtige Tugenden) und den Roman »El cementerio de sillas« (2002; Ü: Der Friedhof der Stühle), der 2003 vom mexikanischen Literaturmagazin »Tempestad« als bester Roman gekürt wurde.
Im Gegensatz zu den jüngeren aufstrebenden mexikanischen Autoren, von denen sich viele in Bewegungen wie »Crack« oder »Boomerang« zusammengeschlossen haben, nimmt Enrigue eine unabhängige Stellung für sich in Anspruch. Obwohl er mit einem Gründungsmitglied von »Crack«, Ignacio Padilla, die Universität besuchte, ziehe er, so Enrigue, die Arbeit außerhalb der Grenzen eines kollektiven Programms oder einer Doktrin vor. Seine Literatur wird oft als postmodern bezeichnet, doch wäre die Beobachtung wohl treffender, dass er historische Themen innerhalb eines zeitgenössischen und geographisch kaum fixierten Rahmens entwickelt. In »El cementerio de sillas« verfolgt er die Familiengeschichte einer kleinen Gruppe von »garamantes« – mythologischen Wesen, die ihren Ursprung in Afrika haben und gegen die Zyklopen kämpften – bis hin zu den Beschwerlichkeiten ihrer Nachfahren in der Neuen Welt. Unter Verwendung verschiedener narrativer Techniken wie der Tagebuchform, auktorialem Erzählstil und der Polyphonie verschiedener Stimmen widmet sich der Roman einer Vielzahl unterschiedlichster Themen, die vom afrikanischen Exodus bis zum gegenwärtigen Exil, von individueller Erlösung bis zur Auflösung von ethnischer und persönlicher Identität reichen. Kritiker nannten das Buch eine beißende Satire, in der sich gegenwärtige Ereignisse und weit Zurückliegendes, Legende und Geschichte, Tragödie und Komödie durchdringen.
Für verschiedene mexikanische Radioprogramme produzierte Enrigue Literaturbeiträge und trat auch live in Sendungen für Kinder- und Erwachsenenliteratur auf. Zusammen mit zwei anderen Literaturwissenschaftlern leitete er die ebenfalls live ausgestrahlte Sendung zu Literatur und literarischem Leben »La conjura de necios«. Álvaro Enrigue lebt derzeit in Washington, D. C.

aritha van herk

biography

Aritha van Herk, the daughter of Dutch immigrants, was born in Wetaskiwin, Alberta, Canada. She grew up on a farm and then studied Canadian Literature and Creative Writing in Edmonton. Her debut novel »Judith« appeared in 1978 and won the Seal First Novel Award. Judith is a young woman who works as a secretary. She decides to leave behind a rather ambivalent relationship with an older man from the city in favour of moving to the country and starting her own pig farm. Aritha van Herk writes about women striving to be independent and about the search for complex female identity. This can be seen in her choice of evocative strong female roles which are inspired by representative women in Biblical and ancient mythology. The character of Judith falls into this category; linked to both the Old Testament figure of the same name, who beheaded the warlord Holofernes, and the Greek sorceress Circe, who turned Odysseus' men into swine. This feminist perspective has both provoked and nterested literary critics. Her other novels also set out to question and to trouble gender stereotypes. J. L., the protagonist in »The Tent Peg« (1981), works as a cook for an all-male bush camp of exploration geologists in northern Canada, a situation that sets up a complex battle for respect. The narrative begins realistically, but becomes progressively more mystical and fantastical, coloured by the landscape and the multiple perspective from which the novel is revealed. The Canadian wilderness plays a metaphorical role, nature influencing the socially determined categories of male and female and ultimately dissolving them. Van Herk is persistently interested in the contradictory roles of woman as 'mother-earth' as opposed to temptress or murderess. J. L.'s name derives from the Biblical heroine Ja-el, who actually killed her oppressor by driving a tent peg through his temple. Her third novel, »No Fixed Address« (1986) follows a contemporary picara who looks for trouble and adventure on the backroads of the prairies.

Since 1983 Aritha van Herk has been teaching Creative Writing and Canadian Literature at the University of Calgary. She has also published a range of critical books, articles, and reviews, including »Places far from Ellesmere« (1990), »In Visible Ink: Cryptofrictions« (1991), »A Frozen Tongue« (1992), and »Mavericks: An Incorrigible History of Alberta« (2001). These consist of experimental and subversive essays in which she puts together elements of Canadian history, fiction, literary theory and biography. Her latest novel, »Restlessness« (1998), explores the melancholia of travel and the temptations of homesickness. Aritha van Herk lives in Calgary.

Alle meine Schweine
Zsolnay
Wien, 1979
Mackenzies Koch
Zsolnay
Wien, 1983
Unter Männern
Rowohlt
Reinbek, 1987
Adresse unbekannt
Rowohlt
Reinbek, 1989
In Visible Ink
NeWest
Edmonton, 1991
A Frozen Tongue
Dangaroo
Sydney, 1992
Restlessness
Red Deer College Press
Red Deer, 1998
Mavericks – An Incorrigible History of Alberta
Penguin
Toronto/London, 2001

Aritha van Herk wurde in Wetaskiwin/Alberta, Kanada, geboren. Die Tochter niederländischer Immigranten wuchs auf einer Farm auf. Sie studierte Kanadische Literatur und Kreatives Schreiben in Edmonton. Ihr Debütroman »Judith« (dt. »Alle meine Schweine«, 1979), erschien 1978 und wurde mit dem Seal First Novel Award ausgezeichnet. Judith ist eine junge Frau, die ihr Leben als Sekretärin und ihre ambivalente Beziehung zu einem älteren Mann in der Stadt hinter sich lässt, um allein auf einer abgelegenen Farm Schweine zu züchten. Aritha van Herk erzählt vom Streben nach Unabhängigkeit und der Suche nach einer komplexen weiblichen Identität, indem sie starke Frauenfiguren aus Mythen sowie aus der Bibel adaptiert: in diesem Fall sind es die alttestamentarische Judith, die den Kriegsherrn Holofernes enthauptete, und die griechische Zauberin Circe, die die Männer des Odysseus in Schweine verwandelte. Die feministische Erzählperspektive interessierte und provozierte die Literaturkritik gleichermaßen. Auch in ihren weiteren Romanen fordert Aritha van Herk Geschlechterstereotype heraus. J. L., die Protagonistin ihres zweiten Romans »The Tent Peg« (1981; dt. »Mackenzies Koch«, 1983), muss sich als Köchin bei den Männern eines Geologenteams, das im Norden Kanadas ein Forschungsprojekt durchführt, ihren Respekt erkämpfen. Die Erzählung beginnt realistisch, verlagert sich im Verlauf jedoch mehr und mehr ins Mythisch-Phantastische, untermalt von der Landschaft und wechselnden Erzählperspektiven. Parallel dazu lösen sich in der ursprünglichen Natur Kanadas die gesellschaftlich festgelegten Rollenklischees des Männlichen und des Weiblichen metaphorisch auf. Die Autorin lässt aber auch weibliche Rollenbilder in ihrer Ambivalenz aufeinandertreffen: J. L. erfüllt als Köchin die mütterlich-versorgende Rolle, aber ihr Name sowie der Originaltitel des Buches verweisen auf die biblische Heldin Jael, die ihren Widersacher tötete, indem sie ihm einen Pflock in die Schläfe schlug. Ihr dritter Roman, »No Fixed Address« (1986; dt. »Adresse unbekannt«, 1989), folgt einem weiblichen Schelm auf einsamen Wegen durch die Prärie, in der sie Ärger und Abenteuer sucht.

Seit 1983 unterrichtet Aritha van Herk Kreatives Schreiben und Literaturwissenschaft an der Universität Calgary. Sie publizierte eine Reihe von Literaturkritiken sowie literaturwissenschaftliche Aufsätze und Bücher, darunter »Places Far from Ellesmere« (1990), »In Visible Ink. Crypto-frictions« (1991) und »A Frozen Tongue« (1992) und »Mavericks: An Incorrigible History of Alberta« (2001). In diesen experimentellen und subversiven Essays verbindet sie die Geschichte Kanadas mit fiktiven, biographischen und literaturtheoretischen Elementen. »Restlessness« (1998), ihr bisher letzter Roman, erforscht die Melancholie des Reisens und die Versuchungen des Heimwehs. Aritha van Herk lebt in Calgary.

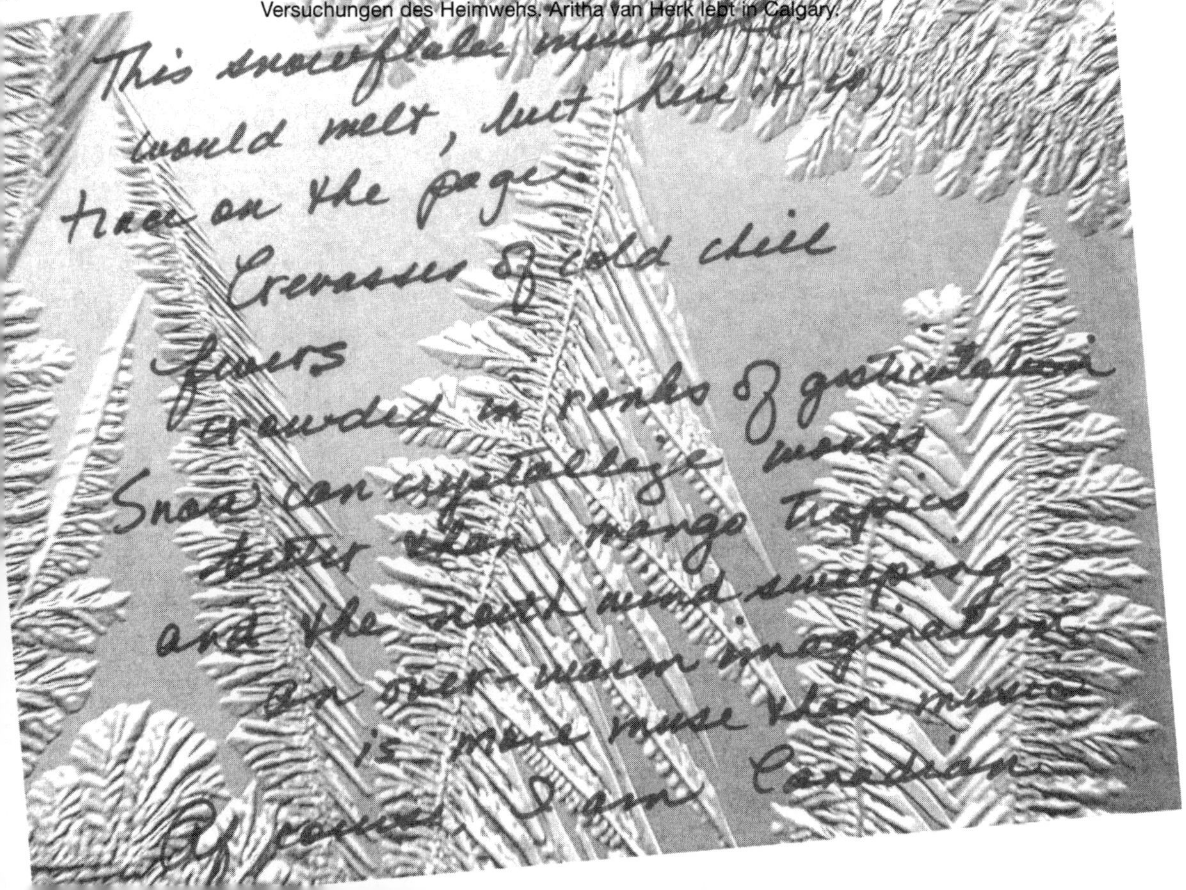

k. s. maniam

biography

K. S. Maniam was born under the name Subramaniam Krishnan into an Indian family in Bedong/Kedah, Malaysia, in 1942. His childhood bore the mark of the everyday life of the Indian minority group in Malaysia. Following his father's wish that he should have an education that would fit his cultural background, he attended a Tamil school. After a year however his father gave in to his pleas and let him attend an English school, so that during his adolescence K. S. Maniam was strongly influenced by British and western culture. In the 1960's he completed his training as teacher at the Malayan Teacher's College in Great Britain. He began to write poems, some of which were published in »The Sunday Times«. After his return he worked as a teacher for several more years, before beginning studies for a degree in English at the University of Malaya in 1970. He worked on poetry written in English in Malaysia and Singapore for his MA. Then followed a long lasting job at the University of Malaya, where he was Associate Professor of Literature and Creative Writing until 1997. Inspired by the new postcolonial literature, he began to focus more intensely on his own writing in the mid 1970's. K. S. Maniam writes in English.

His first short story, »The Eagles«, appeared in 1976, and in 1981 his first novel »The Return«, which is largely autobiographical. The young Ravi, from a third-generation Indian immigrant family in Malaya, feels lost in the conflict between cultures. In an effort to avoid demands to preserve his grandparent's ancestral culture, as well as the expectations of the Malaysian society for cultural and linguistic assimilation, Ravi flees to an English school. There he learns not only the language, but also the mindset and customs of the former colonial power, and this increasingly distances him from his family. The question of cultural identity in an immigrant society prevails in other works by K. S. Maniam. In addition to numerous stories and three novels, the other two being »In a Far Country« (1993) and »Between Lives« (2003), he has written a number of plays. He received the Raja Rao Award for his Outstanding Contribution to the Literature of the South Asian Diaspora in New Delhi in 2000. His most recent volume of short stories is entitled »Faced Out« (2004). K. S. Maniam lives in Subang Jaya/Selangor, Malaysia.

Writing, for me, comes from a deep stillness. When it falters or trickles to a stop, it means I've been distracted from that stillness. So, I wake up earlier than the earliest dawn, when the physical stillness is there to touch. I sit at my blank page, and wait. Gazing at all that whiteness is praying. The distractions crumble and dissolve. My Muse, stillness, hears. It — don't ask me what — comes slowly like a soft but soul-warming rain from the hills; soon I'm wrestling with my characters, their conflicts, their yearnings. I've begun the inexorable struggle again. I'm writing!

KSManiam

Plot, The Aborting, Parablames and Other Stories
AMK Interaksi Sdn. Bhd.
Kuala Lumpur, 1989
In A Far Country
Skoob Books
London, 1993
The Return
Heinemann Asia
Petaling Jaya, 1996
Between Lives
Maya Press
Petaling Jaya, 2003
Faced Out
Maya Press
Petaling Jaya, 2004

K. S. Maniam wurde 1942 unter dem Namen Subramaniam Krishnan in eine indische Familie in Bedong/Kedah, Malaysia, geboren. Seine Kindheit war geprägt vom Alltag der indischen Minderheit in Malaysia. Auf Wunsch des Vaters, der ihm eine Schulbildung gemäß der kulturellen Herkunft zukommen lassen wollte, besuchte er eine Tamil-Schule. Nach einem Jahr gab der Vater jedoch dem Drängen seines Sohnes nach und ließ ihn eine englische Schule besuchen, so dass K. S. Maniam in seiner Jugend stark von der britischen bzw. westlichen Kultur beeinflusst wurde. In den sechziger Jahren schloss er eine Lehrerausbildung am Malayan Teachers' College in Großbritannien ab. Er begann mit dem Schreiben von Gedichten, von denen einige in der »Sunday Times« veröffentlicht wurden. Nach seiner Rückkehr arbeitete er zunächst mehrere Jahre als Lehrer, bevor er 1970 ein Englischstudium an der University of Malaya aufnahm. In seiner Abschlussarbeit beschäftigte er sich mit englischsprachiger Lyrik in Malaysia und Singapur. Es folgte eine langjährige Tätigkeit an der University of Malaya, wo er bis 1997 als Associate Professor Literatur und Kreatives Schreiben lehrte. Inspiriert von der neuen postkolonialen Literatur, wandte er sich Mitte der siebziger Jahre verstärkt dem eigenen Schreiben zu. K. S. Maniam schreibt in Englisch.
Seine erste Kurzgeschichte »The Eagles« erschien 1976, einige Jahre später folgte sein erster Roman »The Return« (1981), der starke autobiographische Züge aufweist. Der junge Ravi, der aus der dritten Generation einer indischen Einwandererfamilie in Malaysia stammt, fühlt sich verloren im Spannungsfeld zwischen den Kulturen. Im Versuch, sich sowohl den Ansprüchen zur Bewahrung der Herkunftskultur seiner Großmutter und seines Vaters zu entziehen als auch den Erwartungen der malaysischen Gesellschaft zur kulturellen und sprachlichen Assimilation, flüchtet sich Ravi in die englische Schule. Dort lernt er nicht nur die Sprache, sondern auch Denkweise und Gebräuche der ehemaligen Kolonialmacht, was ihn zunehmend von seiner Familie entfremdet. Auch in anderen Werken von K. S. Maniam ist die Frage nach der kulturellen Identität in der Migrationsgesellschaft vorherrschend. Neben zahlreichen Erzählungen und zwei weiteren Romanen, »In a Far Country« (1993) und »Between Lives« (2003), verfasste er einige Theaterstücke. 2000 wurde ihm in Neu Delhi für seinen herausragenden Beitrag zur Literatur der südasiatischen Diaspora der renommierte Raja Rao Award verliehen. Sein jüngster Erzählband erschien 2004 unter dem Titel »Faced Out«. K. S. Maniam lebt in Subang Jaya/Selangor, Malaysia.

Schreiben entsteht für mich aus einer tiefen Stille. Wenn es nur noch zögerlich kommt oder tröpfelnd zu versiegen droht, bedeutet es, dass ich aus dieser Stille gerissen bin. Also wache ich noch vor der ersten Dämmerung auf, wenn die körperliche Stille greifbar ist. Ich sitze vor meiner weißen Seite und warte. Dieses ganze Weiß zu betrachten ist ein Gebet. Die Ablenkungen bröckeln und lösen sich auf. Meine Muse, die Stille hört. Es – fragen Sie nicht was – kommt langsam wie ein sanfter aber seelenwärmender Regen von den Hügeln. Bald kämpfe ich mit meinen Figuren, ihren Konflikten, ihren Sehnsüchten. Ich habe den unerbittlichen Kampf wieder aufgenommen. Ich schreibe!

zakes mda
biography

Zakes Mda, full name Zanemvula Kizito Gatyeni Mda, was born in Herschel, Eastern Cape, South Africa, in 1948. His father, Ashby P. Mda, was an anti-Apartheid activist, a founding member and president of the African National Congress (ANC) Youth League.
In the 1960's, his father was imprisoned and the family had to leave South Africa. Zakes Mda finished his schooling in exile in Lesotho. Later on, he went to the USA, studied drama and mass communication at Ohio University, and received his Ph.D. from the University of Cape Town in 1990. After thirty two years in exile, he decided to return to South Africa where he worked as a Professor of Drama at the University of the Witwatersrand, and later became a full-time writer, painter and film maker. He is currently a literary consultant at the Market Theatre in Johannesburg and Professor of Creative Writing at Ohio University in the US.
During the 1970's and 80's, the theatre was Mda's foremost interest. Beginning with the early drama »We Shall Sing for the Fatherland« (1977) many of his around thirty plays have repeated the premonition that a new government, being as corrupt and craving for power as the old one, would betray the ideals of resistance. In Mda's style, the African oral narrative tradition is interwoven with elements of the Xhosa Intsomi Theatre, with magical realism and the European Theatre of the Absurd. His plays have been awarded numerous prizes. »The Plays of Zakes Mda« (1990) has been translated into South Africa's eleven official languages. Mda's novels reflect the collective internal conflict of tradition and materialist consumerism prevalent in post-Apartheid South Africa. They are told from the blacks' perspective; whites only play a peripheral role. The much acclaimed novel »Ways of Dying« (1995) depicts Toloki, a self-proclaimed mourner, wandering from one township funeral to the next. Slowly, the reader learns that almost all the victims' ways of dying were inflicted on them by their own fanatic, greedy and violent community. »Heart of Redness«, published in 2000, looks back at the colonial past. The Xhosa were prophesied by ancestral spirits a victory over the British if they slew their cattle, which left the tribe ultimately divided. Mda vivedly describes how the tragic effects of this rift have continued up to the present day. His latest book »Madonna of Excelsior« (2002) is based on a sex scandal between white Africans and their black maids in the 1970's. The book will soon appear in German translation. Zakes Mda lives in Johannesburg and Ohio.

My Muse always answers.
I am surrounded by women who love me.
These include my daughters, my fiancee,
my mother, my nieces, my friends who are
actresses and filmmakers and traditional
healers and diviners ...
It is this positive female energy that
fuels my creativity. Females are the source
of life and the female well never runs dry.
I myself was part of a woman's body for
nine months.

We Shall Sing for the Fatherland
Ravan Press
Johannesburg, 1977
The Plays of Zakes Mda
Ravan Press
Johannesburg, 1990
Ways of Dying
Picador
New York, 2002
Fools Bells and the Habit of Eating
Witwatersrand University Press
Johannesburg, 2002
The Heart of Redness
Farrar, Straus and Giroux
New York, 2002
The Madonna of Excelsior
Farrar, Straus and Giroux
New York, 2004
She Plays with the Darkness
Picador
New York, 2004

Zakes Mda wurde 1948 in Herschel/Eastern Cape, Südafrika, geboren. Sein vollständiger Name lautet Zanemvula Kizito Gatyeni Mda. Sein Vater Ashby P. Mda war Anti-Apartheidsaktivist und prominenter Mitbegründer und Präsident der African National Congress (ANC) Youth League. In den sechziger Jahren wurde der Vater inhaftiert, und die Familie musste Südafrika verlassen. Im Exil in Lesotho beendete Zakes Mda seine Schulausbildung.
Später ging er in die USA, wo er an der Ohio University Theater und Mass Communication studierte. 1990 promovierte er an der University of Cape Town. 1995 entschloss er sich, nach zweiunddreißigjährigem Exil wieder in Südafrika ansässig zu werden, wo er an der University of the Witwatersrand Professor für Drama war. Später arbeitete er ausschließlich als Schriftsteller, Maler und Filmemacher. Zur Zeit ist er als Dramaturg am Market Theatre in Johannesburg und als Dozent für kreatives Schreiben an der Ohio University tätig.
In den siebziger und achtziger Jahren galt Mdas Interesse vor allem dem Theater. In mehreren seiner rund dreißig Dramen warnt er vor dem Verrat der Widerstandsideale durch eine neue Regierung, die sich als ebenso korrupt und machtgierig entpuppt wie die abgelöste. So auch in dem frühen »We Shall Sing for the Fatherland« (1977). Über die Jahre entwickelte er einen besonderen Stil, indem er mündliche Erzähltraditionen Afrikas, Elemente des Intsomi-Theaters der Xhosa und des magischen Realismus mit dem Absurden Theater Europas verbindet. Seine Theaterstücke wurden mit zahlreichen Preisen gewürdigt. »The Plays of Zakes Mda« (1990) wurde in alle elf offiziellen Sprachen Südafrikas übersetzt.
In seinen Romanen spiegelt Mda den kollektiven inneren Konflikt zwischen Tradition und materialistischem Konsum, der für das Südafrika der Post-Apartheid charakteristisch ist. Er erzählt aus der Perspektive von Schwarzen und ihren Lebenswelten, in denen Weiße nur am Rande vorkommen. Im mehrfach preisgekrönten »Ways of Dying« (1995) zieht Toloki, ein selbsternannter professioneller Trauernder, von Begräbnis zu Begräbnis. Im Verlauf des Romans wird deutlich, dass nahezu alle diese Toten Opfer von Fanatismus, Gier und Gewalt innerhalb der eigenen Gemeinschaft wurden. Der Roman »Heart of Redness« (2000) blickt zurück in die koloniale Vergangenheit. Die Prophezeiung vom Sieg der Xhosa über die Briten, unter der Bedingung, dass sie ihr Vieh schlachteten, spaltete das Xhosa-Volk nachhaltig. Mda erzählt auf sehr lebendige Weise von dieser Tragödie und ihren Auswirkungen bis heute. Mit einem Sexskandal zwischen weißen Afrikanern und ihren schwarzen Hausangestellten in den siebziger Jahren setzt er sich in seinem jüngsten Buch »Madonna of Excelsior« (2002) auseinander. Das Buch erscheint demnächst in deutscher Übersetzung.
Zakes Mda lebt in Johannesburg und Ohio.

Meine Muse antwortet immer.
Ich bin umgeben von Frauen, die mich lieben. Darunter meine Töchter, meine Verlobte, meine Mutter, meine Nichten, meine Freundinnen, die Schauspielerinnen und Filmemacherinnen sind, Heilerinnen und Wahrsagerinnen...
Diese positive weibliche Energie treibt meine Kreativität an. Frauen sind der Ursprung des Lebens und die weibliche Quelle trocknet niemals aus.
Ich selbst war neun Monate lang Teil des Körpers einer Frau.

semezdin mehmedinović

biography

Semezdin Mehmedinović was born in Kiseljak, Bosnia-Herzegovina, in 1960. After studying Comparative Literature and Librarianship in Sarajevo, he worked as an editor for the opposition magazines for young people »Lica« and »Valter«. He also did performance art. He published his first book of poetry »Modrac« in 1984, and his second book »Emigrant« in 1990. In 1991 he founded the cultural magazine »Fantom slobode« (t: Phantom of Freedom), of which only six issues appeared – three pre-war and three war editions. When war broke out in 1992, Mehmedinović remained with his family in Sarajevo during the attacks. In this year he published an early version of »Sarajevo Blues«; the more extensive version was published in Zagreb in 1995. With friends he founded the weekly political magazine »Dani« (t: Days) in 1992, to create a voice for democracy and pluralism in times of genocide. Today, its objectivity and lucidity still make it Bosnia's best magazine.

In 1996 Mehmedinović emigrated to the US and now lives in Alexandria, Virginia. »Sarajevo Blues« was published in English in 1998 and was praised by the »Washington Post« as one of the best literary documents of the Bosnian war. »Sarajevo Blues« was translated into German in 1999. In 2002 Mehmedinović published another book of poems entitled »Devet Alexandrija«, in Zagreb, Croatia. Since autumn 2003 the book has been available in English translation under the title »Nine Alexandrias«.

Modrac
Svjetlost
Sarajevo, 1984
Emigrant
Zadrugar
Sarajevo 1990
Sarajevo Blues
Hainholz,
Göttingen, 1999
[Ü: Harris Džajić]
Devet Alexandrija
Durieux
Zagreb, 2002
Nine Alexandrias
City Lights
San Francisco 2003
[Ü: Ammiel Alcalay]

Semezdin Mehmedinović wurde 1960 in Kiseljak, Bosnien-Herzegowina, geboren. Im Anschluss an sein Studium der Vergleichenden Literaturwissenschaft und Bibliothekswissenschaften in Sarajevo arbeitete er als Redakteur der oppositionellen Jugendzeitschriften »Lica« und »Valter« und trat als Performancekünstler auf. Seinen ersten Gedichtband »Modrac« veröffentlichte er 1984. Im Jahr 1991 gründete er die Kulturzeitschrift »Fantom slobode« (Ü: Phantom der Freiheit), von der insgesamt nur sechs Ausgaben erschienen – drei Vorkriegs- und drei Kriegsausgaben. Bei Ausbruch des Krieges 1992 blieb Mehmedinović mit seiner Familie im belagerten Sarajevo. In diesem Jahr veröffentlichte er eine frühe Fassung von »Sarajevo Blues«, einer Sammlung von Texten über den Krieg, die 1995 in einer erweiterten Ausgabe in Zagreb erschien. Mit Freunden gründete er die politische Wochenzeitschrift »Dani« (Ü: Tage), um eine Stimme der Demokratie und des Pluralismus in Zeiten des Genozids zu schaffen. Sie gilt noch heute aufgrund ihrer Objektivität und Klarsicht als die beste Zeitschrift Bosniens.
1996 emigrierte Mehmedinović in die Vereinigten Staaten, wo er mittlerweile in Alexandria, Virginia, lebt. »Sarajevo Blues«, sein international am stärksten beachtetes Werk (in deutscher Übersetzung 1999 unter dem gleichen Titel erschienen), erschien 1998 in englischer Übersetzung und wurde von der »Washington Post« als eines der besten literarischen Dokumente über den Bosnien-Krieg hervorgehoben. 2002 veröffentlichte Mehmedinović einen weiteren Gedichtband mit dem Titel »Devet Alexandrija« (Ü: Neun Alexandrien). 2003 erschien der Band unter dem Titel »Nine Alexandrias« in englischer Übersetzung.

adrian mitchell

biography

Adrian Mitchell was born in 1932. He studied at Christ Church College Oxford, and began as a reporter and theatre critic at the »Oxford Mail« in 1955. He then moved to the »Evening Standard«. From 1963 to 1965 he worked as a freelance music journalist for various newspapers. During this period, he published the first interview with the Beatles in a national newspaper. The interview was the basis for a long term friendship between him and Paul McCartney. As a result of this friendship they published an edition of Mc Cartney's poems and lyrics under the title »Blackbird Singing« (2001.)
Mitchell's literary career started in 1961, when he received an inheritance. This made it possible for him to dedicate himself freely to write not only his first TV script, but also his first prose writing: »If You See Me Comin'« (1962.) Three novels followed, many TV scripts, as well numerous unconventional plays and musicals for both adults and children, which were produced and successfully played on the main British theatre circuit. An example of which is »Tyger« (1971), a musical about William Blake's life and work. He also wrote the Libretto for Peter Schat's Opera »Houdini« (1977) and in addition he adapted popular stories such as Ibsen's »Peer Gynt« (1995) and Lewis Carroll's »Alice in Wonderland« (2000) into Musicals. In 1964 he celebrated his successful adaptation of Peter Weiss' play on Marat/Sade for the Royal Shakespeare Company, which was directed by Peter Brook.
Mitchell's lyrics are characterised by his humourous note and wit, and above all for his critical sharpness. Mitchell is renowned for his ability to present current and relevant themes from a political standpoint in the form of conversational style melodic poetry. The memorable »To Whom it May Concern« was presented as a reading in 1965 by Mitchell and Allen Ginsberg in the Royal Albert Hall as an angry cry against the official cover-up relating to the Vietnam war. In the 1990's he put together a retrospective of his poetic life's work from the past five decades into three volumes. At that time the author took a new direction into writing powerful children's poetry and stories. This is being further explored in his latest publication, a children's book due to appear this autumn in the UK.

If You See Me Comin'
Jonathan Cape
London, 1962
Man Friday
Methuen
London, 1974
Adrian Mitchell's Greatest Hits – The Top Forty
Bloodaxe Books
Tarset, 1992
The Thirteen Secrets of Poetry
Macdonald Young Books
London, 1993
Heart on the Left
Bloodaxe Books
Tarset, 1997
Nobody Rides the Unicorn
Transworld Publishers
London, 1999
All Shook Up
Bloodaxe Books
Tarset, 2000

Me, I take my beautiful golden retriever, Daisy the Dog of Peace, for a walk on Hampstead Heath, where Blake and Keats and Coleridge used to walk.
Or I sit on stairs with her and listen to her thinking.

Adrian Mitchell wurde 1932 in London geboren. Er studierte am Christ Church College in Oxford und begann 1955 als Reporter und Theaterkritiker bei der »Oxford Mail«. 1957 wechselte er zum Londoner »Evening Standard«. Von 1963 bis 1965 arbeitete er als freier Musikjournalist für verschiedene Zeitungen. In dieser Zeit veröffentlichte er unter anderem das erste Interview mit den Beatles in einem überregionalen Blatt. Das Gespräch legte den Grundstein für eine anhaltende Freundschaft Mitchells mit Paul McCartney, aus welcher zuletzt die gemeinsame Publikation von Gedichten und Songtexten McCartneys unter dem Titel »Blackbird Singing« (2001) hervorging.
Mitchells literarische Laufbahn begann 1961. Eine Erbschaft, die ihn für ein Jahr von den Zwängen der Erwerbstätigkeit befreite, ermöglichte ihm nicht nur ein erstes Fernsehstück zu schreiben, sondern auch den Prosaerstling »If You See Me Comin'« (1962). Dem folgten bisher drei weitere Romane, zahlreiche TV-Drehbücher sowie eine Reihe von unkonventionellen Theaterstücken und Musicals für Erwachsene und Kinder, die – wie zunächst »Tyger« (1971), ein musikalisches Schauspiel zu Leben und Werk William Blakes – mit großem Erfolg an den bedeutendsten Bühnen Großbritanniens uraufgeführt wurden. Auch das Libretto zu Peter Schats Oper »Houdini« (1977) stammt aus Mitchells Feder. Darüber hinaus adaptierte der Autor beliebte Stoffe wie Ibsens »Peer Gynt« (1995) oder Carrolls »Alice in Wonderland« (2000) für das musikalische Theater. Einen Erfolg feierte er 1964 mit seiner Bearbeitung des Marat/Sade-Stücks von Peter Weiss für die Royal Shakespeare Company in der Regie von Peter Brook.
Besondere Berühmtheit aber erlangte Mitchell mit seiner Lyrik, die sich durch einen oft humorvollen Tenor, vor allem aber durch kritische Schärfe auszeichnet. Der Autor hat in seinen sprachlich schlichten, dennoch aber hoch melodiösen Gedichten ästhetisches Wirken stets unmittelbar mit politischen Zielsetzungen verbunden und zu den wichtigen Themen seiner Zeit Stellung bezogen. Unvergessen ist »To Whom It May Concern«, ein wütender Aufschrei gegen das von oben verordnete Schweigen zum Vietnamkrieg, den Mitchell 1965 bei einer Lesung Allen Ginsbergs in der Royal Albert Hall vortrug. In den neunziger Jahren hat Mitchell sein poetisches Lebenswerk aus fünf Jahrzehnten in drei Bänden zusammengetragen, parallel dazu hat er verstärkt auch Gedichte und Geschichten für Kinder geschrieben. Eine Tendenz, die der Autor auch in Zukunft fortzusetzen gedenkt – noch im Herbst wird in Großbritannien sein neuestes Kinderbuch erscheinen.

Ich gehe mit meinem wunderschönen Golden Retriever Daisy, dem Hund des Friedens, in der Hampstead Heath spazieren, wo Blake und Keats und Coleridge gern liefen. Oder ich sitze mit ihr auf einer Treppe und höre ihr beim Denken zu.

Daisy the Dog of Peace
by
Adrian Mitchell
2004

alberto mussa

biography

Alberto Mussa was born in Rio de Janeiro, Brazil, in 1961. He studied mathematics briefly, before taking up Language and Literature Studies at the University of Rio de Janeiro. Aside from Tupi, the language of Brazil's original inhabitants, he studied various African languages, amongst them Yoruba, the language of the Afro-Brazilian religious communities, and Arabic. He completed his studies in 1991 with a work on the history of the oral Portuguese of slaves. After that he worked as a sixth form teacher and lexicographer. Because of family roots (his father's family originated from Lebanon and Palestine), he has a special interest in Arabic literature. He has translated several short stories by African and Arab writers into Portuguese, as well as compiling the pre-Islamic anthology »Muallaquat«, a collection of seven odes by the greatest Arabic poets of the sixth and early seventh centuries. He also has been a lecturer in pre-Islamic poetry at the University of Rio de Janeiro.
In 1997 he published his first volume of stories: »Elegbara«, named after the Yoruba deity Eshu-Elegbara, the crafty messenger of the gods. Elegbara's traits, be they extreme cruelty or profound wisdom, are mirrored in the protagonists of these ten short stories, which directly, or indirectly, refer to Brazil's colonial history. He also revisits the colonial past in his first novel »O trono da rainha Jinga« (1999; t: Queen Jinga's throne). In seventeenth century Rio de Janeiro there was a secret society of blacks who sought the liberation of slaves through the brutal murder of white colonial rulers and representatives of the Catholic Church. There is a strange connection between the slave trade and the north Angolan Mbundu queen Jinga. The story unfolds through shifts in the perspectives of the different protagonists. Alberto Mussa maps out a panorama of the society upon which the state of Brazil was founded. Alberto Mussa was awarded the Premio Biblioteca Nacional for »O trono da rainha Jinga«, the first of five planned novels about the history of Rio de Janeiro from its founding to the end of the twentieth century. With his most recent novel, »O enigma de Qaf« (2004; t: The Qaf's riddle), Mussa drew upon his knowledge of myriad philosophical, mythological and literary references and combined them in a story about the origins of Arabic language and civilisation, at whose centre stands the fictitious poet al-Gatash, author of the eight odes of »Muallaquat«. Alberto Mussa lives in Rio de Janeiro.

Elegbara
Revan
Rio de Janeiro, 1997
O trono da rainha Jinga
Nova Fronteira
Rio de Janeiro, 1999
O enigma de Qaf
Record
Rio de Janeiro, 2004

Alberto Mussa wurde 1961 in Rio de Janeiro, Brasilien, geboren. Ein Studium der Mathematik gab er bereits nach kurzer Zeit zugunsten eines Literatur- und Sprachenstudiums an der Universität Rio de Janeiro auf. Neben Tupi, der Sprache der brasilianischen Ureinwohner, studierte er verschiedene afrikanische Sprachen, darunter Yoruba, die Sprache der afro-brasilianischen Religionsgemeinschaften, sowie Arabisch. 1991 schloss er sein Studium mit einer Arbeit über die Geschichte des mündlichen Portugiesisch der Sklaven ab. Anschließend arbeitete er zunächst als Lehrer für die Oberstufe und als Lexikograph. Nicht zuletzt wegen seiner familiären Wurzeln (die Familie väterlicherseits stammt aus dem Libanon und aus Palästina) hat er ein besonderes Interesse an der arabischen Literatur. Er übersetzte mehrere Kurzgeschichten afrikanischer und arabischer Autoren ins Portugiesische sowie die prä-islamische Anthologie »Muallaquat«, eine Zusammenstellung von sieben Oden der größten arabischen Dichter des 6. und frühen 7. Jahrhunderts. Mussa war auch als Dozent für prä-islamische Lyrik an der Universität in Rio de Janeiro tätig.
1997 veröffentlichte er seinen ersten Erzählband »Elegbara«, mit dessen Titel er auf den trickreichen Götterboten Eshu-Elegbara verweist. In den Protagonisten der zehn Kurzgeschichten, die sich direkt oder indirekt auf die Kolonialgeschichte Brasiliens beziehen, spiegeln sich Elegbaras Eigenschaften als extreme Grausamkeit oder tiefe Weisheit. Auch in seinem ersten Roman »O trono da rainha Jinga« (1999; Ü: Königin Jingas Thron) geht es um die koloniale Vergangenheit. Im Rio de Janeiro des 17. Jahrhunderts begeht ein Geheimbund von Schwarzen, der die Befreiung der Sklaven anstrebt, grausame Morde an den weißen Kolonialherren und Vertretern der katholischen Kirche. Über die Wege des Sklavenhandels besteht zugleich eine mysteriöse Verbindung zur nordangolanischen Mbundu-Königin Jinga. Die Geschichte entfaltet sich durch die Perspektivwechsel der Protagonisten. Alberto Mussa entwirft ein Panorama jener Gesellschaft, auf der sich der Staat Brasilien gründet. Für »O trono da rainha Jinga«, den ersten von fünf geplanten Teilen über die Geschichte Rio de Janeiros von der Gründung bis zum Ende des 20. Jahrhunderts, wurde Alberto Mussa mit dem Premio Biblioteca Nacional ausgezeichnet. Mit seinem jüngsten Roman »O enigma de Qaf« (2004; Ü: Das Qaf-Rätsel) erfand Alberto Mussa unter Verwendung von zahlreichen philosophischen, mythologischen und literarischen Verweisen eine zweite Entstehungsgeschichte der arabischen Zivilisation und Sprache, in deren Mittelpunkt der fiktive Dichter al-Gatash steht, Verfasser der achten Ode des Muallaquat. Der Autor lebt in Rio de Janeiro.

nabil naoum

biography

Nabil Naoum was born in Cairo, Egypt, in 1944. He studied Engineering in Cairo and then went to the United States, where he worked as an engineer in New York for ten years. During this time he wrote his first short stories, some of which were published in Egyptian literary magazines. In 1977 his first novel, »Al-bâb« (t: The door) came out, in Egypt. In 1979 he returned to Cairo, where he opened a gallery for modern art and turned more seriously towards writing. In the 1980's he published a series of short story collections, among them for example the French-Arabic volume »Le Caire est petit« (1985; t: Cairo is small). A collection of twenty stories came out in English translation under the title »The Slave's Dream and Other Stories« (1991).
Nabil Naoum's narratives are infused with subtle and objective irony. He foregoes detailed descriptions of landscapes, places and customs. Thus events, even when Egypt is named, can only vaguely be located. Instead, his texts unfold largely detached from real clues, in their own space and time. The characters too are only roughly sketched out and only over the course of a story does their distinct character emerge, all the same, the reader comes to know little about their emotional and mental worlds. Most of Naoum's stories are constructed via a linear narrative flow. Without the moral appraisal of a higher entity, surprising turns take place which suddenly open up room for the horrible and nightmarish. In the novel »Jasad Awal« (1998) the architect and writer Fouad, upon his return from abroad reunites with his family, in particular the older relatives, who are again sharing life and housing. Being thus confronted with loss, old age and death, he searches for a fusion between the secular and the otherworldly. The protagonists of his most recent novel »Hafat el wed« (2000) are driven by their longing for love. They are ensnarled in a web of seduction, power, and unfulfilled longing. In addition to his prose, Nabil Naoum has published several essays on contemporary Arab art and photography. Since 2000 he has been a member of the selection committee of the Biennale for Arabic Film at the Institut du Monde Arabe in Paris. Nabil Naoum has lived in Cairo and Paris since 1993.

Le Caire est petit
Centre de traduction
franco-égyptien
Paris, 1985
[Ü: Ghislaine Alleaume
Luc Barbulesco
Philippe Cardinal]
Le rêve de l'esclave
Actes Sud
Paris, 1994
[Ü: Jean Tardy
Anne Wade Minkowski]
Corps premier
Actes Sud
Paris, 1998
[Ü: Luc Barbulesco]
Jasad Awal
Dar al hilal
Kairo, 1998
Hafat el wed
Kossour al-Thakafa
Kairo, 2000
Textes sur images: art contemporain arabe
ACR, Institut du
monde arabe
Paris, 2000
[Ü: Luc Barbulesco]
Les rivages de l'amour
Actes Sud
Paris, 2003
[Ü: Luc Barbulesco]

It just I like to read this writer and
make drawings, when the music hides away.

And he said to me:
Write who are you, to know
who you are.
Are if you do not know
who you are
you are not of those
who merit to know me.
(El Nefari)

When letters stray away
Ecstasy takes place,
time too.
Nearness would not be allowed,
and the muse would be prevention
(Nabil Naoum)

Nabil Naoum wurde 1944 in Kairo, Ägypten, geboren. Er studierte Ingenieurswesen in Kairo. Nach dem Studium ging er in die USA, wo er zehn Jahre lang als Ingenieur in New York lebte und arbeitete. Während dieser Zeit verfasste er seine ersten Kurzgeschichten, von denen einige in ägyptischen Literaturmagazinen veröffentlicht wurden. In Ägypten erschien 1977 auch sein erster Roman »Al-bâb« (Ü: Die Tür). 1979 kehrte er nach Kairo zurück, wo er eine Galerie für Moderne Kunst eröffnete und sich verstärkt dem Schreiben zuwandte. In den achtziger Jahren veröffentlichte er eine Reihe von Erzählbänden, darunter beispielsweise der französisch-arabische Band »Le Caire est petit« (1985; Ü: Kairo ist klein). In englischer Übersetzung erschien eine Sammlung von zwanzig Kurzgeschichten unter dem Titel »The Slave's Dream and Other Stories« (1991).
Nabil Naoum erzählt mit subtiler Ironie und kühler Distanz. Er verzichtet auf detaillierte Beschreibungen von Landschaften, Orten und Bräuchen. So bleibt das Geschehen, selbst wenn Ägypten genannt wird, nur vage lokalisierbar. Statt dessen entfalten sich seine Texte weitgehend losgelöst von realen Anhaltspunkten in ihrem eigenen Raum und ihrer eigenen Zeit. Auch die Figuren werden in ihren Konturen nur grob skizziert. Erst im Verlauf einer Geschichte treten sie etwas deutlicher in ihren Eigenarten hervor. Dennoch erfährt der Leser wenig über ihre Gefühls- und Gedankenwelten. Die meisten Erzählungen konstituieren sich durch einen linearen Narrationsfluss. Ohne die moralische Wertung einer höheren Instanz kommt es zu überraschenden Wendungen, die unversehens Räume für das Beklemmende und Grausame öffnen. In dem Roman »Jasad Awal« (1998) hat der Architekt und Schriftsteller Fouad nach seiner Rückkehr aus dem Ausland seine Familie, insbesondere die älteren Verwandten, in einer Wohn- und Lebensgemeinschaft wieder vereint. Dadurch konfrontiert mit Verlust, Alter und Tod, sucht er nach der Verbindung zwischen der diesseitigen und der jenseitigen Welt. Die Protagonisten des jüngsten Romans »Hafat el wed« (2000) sind getrieben von ihrer Sehnsucht nach Liebe. Sie verstricken sich in ein Netz aus Verführung, Macht und unerfülltem Verlangen. Neben Prosa publizierte Nabil Naoum mehrere Essays zur zeitgenössischen arabischen Kunst und Fotografie. Seit 2000 ist er Mitglied des Auswahlkomitees für die Biennale des Arabischen Films am Institut du Monde Arabe in Paris. Nabil Naoum lebt seit 1993 abwechselnd in Kairo und in Paris.

وقال لي اكتب من أنت
لتعرف من أنت فإن لم تعرف
من أنت فما أنت من أهل
معرفتي.
النفري ٣٥٤ هـ

فإن تبعثرت الحروف حل
الوجد.
وحل
الوقت،
ولغى
القرب،
وصار الوحي
هو المنع.

ن. ن،

15.03.04

Und Er sprach zu mir:
Schreib wer du bist, um zu wissen
wer du bist.
Und wenn du nicht weißt
wer du bist
bist du keiner von denen
die es wert sind mich zu kennen.
(El Nefari)

Wenn Buchstaben sich zertreuen,
tritt Ekstase an ihre Stelle
und Zeit.
Nähe wäre nicht gestattet
und die Muse wäre Verhinderung.
(Nabil Naoum)

bernard noël

biography

Bernard Noël was born in Sainte-Genevieve-sur-Argence/Aveyron, France, in 1930. He went to Journalism school at the beginning of the 1950's, though his real interest lay in literature. The committed literature of Jean-Paul Sartre and Albert Camus fascinated him, as did the radicalism of Georges Bataille and Antonin Artaud. He was working as an editor and translator when his first volume of poetry came out in 1953. Five years later, »Extraits du corps« (1958), a collection of prose poems, appeared. In this collection, he attempts an unique »reciprocal fusion«. He tries to give words a body and the body, words. The main concern of his »écriture du corps« is the interpenetration of the material and immaterial dimensions. After its publication, Bernard Noël discussed in a letter to his editor his radical break with literature and his abandonment of writing. Around ten years later he published »Le Château de cène« (1969) under a pseudonym. In this boundary-breaking novel, intended as an allegory of brutal experiences in the Algerian War, Noël depicts drastic and explicitly sexual excesses and violence, which led to censorship of the book and a lawsuit concerning the circulation of obscene writing.
»Le Château de cène« marked a turning point in Noël's literary output. Having previously turned away from literature, he now became a freelance writer. Since the 1970's he has produced an oeuvre which is as extensive as it is complex, and which today includes over sixty titles, among them poems, novels, the »Dictionnaire de la Commune« (1971), travelogues, literary criticism and political essays, as well as a series of texts on art, artists and questions concerning perception. In 1983 he founded the literary centre the Abbey of Royaumont, where he aimed to carry out the translation of contemporary poets such as Nuno Judice, Oskar Pastior and Yadollah Royai. In 1992 he was awarded the Prix National de Poésie.
As early as 1975 he had coined the neologism »la sensure«, meaning the ›prohibition of thought‹, an allusion to »la censure« (censorship of word). In the collection of essays »La Castration mentale« (1997), Noël warned of how freedom of speech is threatened by the creeping damage brought about in particular by inundation with visual mass media. Since then his most recent work is »Un trajet en hiver« (2004), a poetic reflection on travel. Bernard Noël lives in Northern French Maurigny.

Extraits du corps
Unes
Draguignan, 1988
Le Château de cène
Gallimard
Paris, 1990
La Castration mentale
P.O.L
Paris, 1997
La Langue d'Anna
P.O.L
Paris, 1998
La Peau et les Mots
P.O.L
Paris, 2002
Les premiers mots
Flammarion
Paris, 2003
Romans d'un regard
P.O.L
Paris, 2003
Un trajet en hiver
P.O.L
Paris, 2004

Bernard Noël wurde 1930 in Sainte-Geneviève-sur-Argence/Aveyron, Frankreich, geboren. Zu Beginn der fünfziger Jahre besuchte er eine Journalistenschule in Paris. Doch sein wirkliches Interesse galt der Literatur. Die Engagierte Literatur von Jean-Paul Sartre und Albert Camus faszinierte ihn ebenso wie die Radikalität von Georges Bataille und Antonin Artaud. Als er 1953 seinen ersten Gedichtband veröffentlichte, arbeitete er als Lektor und Übersetzer. Fünf Jahre später erschien »Extraits du corps« (1958; Ü: Körperextrakte), eine Sammlung von Prosagedichten. In ihnen unternimmt er eine einzigartige, »reziproke Fusion«: Er versucht, den Wörtern einen Körper zu geben und dem Körper die Wörter. Das Anliegen seiner »écriture du corps« ist die gegenseitige Durchdringung der materiellen und immateriellen Dimension. Nach dieser Veröffentlichung erklärte Bernard Noël in einem Brief an seinen Herausgeber seinen radikalen Bruch mit der Literatur und seinen Verzicht auf das Schreiben.
Rund zehn Jahre später publizierte er unter Pseudonym »Le Château de cène« (1969; Ü: Das Schloss des Abendmahls). In diesem grenzüberschreitenden Roman, der als Allegorie auf die brutalen Ereignisse im Algerienkrieg intendiert war, schildert er drastisch sexuelle Exzesse und Gewalt, was zur Zensur des Buches und einem Prozess wegen Verbreitung unzüchtiger Schriften führte. »Le Château de cène« markiert einen Wendepunkt in Bernard Noëls literarischem Schaffen. Er, der sich zuvor von der Literatur abgewandt hatte, wurde nun freier Schriftsteller. Seit den siebziger Jahren schuf er ein ebenso umfangreiches wie komplexes Œuvre, das heute mehr als sechzig Titel umfasst, darunter Gedichte, Romane, das »Dictionnaire de la Commune« (1971; Ü: Wörterbuch der Kommune), Reisebeschreibungen, literaturkritische und politische Essays sowie eine Reihe von Texten über Kunst, Künstler und Fragestellungen zur Wahrnehmung. 1983 gründete er das Literarische Zentrum der Abtei von Royaumont, das sich die Übersetzung zeitgenössischer Dichter wie Nuno Judice, Oskar Pastior und Yadollah Royai zum Ziel gesetzt hat. 1992 wurde ihm der Prix National de Poésie verliehen.
Bereits 1975 prägte er in Anlehnung an »la censure« (›Zensur des Wortes‹) den Neologismus »la sensure« mit der Bedeutung ›Verbot des Denkens‹. In der Essaysammlung »La Castration mentale« (1997; Ü: Die Kastration des Geistes) warnt er vor dem schleichenden Verlust der Freiheit des Denkens, die er insbesondere durch die visuelle Überflutung der Massenmedien bedroht sieht. Sein bisher letztes Werk ist »Un trajet en hiver« (2004), eine poetische Reflexion über das Reisen. Bernard Noël lebt im nordfranzösischen Maurigny.

joseph olshan

biography

Joseph Olshan was born in the USA. He taught Creative Writing at New York University in the 1990s and was the editor-in-chief of Delphinium Books until 2002. In 1985, his debut novel »Clara's Heart« won him The London Times/Jonathan Cape Young Writers' Competition. Three years later the book was filmed starring Whoopi Goldberg in the leading role. The theme of the novel revolves around an unusual relationship developing between the American puberty-stricken boy David and the Jamaican housekeeper Clara. Since David's parents are totally absorbed in their own affairs, they are not able to recognise their son's needs, and Clara takes over the important role of the ›substitute mother‹. David opens up to her and even learns to speak her Jamaican Patois. But his desire for closeness and acceptance goes too far and their intimate friendship is put to the test when he violates Clara's privacy by digging for dark secrets in her past. The sequel, »In Clara's Hands«, appeared some fifteen years later in 2001. Olshan places the main emphasis on the complexities and the emotional and psychological dynamics of relationships – as he does in all his other novels.
In the New York setting of the 1990's, »Nightswimmer« (1994) tells the love story of Will Kaplan and Sean Paris, dealing with longing and loss, with closeness and distance, and with sex and the »fear of drowning in love«. The novel was praised by the critics for its psychological accuracy and realist narrative style, which are strengths that it also shares with »Vanitas« (1988). In that novel, the protagonist and art dealer Elliott Garland, who suffers from AIDS, hires author Sam Solomon to write his memoirs. He also asks Sam to return a drawing to his ex-lover Bobby LaCour, who lives in London, all of which sets a complicated relationship in motion. The three men engage in a triangular network of obsessions, lust and jealousy. Apart from his seven novels, Joseph Olshan has contributed to various American and British newspapers including »The New York Times«, »The Washington Post«, and »The London Times«. In addition, he writes book reviews for »The Wall Street Journal« on a regular basis. Together with neuropathologist Mahlon Johnson, who acquired HIV while performing an autopsy, he reported Dr Johnson's battle against the virus in »Working on a Miracle« (1997). At the moment he is working on a new novel. Joseph Olshan lives in Woodstock/ Vermont and in New York.

A Warmer Season
Bloomsbury
London, 1987
Claras Herz
dtv
München, 1992
[Ü: Matthias Müller]
Sound of Heaven
Bloomsbury
London, 1992
Arbeit an einem Wunder
mit Mahlon Johnson
Berlin Verlag
Berlin, 1997
[Ü: Barbara Schaden]
Vanitas
Bloomsbury
London, 1998
In Clara's Hands
Bloomsbury
London, 2001
Nachtschwimmer
dtv
München, 2003
[Ü: Gerold Hens]

So sehr das Schreiben fachspezifische Fähigkeiten erfordert, ist es doch alles andere als wissenschaftlich. Aus meiner Sicht wird das Schreiben von einem gewissen primitiven Impuls getrieben, der vielleicht ein Zwitter aus Sehnsucht und Inspiration ist.

Als Autoren haben wir immer unsere Antennen ausgefahren und hoffen, die Signale empfangen zu können, die diesen primitiven Impuls reizen und uns ermöglichen, uns selbst – im Akt des Schreibens – zu übersteigen. Denn im Vergleich zu unserem besten Schreiben sind unsere besten Alltagsgedanken ziemlich banal.

Wir haben gelernt, jene Signale zu erkennen, die unserem geschriebenen Werk die größte Resonanz verleihen könnten. Wir kennen das seltsame Gefühl in der Magengrube, das die Schöpfung von Absätzen und Seiten ankündigt, die hoffentlich noch bestehen werden, lange nachdem bei uns das Licht ausgegangen ist. Womit beginnt diese seltsame Alchemie?

Gewissermaßen zeigt sich meine Muse oft, aber nicht immer, in zwei verschiedenen Formen: in der Form einer Person, die einen tiefen Eindruck auf mich macht, oder als merkwürdiges Ereignis in der natürlichen Welt.

Einer meiner Romane handelt von einem kraftvollen Schwimmer, der vielleicht, vielleicht aber auch nicht, beim Schwimmen im Pazifik verschwindet. Obwohl diese Figur zu Beginn des Romans tot ist, hat er in Rückblicken doch immer wieder kurze Gastauftritte. Viele Leser haben auf diese Figur reagiert, die sicherlich nicht die am besten ausgearbeitete Figur des Romans ist, die aber auf irgendeine Weise einen starken Eindruck hinterlässt. Obwohl er nur wenig spricht, meinen die Leute ihn sehr gut zu kennen und nehmen großen Anteil daran, was ihm passiert sein mag.

Meine „Muse" für diese Figur war ein Schwimmer, der in den frühen neunziger Jahren das Darmouth College besuchte. Dieser Mann las einen meiner Romane,

Joseph Olshan wurde in den USA geboren. In den neunziger Jahren unterrichtete er Kreatives Schreiben an der New York University. Bis 2002 war er Lektor des Verlags Delphinium Books. 1985 gewann Olshan mit seinem Debütroman »Clara's Heart« (1985; dt. »Claras Herz«, 1986) den Jonathan Cape Literaturwettbewerb junger Autoren der Londoner »Times«. Drei Jahre später wurde das Buch mit Whoopi Goldberg in der Hauptrolle verfilmt. Thema des Romans ist die ungewöhnliche Beziehung, die sich zwischen David, einem pubertierenden amerikanischen Jungen, und seiner jamaikanischen Erzieherin Clara entwickelt. Clara nimmt eine wichtige Rolle als ›Ersatzmutter‹ für David ein, dessen Eltern mehr mit ihrem eigenen Leben beschäftigt sind, als dass sie sich für die Bedürfnisse ihres Sohnes interessierten. David vertraut ihr seine Sorgen an und lernt sogar jamaikanisches Patois, aber er geht in seiner Sehnsucht nach Nähe und Akzeptanz zu weit. In der innigen Beziehung kommt es zum Bruch, weil David Claras Grenzen verletzt, um ihr Geheimnis zu ergründen. Rund fünfzehn Jahre später entstand mit »In Clara's Hands« (2001) eine Fortsetzung der Geschichte. Auch in seinen anderen Romanen gilt das Interesse des Autors der emotionalen und psychologischen Dynamik in komplexen Beziehungskonstellationen.
»Nightswimmer« (1994; dt. »Nachtschwimmer«, 1999) erzählt anhand der Liebesgeschichte zwischen Will Kaplan und Sean Paris im New York der neunziger Jahre von Begehren und Verlust, Nähe und Distanz, dem Sex und »der Angst vor dem Ertrinken in der Liebe«. Die Kritik lobte den Roman für die psychologische Genauigkeit und die realistische Erzählweise. Hierin liegt auch die Stärke von »Vanitas« (1988). In diesem Roman beauftragt der aidskranke New Yorker Kunsthändler Elliott Garland den Autor Sam Solomon mit dem Schreiben seiner Memoiren und bittet ihn, seinem Ex-Freund Bobby LaCour, der in London lebt, eine Zeichnung zurückzugeben. Es entspinnt sich ein kompliziertes Verhältnis zwischen den drei Männern, geprägt von Obsessionen, Eros und Eifersucht. Neben bisher sieben Romanen schrieb Joseph Olshan Artikel für verschiedene amerikanische und britische Zeitungen, darunter die »New York Times«, »Washington Post« und die »London Times«. Außerdem veröffentlichte er regelmäßig Buchkritiken im »Wall Street Journal«. Zusammen mit dem Arzt Mahlon Johnson, einem Neuropathologen, der sich bei einer Obduktion mit HIV infizierte, verfasste er unter dem Titel »Working On A Miracle« (1997; dt. »Arbeit an einem Wunder«, 1998), einen Bericht über Johnsons Versuche, die Krankheit zu überwinden. Joseph Olshan arbeitet derzeit an einem neuen Roman und lebt in Woodstock/Vermont sowie in New York.

schrieb mir in einem Brief, was das Buch ihm bedeutet habe, und wir trafen uns einmal zu Mittagessen. Ich bin selbst ein Schwimmer, und so sah ich ihn oft im campuseigenen Pool trainieren. Er war ein kleiner, aber kräftiger Schmetterlingsschwimmer. In meiner Phantasie intensivierte sich unser langes Gespräch beim Mittagessen dadurch, wie dieser Mann den schwierigsten (und wohl auch schönsten) aller Schwimmstile beherrschte. Diese Verbindung inspirierte viele gefühlvolle Textpassagen.

Als ich sechs Jahre alt war, sah ich ein zweijähriges Kind ertrinken. Obwohl dieses Ereignis vierzig Jahre zurückliegt, kann ich mich besser an Details und Gespräche jenes Tages erinnern als daran, was mir gestern passierte. Der Vorfall verfolgte mich, bis ich darüber zu schreiben wagte. Als ich mit dem Roman fast fertig war, fuhr ich nach Kalifornien. Dort hatte ich einen Traum, an den ich mich vielleicht nicht erinnert hätte, wäre ich nicht vom Tumult geweckt worden, den ein Hund verursachte, der eine Ratte jagte, die sich vom Festschmaus auf einem Avocadobaum herunterwagte. Der Traum handelte von einem Friedhof, der sich von einem Horizont zum anderen erstreckte; anstelle von Grabsteinen war jedes Grab durch einen toten Jungen markiert. Sie trugen Blazer, und ihr Haar war adrett gekämmt. Ich verwende normalerweise keine Träume in Romanen, und dennoch wusste ich, dass und an welcher Stelle dieser Traum verarbeitet werden müsse: zu Beginn des dritten Abschnitts. Die Beschreibung dieses Traums ist noch immer meine Lieblingsstelle im ganzen Roman.

Es gibt noch eine Zutat in der Alchemie der Muse – und das ist ein Hund. Schreiben erfordert Einsamkeit und tiefe Kontemplation. Schnarcht ein Hund neben mir, wenn ich schreibe, oder springt er vor mir her, wenn ich im Wald spazieren gehe, so befördert dies den Prozess aus einem einfachen Grund. Denn das, was zwischen dem Hund und mir besteht, ist die Reinheit unausgesprochener Hingabe. Mit einem Tier zusammen zu sein ist wie beten. Tatsächlich war die beste Beschreibung Gottes, die ich jemals gehört habe, das was zwischen dir und deinem Hund während eines Waldspaziergangs besteht.

hagar peeters

biography

Hagar Peeters was born in Amsterdam, the Netherlands, in 1972. She studied Philosophy, General Literature Studies and Cultural History in Utrecht. In her dissertation she documented the development of Dutch penal systems through the biography of the notorious criminal Gerrit de Stotteraar, who was as notorious for the large number of burglaries he committed as for his jailbreaks. For this scholarly work, which also reads as an exciting novel, Peeters soon received two important distinctions: first the renowned prize for scholarly texts, the Nationale Scriptieprijs, and then, following the publication of the work under the title »Gerrit de Stotteraar – Biographie van een boef« (2002; t: Gerrit de Stotteraar – biography of a criminal), the Utrecht booksellers' award 2002. After completing her studies she worked as an editor for the newspaper »Historisch Nieuwsblad« and as a PR consultant for a non-profit organisation. During her adolescence she discovered her love of poetry. Her first appearance as a ›performing poet‹ was in a youth centre in front of an extremely critical audience, whose attention she had to fight for. Through this experience she developed a flair for knowing which poems worked best performed on stage, and which were fit for poetry collections. The balance between content and presentation is therefore very important to Peeters. Some poems function through their ›flow‹, that is: through clipped rhymes and distinct rhythms of speech, as raps. At other times she performs with a guitarist, in an interplay between music and language. Although the title of her first poetry collection is called »Genoeg gedicht over de liefde vandaag« (1999; t: I've had enough poems about love for one day), her poems are largely about the possibility and impossibility of love, about expectations and disappointments. She prefers to address situations in life and love whose particular tragedy lies in the fact that they are nearly perfect, but remain just a pinch away from perfection. She succeeds in confronting serious themes with a carefree, ironic ease. »Dancing arises from beautiful ways of walking, singing from beautiful ways of speaking. Poetry is the art of expressing as purely as possible beautiful thoughts and the amazement at the inscrutability of being.« From her most recent book, »Koffers Zeelucht« (2003; t: A suitcase of sea air), the poem »Droombeeld« was awarded the Gedichtendagprijzen 2004 as one of the best Dutch poems of 2003. Hagar Peeters lives in Amsterdam.

Genoeg gedicht over de liefde vandaag
Podium
Amsterdam, 1999
Gerrit de Stotteraar – Biografie van een boef
Podium
Amsterdam, 2002
Koffers Zeelucht
De Bezige Bij
Amsterdam, 2003

Kanttekeningen van de muze IV.

Leg je hand niet op mijn hand als ik een pen vasthoud.
Zelfs als ik geen pen vasthoud omklem ik er een.
Het is de lucht tussen mijn vingers die ik koester.
Soms streel ik er de wereld mee.

Je gekwelde hart is me te bloedig.
Het bonst te hard, daar krijg ik hoofdpijn van.
Van alle tastbaarheid ontdaan wil ik het.

Je geschreven stem is meer welluidend
dan de woorden die je dagelijks tot mij spreekt.
Bij het zwart op wit verbleekt toch alles.

Je mond kan eenvoudigweg niet tippen
aan de beschrevenheid van je lippen.
Je geest is me te vol, je gedachten passen
niet naast de mijne.
Alleen op papier vind ik ze verrassend.

Een acteur kan werkelijk huilen terwijl hij niets voelt
maar mijn tranen stollen
nog voor ze vallen tot papieren bootjes
omdat er een schip in mij kapseisde.

Ieder woord is een matroos op een boot van papier,
elke letter een liefje dat tuurt naar de mast,
de betekenis een anjer, een anker
maar houd me alsjeblieft met echte armen vast.

Hagar Peeters wurde 1972 in Amsterdam, Niederlande, geboren. Sie studierte Philosophie, Allgemeine Literaturwissenschaft und Kulturgeschichte in Utrecht. In ihrer Dissertation dokumentierte sie die Entwicklung des niederländischen Strafsystems anhand der Biographie des notorischen Kriminellen Gerrit de Stotteraar, der für seine zahlreichen Einbrüche ebenso berühmt-berüchtigt war wie für seine Ausbrüche aus dem Gefängnis. Für diese wissenschaftliche Arbeit, die sich zugleich wie ein spannender Roman liest, erhielt sie gleich zwei wichtige Auszeichnungen: zunächst 2001 den renommierten Preis für Wissenschaftstexte Nationale Scriptieprijs und nach der Veröffentlichung des Werkes unter dem Titel »Gerrit de Stotteraar – Biografie van een boef« (2002; Ü: Gerrit de Stotteraar – Biographie eines Verbrechers) den Utrechter Buchhandelspreis 2002. Nach dem Studium arbeitete sie als Redakteurin für die Zeitung »Historisch Nieuwsblad« und als PR-Beraterin für eine Non-Profit-Organisation.
Die Liebe zur Poesie entdeckte sie bereits als Jugendliche. Ihre ersten Auftritte als ›Performing Poet‹ hatte sie in Jugendzentren vor einem äußerst kritischen Publikum, dessen Aufmerksamkeit sie sich hart erkämpfen musste. Dadurch entwickelte sie ein Gespür dafür, welche Gedichte besser für die Performance auf der Bühne und welche besser für Gedichtsammlungen geeignet sind. Die Suche nach der Balance von Inhalt und Präsentation ist ihr sehr wichtig. Einige Gedichte funktionieren durch ihren ›Flow‹, d. h. durch prägnante Reime und einen ausgeprägten Sprechrhythmus, als Rap-Stücke. Andere präsentiert sie zusammen mit einem Gitarristen als Wechselspiel zwischen Sprache und Musik. Anders als der Titel ihrer ersten Gedichtsammlung »Genoeg gedicht over de liefde vandaag« (1999; Ü: Für heute reicht's mit Gedichten über die Liebe) vermuten lässt, handeln ihre Gedichte größtenteils von der Möglichkeit und Unmöglichkeit der Liebe, von Erwartungen und Enttäuschungen. Bevorzugt richtet sie den Blick auf Lebens- und Liebessituationen, deren besondere Tragik darin liegt, dass sie nur fast perfekt sind, ihnen zur Vollkommenheit das gewisse Quentchen fehlt. Auch gelingt es ihr, ernsten Themen mit einer heiteren, ironischen Leichtigkeit zu begegnen. »Tanzen ist aus dem schönen Gehen entstanden, Singen aus dem schönen Reden. Poesie ist die Kunst, schöne Gedanken und das Erstaunen über die Unergründlichkeit des Seins so rein wie möglich auszudrücken.« Aus ihrem jüngsten Band »Koffers Zeelucht« (2003; Ü: Ein Koffer Seeluft) wurde »Droombeeld« (Ü: Traumbild) mit dem Gedichtendagprijzen 2004 als eines der besten niederländischen Gedichte aus dem Jahr 2003 ausgezeichnet. Hagar Peeters lebt in Amsterdam.

Randbemerkungen der Muse IV

Leg deine Hand nicht auf meine Hand, wenn ich
eine Feder halte. Auch wenn ich keine Feder halte,
umklammere ich eine. Die Luft zwischen den Fingern
ist es, die ich liebkose. Manchmal streichle ich
die Welt damit.

Dein gequältes Herz ist mir zu blutig.
Es klopft zu laut, mir schmerzt der Kopf davon.
Frei von allem Ertastbaren will ich es.

Deine geschriebene Stimme hat mehr Wohllaut
als die Worte, die du täglich zu mir sprichst.
In Schwarz auf Weiß verblasst doch alles.

Dein Mund kann sich einfach nicht messen
mit der Beschriebenheit deiner Lippen.
Dein Geist ist mir zu voll,
deine Gedanken passen nicht zu den meinen.
Nur auf Papier find ich sie überraschend.

Ein Schauspieler kann richtig weinen,
obwohl er nichts fühlt,
doch meine Tränen erstarren,
noch ehe sie fallen, zu papierenen Schiffchen,
weil ein Schiff in mir kenterte.

Jedes Wort ist ein Matrose auf einem Papierschiff,
jeder Buchstabe eine Liebste, die den Mast erspäht,
die Bedeutung eine Nelke, ein Anker,
doch bitte halte mich mit echten Armen fest.

susanne riedel

biography

Susanne Riedel was born in Unna, Germany, in 1959. She first worked at the »Westdeutsche Allgemeine Zeitung« in Essen, before moving to Berlin in 1986. There she worked as an editor and presenter for various children's radio programmes, and then as freelance journalist for the »Sender Freies Berlin« and other radio stations. Her first novel, »Kains Tochter« (t: Kain's daughter), was published in 2000. With nightmarish intensity Riedel portrays death, suicide, incest and violence within the family history of sisters Joa and Timpie Leghorn. The older Joa tells in retrospect of the heavy physical and psychological abuse to which the girls had been exposed since early childhood at the hands of their mother, and its consequences in their lives and later actions. As adults they also fail to escape from family entanglements and the vicious circle of violence, guilt and renewed violence. At the time of the account, both Timpie and Joa's daughter Ruth are dead, while Joa finds herself in psychiatric care, deeply afflicted by feelings of guilt and self-loathing. The novel's dark-archaic atmosphere unfolds through Susanne Riedel's extraordinary style, and her forceful deployment of lyrical images, biblical names and bizarre analogies. The novel's unusual imagery offered at the time occasion for great controversy amongst Germany's best-known literary critics.

Her second book, »Die Endlichkeit des Lichts« (2001; t: The finitude of light), a whimsical love story between the quiz show presenter Verna Albrecht and the mushroom expert Alakar Macody, further testified to the author's fascination with the poetic content of language. Her protagonists quote poems by T. S. Eliot and Anne Sexton and do not doubt that poetry is superior to physics in perceiving »the hidden symmetry of the universe«, and thus able to discover the true essence of the world. The novel itself is formally and symmetrically designed through its mirroring, doubling, and twin motifs.

At the centre of the third novel, »Eine Frau aus Amerika« (2003; t: A woman from America), stands an ageing German-American couple who, during a university cultural exchange programme, must come to terms with the lifelong lies of their decades-long relationship.

In 2000, Susanne Riedel was awarded the Jury Prize of the Ingeborg Bachmann competition for a passage from »Die Endlichkeit des Lichts«. In 2002, she received the Wolfgang Koeppen Prize of the city of Greifswald. Susanne Riedel lives in Berlin.

Kains Töchter
Rowohlt Berlin
Berlin, 2000
Die Endlichkeit des Lichts
Berlin Verlag
Berlin, 2001
Eine Frau aus Amerika
Berlin Verlag
Berlin, 2003

Susanne Riedel wurde 1959 in Unna, Nordrhein-Westfalen, geboren. Zunächst war sie für die »Westdeutsche Allgemeine Zeitung« in Essen tätig, bevor sie 1986 nach Berlin zog. Dort arbeitete sie als Redakteurin und Moderatorin verschiedener Jugendradiosendungen, später als freie Journalistin für den »Sender Freies Berlin« und andere Hörfunksender. 2000 wurde ihr erster Roman »Kains Töchter« veröffentlicht. Mit beklemmender Intensität schildert sie die von Mord, Selbstmord, Inzest und Gewalt bestimmte Familiengeschichte der beiden Schwestern Joa und Timpie Leghorn. Die ältere Joa erzählt im Rückblick von den schweren physischen und psychischen Misshandlungen, denen die Mädchen seit frühester Kindheit durch die Mutter ausgesetzt waren und deren Folgen ihr weiteres Leben und Handeln bestimmen. Auch als sie erwachsen sind, gelingt es ihnen nicht, sich aus den familiären Verstrickungen zu lösen und dem Teufelskreis aus Gewalt, Schuld und erneuter Gewalt zu entfliehen. Zum Zeitpunkt des Berichts sind Timpie und Joas Tochter Ruth tot, während Joa sich in psychiatrischer Behandlung befindet, zutiefst gequält von Schuldgefühlen und Selbsthass. Die dunkel-archaische Atmosphäre des Romans entfaltet sich durch Susanne Riedels außergewöhnlichen Stil, durch die konsequente Verwendung lyrischer Bilder, biblischer Namen und bizarrer Vergleiche. Diese für ein Prosawerk ungewohnte Metaphorik bot seinerzeit Anlass zum Streit zwischen Deutschlands bekanntesten Literaturkritikern.
Auch mit dem zweiten Buch »Die Endlichkeit des Lichts« (2001), der skurrilen Liebesgeschichte zwischen der Quizshow-Moderatorin Verna Albrecht und dem Pilzexperten Alakar Macody, zeigt sich die Autorin fasziniert vom poetischen Gehalt der Sprache. Ihre Protagonisten zitieren Gedichte von T. S. Eliot und Anne Sexton und zweifeln nicht daran, dass die Poesie der Physik in der Fähigkeit überlegen ist, »die versteckte Symmetrie des Universums« und somit das wahre Wesen der Welt zu erkennen. Der Roman selbst ist formal in Spiegelungen, Doppelungen und Zwillingsmotiven symmetrisch konstruiert. Im Zentrum des dritten Romans »Eine Frau aus Amerika« (2003) steht ein alterndes deutsch-amerikanisches Paar, das sich während eines universitären Kulturaustauschs die Lebenslüge seiner jahrzehntelangen Beziehung eingestehen muss.
Für eine Passage aus »Die Endlichkeit des Lichts« wurde Susanne Riedel 2000 mit dem Preis der Jury des Ingeborg-Bachmann-Wettbewerbs ausgezeichnet. 2002 wurde ihr der Wolfgang-Koeppen-Preis der Hansestadt Greifswald verliehen. Susanne Riedel lebt in Berlin.

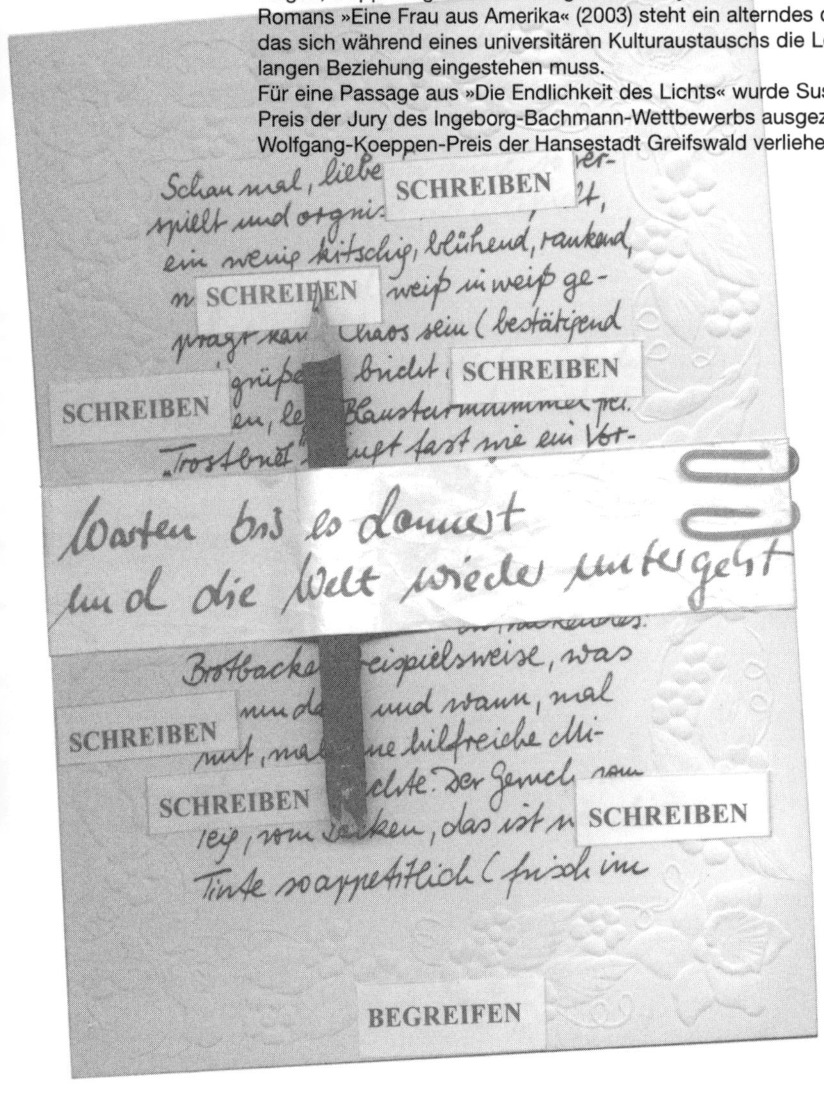

fuad rifka

biography

Fuad Rifka was born in Syria in 1930 and moved to Lebanon with his Christian parents in the 1940s. He studied philosophy in Beirut and obtained a Ph.D. in philosophy from the University of Tübingen in 1965 with a dissertation on the aesthetics of Martin Heidegger. Since 1966 he has taught philosophy at the Lebanese American University Beirut. In addition, he has spent numerous semesters as a visiting lecturer and scholar in the USA Great Britain, Italy and Germany. German philosophers still hold a prominent place in his syllabus. His ardent interest in German poets and thinkers came about accidentally more than forty years ago at the Beirut Goethe Institute, when he discovered an English edition of Rilke's »Duino Elegies«. This volume of poetry was to have such a lasting influence on him that he developed the urgent wish »to translate German poetry into Arabic, in order to make it known throughout the Arab world«. Rendering contemporary poetry into Arabic has also been the declared aim of the group associated with the avant-garde poetry magazine »Shi'r«, which Rifka co-founded with Yusuf al-Khan, Adonis, and others in 1957. »Shi'r« aimed at nothing less than the liberation of classical Arabic poetry from its subjection to strict rules of form and content, and the admission of freer, more experimental poetry.

The first volume of Rifka's own poetry was published in 1961, followed by further poems and essays, as well as translations from German and English. In 1993, a translation of the Bible was issued in which he had participated. This translation resulted in a volume of 365 Bible stories for children retold by Rifka. Throughout his lyrical work, Fuad Rifka perpetually searches for the »absolute poem«. He radically abstains from ornamentation. In short, concise lines he conveys both his love of nature and his sense of transitoriness. Using language stripped to its essentials he attempts to penetrate the depths of meaning beyond actual words. Or, as Rifka himself puts it: »In all my poetry I have been writing on one single poem – to achieve greater and greater clarity«. In 2002, »Das Tal der Rituale« (t: The valley of rituals) was published, a dual language selection of his poetry of the last fifteen years. For his Arabic translations of German poetry, including Goethe, Hölderlin, Novalis, Rilke, and Trakl, Fuad Rifka was awarded the Friedrich-Gundolf-Prize in 2001 by the German Academy for Language and Poetry, which also selected him for membership one year later. Fuad Rifka lives in Beirut.

Tagebuch eines Holzsammlers
Heiderhoff
Eisingen, 1990
[Ü: Ursuala und Siman Yussuf Assaf]

Gedichte eines Indianers
Heiderhoff
Eisingen, 1994
[Ü: Ursuala und Siman Yussuf Assaf]

Das Tal der Rituale
Straelener Manuskripte
Straelen, 2002
[Ü: Ursuala und Siman Yussuf Assaf, Stefan Weidner]

Fuad Rifka wurde 1930 in Syrien geboren. In den vierziger Jahren übersiedelte er mit seiner christlichen Familie in den Libanon. Er studierte Philosophie in Beirut, 1965 promovierte er über die Ästhetik Martin Heideggers in Tübingen. Seit 1966 unterrichtet er Philosophie an der Lebanese American University Beirut. Diese Tätigkeit wurde ergänzt durch zahlreiche Lehr- und Forschungsaufenthalte in den USA, Großbritannien, Italien und Deutschland. Bis heute nehmen die deutschen Philosophen einen festen Platz in seinem Lehrplan ein. Sein leidenschaftliches Interesse für deutsche Dichter und Denker basiert auf einer zufälligen Entdeckung im Goethe-Institut Beirut vor mehr als vierzig Jahren. Rifka stieß dort auf eine englische Ausgabe der »Duineser Elegien« von Rilke. Dieser Gedichtband beeindruckte ihn nachhaltig und weckte in ihm den Wunsch, »deutsche Lyrik ins Arabische zu übersetzen, um sie der gesamten arabischen Welt zugänglich zu machen«. Die Übertragung von zeitgenössischer Dichtung ins Arabische war auch eines der erklärten Ziele des Kreises um die avantgardistische Lyrikzeitschrift »Shi'r« (Ü: Poesie), die 1957 u. a. von Yusuf al-Khal, Adonis und Fuad Rifka ins Leben gerufen wurde. Das zentrale Anliegen von »Shi'r« war nichts Geringeres als die Revolutionierung der klassischen arabischen Dichtung, die thematisch und formal strengen Regeln unterworfen ist, hin zu einer freieren, experimentellen Dichtung.
Rifkas erster eigener Gedichtband erschien 1961. Weitere Gedichte und Essays sowie Übersetzungen aus dem Deutschen und Englischen folgten.1993 erschien eine arabische Bibelübersetzung, an der Rifka beteiligt war. Aus dieser Arbeit resultierte 1994 eine Publikation, in der Rifka 365 biblische Geschichten für Kinder erzählte. In seiner Dichtung ist Fuad Rifka fortwährend auf der Suche nach dem »absoluten Gedicht«. Er verzichtet radikal auf Ornamente. Seine Liebe zur Natur fasst er ebenso wie die Auseinandersetzung mit der Vergänglichkeit in kurze, verdichtete Verse. In der betont schlichten Sprache zeigt sich der Wunsch, durch Reduzierung in die Tiefe zu dringen, gleichsam hinter die Worte. Fuad Rifka sieht es so: »Ich habe in allen meinen Werken nur an einem Gedicht geschrieben – um es immer klarer zu fassen.« 2002 erschien unter dem Titel »Das Tal der Rituale« in einer zweisprachigen Ausgabe eine Auswahl von Gedichten aus den letzten fünfzehn Jahren.
Für seine Übertragungen deutscher Lyrik ins Arabische, darunter Goethe, Hölderlin, Novalis, Rilke und Trakl, wurde er 2001 von der Deutschen Akademie für Sprache und Dichtung mit dem Friedrich-Gundolf-Preis ausgezeichnet. Ein Jahr später wurde er zum Mitglied der Akademie gewählt. Fuad Rifka lebt in Beirut.

Brod und Wein
An Heinze

7

Aber Freund! wir kommen zu spät. Zwar leben die Götter,
        Aber über dem Haupt droben in anderer Welt.
Endlos wirken sie da und scheinens wenig zu achten,
        Ob wir leben, so sehr schonen die Himmlischen uns.
Denn nicht immer vermag ein schwaches Gefäß sie zu fassen,
        Nur zu Zeiten erträgt göttliche Fülle der Mensch.
Traum von ihnen ist drauf das Leben. Aber das Irrsaal
        Hilft, wie Schlummer und stark machet die Noth und die Nacht,
Biß daß Helden genug in der ehernen Wiege gewachsen,
        Herzen an Kraft, wie sonst, ähnlich den Himmlischen sind.
Donnernd kommen sie drauf. Indessen dünket mir öfters
        Besser zu schlafen, wie so ohne Genossen zu seyn,
So zu harren und was zu thun indeß und zu sagen,
        Weiß ich nicht und wozu Dichter in dürftiger Zeit?
Aber sie sind, sagst du, wie des Weingotts heilige Priester,
        Welche von Lande zu Land zogen in heiliger Nacht.

alfian bin sa'at

biography

Alfian Bin Sa'at was born in Singapore in 1977. A Malay-Muslim of Minang, Javanese and Hakka descent, he is regularly referred to as his country's ›enfant terrible‹, known for his provocative works that span the genres of poetry, fiction and plays. He published his first collection of poetry, »One Fierce Hour« when he was only 21. The book was hailed by »The Straits Times« as »truly a landmark for poetry (in Singapore)« and the author was described by Malaysia's »The New Straits Times« as »one of the most acclaimed poets in his country...a prankish provocateur, libertarian hipster«. A year later, Alfian Bin Sa'at published a collection of short stories called »Corridor«, which was a Singapore Literature Prize Commendation Award winner. Seven of the short stories from the collection have been adapted and filmed for television. In 2001, he published his second collection of poetry, »A History of Amnesia«, which was shortlisted for a Kiriyama Asia-Pacific Book Prize. The sophomore poetry collection was acclaimed as »one of the most powerful collections by a Singaporean« by »The Straits Times«, which commented that the poetry was of a type that reminded »relentlessly of the human potential – and therefore a society's potential – for shutting our senses to disease we might have helped aggravate, or for daring to look unflinchingly at the roots of our suffering«.

At 24, Alfian won both the inaugural National Arts Council-Singapore Press Holdings Golden Point Award for Poetry, as well as the National Arts Council's Young Artist Award for Literature. Alfian Bin Sa'at's plays, written in English and Malay, have received broad attention in both Singapore and Malaysia. His first play was produced when he was 19, and he has had a long and fruitful association as a playwright with the socially-conscious English theatre group »The Necessary Stage« as well as »Teater Ekamatra«, a Malay theatre group known for articulating minority concerns in Chinese-majority Singapore. Some of his more notable plays include »sex.violence.blood.gore«, which suffered from censorship cuts at the hands of the State, »Asian Boys Vol.1« which employed camp aesthetics to examine the homosexual milieu in Singapore, »The Optic Trilogy«, an attempt to recuperate personal and idiosyncratic ways of perception under a surveillance State, and »Fugitives«, a play about inter-racial relations translated from English and which had its premiere in Mandarin. The latter three plays have been nominated for Best Script at the DBS-Life! Theatre Awards for three consecutive years.

Alfian Bin Sa'at's interests range from gender politics, to Malay identity, to strategies of resistance to censorship as well as hegemonising discourses. He is currently a Resident Playwright with W!ld Rice, a theatre company which recently staged his highly-regarded play, »Landmarks: Asian Boys Vol. 2.«

One Fierce Hour
Landmark Books
Singapur, 1998
Corridor
Raffles Publications
Singapur, 1999
A History of Amnesia
Ethos Books
Singapur, 2001

Alfian Bin Sa'at wurde 1977 in Singapur geboren. Der malaysische Moslem aus Minang von javanesischer und Hakka-Herkunft wird regelmäßig als ›enfant terrible‹ seines Landes bezeichnet. Sein provokatives Werk umfasst Lyrik, Prosa und Theaterstücke. Bereits im Alter von 21 Jahren veröffentlichte er seine erste Lyriksammlung »One Fierce Hour«. Das Buch wurde von »The Straits Times« als »ein wirkliches Wahrzeichen der Dichtung« Singapurs bejubelt, und der Autor wurde von der malaysischen »The New Straits Times« als »einer der am meisten gefeierten Dichter seines Landes, als frecher Provokateur und libertinärer Hipster« beschrieben. Ein Jahr später veröffentlichte Alfian Bin Sa'at den Erzählband »Corridor«, für den er mit dem Singapore Literature Prize Commendation Award ausgezeichnet wurde. Daraus wurden sieben Geschichten für das Fernsehen adaptiert und verfilmt. 2001 erschien seine zweite Lyriksammlung »A History of Amnesia«, die in die engere Wahl für den Kiriyama Asia-Pacific Book Prize kam. Das Buch wurde von »The Strait Times« als »eine der beeindruckendsten Sammlungen eines Singapurers« bejubelt; laut der Zeitung erinnere die Lyrik »schonungslos an das menschliche und daher gesellschaftliche Potential, unsere Sinne vor Krankheiten zu verschließen, an deren Ausbreitung wir vermutlich nicht unschuldig waren, und ohne Scheu auf die Wurzeln unseres Leidens zu schauen.«

Im Alter von 24 Jahren wurde Alfian Bin Sa'at sowohl mit dem National Arts Council-Singapore Press Holdings Golden Point Award for Poetry als auch mit dem National Arts Council's Young Artist Award for Literature ausgezeichnet. Seine Stücke, die er auf Englisch und Malaysisch schreibt, erhielten sowohl in Singapur als auch in Malaysia große Beachtung. Sein erstes Schauspiel wurde produziert, als er 19 Jahre alt war. Als Dramatiker unterhielt er eine lange und von Erfolg gekrönte Verbindung zu der gesellschaftskritischen englischen Theatergruppe »The Necessary Stage« sowie zum »Teater Ekamatra«, einer malaysischen Theatergruppe, die dafür bekannt ist, die Stellung von Minderheiten in der chinesischen Mehrheit von Singapur zu thematisieren. Zu seinen bemerkenswertesten Stücken gehören: »sex.violence.blood.gore«, das von der staatlichen Zensur gekürzt wurde; »Asian Boys Vol. 1«, das sich mit Ästhetik und Gemeinschaft der Homosexuellenszene in Singapur auseinandersetzt; »The Optic Trilogy«, ein Versuch, persönliche und eigenwillige Wahrnehmungsweisen in einem Überwachungsstaat zu behaupten; »Fugitives«, ein Stück über Beziehungen zwischen verschiedenen Rassen, das aus dem Englischen übersetzt wurde und in Mandarin erstaufgeführt wurde. Die letzten drei Stücke wurden in drei aufeinanderfolgenden Jahren für den Best Script at the DBS-Life! Theatre Awards nominiert.

Alfian Bin Sa'ats Interessen erstrecken sich von der Geschlechterfrage über die malaysische Identität bis hin zu Widerstandsstrategien gegen die Zensur sowie hegemoniales Denken. Gegenwärtig ist er Hausautor bei »W!ld Rice«, einem Theaterensemble, das kürzlich sein hoch gelobtes Stück »Landmarks: Asian Boys Vol. 2« aufführte.

alka saraogi

biography

Alka Saraogi was born in Calcutta (now Kolkata), India, in 1960. Eight years after her marriage, and after having two children, she went to university to do a Master's and a Ph.D. in Hindi literature – an unusual step in her conservative community. She published newspaper articles about health and women's issues before beginning writing prose. Her first volume of short stories, »Kahaniki Talash Mein«, appeared in 1996; two years later she published her debut novel, »Kali-Katha Via Bypass« (1998; Engl. »Kalikatha, Via Bypass«, 2002), for which she received the acclaimed Sahitya Akademi Award in 2001. The book was proposed to be translated into India's official twenty-two official languages. Alka Saraogi pens her texts in her Hindi mother tongue, and through this consciously distances herself from many Indian authors who write in English. According to the author, English remains, more than fifty years after the end of the British colonisation, a symbol of inequality as well as evidence of the continuity of colonial presence in postcolonial Indian society. The setting for her multi-faceted novel »Kalikatha, Via Bypass« is Calcutta. After a bypass operation, the seventy-two year old Marwari patriarch Kishore Babu becomes a vagrant as he wanders the city streets, along the tracks of his long suppressed memories of the idealistic days of the freedom struggle. Calcutta, once the second capital of the British Empire, was the seat of the East India Company and thus attractive to immigrants. The Marwaris, traditionally business people from Rajasthan, the far west desert land of India, also came, and their way of life amongst the progressive local Bengalis provoked disapproval.

Alka Saraogi not only narrates the story of an old man up against a lack of understanding from his fellow men and family for following his own logic as he recalls the long-forgotten idealism of his youth. She also recounts the history of the Marwari Diaspora – of their ancestry, their traditions, and their family structures. Above all, she writes about India's colonial and postcolonial history. Calcutta was the stage for nationalist independence struggles (inspired by Mahatma Gandhi and Netaji Subhash Chandra Bose) as well as for the bloody conflict between Hindus and Muslims which led to the division of land between India and Pakistan. In apparently spontaneous flashbacks, the author interweaves historical facts with the protagonist's own memories, who, becoming the wise fool after a heart bypass, poses uncomfortable questions about postcolonial Indian identity. Another volume of stories by Alka Saraogi, »Doosri Kahani« (2000), has recently been published, as well as two novels: »Shesh Kadambari« (2002; Engl. »Over to You Kadambari«, 2004) and »Koi Baat Bahin« (2004; t: Never mind, it's okay). She lives in Calcutta.

Kahaniki Talash Mein
Aadhar
Panchkula, 1996
Doosri Kahani
Radhakrishna
New Delhi, 2000
Over To You Kadambari
Katha
New Delhi, 2004
Koi Baat Bahin
Rajkamal
New Delhi, 2004
Kali-Katha via Bypass
Insel
Frankfurt am Main, 2004
[Ü: Margot Gatzlaff]

Alka Saraogi wurde 1960 in Kalkutta (heute Kolkata), Indien, geboren. Nachdem sie bereits acht Jahre verheiratet war und zwei Kinder bekommen hatte, nahm sie – ein in ihrer konservativen Umgebung ungewöhnlicher Schritt – ein Studium der Hindi-Literatur an der Universität Kalkutta auf, das sie mit einer Promotion abschloss. Sie veröffentlichte Zeitungsartikel über Gesundheits- und Frauenthemen, bevor sie mit dem Schreiben von fiktiven Geschichten begann. Ihr erster Band mit Kurzgeschichten »Kahaniki Talash Mein« erschien 1996, zwei Jahre später veröffentlichte sie ihren Debütroman »Kali-Katha Via Bypass« (1998; dt. »Kali-Katha via Bypass«, 2004), für den sie 2001 mit dem renommierten Sahitya Akademi Award ausgezeichnet wurde. Das Buch wurde zur Übersetzung in zweiundzwanzig weitere offizielle Sprachen Indiens vorgeschlagen. Alka Saraogi verfasst ihre Texte in ihrer Muttersprache Hindi und setzt sich dadurch bewusst von vielen indischen Schriftstellern ab, die auf Englisch schreiben. Nach Meinung der Autorin ist Englisch auch mehr als fünfzig Jahre nach dem Ende der britischen Kolonialzeit immer noch sowohl Symbol für Ungleichheit als auch ein Indiz für den Fortbestand kolonialer Präsenz in der postkolonialen Gesellschaft Indiens. Schauplatz ihres vielschichtigen Romans »KaliKatha via Bypass« ist Kalkutta. Nach einer Bypass-Operation wandert der zweiundsiebzigjährige Marwari-Patriarch Kishore Babu ziellos auf den Spuren seiner lang verdrängten Erinnerungen an die idealistischen Tage der Freiheitskämpfe durch die Straßen der Stadt. Die ehemalige zweite Hauptstadt des British Empire mit Sitz der East India Company war für Zuwanderer sehr attraktiv. Auch die Marwaris kamen, traditionell Geschäftsleute aus Rajasthan im westlichen Indien, deren Lebensweise bei den progressiven heimischen Bengalis Ablehnung hervorrief.

Alka Saraogi erzählt nicht nur die Geschichte eines alten Mannes, der auf das Unverständnis seiner Mitmenschen und seiner Familie stößt, weil er seiner eigenen Logik folgt und sich wieder dem lang vergessenen Idealismus seiner Jugend zuwendet. Sie erzählt auch die Geschichte der Marwari-Diaspora, von ihrer Herkunft, ihren Traditionen und ihren Familienstrukturen. Vor allem erzählt sie die koloniale und postkoloniale Geschichte Indiens. Kalkutta war Bühne für nationalistische Unabhängigkeitsbestrebungen (von Mahatma Gandhi bis Netaji Subhash Chandra Bose mitgeprägt) sowie für den blutigen Konflikt zwischen Hindus und Moslems, der schließlich zur Teilung in die beiden Staaten Indien und Pakistan führte. In überraschenden Rückblenden verbindet die Autorin historische Fakten mit den Erinnerungen ihres Protagonisten, der nach seiner Bypass-Operation zum weisen Narr wird, der unbequeme Fragen nach der postkolonialen indischen Identität stellt. In letzter Zeit erschienen von Alka Saraogi ein weiterer Band mit Erzählungen (»Doosari Kahani«, 2000) sowie zwei Romane, »Shesh Kadambari« (2002; Engl. »Over To You, Kadambari«, 2004) und »Koibaat Nahin« (2004; Ü: Macht nichts, ist schon gut). Alka Saraogi lebt in Kalkutta.

jelena schwarz

biography

Elena Schwarz was born in 1948 in St. Petersburg, where she still lives. She wrote her first poems at the age of thirteen. After finishing her studies at the Leningrad Institute for Drama, Music and Film in 1971, she worked as a translator, poet and essayist. She has issued her texts in the Samizdat underground scene since the 1960's, because she was not allowed to publish a single line until the collapse of the Soviet Union. The censors were wary of the metaphysical-mystic themes, which, however, could not prevent her experimental lyric and epic verse poetry from enjoying an ever-increasing, though secret, popularity. Owing to the fact that her texts could be published in western periodicals, Elena Schwarz became acknowledged outside Russia from early on. It is not surprising therefore that her first volume of poetry in Russian »Tanzuyushzy David« (1985; Eng. »Dancing David«) came out in New York and not in her native country. The following volume »Stichi« (t: Poems) was published in Paris and Munich in 1987. When finally in 1989, Perestroika made it possible for her first volume of poetry to be published in the Soviet Union, »Storony svieta« (t: Four quarters of the globe) was sold out the day of its appearance. Since then, she has published one book of poems a year. In 1999, Elena Schwarz was awarded the renowned Northern Palmyra prize for literature. Four years later, she received the Triumph Prize for her collected poetry in two volumes »Sochinenia Eleny Schwarz« (2002; t: Works of Elena Schwarz).
Elena Schwarz' writing is characterised by a combination of counterpoint elements. Her power of imagination creates a unique relationship between the ordinary and the mythical. Her poetry has its roots in the lyrical-religious tradition as well as in the ludic experiment. Its structure and theme are both simple and complex, its mood and diverse imagery both poetical and ironic-grotesque. »Like in a shelter in the Taiga, the wanderer should also find in poems all his basic requirements: matches, bread, salt, an axe, and a nearby well. But then it so happens he can imagine and discover the unexpected in it.« Though she calls her poems very close and personal »aphoristic descriptions of life« she is well aware that they have a life of their own: »Poems are living beings, they fly away, very far away.«
Her texts have been translated into several European languages. Her poems are available in German in two volumes, »Ein kaltes Feuer brennt an den Knochen entlang...« (1997; t: A cold fire burns along the bones...) and »Das Blumentier« (1999; t: The flower animal).

Tanzujuschzij Dawid
Russica Publishers
New York, 1985
Storonij swjeta
Sowjetski pisatjel
Leningrad, 1989
Ein kaltes Feuer brennt an den Knochen entlang...
Oberbaum
Chemnitz, 1997
[Ü: Bettina Eberspächer]
Das Blumentier
Grupello Verlag
Düsseldorf, 1999
[Ü: Alexander Nitzberg]
Stichotworenija i poemi
Inapress
St. Petersburg, 1999
Widimaja storona schisni
Limbuspress
St. Petersburg, 2003

Jelena Schwarz wurde 1948 in St. Petersburg geboren, wo sie auch heute lebt. Bereits im Alter von dreizehn Jahren schrieb sie ihre ersten Gedichte. 1971 absolvierte sie ihr Studium am Leningrader Institut für Theater-, Musik- und Filmwissenschaften und arbeitete anschließend als Übersetzerin, Lyrikerin und Essayistin. Seit den sechziger Jahren publizierte sie ihre Texte und Gedichte in der Samisdat-Untergrundliteraturszene. Bis zum Ende der Sowjetzeit durfte sie offiziell keine einzige Zeile veröffentlichen. Die metaphysisch-mystische Thematik ihrer Gedichte war der Zensur suspekt, was jedoch die Beliebtheit ihrer experimentell-lyrischen Gedichte und epischen Versdichtungen keineswegs schmälerte. Da ihre Texte jedoch in westlichen Periodika publiziert wurden, nahm man Jelena Schwarz schon früh außerhalb Russlands wahr. So verwundert es kaum, dass ihr erster Gedichtband in russischer Sprache »Tanzujuschzij David« (Ü: Der tanzende David) 1985 nicht in ihrer Heimat, sondern in New York erschien. Es folgten 1987 »Stichi« (Ü: Gedichte), veröffentlicht in Paris und München. Als 1989 im Zuge der Perestroika endlich ihr erster Gedichtband »Storonij swjeta« (Ü: Himmelsrichtungen) in der Sowjetunion herauskommen konnte, war das Buch bereits am ersten Erscheinungstag ausverkauft. Seitdem erschien jedes Jahr ein Gedichtband. 1999 erhielt Jelena Schwarz den angesehenen Literaturpreis Palmyra des Nordens. Vier Jahre später wurde ihre zweibändige Werkausgabe »Sochinenia Eleny Schwarz« (2002) mit dem Triumph-Preis ausgezeichnet.

Das Schreiben Jelena Schwarz' ist durch die Kombination konträrer Elemente geprägt. Mit imaginativer Kraft entstehen eigenwillige Symbiosen von Alltäglichem und Mythischem. In der Struktur und Thematik einfach und komplex zugleich, in der Bildervielfalt und Stimmung teils poetisch, teils ironisch-grotesk, ist ihre Dichtung sowohl in lyrisch-religiösen Traditionen als auch im Spielerisch-Experimentellen verwurzelt. »In Gedichten sollte der Wanderer, wie in einer Taiga-Hütte, all das finden, was er fürs erste benötigt: Streichhölzer, Brot, Salz, eine Axt, daneben einen Brunnen. Doch dann stellt sich heraus, dass sich in ihnen alles Mögliche finden lässt, was von sich aus niemand erwartet.« Und obwohl sie ihre Gedichte als sehr nahe und persönliche »Lebensbeschreibung in Aphorismen« bezeichnet, weiß sie auch um deren Eigenleben: »Gedichte sind Wesen, sie fliegen fort und zwar sehr weit.«

Ihre Texte wurden in mehrere europäische Sprachen übersetzt. Mit den Bänden »Ein kaltes Feuer brennt an den Knochen entlang« (1997) und »Das Blumentier« (1999) liegen ihre Gedichte auch in deutscher Sprache vor.

aharon shabtai

biography

Aharon Shabtai was born in Tel Aviv during the British mandate over Palestine in 1939. He spent his childhood on a kibbutz, and he later read philosophy and Greek at the Hebrew University in Jerusalem and at the Sorbonne in Paris. After earning his Ph. D. with a dissertation on Aeschylus' tragedies in 1979, he taught Greek drama at the Hebrew University up to the mid 1980's, and he has been lecturing on poetry and Greek literature at Tel Aviv University since 1990. As the foremost Hebrew translator of Greek drama including Aeschylus, Sophocles, Euripides, and Aristophanes, Shabtai was awarded the 1993 Prime Minister's Prize for Translation as well as the 1999 Tchernichowsky Prize.
To date he has published seventeen volumes of poetry which also received several prizes.
In his long poem »Kibbutz« (1973) Aharon Shabtai describes life in the Zionist-socialist Israel of the 1950's. »ha-Poema ha-betit« (1976; Eng. »The Domestic Poem«, 1987) consists of 363 vignettes strung on a mythical thread of concrete situations. Several of his poems are mercilessly intimate in their reference to his personal experience of depression, erotic sprees and an unhappy marriage; the tone of these poems is direct and uncompromising. »Love & Selected Poems«, which is the English selection of his poems of the past 30 years, was published in 1997. Recently, »J'accuse« has incensed the readers' passionate response. This collection of political poems had first appeared in the literary pages of the weekend edition of the newspaper »Ha'aretz« and was translated into English in 2003. The title alludes to Emile Zola's famous letter denouncing the French government's anti-Semitic bias during the Dreyfus affair. Stylistically and morally drawing from Hebrew liturgy, Aharon Shabtai accentuates his contempt for Israeli politics in the Israeli-Palestinian conflict in scornful pointed rhetoric. The poems cover the years from Netanyahu's election in 1996 to the second Intifada and it unleashed a storm of indignation. Readers accused him of ignorantly underestimating the actual terrorist threat and implied that he had deep anti-Israeli convictions. But it is the poem »Artsenu« (2002; t: Our Country) which gave his latest volume of poetry its title, that reveals Shabtai's intention; recalling as it does, his childhood prior to the foundation of the State of Israel, the author clearly expresses that his criticism is meant as a defence of his ideal vision of Israel. Aharon Shabtai lives in Tel Aviv.

La première lecture
Editions de l'Eclat
Paris, 1990
ha-Poema ha-betit
Am Oved
Tel Aviv, 1990
Love & Selected Poems
The Sheep Meadow Press
New York, 1997
[Ü: Peter Cole]
Artsenu. Shirim 1987-2002
Hotsa'at ha-Kibuts
ha-me'uhad
Tel Aviv, 2002
J'accuse
New Directions
New York, 2003
[Ü: Peter Cole]

Aharon Shabtai wurde 1939 in Tel Aviv, im unter britischem Mandat stehenden Palästina, geboren. Seine Kindheit verbrachte er in einem Kibbuz. Er studierte Philosophie und Griechisch an der Hebrew University in Jerusalem und an der Sorbonne in Paris. 1979 promovierte er mit einer Arbeit über die Tragödien von Aischylos. Bis Mitte der achtziger Jahre lehrte er Griechisches Drama an der Hebrew University. Seit 1990 ist er Dozent für Griechische Literatur und Lyrik an der Tel Aviv University. Er übersetzte Theaterstücke von Aischylos, Sophokles, Euripides und Aristophanes ins Hebräische. Für seine Übersetzungen erhielt er u. a. den Prime Minister's Prize for Translation 1993 und den Tchernichowsky Prize 1999. Seit 1966 veröffentlichte er bislang siebzehn Gedichtbände, die ebenfalls mit wichtigen Auszeichnungen geehrt wurden.

In seinem langen Gedicht »Kibbutz« (1973) beschreibt er das Leben im zionistisch-sozialistischen Israel der fünfziger Jahre. »ha-Poema ha-betit« (1976; Ü: Das häusliche Poem) ist eine Aneinanderreihung von 363 Miniaturen, eine mythische Gestaltung des Gegenständlichen. Andere Gedichte sind schonungslos persönlich. In direkter, sperriger Sprache thematisiert er eigene Erfahrungen mit Depressionen, erotische Abenteuer und das Scheitern seiner Ehe. Eine Auswahl von Gedichten aus dreißig Jahren erschien 1997 auf englisch unter dem Titel »Love & Selected Poems«. In letzter Zeit erregte der Dichter die Gemüter mit »J'accuse«, einer Sammlung politischer Gedichte, die zuvor in der Wochenendausgabe der Tageszeitung »Ha'aretz« erschienen waren. Seit 2003 liegt der Band auch in englischer Übersetzung vor. Der Titel spielt auf Emile Zolas berühmten Brief an, mit dem er den Antisemitismus der französischen Regierung während der Dreyfus-Affäre anklagte. Aharon Shabtai fasst in kritischen Gedichten seine Ablehnung der Politik Israels im israelisch-palästinensischen Konflikt in zornige, klare Worte. Stilistisch und moralisch bezieht sich Shabtai auf die hebräische Schrifttradition. Die Texte entstanden in einem Zeitraum, der von Netanjahus Wahlsieg 1996 bis zur Zeit der zweiten Intifada reicht. Sie entfesselten einen Sturm der Entrüstung unter den Lesern, die ihm Ignoranz gegenüber der realen Bedrohung Israels durch den Terror vorwarfen und ihm eine anti-israelische Haltung unterstellten. Dass er in seiner Kritik vielmehr sein Ideal von Israel verteidigt, wird im Titelgedicht seines jüngsten Gedichtbandes »Artsenu« (2002; Ü: Unser Land) deutlich, mit dem er sich an seine Kindheit vor der Staatsgründung Israels erinnert. Aharon Shabtai lebt in Tel Aviv.

jean-philippe toussaint

biography

Jean-Philippe Toussaint was born in Brussels, Belgium, in 1957. He spent a large part of his youth in Paris, where later he studied Politics and Modern History. From 1982 to 1984 he taught French in Algeria, where he started writing. Incidentally, his first book »La salle de bain« (1985; Eng. »The Bathroom«, 1989) attracted the attention of Jérôme Lindon, head of the Paris based publishing house Éditions de Minuit, which had published the most important writers of the »nouveau roman« in the 1950's, and he decided spontaneously to bring out the book. After all, in this story of a man who in his quest for an ›abstract life‹ turns his bathroom into his living room, Toussaint employs several narrative elements reminiscent of the »nouveau roman's« aesthetics. For example, he abstains from any psychological rendering of his characters, but instead he maintains a detached perspective of the minutiae. Critics regard him as an exponents of the »nouveau nouveau roman«. His minimalist style, which seems to linger in phenomenological precision, always corresponds with a subjacent layer: »Just as my books are void of sociology and politics, philosophy and metaphysics are always apparent, even if not explicitly named. They are always a reflection on time and death.«
In his novels »Monsieur« (1986; Eng. »Monsieur«, 1991) and »L'appareil-photo« (1989; t: The camera) the focus is on melancholic protagonists who try to evade life's demands by passivity. During a scholarship in Berlin Toussaint wrote »La télévision« (1997; t: The TV). In the text, the first-person narrator decides to abstain from watching TV and spends the time saved in the swimming pool, in the museum and on small trips. The loss of immediate perception is rendered in a subtle and ironic manner. The consequently subjective travel book »Autoportrait (à l'étranger)« (2000; t: Self portrait (abroad)) was recently published, as well as »Faire l'amour« (2002; Eng. »Making Love«, 2004). On their trip to Japan a French couple is not only confronted with being alien in another culture, but also with a deep estrangement in their relationship. Toussaint manages to find impressive images for the interior emotional states. At the same time, in his numerous descriptions of light, he casually refers to Jun'ichiro Tanizaki's classical book »In Praise of Shadows«.
Jean-Philippe Toussaint alternately lives in Corsica and Brussels.

Monsieur
Hanser
München/Wien, 1988
[Ü: Sigrid Vagt]
Der Photoapparat
Suhrkamp
Frankfurt am Main, 1991
[Ü: Joachim Unseld]
Der Köder
Suhrkamp
Frankfurt am Main, 1993
[Ü: Achim Russer]
Fernsehen
Suhrkamp
Frankfurt am Main, 2001
[Ü: Bernd Schwibs]
Selbstporträt (in der Fremde)
FVA
Frankfurt am Main, 2001
[Ü: Bernd Schwibs]
Sich lieben
FVA
Frankfurt am Main, 2003
[Ü: Bernd Schwibs]
Das Badezimmer
FVA
Frankfurt am Main, 2004
[Ü: Joachim Unseld]

Jean-Philippe Toussaint wurde 1957 in Brüssel, Belgien, geboren. Einen Teil seiner Jugend verbrachte er in Paris, wo er später Politikwissenschaft und Neuere Geschichte studierte. Von 1982 bis 1984 arbeitete er als Französischlehrer in Algerien. Dort begann er mit dem Schreiben. Durch einen Zufall wurde Jérôme Lindon, Verleger des Pariser Verlags Éditions 0de Minuit, der in den fünfziger Jahren die wichtigsten Autoren des ›nouveau roman‹ publizierte, auf Toussaints Manuskript »La salle de bain« (1985; dt. »Das Badezimmer«, 2004) aufmerksam und entschied spontan, das Buch herauszubringen. Jean-Philippe Toussaint verwendet in seiner Geschichte von einem Mann, der auf der Suche nach dem »abstrakten Leben« das Badezimmer zu seinem Wohn- und Lebensraum macht, verschiedene narrative Elemente, die an die Ästhetik des ›nouveau roman‹ erinnern. So verzichtet er auf jegliche Psychologisierung der Figuren und schreibt statt dessen mit distanziertem Blick aufs Detail. Die Kritik zählt ihn zu den Vertretern des ›nouveau nouveau roman‹. Sein minimalistischer Stil, der in phänomenologischer Präzision zu verharren scheint, korrespondiert immer mit einer untergründigen Ebene: »Ebenso, wie meine Bücher völlig frei von Soziologie und Politik sind, sind Philosophie und Metaphysik in ihnen immer gegenwärtig, auch wenn sie nicht direkt thematisiert werden. Sie sind immer eine Reflexion über die Zeit und den Tod.«
In seinen Romanen »Monsieur« (1986; dt. »Monsieur«, 1988) und »L'appareil-photo« (1989; dt. »Der Photoapparat«, 1991) stehen melancholische Antihelden im Mittelpunkt, die sich den Anforderungen der Realität durch Passivität entziehen. Während eines Stipendienaufenthaltes in Berlin entstand »La télévision« (1997; dt. »Fernsehen«, 2001). Der Ich-Erzähler beschließt, auf das Fernsehen zu verzichten. Die gewonnene Zeit verbringt er im Schwimmbad, im Museum und mit kleinen Ausflügen. Der Verlust der unmittelbaren Wahrnehmung wird hier subtil und ironisch thematisiert. Zuletzt erschienen »Autoportrait (à l'étranger)« (2000; dt. »Selbstporträt (in der Fremde)«, 2001), ein überaus subjektives Reisebuch, sowie der Roman »Faire l'amour« (2002; dt. »Sich lieben«, 2003). Während einer Japanreise sieht sich ein französisches Paar nicht nur mit dem Gefühl des Fremdseins in einer anderen Kultur konfrontiert, sondern auch mit starker Entfremdung in der Beziehung. Für die inneren, emotionalen Zustände findet Toussaint eindrucksvolle Bilder. Zugleich verweist er in zahlreichen Schilderungen des Lichts auf Jun'ichiro Tanizakis Klassiker »Lob des Schattens«. Jean-Philippe Toussaint lebt auf Korsika und in Brüssel.

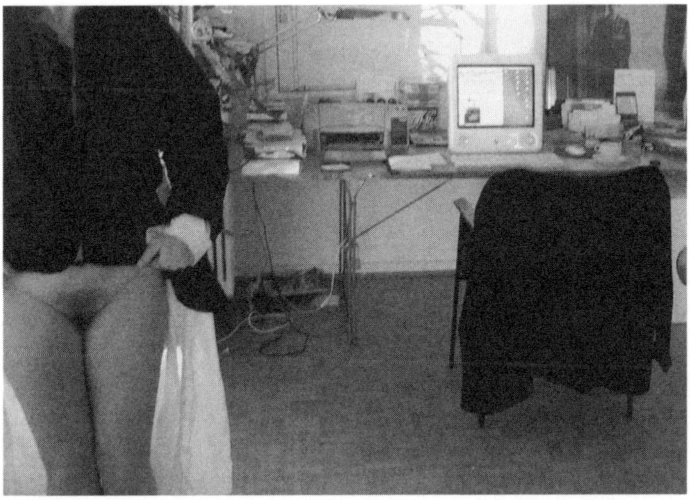

m.t. vasudevan nair

biography

M. T. Vasudevan Nair was born in Kudallur, a village in the southern Indian state of Kerala, in 1933. His first short stories, written in his native language, Malayalam, were published in several magazines while he was a youth. The young author's first volume of narratives came out in 1952. His debut novel »Nalukettu« (1958; Eng. »The Ancestral House«,1959) won him the Kerala Sahitya Akademi Award in 1959. The National Book Trust made it possible for him to have the book translated into all the official languages of India. Since then he has written eight more novels, including »Asuravithu« (1962; Eng. »The Demon Seed and Other Writings«,1998), »Manju« (1964; t: Snow) and »Kaalam« (1969; Eng. »Kaalam«, 1998). He has also published eighteen volumes of short stories, as well as travelogues, literary essays and children's books. He has been honoured with the Jnanpith Award, the most prestigious Indian literary award, and numerous other accolades. But M. T. Vasudevan Nair has not only made a reputation for himself as an author and long time editor of the influential weekly literary magazine »Mathrubhumi«, but also as the prize winning script writer and director of Malayalam movies. His cinema work includes more than forty film scripts, and the direction of six feature films, three documentaries and one TV series.

His literary and cinematographic oevres focus on rural south Indian society. British colonialism and the independence of India led to fundamental changes of traditional matrilineal structures in the northern Kerala (Nair) communities. M. T. Vasudevan Nair is considered the principal chronicler of the breakdown of the family system. Many narratives draw from the history of Kudallur, Nair's home village, which is characterised by the dissolving of feudal structures and values. Nair uses a concise and lyrical language to depict the correlation between conditions of society and the anxieties and emotional involvements of his characters. This is true also in his novel »Randamoozham« (1984; Eng. »Second Turn«, 1997) which is based on the Indian epic »Mahabharata«. Nair's respectful recreation of the classic is told from the point of view of the war hero Bhima, who gains, through the author's ironic undertones, a new psychological depth. »I have not changed the framework of the story by the first Vyasa, Krishna-Dwaipayana. I have read between his lines and expanded on his pregnant silences.« M. T. Vasudevan Nair lives in Calicut/Kerala, India.

The Legacy
Vikas
Neu Delhi, 1975
[Ü: Celine Matheu]

Nalukettu
Poorna
Kalkutta,1979

Catching An Elephant and Other Stories
Rupa & Co.
Kalkutta, 1991
[Ü: V. Abdulla]

Second Turn
MacMillan India
Chennai, 1997
[Ü: P. K. Ravindranath]

The Demon Seed and Other Writings
Penguin Books
Neu Delhi, 1998
[Ü: V. Abdulla und Gita Krishnankutty]

Kaalam
Sangam
London, 1998
[Ü: Gita Krishnankutty]

M. T. Vasudevan Nair wurde 1933 in Kudallur, einem Dorf im südindischen Bundesstaat Kerala, geboren. Bereits als Jugendlicher veröffentlichte er in Zeitschriften erste Kurzgeschichten in seiner Muttersprache Malayalam. Der erste Erzählband des jungen Autors erschien 1952. Für seinen Debütroman »Nalukettu« (1958; engl. »The Ancestral House«, 1959) wurde er 1959 mit dem Kerala Sahitya Akademi Award ausgezeichnet. Der National Book Trust ermöglichte die Übersetzung des Buches in alle anderen offiziellen Sprachen Indiens. Seither schrieb er acht weitere Romane, darunter »Asuravithe« (1962; engl. »The Demon Seed and Other Writings«,1998), »Manju« (1964; Ü: Schnee) und »Kaalam« (1969; engl. »Kalaam«, 1998) sowie achtzehn Bände mit Kurzgeschichten, außerdem Reiseberichte, literarische Essays und Kinderbücher. Er wurde mit zahlreichen Literaturpreisen gewürdigt, u. a. 1996 mit der höchsten literarischen Auszeichnung Indiens, dem Jnanpith Award. M. T. Vasudevan Nair ist jedoch nicht nur als Schriftsteller sowie als langjähriger Herausgeber der Wochenzeitung »Mathrubhumi« bekannt, sondern insbesondere auch als mehrfach preisgekrönter Drehbuchautor und Filmregisseur des Malayalam-Kinos. Er verfasste mehr als vierzig Drehbücher und führte selbst Regie bei sechs Spielfilmen, drei Dokumentarfilmen und einer Fernsehserie.

Im Mittelpunkt seiner literarischen und filmischen Werke steht die dörfliche Gesellschaft Südindiens. Die britische Kolonisierung und die indische Unabhängigkeit führten in Kerala zu gravierenden Veränderungen in den althergebrachten matrilinearen Strukturen der Nair-Gemeinschaften Nord-Keralas. M. T. Vasudevan Nair gilt als der Chronist des Niedergangs dieser Familienverbände. Inspiration für viele seiner Erzählungen ist die Geschichte seines Heimatdorfes Kudallur, das von der Auflösung feudalistischer Strukturen und Werte geprägt ist. In dichter, lyrischer Sprache schildert er das Wechselspiel zwischen den Bedingungen der äußeren Welt und den Ängsten und emotionalen Verstrickungen der Protagonisten. So auch im Roman »Randamoozham« (1984; engl. »Second Turn«, 1997), der auf dem großen indischen Epos »Mahabharata« basiert. M. T. Vasudevan Nairs respektvolle Interpretation des Klassikers folgt dem Blickwinkel des Kriegerhelden Bhima, dem er unter Verwendung von leisen ironischen Untertönen eine neue psychologische Dimension hinzufügt. »Ich habe die Grundzüge der Geschichte des ersten Vyasa, Krishna-Dwaipayana, nicht verändert. Ich habe zwischen seinen Zeilen gelesen und sein bedeutsames Schweigen ausgearbeitet.«
M. T. Vasudevan Nair lebt in Calicut/Kerala, Indien.

M.T. Vasudevan Nair

(To the Muse)

In the Past
when you went into your tantrums
I felt miserable.
Then I was like a young lover!
Now we know each other
thoroughly as an old couple
So I wait with a subtle smile.
I know you cannot keep it
for long
as you will choke of anger
and despair
I know that you know
I am your only chosen
oracle!

homero aridjis
constantin virgil bănescu
frédéric beigbeder
wolf biermann
volker braun
tianxin cai
peter carey
rafael chirbes
bora ćosić
peter cole
dimitré dinev
marjana gaponenko
durs grünbein
lars gustafsson
christoph hein
rolf hochhuth
viktor jerofejew
navid kermani
nicole krauss
antjie krog
jonathan lethem
ma yuan
claudio magris
les murray
oskar pastior
boualem sansal
marie-luise scherer
alan sillitoe
burkhard spinnen
peter truschner
ayu utami
gore vidal
eliot weinberger
xi chuan

homero aridjis

biography

The youngest of five brothers, Homero Aridjis was born in 1940, in the village of Contepec, Michoacán, Mexico, to a Mexican mother and a Greek father. He began writing at the age of 11, after surviving an accident which nearly cost him his life. At age of 19 he won a fellowship from the Mexican Writers' centre, and in 1964 was the youngest-ever recipient of the Xavier Villaurrutia Prize for best book of the year, for »Mirándola dormir«, a classic of Mexican erotic poetry. After two years in Europe on a Guggenheim Fellowship, he taught at American universities until entering the Mexican diplomatic service and serving as Ambassador to both Switzerland and then The Netherlands while still in his thirties. Back in Mexico, in 1985 Aridjis and 99 other renowned artists and intellectuals founded the legendary »Grupo de los Cien,« an activist organization based in Mexico which addresses national and international environmental and ethical issues. From 1997 through 2003 he served two terms as president of International PEN, where he strove to make PEN less Eurocentric.
In addition to fourteen volumes of poetry and eleven novels, Aridjis has written children's books, essays and plays, and for the past ten years has been an editorial page columnist for the Mexican newspaper »Reforma«. His work has been translated into a dozen languages and recognized with literary prizes such as the Grinzane Cavour in Italy, for »1492 Vida y tiempos de Juan Cabezón de Castilla« (1985). In 1997 he received the Prix Roger Caillois in France, and most recently, the Smederevo Golden Key poetry prize. »Eyes to See Otherwise: Selected Poems of Homero Aridjis«, a wide-ranging bilingual anthology of his poetry, was published in England (2001) and the United States (2002). Kenneth Rexroth called Aridjis a »visionary poet of lyrical bliss, crystalline concentrations and infinite spaces.«
A champion of grey whales, monarch butterflies, sea turtles and rain forests, Aridjis has been termed the »green conscience« of his country, and for his passionate defence of the Earth has received numerous international awards, including the UNEP Global 500 Award, the Orion Society's John Hay Award, and the International Environmental Leadership Award given by Mikhail Gorbachev and Global Green.
Aridjis and his wife Betty live in Mexico City, too far from their daughters, the writer Chloe Aridjis, in Berlin, and the filmmaker Eva Aridjis, in New York.

Los espacios azules
Joaquín Mortiz
Mexiko, 1969
Construir la muerte
Joaquín Mortiz
Mexiko, 1982
1492 – Die Abenteuer des Juan Cabezón von Kastilien
Benziger
Zürich, 1992
[Ü: Harald Riemann]
El señor de los últimos días, visiones del año mil
Alfaguara
Mexiko, 1994
Tiempo de ángeles
Fondo de Cultura Económica
Mexiko 1997
Eyes to See Otherwise. Ojos de otro mirar
New Directions
New York, 2001
Obra poética 1960 – 2001
Fondo de Cultura Económica
Mexiko, 2001

Defending the grey whale nursery at Laguna San Ignacio in Mexico from construction of the world's largest salt works.

Als jüngster von fünf Brüdern wurde Homero Aridjis, Sohn einer mexikanischen Mutter und eines griechischen Vaters, 1940 im Dorf Contepec in Michoacán, Mexiko, geboren. Nachdem er im Alter von elf Jahren einen schweren Unfall nur knapp überlebt hatte, begann er zu schreiben. Mit 19 Jahren gewann er das Stipendium des mexikanischen Writers' Center, und 1964 wurde er mit seinem Werk »Mirándola dormir« jüngster Träger des Xavier-Villaurrutia-Preises für das beste Buch des Jahres, das zu einem Klassiker der mexikanischen erotischen Poesie avancierte. Nach einem zweijährigen Aufenthalt in Europa, der durch ein Stipendium der Guggenheim-Foundation ermöglicht wurde, lehrte Aridjis zunächst an amerikanischen Universitäten, trat dann in den mexikanischen diplomatischen Dienst ein und vertrat sein Land – noch nicht vierzigjährig – als Botschafter in der Schweiz und den Niederlanden.
1985 kehrte er nach Mexiko zurück und gründete gemeinsam mit 99 anderen bekannten Künstlern und Intellektuellen die legendäre Gruppe »Grupo de los Cien«, eine Aktivistenvereinigung mit Sitz in Mexiko, welche sich nationaler und internationaler Umweltbelange und ethischer Fragen annimmt. Von 1997 bis 2003 war Aridjis zwei Mal in Folge Präsident des PEN International und setzte sich dafür ein, der eurozentristischen Ausrichtung des PEN entgegenzuwirken.
Zusätzlich zu vierzehn Bänden mit Poesie und elf Romanen verfasste Aridjis Kinderbücher, Essays und Theaterstücke, und in den vergangenen zehn Jahren arbeitete er als Kolumnist für die mexikanische Zeitung »Reforma«. Seine Arbeiten wurden in ein Dutzend Sprachen übersetzt und mit Literaturpreisen wie dem italienischen Grinzane-Cavour-Preis für »1492. Vida y tiempos de Juan Cabezón de Castilla« (1985, dt. »1492. Die Abenteuer des Juan Cabezón von Kastillien«, 1992) ausgezeichnet. 1997 erhielt er den Roger-Caillois-Preis in Frankreich und zuletzt den Poesie-Preis Smederevo Golden Key. »Eyes to See Otherwise: Selected Poems of Homero Aridjis«, eine umfangreiche zweisprachige Anthologie seiner Gedichte, wurde 2001 in England und 2002 in den USA publiziert. Kenneth Rexroth nannte ihn einen »visionären Poeten von lyrischer Glückseligkeit, kristalliner Konzentration und unendlichen Weiten.«
Als Kämpfer für die grauen Wale, die Monarchschmetterlinge, Wasserschildkröten und Regenwälder wurde Aridjis als »grünes Gewissen« seines Landes bezeichnet, und für seinen engagierten Einsatz für die Umwelt erhielt er zahlreiche internationale Auszeichnungen, darunter den UNEP Global 500 Award, den Orion Society's John Hay und den International Environmental Leadership Award, der von Michail Gorbatschow und Global Green vergeben wird.
Aridjis und seine Frau Betty leben in Mexiko City, viel zu weit entfernt von ihren Töchtern, der Berliner Schriftstellerin Chloe Aridjis und der New Yorker Filmemacherin Eva Aridjis.

Wenn die Muse nicht antwortet, suche ich sie in mir und außerhalb meiner selbst. Die Muse kann den Namen einer Straße tragen, eines Landes, eines Menschen. Wenn ich sie fange, beginne ich zu dichten. Sobald das Gedicht fertig ist, zieht die Muse wieder ihrer Wege.

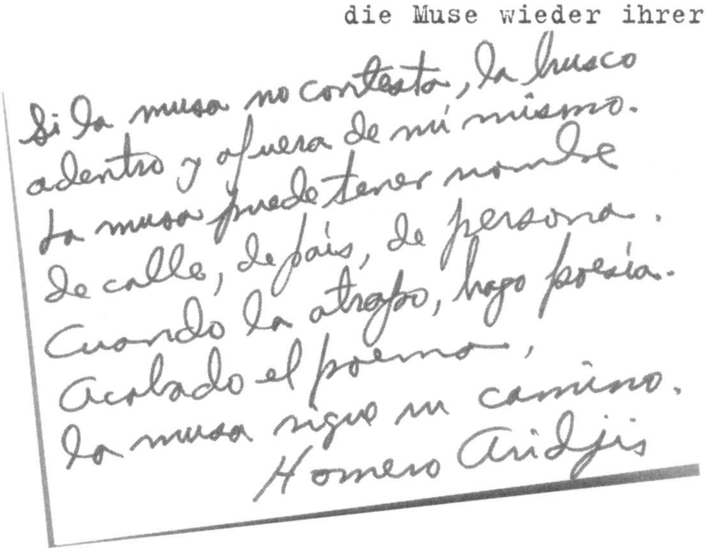
Si la musa no contesta, la busco
adentro y afuera de mí mismo.
La musa puede tener nombre
de calle, de país, de persona.
Cuando la atrapo, hago poesía.
Acabado el poema,
la musa sigue su camino.
Homero Aridjis

constantin virgil bănescu

biography

Constantin Virgil Bănescu was born in Târgovişte, Romania, in 1982. He studied Communication and Public Relations at the National School for Administrative and Political Studies in Bucharest. Since his early youth he has always enjoyed poetry, and when he was ten years old, he wrote his first poem – in French. His poems appeared in numerous magazines, among them »Ziua Literara«, »Literatorul« and »Viata Romaneasca«. They were translated into Slovenian, German, Spanish and English. In the German translation by Oskar Pastior they were published in literary magazines such as »Manuskripte« and »Schreibheft«. His first volume of poetry »Câinele, femeia şi ocheada« (t: The dog, the woman and the glance) appeared in 2000 and was received by critics with enthusiasm. For his debut, the young writer was awarded the renowned Prize of the Bucharest Writers Association. He published his second volume of poetry »Floarea cu o singură petală« (t: The flower with the single petal) in 2002. Constantin Virgil Bănescu's lyrical cosmos appears both tender and frightening. While in a love poem such as »ocheadă (vino)« a gentle seduction by cajoling cadences is practised, in poems such as »Câinele« and »Femeia« he indulges in violent fantasies of possession and power as if a godlike creator. He forms verbal spaces that often open up surprisingly towards the surreal and nightmarish. Some of the poems from his second volume he arranged in accordance with the Hindu principles of »Jagrat« and »Svapna«. »Jagrat« refers to the ›state of being awake‹, whereas »Svapna« is the Sanskrit term for the ›dreamy consciousness of sleep‹. Sleep, as the space of dreams, is the most important precondition for accessing an ephemeral, secret world defined purely by individual experience. For the poet Constantin Virgil Bănescu too, dreaming is inhabited by a special creative potential that has to be harnessed. As he writes in his poem »svapna-gata (dorm ca să visez)« quote: »chiar acum / mi se întoarce / sufletul / în / trup / chiar acum / mă văd scriind pe dealuri / aşteptându-mi fluturii / ascuns într-un zid de apă / chiar acum spun: / dorm ca să visez / dorm numai ca să visez / dorm«
Constantin Virgil Bănescu was awarded the Hubert Burda Prize for young poets from the south and south east of Europe. He lives in Bucharest.

Câinele, femeia şi ocheada
Timpul
Iasi, 2000
Floarea cu o singură petală
Junimea
Iasi, 2002

Constantin Virgil Bănescu wurde 1982 in Târgovişte, Rumänien, geboren. Er studiert Kommunikation und Public Relations an der nationalen Schule für administrative und politische Studien in Bukarest. Bereits in früher Jugend begeisterte er sich für Lyrik. Als Zehnjähriger verfasste er sein erstes Gedicht – in französischer Sprache. Später wurden seine Gedichte in zahlreichen rumänischen Zeitschriften veröffentlicht, darunter »Ziua Literara«, »Literatorul« und »Viata Romaneasca«. Sie wurden ins Slowenische, Deutsche, Spanische und Englische übersetzt. In der deutschen Übersetzung von Oskar Pastior wurden sie in Literaturmagazinen wie »Manuskripte« und »Schreibheft« publiziert. 2000 erschien sein erster Gedichtband »Câinele, femeia şi ocheada« (Ü: Der Hund, die Frau und der Liebäugler), der von der Kritik mit Begeisterung aufgenommen wurde. Der junge Dichter erhielt für sein Debüt u. a. den Preis des Bukarester Schriftstellerverbandes 2001.
Den zweiten Lyrikband »Floarea cu o singură petală« (Ü: Die Blüte mit einem Kelchblatt) veröffentlichte er 2002. Constantin Virgil Bănescus poetischer Kosmos mutet ebenso zart wie erschreckend an: Mal übt er in einem Liebesgedicht wie »liebäugler (lass uns)« die sanfte Verführung durch einen schmeichelnden Tonfall, mal ergeht er sich in Gedichten wie »der hund« und »die frau« in den gewaltsamen Besitz- und Machtphantasien eines gottgleichen Schöpfers. Er kreiert Worträume, die sich oftmals überraschend ins Surreale und Alptraumhafte öffnen. Einige der Gedichte seines zweiten Bandes hat er nach den hinduistischen Prinzipien »Jagrat« und »Swapna« geordnet. »Jagrat« bezeichnet den Wachzustand, während »Swapna« die Sanskrit-Bezeichnung für das Traumbewusstsein während des Schlafs ist. Der Schlaf als Ort des Traums bildet die wichtige Voraussetzung für den Träumenden, Zugang zu einer flüchtigen, verborgenen Welt zu finden, die allein durch sein subjektives Erleben bestimmt ist. Auch für den Dichter Constantin Virgil Bănescu wohnt dem Traum ein besonderes kreatives Potential inne, das es zu fassen gilt. Wie er in seinem Gedicht »Swapna-Gatter (ich schlafe um zu träumen)« schreibt: »eben / kehrt die seele / mir wieder zum leib. / eben / seh ich mich / auf ein paar hügeln schreibend / warten auf die flügel / im verborgenen einer / wassermauer. / eben / sah ich / ich schlafe um zu träumen / schlafe nur um zu träumen / schlafe eben.« Der Autor wurde 2003 mit dem Hubert-Burda-Preis für junge Lyriker aus Süd- und Südosteuropa ausgezeichnet. Constantin Virgil Bănescu lebt in Bukarest.

The Muse isn't coming.
What do I do about it?
I remember Her.
I remember Her until She remembers me too.

frédéric beigbeder

biography

Frédéric Beigbeder was born in Neuilly-sur-Seine, France, in 1965. While studying politics he became involved in the organisation of parties in the Parisian night scene. After the publication of his first novel »Memoires d'un jeune homme dérangé« (1990; t: Memoirs of a deranged young man), he embarked on a career in advertising as a copywriter, and worked successfully with various agencies for ten years. Simultaneously he made a reputation for himself through his literary reviews for a variety of magazines including »Elle«, »Paris Match«, and »Voici« along with cultural programmes on French TV. Feeling at home in the world of glamour and scandal, the provocative dandy soon became the controversial as well as the admired enfant terrible of the French literary scene. In 1994, he founded the Prix de Flore for young authors (named after the famous Café de Flore in St.-Germain-des-Prés), whose award winners include Michel Houellebecq and Virginie Despentes.

Beigbeder's work could be labelled ›autofiction‹. His alter ego Marc Maronnier, the typical society hedonist of the 1990's fun and party generation, is portrayed in a narcissistic-ironical way in the trilogy of »Memoires d'un jeune homme dérangé«, »Vaçances dans le coma« (1994; t: Holidays in a coma), and »L'amour dure trois ans« (1997; t: Love lasts three years). In his scandalous novel »99 francs« (2000; Eng. »£9.99«, 2002) Beigbeder casts a gaze over a society based on sham, brand names, and superficialities, thus lampooning the advertising industry. The ›world power of advertising‹ that he polemically warns of, consequently put an abrupt end to his copywriting career. Since then he has, on the one hand, supported the activities of the anti-globalisation »Antipub«-movement, and on the other hand, devised the advertising for the 2002 election campaign of the Communist Party candidate, Robert Hue. His most recent novel has again given rise to international criticism and heated debate.

With the title referring to the name of the restaurant at the World Trade Center, the 119 brief chapters of »Windows on the World« (2003) report the last 119 minutes of a real estate agent who is having breakfast there with his two sons on 9/11. In a parallel strand of the story, the narrator, called Frédéric Beigbeder, is sitting in the topfloor restaurant of the Tour Montparnasse in Paris. The time is one year later and he is musing on the effects of the terrorist attack on the western world, on Franco-American relations, and on his own life. In France, the book was widely acclaimed and awarded the Prix Interallié in 2003.

Frédéric Beigbeder lives in Paris and works as a writer, literary critic and editor-in-chief for the publishing house Flammarion.

Neununddreissigneunzig
Rowohlt
Reinbek, 2001
[Ü: Brigitte Große]
Memoiren eines Sohnes aus schlechtem Hause
Rowohlt
Reinbek, 2001
[Ü: Brigitte Große]
Ferien im Koma
Rowohlt
Reinbek, 2002
[Ü: Brigitte Große]
Die Liebe währt drei Jahre
Rowohlt
Reinbek, 2003
[Ü: Brigitte Große]
Letzte Inventur vor dem Ausverkauf. Die 50 besten Bücher des Jahrhunderts
Rowohlt
Reinbek, 2004
[Ü: Juliane Gräbener-Müller]
Windows on the World
Ullstein
Berlin/München, 2004
[Ü: Brigitte Große]

Frédéric Beigbeder wurde 1965 in Neuilly-sur-Seine, Frankreich, geboren. Neben dem Studium der Politikwissenschaften organisierte er Partys im Pariser Nachtleben. Nach der Veröffentlichung seines ersten Romans »Memoires d'un jeune homme dérangé« (1990; dt. »Memoiren eines Sohnes aus schlechtem Hause«, 2001) nahm er ein Jobangebot als Werbetexter an. Zehn Jahre lang arbeitete er erfolgreich für verschiedene Werbeagenturen. Zur selben Zeit machte er sich als Literaturkritiker für Magazine wie »Elle«, »Paris Match« und »Voici« sowie in Kultursendungen des französischen Fernsehens einen Namen. Durch seine Vorliebe für die Welt des Glamours und der Skandale sowie durch seine Lust an Provokationen wurde er schon bald zum ebenso umstrittenen wie bewunderten enfant terrible der französischen Literaturszene. 1994 rief er den Prix de Flore für junge Autoren (benannt nach dem berühmten Café Flore in St.-Germain-des-Prés) ins Leben, zu dessen Preisträgern Michel Houellebecq und Virginie Despentes zählen.

Seine eigenen Werke könnte man als ›Autofiktionen‹ bezeichnen. In der Trilogie »Memoires d'un jeune homme dérangé«, »Vacançes dans le coma« (1994; dt. »Ferien im Koma«, 2002) und »L'amour dure trois ans« (1997; dt. »Die Liebe währt drei Jahre«, 2003) porträtiert er auf narzisstisch-ironische Art sein alter ego Marc Maronnier als typischen Vertreter der hedonistischen Party- und Spaßgeneration der neunziger Jahre. Um die Welt des Scheins, der Marken und der Oberflächen geht es auch in seinem Skandalroman »Neununddreißigneunzig« (2001), einer Abrechnung mit der Werbebranche und zugleich polemischen Warnung vor der ›Weltmacht Werbung‹, die prompt Beigbeders Karriere als Werbetexter beendete. Seither unterstützt er einerseits die Aktionen der globalisierungskritischen »Antipub«-Bewegung, arbeitete andererseits aber auch als Berater für die Wahlkampagne des kommunistischen Kandidaten Robert Hue. Auch sein jüngster Roman »Windows on the World« (2003) bietet genügend Angriffsfläche für Kritiker. In 119 kurzen Kapiteln imaginiert Frédéric Beigbeder die 119 letzten Minuten eines Immobilienmaklers, der mit seinen beiden Söhnen am 11.09. 2001 im Restaurant des World Trade Centers frühstückt. In einer Parallelkonstruktion zu diesem Handlungsstrang denkt ein Jahr später der Erzähler namens Frédéric Beigbeder im Pariser Tour Montparnasse über die Auswirkungen des Terroranschlags auf die westliche Welt, das amerikanisch-französische Verhältnis und sein eigenes Leben nach. Das Buch wurde in Frankreich begeistert aufgenommen und 2003 mit dem Prix Interallié ausgezeichnet. Frédéric Beigbeder lebt als Schriftsteller und Literaturkritiker in Paris. Er ist zudem Programmchef des Verlags Flammarion.

wolf biermann

biography

Wolf Biermann was born in Hamburg in 1936. When he was six years old he lost his father, a Communist and a Jew who was killed in Auschwitz. Shortly afterwards Biermann survived the bombing of Hamburg. In 1953 he settled in the GDR and studied Political Economy, Mathematics and Philosophy at Humboldt University. Upon the encouragement of Hanns Eisler, he began to write poems and songs. With the skilled sound of Brecht, Heine and Villon, he did not adhere to the individual demands of Socialism, which led to conflict early on with the SED. In 1963 his first play, »Berliner Brautgang«, was not allowed to premiere. Thereafter, his work was only allowed to appear in the West: first the volumes of poetry »Die Drahtharfe« (1965) and »Mit Marx- und Engelszungen« (1968), then the long record »Chausseestraße 131« (1969). Biermann received an indefinite ban on any kind of performance, publication or travel. Meanwhile, he popularised his songs and writings, and his home became a meeting place for opponents and artists critical of the regime. The Stasi responded by spying on him, an operation in which over a hundred secret agents and informers participated.

In 1976, while Biermann was on a concert tour in West Germany, the SED expatriated the popular yet unrelenting artist. The protest which he thereupon raised is often considered the beginning of the end of the GDR. In the aftermath many other writers left the GDR, including: Thomas Brasch, Jürgen Fuchs, Jurek Becker, Günter Kunert, Sarah Kirsch and Manfred Krug. For a long time, Biermann himself felt tied to Socialism, from which he finally broke away. After the reunification he emerged as a sharp critic of the perpetrators and followers of the State's SED. Biermann's cavalier and often provocative language, with its desire for dialectical climax, is especially accounted for in his poems and lyrics, which achieve spectacular effect through the songwriter's stage presence. Biermann is also active as a brilliant essayist for different newspapers. The freshness and immediacy of his style are rare and also preserved in his translations from French, Russian, Finnish and English. Over the past few years Biermann has grappled increasingly with his Jewish roots and contemporary Jewish life, at present stimulated by his friendship with Arno Lustiger and George Tabori. His adaptation of the Yiddish epic »Großer Gesang vom ausgerotteten jüdischen Volk« by Jitzchak Katzenelson, who was killed in Auschwitz, was met with wide interest. An adaption of forty Shakespeare sonnets, under the title »Das ist die feinste Liebeskunst«, will appear shortly. Wolf Biermann has received many distinctions for his extensive body of work, among them Berlin's Fontane Prize (1969), the Georg Büchner Prize (1991) and the National Prize of the German National Foundation (1998). The father of nine children lives and works in his birthplace, Hamburg.

Alle Gedichte
Kiepenheuer & Witsch
Köln, 1995
Jitzchak Katzenelson: Großer Gesang vom ausgerotteten jüdischen Volk
dtv
München, 1996
Die Drahtharfe
dtv
München, 1999
Paradies uff Erden
Kiepenheuer & Witsch
Köln, 1999
Mit Marx- und Engelszungen
dtv
München, 2000
Über Deutschland. Unter Deutschen
Kiepenheuer & Witsch
Köln, 2002
Das ist die feinste Liebeskunst. 40 Shakespeare Sonette
Kiepenheuer & Witsch
Köln, 2004

Wolf Biermann wurde 1936 in Hamburg geboren. Mit sechs Jahren verlor er seinen Vater, Kommunist und Jude – er wurde im Konzentrationslager Auschwitz ermordet. Wenig später erlebte er die Bombardierung Hamburgs. 1953 übersiedelte er in die DDR. Biermann studierte an der Humboldt-Universität Politische Ökonomie, Mathematik und Philosophie. Von Hanns Eisler ermutigt begann er, Gedichte und Lieder zu schreiben. Mit einem an Brecht, Heine und Villon geschulten Ton hielt Biermann auch individuelle Forderungen an den Sozialismus nicht zurück, was früh zum Konflikt mit der SED führte. Schon sein erstes Theaterstück »Berliner Brautgang« wurde 1963 nicht zur Aufführung zugelassen. Seither konnten seine Werke nur noch im Westen erscheinen: zunächst die Gedichtbände »Die Drahtharfe« (1965) und »Mit Marx- und Engelszungen« (1968), dann die Langspielplatte »Chausseestraße 131« (1969). Biermann erhielt ein unbefristetes Auftritts-, Publikations- und Reiseverbot. Gleichzeitig verbreiteten sich seine Lieder und Schriften unter der Hand, und seine Wohnung wurde zum Treffpunkt von regimekritischen Künstlern und Oppositionellen. Der Staatssicherheitsdienst reagierte mit einer Bespitzelung, an der mehrere hundert Geheimdienstler und informelle Mitarbeiter beteiligt waren.
Während er sich 1976 auf einer Konzerttournee in der Bundesrepublik befand, bürgerte die SED den ebenso populären wie unbeugsamen Künstler kurzerhand aus. Der Protest, der sich daraufhin erhob, wird oft als Anfang vom Ende der DDR gewertet. In der Folgezeit kam es zu zahlreichen weiteren Ausreisen, u. a. von Thomas Brasch, Jürgen Fuchs, Jurek Becker, Günter Kunert, Sarah Kirsch und Manfred Krug. Biermann selbst fühlte sich weiterhin dem Sozialismus verbunden, von dem er sich schließlich dennoch lossagte. Nach der Wiedervereinigung trat er als scharfer Kritiker der Täter und Mitläufer des SED-Staates auf. Biermanns ungenierte und oft provokative Sprache mit ihrer Lust an dialektischer Zuspitzung entfaltet sich besonders in Gedichten und Liedtexten, die wiederum durch die performative Präsenz des Liedermachers eindrucksvoll zur Wirkung kommen. Biermann betätigte sich zudem als brillanter Essayist für verschiedene Zeitungen. Die im Deutschen seltene Frische und Direktheit seiner Sprachgebung erhält sich auch in Übertragungen, so z. B. aus dem Französischen, Russischen, Finnischen und Englischen. In letzter Zeit setzte sich Biermann zunehmend mit seinen jüdischen Wurzeln und dem zeitgenössischen jüdischen Leben auseinander, wesentlich angeregt durch die Freundschaften mit Arno Lustiger und George Tabori. Seine Nachdichtung des jiddisch verfassten Epos »Großer Gesang vom ausgerotteten jüdischen Volk« von Jitzchak Katzenelson, der in Auschwitz ermordet wurde, fand weithin Beachtung. In Kürze erscheinen unter dem Titel »Das ist die feinste Liebeskunst« die Übertragungen von vierzig Sonetten Shakespeares. Wolf Biermann erhielt für sein umfangreiches Werk zahlreiche Auszeichnungen, darunter den Berliner Fontane-Preis (1969), den Georg-Büchner-Preis (1991) und den Nationalpreis der Deutschen Nationalstiftung (1998). Der Vater von neun Kindern lebt und arbeitet in seiner Geburtsstadt Hamburg.

volker braun

biography

Volker Braun was born in Dresden in 1939. After finishing school he worked for three years in printing, in underground engineering, and in strip mining before studying Philosophy. In 1962 he was threatened with expulsion after Stephan Hermlin recited Braun's poems at a reading at the Akademie der Künste. In 1965 Helene Weigel brought him to the Berliner Ensemble, where his first piece, »Die Kipper« (t: The dumpers), was staged (and banned). Following the put down of the Prague Spring, he wrote »T« (Trotzki) and »Lenins Tod« (t: Lenin's death). Between 1972 and 1977 he collaborated with the Deutsche Theater, and in 1990 he became house author of the Berliner Ensemble. Many of his later works were printed and, in some cases, performed, years after their conception: among them »Unvollendete Geschichte« (t: Unfinished story), »Hinze-Kunze-Roman« (t: Hinze-Kunze novel), the volumes of poetry »Training des aufrechten Gangs« (t: Training to walk erect) and »Langsamer knirschender Morgen« (t: Slowly grinding morning), the theatre pieces »Dmitri« and »Die Übergangsgesellschaft« (t: The transformation society), and the essay collection »Verheerende Folgen mangelnden Anscheins innerbetrieblicher Demokratie« (t: Devastating consequences of lacking appearance of internal democracy). Braun calls it all »work against the rock crust of promises«. Despite the fundamental criticism he received, Braun considers himself a socialist, who through his »conspiratorial Realism« pushes for changes of circumstances. »One searches for a perspective which does not comply with the official way of thinking, nor with appeasing or conformist thinking – in other words, a view on things from below.« He remained true to this attitude after the German reunification, be it with the abyssal novella »Die vier Werkzeugmacher« (t: The four tool makers), the cycle of poems »Rot ist Marlboro« (t: Red is Marlboro) and »Tumulus«, or the theatre pieces »Der Staub von Brandenburg« (t: Brandenburg dust) and »Limes. Mark Aurel«. The Academy in Darmstadt awarded the Büchner Prize 2000 »to the poet, who with wit and mercy has created a lively chronicle of his historical world«, and »has renewed and transformed the language and forms of the philosophical era of German literature«.

DIE KUNST

Sie tanzt auf den Gräbern, mit Grazie
Mit ihrem wilden Gedächtnis.
WIR KÖNNEN JA NICHTS BEHALTEN. Sie
Ruft die Verreckten herauf, die Vergessenen
Mit ihren Messern und Forderungen. Erloschene
Liebe, kalter Zorn, vertane Zeiten. Was
Ist der Gedanke, daß wir sterblich sind
Gegen das GROSSE UMSONST. Sie wagt es zu denken
Im Untergrund, wo alles lebt.
Wie, ist es möglich? daß die Verhältnisse tanzen

Provokation für mich
Mitteldeutscher Verlag
Halle, 1965
Wir und nicht sie
Mitteldeutscher Verlag
Halle, 1970
Hinze-Kunze-Roman
Mitteldeutscher Verlag
Halle, 1985
Unvollendete Geschichte
Mitteldeutscher Verlag
Halle, 1988
Iphigenie in Freiheit
Suhrkamp
Frankfurt am Main, 1992
Wir befinden uns soweit wohl. Wir sind erst einmal am Ende
Suhrkamp
Frankfurt am Main, 1998
Die unvollendete Geschichte und ihr Ende
Suhrkamp
Frankfurt am Main, 1998
Tumulus
Suhrkamp
Frankfurt am Main, 1999
Wie es gekommen ist
Suhrkamp
Frankfurt am Main, 2002
Das unbesetzte Gebiet
Suhrkamp
Frankfurt am Main, 2004

Volker Braun wurde 1939 in Dresden geboren. Nach dem Abitur arbeitete er drei Jahre als Drucker, im Tiefbau und als Tagebaumaschinist, ehe er in Leipzig Philosophie studieren konnte. Wegen seiner Gedichte, die Stephan Hermlin 1962 auf der Lesung der Akademie der Künste vortrug, drohte ihm die Exmatrikulation. 1965 holte ihn Helene Weigel an das Berliner Ensemble, wo sein erstes Stück, »Die Kipper«, inszeniert (und verboten) wurde. Nach der Niederschlagung des Prager Frühlings schrieb er »T.« (Trotzki) und »Lenins Tod«. 1972 bis 1977 war er Mitarbeiter des Deutschen Theaters, anschließend bis 1990 Hausautor am Berliner Ensemble. Auch viele seiner späteren Werke – die »Unvollendete Geschichte«, der »Hinze-Kunze-Roman«, die Gedichtbände »Training des aufrechten Gangs«, »Langsamer knirschender Morgen«, die Stücke »Dmitri«, »Die Übergangsgesellschaft« oder die Essay-Sammlung »Verheerende Folgen mangelnden Anscheins innerbetrieblicher Demokratie«, mit immenser Verzögerung gedruckt bzw. aufgeführt, waren »Arbeit gegen die Deckgebirge der Verheißungen«. Trotz der fundamentalen Kritik verstand sich Braun als Sozialist, der durch seinen ›konspirativen Realismus‹ auf Veränderung der Verhältnisse drängte. »Man sucht einen Blickwinkel zu wählen, der dem offiziellen Denken, dem beschwichtigenden und sich einrichtenden Denken nicht nachkommt – also einen Blick von unten auf die Dinge.« Dieser Einstellung ist er auch nach der deutschen Vereinigung treu geblieben, sei es mit der abgründigen Novelle »Die vier Werkzeugmacher«, mit den Gedichtzyklen »Rot ist Marlboro« und »Tumulus« oder den Stücken »Der Staub von Brandenburg« und »Limes. Mark Aurel«. Die Darmstädter Akademie verlieh den Büchner-Preis 2000 »dem Dichter, der mit Erbarmen und Witz eine lebendige Chronik seiner geschichtlichen Welt geschaffen« und »die Sprache und die Formen der philosophischen Epoche der deutschen Literatur erneuert und verwandelt hat«.

Die Kunst

Die Kunst mit den Gräbern, mit Grazie
Mit ihrem vollen Gedächtnis.
WIR KÖNNEN JA NICHTS BEHALTEN. Die
Rückt die Verrückten heraus, die Versprechen
Mit ihren Namen und Forderungen. Erbitterte
Liebe, kalter Zorn, verlorene Zeiten. Was
ist der Gedanke, sagt mir schließlich sind
Gegen die GROSSE UMSONST. Die wagt es zu denken
Im Untergrund, am hellen Licht.
wie, ist es möglich? sagt die Verhältnisse tanzen

tianxin cai

biography

Tianxin Cai was born in Huangyan, in the south east of the People's Republic of China, in 1963. He studied mathematics and received his doctorate with a dissertation on number theory from Shandong University in 1987. For several years Cai was a visiting lecturer and professor in France and North and South America. His publications include many research papers on mathematics in prestigious journals. Tianxin Cai is also considered to be among the most active young Chinese avant-garde authors. He participated in international poetry festivals in Medellín, Colombia, and Rosario, Argentina, as well as in Zurich, Genoa, Vilenica, Slovenia, and Durban, South Africa. Since the publication of his first volume of poetry »Bi An« (t: Shore) in 1992, another three volumes have appeared in China. A Spanish collection of his lyrical work, »La desnudez antigua« was published in Colombia in 2002. Though he prefers to deal with everyday situations the author tends to employ a surrealist perspective – as conveyed in the poem »Sunlight«. Quote: »The sun is mango. / Cut open the day. / Left uncut, the evening. / We swallow sunlight / Making strong muscles. / While we sleep / Sunlight flows into our blood / Travels throughout our body. / On its journey meets / Another piece of sunlight.« Using simplified language, he intensifies images of nature and metaphors of time and infinity; in the same way, he enhances the sensual aesthetic of space by the bare form of his lines.
Since 1995, Tianxin Cai has been editing the biannual literary magazine »Apollinaire«, which has developed into one of the most important underground magazines in China. Apart from poetry he is engaged in writing travelogues and essays. In addition, he has translated into Chinese various authors including Elizabeth Bishop, Margaret Atwood, Jorge Luis Borges, Octavio Paz, and Gabriel García Márquez. His biography on Elizabeth Bishop entitled »Bei Fang, Nan Fang« (t: North and south) was published in 2000, it depicts her journeys as well as her lyrical work. A volume of translations of American poetry and prose appeared in 2003, and another volume of essays in the same year. Cai is regular columnist in the Shanghai magazine »Book City«, considered to be the Chinese »New Yorker«. This year he edited a selection of 20th century poetry in two volumes. Tianxin Cai lives in Hangzhou, where he is a professor of mathematics at Zhejiang University.

Bi An
Zhejiang Art & Literature
Hangzhou, 1992
Meng Xiang Huo
Zai Shi Shang
Zhishi
Peking, 1993
Jiang Shi
Dreaming Factory
Hangzhou, 1995
Mei Guo, Tian Shang
Fei Ji Zai Fei
Dreaming Factory
Hangzhou, 1998
Heng Yue Da Lu
De Lv Xing
Orient
Peking, 1999
Bei Fang, Nan Fang
Orient
Peking, 2000

Tianxin Cai wurde 1963 in Huangyan, einer Stadt im Südosten der Volksrepublik China, geboren. Er studierte Mathematik und erlangte 1987 seinen Doktortitel in Zahlentheorie an der Shandong Universität. Der Mathematiker war mehrere Jahre lang Gastdozent und Gastprofessor in Frankreich sowie in Nord- und Südamerika. Er publizierte eine Reihe von mathematischen Fachaufsätzen. Tianxin Cai zählt zu den aktivsten Autoren der jungen chinesischen Avantgarde. Er nahm an internationalen Poesiefestivals im kolumbianischen Medellín, im argentinischen Rosario sowie in Zürich, Genua, Vilenica, Slowenien, und in Durban, Südafrika, teil. Sein erster Lyrikband »Bi An« (Ü: Das Ufer) wurde 1992 veröffentlicht. Seither sind drei weitere Gedichtbände in China erschienen. In Kolumbien wurde in spanischer Übersetzung »La desnudez antigua« (2002), eine Sammlung seiner Lyrik, herausgegeben. Seine Gedichte basieren zumeist auf ganz alltäglichen Beobachtungen der Umgebung, die er ins Surreale überhöht. So beispielsweise in dem Gedicht »Sonnenlicht«: »Die Sonne gleicht einer Mangofrucht, / aufgeschnitten ist sie der Tag, / unberührt die Nacht, / unser Mund verschlingt Sonnenlicht, / das die Muskeln stärkt, / im Schlaf strömen / die Strahlen in unsere Adern, / wandern durch uns hindurch / und treffen unterwegs / andere Stücke Licht.« Bilder aus der Natur, Metaphern der Zeit und der Unendlichkeit werden in ihrer Intensität durch die Verwendung einer reduzierten Sprache aufgeladen. In der schlichten Form entwickelt sich eine sinnliche Poetik des Raumes.

Seit 1995 ist Tianxin Cai Herausgeber von »Apollinaire«, einer Literaturzeitschrift, die zweimal jährlich erscheint und mittlerweile eines der einflussreichsten Untergrundmagazine im heutigen China ist. Neben Lyrik schreibt er Reiseberichte und Essays. Er übersetzte außerdem Werke von Elizabeth Bishop, Margaret Atwood, Jorge Luis Borges, Octavio Paz und Gabriel García Marquez ins Chinesische. Seine Biographie über Elizabeth Bishop, ihre Reisen und ihre Poesie, kam 2000 unter dem Titel »Bei Fang, Nan Fang« (Ü: Nord, Süd) heraus. 2003 erschien ein Band mit Übersetzungen amerikanischer Lyrik und Prosa sowie ein Band mit Essays. Darüber hinaus schreibt er eine regelmäßige Kolumne für das Magazin »Book City« aus Shanghai, eine Zeitschrift, die mit dem »New Yorker« vergleichbar ist. In diesem Jahr gab er in zwei Bänden eine Auswahl von Gedichten des 20. Jahrhunderts heraus. Tianxin Cai lebt in Hangzhou. Er ist Mathematikprofessor an der Zhejiang Universität.

peter carey

biography

Peter Carey was born in 1943 in Bacchus Marsh, a small town in the State of Victoria, Australia. He began to study Natural Science, but gave that up to write. He made a living as a copywriter, first in Melbourne and then in London. After a few years in Europe, he returned to Australia in 1970, where he lived part of the time in an alternative community in the rainforest of Queensland, and part of the time in Sydney, where he had set up an advertising agency. Since 1990 he has lived in New York. To date Carey has published seven novels – winning several prizes –, three short story collections, a children's book, travel writings, and several filmscripts. After J. M. Coetzee, he is the only author to have received the Booker Prize twice. Peter Carey's style is characteristically an agglomeration of surreal and real elements, creating a nightmarish atmosphere with macabre-ironic, weird, comic characters, which he himself sees »as victims of a particular lifestyle«. His first publication was in 1974 with »The Fat Man in History,« a collection of absurd short stories. In his first novel, »Bliss« (1981), Harry Joy, an adman, dies three times over and wakes up each time into a new life. »The Unusual Life of Tristan Smith« (1994) reveals a colourful universe spilling over into copious footnotes, in which the author created two parallel worlds and two languages. The author's predilection for tall tales is most clearly evident in »Illywacker« (1985), where the division between fact and fiction blur (an Illywacker is an Australian expression for someone who brags). In the novel, the character colourfully depicts the scenes of everyday events between the 1800's and now which have either genuinely or allegedly occurred. Peter Carey grapples further with the theme of Australia's colonial past. In another three novels, he focuses on three aspects: the fate of the Aborigines, the plight of the detainees in the penal colonies, and the heritage of Australia's relationship with Great Britain. The two novels for which he was awarded the Booker Prize, »Oscar & Lucinda« in 1988 and »True History of the Kelly Gang« in 2001 both take place in the 19th century. Carey retells in letter form the myth and real life story of the Australian national hero Ned Kelly, an infamous horse snatcher and police murderer. His most recent novel to have been published is »My Life as a Fake« (2003). Peter Carey currently lives in New York, where he teaches Creative Writing.

Bliss, das Paradies umsonst
Rowohlt
Reinbek, 1987
[Ü: Charlotte Franke]
Illywhacker
Rowohlt
Reinbek, 1994
[Ü: Dirk van Gunsteren]
Oscar und Lucinda
Rowohlt
Reinbek, 1994
[Ü: Dirk van Gunsteren]
Die geheimen Machenschaften des Jack Maggs
Fischer
Frankfurt am Main, 2001
[Ü: Regina Rawlinson]
Die wahre Geschichte von Ned Kelly und seiner Gang
Fischer
Frankfurt am Main, 2002
[Ü: Regina Rawlinson und Angela Schumitz]
Mein Leben als Fälschung
Fischer
Frankfurt am Main, 2004
Wrong About Japan
Faber and Faber
London, 2004

Ich hab auf die Muse geschossen
Ein Gespräch mit Peter Carey

F: Wie in der New York Times zu lesen war, hatten Sie einige Schwierigkeiten mit Ihrer Muse.

A: Ich hab auf die Muse geschossen. Die Kugel traf sie an ihrer rechten Schulter und blieb im Latissimus Dorsi hängen. Das reichte natürlich nicht, um sie zu töten, obwohl sie einiges an Blut verloren hat.

F: Gab es kritische Reaktionen?

A: Naja, meine Freunde haben mir e-mails geschickt und so. Wir sind hier ja in Amerika, deshalb dachten wohl viele von ihnen, ich bräuchte „Hilfe". Aber genau das war der Punkt seit damals, als ich mir die Smith and Wesson gekauft hatte – dass, obwohl ich viele Dinge mit der Muse besprochen hatte, und obwohl ihre Meinung manchmal ganz interessant, sogar unterhaltsam, war, ich doch froh gewesen wäre, wenn sie mich einfach mit meinem Buch hätte weitermachen lassen. Mit anderen Worten, in dieser speziellen Hinsicht gibt es keine „Hilfe". Halt die Klappe, habe ich ihr gesagt. Aber die Muse wollte einfach nicht hören.

F: Sie leben nun seit 14 Jahren in New York. Glauben Sie, das hat Ihre Tat beeinflusst?

A: Ja, Waffen sind in Amerika verhältnismäßig einfach zu beschaffen. Auf der anderen Seite musste ich nach Tampa in Florida fahren, man muss also den Mietwagen miteinbeziehen, wenn man die Kosten berechnet.

F: Haben Sie sich keine Sorgen darüber gemacht, wie Sie ohne Ihre Muse zurechtkommen würden?

A: Keine der möglichen Anworten schien mir attraktiv. Naja, was soll's, ich werd's Ihnen erzählen. Die Muse fing an, sich einzubilden, sie sei der Autor.

Peter Carey wurde 1943 in Bacchus Marsh, einer Kleinstadt im Bundesstaat Victoria, Australien, geboren. Er begann ein Studium der Naturwissenschaften, gab es jedoch zugunsten des Schreibens auf. Seinen Lebensunterhalt verdiente er als Werbetexter zunächst in Melbourne, später in London. 1970 kehrte er nach einem mehrjährigen Aufenthalt in Europa nach Australien zurück. Dort lebte er abwechselnd in einer alternativen Gemeinschaft im Regenwald von Queensland und in Sydney, wo er eine eigene Werbeagentur gründete. Seit 1990 lebt er in New York. Er veröffentlichte bisher sieben mehrfach preisgekrönte Romane, drei Erzählbände, ein Kinderbuch, Reisebeschreibungen und mehrere Drehbücher. Er ist nach J. M. Coetzee der zweite Autor, dem der Booker Prize zweimal verliehen wurde. Charakteristisch für Peter Careys Erzählkunst sind Verdichtung surrealer und realer Elemente zu einer alptraumhaften Atmosphäre, makaber-ironische Komik und skurrile Figuren, die er selbst als »Opfer einer bestimmten Lebensweise« sieht. 1974 erschien sein erster Band »The Fat Man in History« mit absurden Kurzgeschichten. In seinem ersten Roman »Bliss« (1981; dt. »Bliss, das Paradies umsonst«, 1987) stirbt der Werbefachmann Harry Joy dreimal und erwacht jedesmal erneut zum Leben. Ein buntes Universum eröffnet sich in »The Unusual Life of Tristan Smith« (1994; dt. »Das seltsame Leben des Tristan Smith«, 1996), eine bis in die Fußnoten überquellende Geschichte, für die der Autor gleich zwei Welten und zwei Sprachen erfand. Seine Vorliebe für Lügengeschichten, die die Grenze zwischen Fakten und Fiktion verwischen, zeigt sich besonders deutlich in »Illywhacker« (1985; dt. 1994). Kaleidoskopartig schildert der Illywhacker (wie man im australischen Englisch einen Aufschneider nennt) Ereignisse, die sich angeblich oder tatsächlich in Australien zwischen 1880 und heute zugetragen haben. Peter Carey setzt sich in drei weiteren Romanen mit der Kolonialgeschichte Australiens auseinander. Er thematisiert das Schicksal der Ureinwohner und der Häftlinge in den Strafkolonien sowie die Beziehung zwischen Großbritannien und Australien. Beide Romane, die 1988 bzw. 2001 den Booker Prize erhielten, spielen im 19. Jahrhundert: in »Oscar and Lucinda« (1988; dt. »Oskar und Lucinda«, 1994) greift Carey den Entdeckermythos auf und in »True History of the Kelly Gang« (2000; dt. »Die wahre Geschichte von Ned Kelly und seiner Gang«, 2002) lässt er den australischen Nationalhelden Ned Kelly, einen berühmt-berüchtigten Pferdedieb und Polizistenmörder, in einem Brief zu Wort kommen. Zuletzt erschien der Roman »My Life as a Fake« (2003; dt. »Mein Leben als Fälschung«, 2004). Peter Carey lebt in New York, wo er Kreatives Schreiben unterrichtet.

F: Hätten Sie das mit ihr nicht bereden können?

A: Ja, aber schießen war viel effektiver.

F: Sicherlich. Sie meinen nicht, es war viel EFFIZIENTER?

A: Ja, genau. Perfekt. Jeder Autor versteht das. Es ist wie A auf B zu nageln.

F: Welches A und B?

A: Kunst entsteht durch die Verbindung von bislang unverbundenen Gedanken oder Bildern. Es ist wie eine Zündkerze.

F: Wie interessant. Wird es jetzt schwierig werden für Sie, ohne Muse?

A: Natürlich ist es schwierig. Es war einfach, jeder hätte es machen können. Aber wie viele Marquez' gibt es?

F: Und die leere Seite?

A: Wie immer besudele ich ihr Weiß, manchmal mit Dreck, manchmal mit Glimmer oder sogar mit Saphir, aber meistens mit einer ziemlich unappetitlichen Mischung aus den dreien. Wenn Eliot von "Knoblauch und Saphir im Dreck" redet, meint er, wie Sie wissen, genau das. Ich habe einen großen Teil meiner Nächte damit zugebracht, mich durch diesen Tatort zu wühlen und ihn in Ordnung zu bringen.

F: Und der Writer's Block?

A: Was ist das?

F: Wenn die Muse nicht da ist.

A: Es gibt keine Arbeit für Musen an sich. Die besten von ihnen sind damit beschäftigt, den sogenannten „Krieg gegen den Terror" zu rechtfertigen.

rafael chirbes

biography

Rafael Chirbes was born in Tabernes de Valldigna, near Valencia, Spain, in 1949. Early on, he was drawn to big cities like Salamanca, Madrid, and Barcelona. After finishing his studies in modern history in Madrid, he wrote literature and film reviews, as well as reportage for various journals. He lived in Paris and then, for some years, in Morocco, where he gave Spanish lessons. After his return, »Mimoun« was published in 1988 (Engl. »Mimoun«, 1992), the intense character study of a writer who retreats to a Moroccan village to complete his novel. But – due to cultural estrangement, and above all, due to the abysses of his own personality – he fails. The precise description of the maelstrom threatening to suck in the protagonist corresponds with the clear-cut, explicit language that depicts nature. A keen, observant eye is as typical of Chirbes as his empathy with his manifold characters from diverse social and geographical backgrounds. The following novels tackling the Franco regime and its aftermath gained Chirbes (whose paragons are, among others, Max Aub and Juan Marsé) a reputation as an outstanding literary chronicler of Spain. In »Los disparos del cazador« (1994; t: The shots of the hunter) Chirbes lets an old man look back on his career during the dictatorship; in »La buena letra« (1992; t: The beautiful letter) a woman reflects on how the opportunism of some family members affected her personal fate. The internal monologues not only express their hopes and disappointments, but also mirror the course of Spanish history. The plots develop on the basis of these broken memories, a narrative principle also followed by »La larga marcha« (1996; t: The long march) and »La caída de Madrid« (2000; t: The fall of Madrid). Their structure is, however, more complex; here, the varying points of view of the many individual characters compose one large picture. »What I am writing about the Franco era today is, of course, expressed from a distance to the events described. The perspective has changed. It is not a question of historiography, but of memories: my personal memories during the act of writing.« His most recent book »Los viejos amigos« (2003; t: The old friends) reflects upon the end of the civil war generation and their ideals. Apart from his work as an author, Rafael Chirbes writes travel reports for a gourmet magazine. He lives in a village between Valencia and Alicante.

Der Schuss des Jägers
Kunstmann
München, 1996
[Ü: Elke Wehr]
Der lange Marsch
Kunstmann
München, 1998
[Ü: Dagmar Ploetz]
Mimoun
Wagenbach
Berlin, 1998
[Ü: Elke Wehr]
Die schöne Schrift
Kunstmann
München, 1999
[Ü: Dagmar Ploetz]
Der Fall von Madrid
Kunstmann
München, 2000
[Ü: Dagmar Ploetz]
Am Mittelmeer
Kunstmann
München 2001
[Ü: Thomas Brovot,
Stefanie Gerhold,
Christian Hansen,
Dagmar Ploetz]
Alte Freunde
Kunstmann
München, 2004
[Ü: Dagmar Ploetz]

Rafael Chirbes wurde 1949 in Tabernes de Valldigna nahe Valencia, Spanien, geboren. Früh zog es ihn von dort in größere Städte, darunter Salamanca, Madrid und Barcelona. Nach dem Studium der Neueren Geschichte in Madrid schrieb er für diverse Magazine Literatur- und Filmkritiken sowie Reportagen. Er lebte in Paris und mehrere Jahre in Marokko, wo er Spanisch unterrichtete. Nach seiner Rückkehr entstand 1988 »Mimoun«, die eindringliche Charakterstudie eines Schriftstellers, der sich in ein marokkanisches Dorf zurückzieht, um dort einen Roman zu vollenden. Er scheitert – an der fremden Kultur, vor allem aber an den Untiefen der eigenen Persönlichkeit. Die prägnante Schilderung der Abwärtsspirale, deren Sog der Protagonist zu erliegen droht, findet ihre Entsprechung in Naturbeschreibungen, die in einer überaus klaren, bildhaften Sprache gehalten sind. Die treffende Schärfe der Beobachtung ist ebenso charakteristisch für Chirbes wie sein Einfühlungsvermögen in zahlreiche Charaktere unterschiedlichster sozialer und regionaler Herkunft. Mit den darauf folgenden Romanen, die sich intensiv mit der Zeit während des Franco-Regimes und deren Nachwirkungen auseinandersetzen, erwarb Chirbes – zu dessen Vorbildern Max Aub und Juan Marsé zählen – den Ruf eines herausragenden literarischen Chronisten Spaniens. In »Los disparos del cazador« (1994; dt. »Der Schuss des Jägers«, 1996) lässt Chirbes einen alten Mann, der während der Diktatur Karriere machte, zurückblicken, und in »La buena letra« (1992; dt. »Die schöne Schrift«, 1999) ist es eine Frau, deren Schicksal durch den Opportunismus einiger Familienmitglieder geprägt wurde. Die inneren Monologe der Figuren thematisieren nicht nur ihre persönlichen Hoffnungen und Enttäuschungen, sondern spiegeln den Verlauf der Geschichte Spaniens. Die Handlung entfaltet sich ausschließlich anhand dieser gebrochenen Erinnerungen. Auch »La larga marcha« (1996; dt. »Der lange Marsch«, 1998) und »La caída de Madrid« (2000; dt. »Der Fall von Madrid«, 2000) folgen diesem narrativen Prinzip. Sie sind jedoch komplexer angelegt. Hier setzen sich die unterschiedlichen Blickwinkel vieler einzelner Porträts zu einem großen Bild zusammen. »Was ich heute über die Franco-Zeit schreibe, steht natürlich in einer zeitlichen Distanz zu dem Beschriebenen. Die Perspektive ist anders. Es geht auch nicht um Geschichtsschreibung, sondern um Erinnerungen, die eigene Erinnerung beim Schreiben.« Sein jüngstes Werk, »Los viejos amigos« (2003; dt. »Alte Freunde«, 2004), reflektiert das Ende der Bürgerkriegsgeneration und ihrer Ideale. Neben seiner Tätigkeit als Schriftsteller schreibt Rafael Chirbes Reisereportagen für ein Gourmetmagazin. Er lebt in einem Dorf zwischen Valencia und Alicante.

peter cole

biography

Peter Cole was born in Paterson/New Jersey, USA, in 1957. He began studying Hebrew in Jerusalem in 1981, and has since divided his time between Israel and the United States. He has worked intensively on Hebrew literature, with special emphasis on medieval Hebrew poetry. In 1988 he started the ambitious project of translating into English texts by Shmuel HaNagid, whose lyrical work had always been considered untranslatable. »Selected Poems of Shmuel HaNagid« (1996) received the Modern Language Association's Scaglione Prize for Translation. Shmuel HaNagid was the renowned 11th century poet and Jewish prime minister of the Muslim kingdom of Granada. Cole was granted a TLS translation award for »Selected Poems of Solomon Ibn Gabirol« (2001), an equally challenging translation of the philosopher, poet, and mystic, who was a younger contemporary of Shmuel HaNagid and combined Arabic form and aesthetics with a Hebraic world-view. Cole's edition also includes comprehensive annotations and an introduction to Gabirol's work. Cole is now working on a comprehensive anthology of medieval Hebrew poetry, entitled »The Dream of the Poem: Hebrew Poetry from Muslim and Christian Spain, 950-1492«. Further authors translated from modern Hebrew and Arabic into English by Peter Cole include Avraham Ben Yitzhak, Harold Schimmel and Yoel Hoffmann, as well as the poets Aharon Shabtai and Taha Muhammad Ali.
Cole's own poetry has conveyed, from the very beginning, his deep fascination with medieval lyrical structure and technique. The early poem »Rift« won the General Electric Foundation Award for Younger Writers in 1985 and became, in 1989, the title of his first original and highly acclaimed poetry collection. Critics praised the fusion of medieval lyrical elements and realistic colloquialisms as well as the unique sensual power that Cole creates by confronting visionary and actual perception. Ten years later, his second original collection, »Hymns & Qualms« (1998), shows his poetic work to be deeply rooted in medieval Hebrew and Arabic traditions without, however, losing touch with current events. Quotations from sources as disparate as Pentagon spokesmen, Theodor W. Adorno, witnesses to a 1994 massacre in Hebron, and a 9th century court poet from Baghdad are woven into the poetry, thus forming musical incantations and striking counterpoints, while simultaneously expressing a firm political conviction against fanaticism. Peter Cole lives in Jerusalem where he and his wife are the directors of Ibis Editions, which publishes literature of the Levant.

Rift
Station Hill
New York, 1989
Hymns & Qualms
Sheep Meadow
New York, 1998

Peter Cole wurde 1957 in Paterson/New Jersey, USA, geboren. 1981 ging er nach Jerusalem, wo er ein Hebräisch-Studium aufnahm. Seitdem pendelt er zwischen Israel und den USA und setzt sich intensiv mit der hebräischen Literatur auseinander. Ein besonderes Interesse entwickelte er für die hebräische Dichtung des Mittelalters. 1988 begann er mit der Arbeit an einem ambitionierten Projekt: Er wagte sich an die Übersetzung der bis dahin als ›unübersetzbar‹ geltenden Lyrik von Shmuel HaNagid, der im Spanien des 11. Jahrhunderts jüdischer Premierminister des muslimischen Regimes von Granada und ein bedeutender Dichter war. »Selected Poems of Shmuel HaNagid« (1996) erhielt den Scaglione Prize for Translation der Modern Language Association. Für »Selected Poems of Solomon Ibn Gabirol« (2001), einer ebenso anspruchsvollen Übersetzung der Gedichte des Philosophen, Poeten und Mystikers Solomon Ibn Gabirol, eines jüngeren Zeitgenossen HaNagids, der in seiner Dichtung arabische Form und Ästhetik mit hebräischer Weltanschauung verband, erhielt er den TLS Übersetzerpreis. Cole ergänzte die Ausgabe mit einer ausführlichen Einleitung in Gabirols Werk und Anmerkungen zum Text. Cole arbeitet derzeit an einer umfassenden Anthologie hebräischer Poesie des Mittelalters mit dem Titel »The Dream of the Poem: Hebrew Poetry from Muslim and Christian Spain, 950-1492«. Zu den Autoren, die er aus dem modernen Hebräisch und Arabisch ins Englische übersetzt hat, zählen Avraham Ben Yitzhak, Harold Schimmel und Yoel Hoffmann sowie die Lyriker Aharon Shabtai und Taha Muhammad Ali.

In seinem ersten eigenen Gedichtband »Rift« (1986, Ü: Riss), für dessen Titelgedicht er mit dem General Electric Foundation Award for Younger Poets ausgezeichnet wurde, ist Coles Faszination für lyrische Strukturen und Techniken des Mittelalters bereits spürbar. Von der Kritik gelobt wurde vor allem die Art, wie er lyrische Elemente mit umgangssprachlichen Realismen verbindet, wie das Visionäre auf die direkte, unmittelbare Wahrnehmung trifft und dadurch den langen Versen eine besondere sinnliche Kraft verleiht. Rund zehn Jahre später zeigt sich Coles Poesie fest verankert in mittelalterlichen hebräischen und arabischen Traditionen – ohne dass er dabei die Gegenwart aus den Augen verlieren würde. In »Hymns & Qualms« (1998, Ü: Hymnen & Zweifel) verwebt er Zitate solcher disparaten Quellen wie den Verlautbarungen von Pentagonsprechern, Theodor W. Adorno, den Zeugenberichten des Massakers von 1994 in Hebron, einem höfischen Poeten des 9. Jahrhunderts aus Baghdad zu äußerst musikalisch anmutenden Anrufungen und markanten Kontrapunkten. Gleichzeitig aber offenbart sich hier eine entschlossene politische, den Fanatismus ablehnende Haltung. Peter Cole lebt in Jerusalem, wo er zusammen mit seiner Frau den Verlag Ibis Editions leitet, der die Literatur der Levante publiziert.

TWO POEMS ON TRANSLATION
(OR, HOW TO LURE THE MUSE + LOSE YOUR MIND)

I.

Its asymptotic extension
appealed, its narcotic vision,
erotic wounds. It compelled
as a kind of afterworld, or offering,

without which he wouldn't exist,
emerging to make him wonder
if he was or wasn't another
division slain in its split.

II.

Like a pig's snout pierced by a golden ring;
like the ministering angels sent to sing

through one's own throat of another's joy;
like a calling, in the mouth of a decoy.

bora ćosić

biography

Bora Ćosić was born in Zagreb, Croatia, in 1932. In 1937 he moved to Belgrade to study philosophy. During the 50's he worked as an editor for various journals and translated from Russian (Mayakovsky, Khlebnikov). His first novel, »Kuca lopova« (t: House of thieves), a surrealist confrontation with social reality in Yugoslavia, was published in 1956. Soon his name was on the blacklist which the state cultural authorities used to discourage national publishing houses from printing the works of certain authors. The stage version of his satirical novel, »Uloga moje porodice u svetskoj revoluciji« (Eng. »My Family's Role in the World Revolution«, 1997), written in 1969, was banned for many years.
In 1992 Ćosić left Belgrade in protest against the policies of the Serbian regime and settled in Rovinj, Istria. During his exile in Croatia, his country's declared enemy, he wrote »Dnevnik apatrida« (1993), which is filled with reflections on Proust and the Franco-Prussian War. He came to Berlin on a DAAD grant in 1995, and still lives here today. In 1999, when Nato troops were deployed in Kosovo, Ćosić demanded liberation for the Albanians as well as for the Serbs from Milosevic and »from themselves«, i.e., from »ethnic madness«. Ćosić has written more than thirty books, which have been translated into many European languages: German, English, French, Italian, Hungarian and Russian. Only a few have been translated into German. After a first satirical volume, »Wie unsere Klaviere repariert wurden«, in 1968, German publishers' interest in the author was not rekindled until the 90's. Since then German critics have acknowledged him as one of the wittiest and most outrageous contemporary authors. He owes this reputation largely to his novel »My Family's Role in the World Revolution«, which put him in the public eye in 1994, and which has since been labelled a »subversive classic« (Andreas Breitenstein, »NZZ«). Spanning the time from the German occupation to the establishment of the Tito regime, the vicious satire of this novel, in which historic and mundane events merge into a grotesque whole, results from the pseudo-naive perspective of the childlike first-person narrator. Although Ćosić bases this work, long celebrated as a cult book in Serbia, only implicitly on »The Tin Drum's« constructional principle, the playful treatment of Günter Grass and other role models such as Krleža, Musil, Dostoyevsky, Hamsun and Proust is conspicuously deliberate in other cases. This is evident in works such as »Musils Notizbuch«, »Ein zweites Treffen in Telgte«, »Geschichte Myschkins«, »Bergottes Witwe« and the fictional autobiography of »Miroslav Krleža«. »Collaging existing material« is, according to the critic Karl-Markus Gauß, »a popular aesthetic principle«. This has also affected Ćosić's own work, which the author maintains is in a constant state of transformation and abounds in crossreferences. Ćosić's grandmother, for example, who has already been a figure of literature in »My Family's Role in the World Revolution«, becomes the wheelchair bound central character Suarda in the 1982 monologue novel »Bel Tempo«. Bora Ćosić has also been writing poetry for some years. His new novel »Nulta Zemlja« (t: The country zero) appeared in German translation in 2004.

Wie unsere Klaviere repariert wurden
Suhrkamp
Frankfurt am Main, 1968
[Ü: Peter Urban]
Die Rolle meiner Familie in der Weltrevolution
Rowohlt, Reinbek, 1994
[Ü: Mirjana und Klaus Wittmann]
Musils Notizbuch
Droschl, Graz, 1994
[Ü: Barbara Antkowiak]
Bel Tempo: der Jahrhundertroman
Rowohlt, Berlin, 1998
[Ü: Irena Vrkljan und Benno Meyer-Welack]
Die Zollerklärung
Suhrkamp
Frankfurt am Main, 2001
[Ü: Katharina Wolf-Grießhaber]
Die Toten
DAAD, Berlin, 2001
[Ü: Irena Vrkljan und Benno Meyer-Wehlack]
Das Land Null
Suhrkamp
Frankfurt am Main, 2004
[Ü: Katharina Wolf-Grießhaber]

Bora Ćosić wurde 1932 in Zagreb geboren. Ab 1937 lebte er in Belgrad, wo er nach seinem Schulabschluss Philosophie studierte. In den fünfziger Jahren arbeitete er als Redakteur für verschiedene Zeitschriften und als Übersetzer aus dem Russischen (Majakowski, Chlebnikow). 1956 erschien sein erster Roman »Kuca lopova« (Ü: Haus der Diebe), eine surrealistische Auseinandersetzung mit der gesellschaftlichen Wirklichkeit in Jugoslawien. Bald stand sein Name auf der »schwarzen Liste« der Autoren, von deren Publikation die staatliche Kulturbürokratie den einheimischen Verlagen abriet. Die Theaterfassung seines satirischen Romans »Die Rolle meiner Familie in der Weltrevolution« von 1969 zog ein mehrjähriges Publikationsverbot nach sich.
Aus Protest gegen den Kurs des serbischen Regimes verließ Ćosić 1992 Belgrad und ließ sich im istrischen Rovinj nieder. Während des Exils in Kroatien, dem offiziellen Feindesland Serbiens, entstand sein »Tagebuch eines Heimatlosen« (1993), das angefüllt ist mit Reflexionen über Proust und den deutsch-französischen Krieg. Ein Stipendium des DAAD führte ihn 1995 nach Berlin, wo er bis heute lebt. Als serbischer Autor im Exil plädierte Ćosić 1999 (anlässlich des Nato-Einsatzes im Kosovo) dafür, nicht nur die Albaner, sondern auch die Serben von Milosevic und »von sich selbst«, d. h. vom »völkischen Wahn« zu befreien.
Bora Ćosić hat über dreißig Bücher geschrieben, die in viele europäische Sprachen (u. a. ins Deutsche, Englische, Französische und Ungarische) übersetzt wurden. Nach der Veröffentlichung seines ersten Satire-Bands »Wie unsere Klaviere repariert wurden« (1968) interessierten sich deutsche Verlage erst wieder in den neunziger Jahren für den serbischen Schriftsteller. Seither wird er von der deutschen Kritik als einer der witzigsten und skurrilsten Autoren gefeiert. Diesen Ruf verdankt er insbesondere dem inzwischen zum »subversiven Klassiker« (Andreas Breitenstein, »NZZ«) avancierten Roman »Die Rolle meiner Familie in der Weltrevolution«, der 1994 in Deutschland erschien. Der satirisch-polemische Effekt dieser Familienchronik aus der Zeit von der deutschen Besatzung bis zur Etablierung des Tito-Regimes ergibt sich aus der scheinbar naiven Perspektive des kindlichen Ich-Erzählers, in der historische und alltägliche Ereignisse zu einem grotesken Gesamtbild verschwimmen. Orientiert sich Ćosić in diesem in Serbien als Kultbuch gefeierten Werk nur implizit an dem Konstruktionsprinzip der »Blechtrommel«, ist der spielerische Umgang mit Günter Grass und anderen Vorbildern, wie z.B. Krleža, Musil, Dostojewski, Hamsun oder Proust, in anderen Fällen programmatisch. Dies signalisieren Titel wie »Musils Notizbuch«, »Ein zweites Treffen in Telgte«, »Geschichte Myschkins«, »Bergottes Witwe« oder die fiktive Autobiographie »Miroslav Krleža« (1998). Die »Montage vorgefundenen Materials«, so der Kritiker Karl-Markus Gauß, ist bei Ćosić »ein bevorzugtes ästhetisches Prinzip«. Dies gilt auch innerhalb seines eigenen Werkes, das sich dem Autor zufolge in einem fortwährenden Prozess befindet und zahlreiche Querverbindungen aufweist. So entwickelte er etwa die an den Rollstuhl gefesselte Protagonistin Suarda im Monolog-Roman »Bel Tempo« von 1982 aus der Figur der Großmutter Ćosić', die schon in »Die Rolle meiner Familie in der Weltrevolution« literarisch verewigt wurde. Seit einigen Jahren schreibt Bora Ćosić auch Gedichte. Sein neuer Roman »Das Land Null« erscheint 2004 in deutscher Übersetzung.

dimitré dinev

biography

Dimitré Dinev was born in 1968 in Plovdiv, Bulgaria. He started writing at the time of his secondary schooling in a German speaking ›Gymnasium‹ in Pasardshik. His first texts were published in 1986, both in Bulgarian and Russian. By the end of the 1980's he took part in protests against the regime of Todor Shikov. Dimitré Dinev left Bulgaria after the collapse of communism in the winter of 1990. He entered Austria illegally via the Czech border and ended up in the refugee detention centre in Traiskirchen. Whilst studying Philosophy and Russian Philology in Vienna he earned his living doing several odd jobs. Since 1992 he has been writing in German, including film scripts, plays, radio features and prose. His play »Russenhuhn« (t: Russian chicken) is based on the Euripides tragedy »The Trojans,« and had its world premiere in Vienna in 1999. His short story »Boshidar« won first prize in the year 2000 for the annual literature competition with the theme ›Writing Between Cultures‹. Further short stories which received awards include »Ein Licht über dem Kopf« (t: A light above a head). In 2001 »Die Inschrift« (t: The inscription) was Dimitré Dinev's first collection of stories to be published under his name. These epic short stories about migration and estrangement switch between irony and pathos, the comic and the tragic. Dimitré Dinev describes with a light and distinctive touch of humour the difficulties refugees, asylum seekers and illegal immigrants tackle daily. In his debut novel »Engelszungen« (2003; t: Angels speaking in tongues) his two protagonists, Svetljo and Iskren, are stranded in Vienna, stuck in a desperate situation. In the Central Cemetery, the two characters accidentally meet each other in front of the grave of the Serbian criminal Miro, who has become an ›angel for the immigrants‹, and a last port of call for many. Through the use of flashbacks the novel delves into three generations and deals with the parallel destiny of two different families. Through this panorama, we also see the socio-political structure of the last century in Bulgaria. Dimitré Dinev has an abundant and successive string of funny, tragic, fantastic and absurd stories, in which you cannot help but notice the joy he takes in writing them. He makes talented use of poetic images and the style of ›magic realism‹, yet expresses himself in a clear, concise and pithy way. The author takes his inspiration from his own and other people's experiences: »Many of the stories are true, however so absurd that I must invent others that are even more exaggerated, so that at least the true ones remain plausible.« Dimitré Dinev lives in Vienna.

Die Inschrift
Ed. Exil
Wien, 2001
Engelszungen
Deuticke
Wien/Frankfurt am Main
2003

Dimitré Dinev wurde 1968 in Plovdiv, Bulgarien, geboren. Im nahegelegenen Pasardshik besuchte er ein deutschsprachiges Gymnasium. Während seiner Schulzeit begann er mit dem Schreiben und konnte ab 1986 erste Texte in bulgarischer und russischer Sprache veröffentlichen. Ende der achtziger Jahre nahm er an den Protesten der Oppositionellen gegen das Regime von Todor Shivkov teil. Nach dem Zusammenbruch des Kommunismus verließ Dimitré Dinev im Winter 1990 Bulgarien. Er gelangte über die tschechische Grenze illegal nach Österreich, wo er zunächst im Flüchtlingslager Traiskirchen aufgenommen wurde. In Wien schlug er sich mit verschiedenen Gelegenheitsjobs durch. Nebenher studierte er Philosophie und Russische Philologie. Seit 1992 verfasst er in deutscher Sprache Drehbücher, Theaterstücke, Rundfunkfeatures und Prosa. Sein Theaterstück »Russenhuhn«, das auf der Tragödie »Die Troerinnen« von Euripides basiert, wurde 1999 in Wien uraufgeführt. Für die Kurzgeschichte »Boshidar« erhielt er 2000 den ersten Preis des Literaturwettbewerbs »schreiben zwischen den kulturen«. Weitere Kurzgeschichten, darunter »Ein Licht über dem Kopf«, wurden ebenfalls ausgezeichnet. 2001 erschien sein erster eigenständiger Erzählband »Die Inschrift«. Dimitré Dinevs epische Erzählungen über Migration und Fremdheit wechseln zwischen Ironie und Pathos, Komik und Tragik. Mit Humor und einer bemerkenswerten Leichtigkeit berichtet er von den schwierigen Lebensumständen von Flüchtlingen, Asylsuchenden und illegalen Einwanderern, die den alltäglichen Widrigkeiten trotzig und verzweifelt entgegentreten. Auch die beiden Protagonisten seines Debütromans »Engelszungen« (2003), Svetljo und Iskren, sind in Wien gestrandet und stecken in Schwierigkeiten. Auf dem Zentralfriedhof begegnen sie sich zufällig vor dem Grab des serbischen Kriminellen Miro, der nun als ›Engel der Einwanderer‹ für viele die letzte Hoffnung ist. In einer Rückblende entspinnt sich der Roman über drei Generationen, erzählt in zwei Handlungssträngen vom Schicksal zweier Familien und lässt somit ein gesellschaftlich-politisches Porträt Bulgariens der letzten hundert Jahre entstehen. Dimitré Dinev reiht eine Fülle von lustigen, traurigen, phantastischen und absurden Geschichten aneinander, in denen seine Freude am Erzählen spürbar wird. Neben einer klaren, knappen Sprache verwendet er prägnante poetische Bilder im Stil des magischen Realismus. Der Autor schöpft aus eigenen Erfahrungen und beruft sich auch auf die wahren Erlebnisse anderer: »Viele der Geschichten sind echt, aber so absurd, dass ich dazu andere erfinden musste, die viel übertriebener sind, damit zumindest die echten glaubhaft bleiben.« Dimitré Dinev lebt in Wien.

Wäre Schehrezâd auf eine Muse angewiesen, hätte sie ihren Kopf schon nach wenigen Nächten verloren. Wenn es mit dem Schreiben nicht mehr weiter geht, wende ich mich deswegen lieber an sie. „Wie hast du es geschafft durch 1001 Nächte zu erzählen?" will ich dann wissen.

„Ich habe kein einziges Mal über mich und mein langweiliges Leben als Wesirstochter erzählt, sondern den Menschen auf den Märkten genau zugehört. Händlern, Bettlern, Dienern, Handwerkern, Reisenden, Soldaten ... Hast du jemals mit einem Fischer geredet? Wusstest du, dass er mitsamt den Fischen jedesmal auch eine neue Geschichte ans Land zieht. Vor kurzem hat einer diese Flasche hier in seinen Netze gefunden. Möchtest du sie öffnen ....

marjana gaponenko

biography

Marjana Gaponenko was born in Odessa, Ukraine, in 1981. She spent her childhood writing her diary and reading fairytales, which have remained a source of her inspiration. During that time she also became fascinated by the theatre. At the age of fourteen she wrote her first poem in German as an exercise to memorise new vocabulary. From this pragmatic interest she developed a deep love for the German language and has never continued writing poems in German. Since 1998 her poems have been published in literary magazines and anthologies, including »Muschelhaufen«, »Lichtungen«, and »The Book of Hope«. In 2000, her first volume of poetry, »wie tränenlose ritter« (t: Like tearless knights), was published; its subtle nuances in wording and its powerful imagery were enthusiastically received by the critics. She draws much from her childhood memories, from her dreams and hopes, and focuses her attention on the beauty in everyday life. Rain is one of her recurring motifs. »To me, rain is mature, fertile, pure and in autumn something very tragic. As is the night, and also love. In 2001, she published volumes of love poems entitled »Rotes Blatt in der Mähne des reitenden Pferdes« (t: Red leaf in the riding horse's mane) and »Tanz vor dem Gewitter« (t: Dance before the thunderstorm). The same year she was granted a literary scholarship for the artists' village of Schöppingen near Münster, Germany. In 2002, she was a guest author at the House of Literature in Lower Austria. During that year »Freund« (t: Friend), her first volume of prose, appeared. In it she creates cameos of mock autobiographies depicting both a romantic relationship and her affinity for certain landscapes and places. Her latest book, »Reise in die Ferne« (t: Journey into the distance), came out in 2003. »I write about love. A lot of my texts are attempts to maintain love, to prolong its power.« The magazine »Deutsche Sprachwelt« elected Marjana Gaponenko author of the year in 2002. Her texts have been translated into various languages. At present she studies German language and literature at the University of Odessa.

Meine Muse ist stumm. Ich vermute, sie ist immer da und sitzt wie ein Vogel auf meiner Schulter. Ich gehe spazieren und sie hält meinen Kopf in die „richtige" Richtung, so daß ich das sehe, was sie mir zeigen will. Sie zeigt mir das Lebe selbst, so bitter und wunderschö wie es ist. Nonnen, Eisverkäufe Zigeuner, Kinder, Alte, Diebe, Hunde an der Leine, Hunde ohne Leine und ohne Herrche den Wind, schwarze, graue Regenschirme, die wegfliegen, und die Menschen, die ihnen hinterherrennen…

wie tränenlose ritter
Geest
Vechta Langenförden, 2000
Tanz vor dem Gewitter
Neue Münchener Edition
München, 2001
Freund
Majak
Odessa, 2002
Reise in die Ferne
Majak
Odessa, 2003

Marjana Gaponenko wurde 1981 in Odessa, Ukraine, geboren. Ihre Kindheit füllte sie mit Tagebuchschreiben und der Lektüre von Märchenbüchern aus, die sie nachhaltig inspirierten. Auch ihre Faszination für das Theater entdeckte sie in jener Zeit. Im Alter von vierzehn Jahren schrieb sie ihr erstes Gedicht in deutscher Sprache – eine Textübung, mit der sie sich neue Vokabeln besser einprägen wollte. Aus diesem pragmatischen Interesse entwickelte sich eine tiefe Leidenschaft für die deutsche Sprache, in der sie weiterhin Gedichte verfasst. Seit 1998 erschienen ihre Gedichte in Literaturzeitschriften und Anthologien, unter anderem in »Muschelhaufen«, »Lichtungen« und »The Book of Hope«. Im Jahr 2000 wurde ihr erster Lyrikband »wie tränenlose ritter« veröffentlicht, der die Kritiker vor allen Dingen durch die nuancenreiche Sprache und die Kraft der Bilder begeisterte. Gaponenko schöpft aus Kindheitserinnerungen, Träumen und Hoffnungen. Ihr Blick ist auf die Schönheit in der alltäglichen Welt gerichtet. Eines ihrer Leitmotive ist der Regen. »Regen ist für mich etwas Reifes, Fruchtbares, Reines und im Herbst etwas sehr Tragisches.« Und die Nacht und die Liebe. 2001 veröffentlichte sie einen Band mit Liebesgedichten unter dem Titel »Rotes Blatt in der Mähne des reitenden Pferdes« sowie »Tanz vor dem Gewitter«. Im selben Jahr war sie Literaturstipendiatin im Künstlerdorf Schöppingen in der Nähe von Münster. 2002 war sie Gastautorin im Literaturhaus Niederösterreich. Im selben Jahr erschien ihr erster Prosaband »Freund«, in dem sie in Form von vermeintlich autobiographischen Miniaturen eine Liebesbeziehung schildert, aber auch ihre Verbundenheit mit Landschaften und Orten. 2003 erschien ihr jüngstes Buch »Reise in die Ferne«. »Ich schreibe über die Liebe. Viele meiner Texte sind ein Versuch, die Liebe aufzuhalten, ihre Macht zu verlängern.« Marjana Gaponenko wurde von der Zeitschrift »Deutsche Sprachwelt« zur Autorin des Jahres 2002 gewählt. Ihre Texte wurden in verschiedene Sprachen übersetzt. Derzeit studiert sie Germanistik an der Universität Odessa.

Man muß nur dankbar sein.
Dankbar, daß man lebt,
dankbar, daß sich diese
Hände bewegen, wenn es
ihnen befohlen wird.
Erst dann sieht man richtig.
Ich versuche nicht die Menschen
auf der Straße zu sehen, was
man unter „Menschen auf
der Straße" versteht, sondern
das Wunder, das die Menschen
vollbringen, denn in jeder
Handbewegung, in jeder Stimme,
in jeder Träne und in jedem
Lächeln geschieht ein Wunder.
Als Dichterin brauche ich nicht
viel- nur einen Spaziergang...
Marjana Gaponenko

durs grünbein

biography

Durs Grünbein was born in Dresden, GDR, in 1962. In 1985 he moved to East Berlin, where he studied Drama. Soon after he decided to devote himself to writing. He taught himself Quantum Physics and Neurology, but also with philosophical ideas such as those of Ludwig Wittgenstein, the Frankfurt School and the French Structuralists. Through exchanges with painters, photographers and performance artists, he took part in different magazine, exhibition and book projects. In 1986 he met Heiner Müller, who introduced him to the West German publisher Siegfried Unseld. In 1988 Durs Grünbein's first volume of poetry, »Grauzone morgens« (t: Grey area, at morning), was published by Suhrkamp. Texts from the period between 1985 and 1988 provide, through clinical snapshots, an authentic impression of the attitude towards life in the urban centres of the GDR.
In 1991 followed a much noted volume of poetry, »Schädelbasislektion« (t: Lection at the base of the skull), in which Grünbein depicts the times before, during and after the end of the Cold War through a cycle of poems with titles such as »Niemands Land Stimmen« (t: No man's land voices), »Tag X« (t: Day X), and »Portrait des Künstlers als junger Grenzhund« (t: Portrait of the artist as a young watch dog). With a view bereft of illusions, he dissects the place of thought in smooth language, with the use of cerebral motifs (»Schädelnacht«, »Hirn-maschine«, »Nervenbahnen«; t: Skull night, Brain machine, Nerve tracks). One critic noted: »After the end of all religion and ideology, consciousness is, as it appears, reducible to its physiological existence, as a labyrinth and bundle of biochemical synapses within the brain.« In »Falten und Fallen« (1994; t: Folds and falls), Durs Grünbein lays out his poetic concept of analytical poetry between speech and physis: »Ideally, the poem leads thought to a sequence of physiological short circuits. Each discharge immediately follows a buildup of tension, and vice versa. Energy therefore is provided by a complex, which is actually only insufficiently termed by the word ›body‹, for it goes much deeper beneath the skin.« In 1995 Grünbein received the Peter Huchel Prize for Poetry. That same year, he won the Georg Büchner Prize, at the time the youngest recipient ever. He has published five more volumes of poetry, in which he seeks to strengthen, both formally and thematically, the dialogue with great poets and thinkers from world literature, along with several essay collections and new translations of plays from antiquity, among them Aeschylus' »The Persians« (2000), and Seneca's »Thyestes« (2002). His most recent collection, »Vom Schnee« (2003; t: On snow), is a fascinating portrait of philosopher René Descartes, in the form of an epic poem, comprised of forty-two tightly composed chapters. That same year a volume of essays appeared, »Warum schriftlos leben« (2003; Why live without text). This year he was the first non-philosopher to receive the Friedrich Nietzsche Prize. His work, which also includes contributions to catalogues and a libretto for opera, has been translated into many languages. Durs Grünbein lives in Berlin.

Grauzone morgens
Suhrkamp
Frankfurt am Main, 1988
Schädelbasislektion
Suhrkamp
Frankfurt am Main, 1991
Den teuren Toten
Suhrkamp
Frankfurt am Main, 1994
Falten und Fallen
Suhrkamp
Frankfurt am Main, 1994
Von der üblen Seite
Suhrkamp
Frankfurt am Main, 1994
Galilei vermißt Dantes Hölle und bleibt an den Maßen hängen
Suhrkamp
Frankfurt am Main, 1996
Nach den Satiren
Suhrkamp
Frankfurt am Main, 1999
Warum schriftlos leben
Suhrkamp
Frankfurt am Main, 2003
Vom Schnee
Suhrkamp
Frankfurt am Main, 2003

Durs Grünbein wurde 1962 in Dresden, DDR, geboren. 1985 zog er nach Ost-Berlin, wo er ein Studium der Theaterwissenschaft begann. Schon bald entschied er sich für das Schreiben. Er beschäftigte sich autodidaktisch mit Quantenphysik und Neurologie, aber auch mit Philosophie, etwa mit Ludwig Wittgenstein, der Frankfurter Schule und den französischen Strukturalisten. Im Austausch mit Malern, Fotografen und Performance-Künstlern beteiligte er sich an verschiedenen Zeitschriften, Ausstellungs- und Verlagsprojekten. 1986 begegnete er Heiner Müller, der ihn mit dem westdeutschen Verleger Siegfried Unseld bekannt machte. 1988 erschien Durs Grünbeins erster Gedichtband »Grauzone morgens« im Suhrkamp Verlag. Die Texte aus dem Zeitraum 1985 bis 1988 vermitteln in nüchternen Momentaufnahmen einen authentischen Eindruck des Lebensgefühls in den urbanen Zentren der DDR.

1991 folgte der vielbeachtete Band »Schädelbasislektion«, dessen Gedichtzyklen mit Titeln wie »Niemands Land Stimmen«, »Tag X« und »Portrait des Künstlers als junger Grenzhund« die Zeit vor, während und nach der Wende thematisierten. Mit illusionslosem Blick seziert er in geschliffener Sprache unter Verwendung von zerebralen Motiven (»Schädelnaht«, »Hirnmaschine«, »Nervenbahnen«) den Ort des Denkens. Ein Kritiker befand: »Nach dem Ende aller Religionen und Ideologien, so scheint es, ist das Bewusstsein auf seine physiologische Existenz als Labyrinth und Wirrknäuel biochemischer Verbindungen im Gehirn reduzierbar.«

In »Falten und Fallen« (1994) setzt Durs Grünbein sein poetisches Konzept der analytischen Lyrik zwischen Sprache und Physis fort: »Das Gedicht führt idealerweise das Denken in einer Folge physiologischer Kurzschlüsse vor. Jeder Entladung folgt sofort wieder ein Spannungsaufbau und umgekehrt. Die Energie hierfür liefert ein Komplex, der eigentlich nur unzureichend mit ›Körper‹ bezeichnet ist, weil er sehr viel tiefer unter die Haut geht.«

1995 erhielt Grünbein den Peter-Huchel-Preis für Lyrik. Im selben Jahr wurde ihm – als bis dahin jüngstem Autor – der Georg-Büchner-Preis verliehen. Bisher veröffentlichte er fünf weitere Gedichtbände, in denen er formal und thematisch verstärkt den Dialog mit großen Denkern und Dichtern der Weltliteratur sucht, mehrere Essaysammlungen sowie Neuübersetzungen von Theaterstücken der Antike, darunter Aischylos' »Die Perser« (2000) und Senecas »Thyestes« (2002). Sein jüngster Band »Vom Schnee« (2003) ist ein faszinierendes Porträt des Philosophen René Descartes in Form eines epischen Gedichts, bestehend aus zweiundvierzig streng durchkomponierten Kapiteln. Im selben Jahr erschienen Essays unter dem Titel »Warum schriftlos leben« (2003). In diesem Jahr wurde ihm, als bisher einzigem Nicht-Philosophen, der Friedrich-Nietzsche-Preis verliehen. Sein Werk, das neben Essay- und Gedichtbänden auch zahlreiche Katalogbeiträge sowie ein Opernlibretto umfasst, wurde in mehrere Sprachen übersetzt. Durs Grünbein lebt in Berlin.

lars gustafsson

biography

Lars Gustafsson was born in Västerås, central Sweden, in 1936. He completed his philosophy studies at the University of Uppsala and Magdelen College, Oxford, with a dissertation on »three extremists in the philosophy of language« (Friedrich Nietzsche, Alexander Bryan Johnson and Fritz Mauthner). He published his first novel, »Vägvila : ett mysteriespel på prosa«, (t: Rest on the Way – A Mystery Play in Prose), at the age of only 21. Gustafsson himself dates his actual debut from 1959, when »Poeten Brumbergs sista dagar och död« (t: Last Days and Death of the Poet Brumberg) appeared. From 1960 Gustafsson was editor, and from 1965 to 1972 editor-in-chief, of the Swedish literary journal »Bonniers Litterära Magasin«. After this he travelled extensively and accepted various guest lectureships including in West Germany. The offer of a DAAD scholarship brought him to Berlin in 1972. Gustafsson had already made a name for himself internationally as a writer and academic when he decided to change his life dramatically in 1982 by emigrating to the US, remarrying, and converting to Judaism.
He moved to Austin, Texas, and became an American citizen in 1983. He held a position as adjunct professor of Germanic Studies at the University of Texas. His extensive work has won many awards, including the Prix Européen de l'essai Charles Veillon (1983), the Swedish Academy's Bellman Prize (1990) and the Swedish Pilot Prize (1996). Since 2000, he has been a member of the »Academy of Fine Arts« in Munich. In Germany, Gustafsson first gained renown with his poetry during the 1970's. His poems focus on questions which he also tackles as a novelist and essayist. The search for identity, moral consciousness, the relationship between personal experience and self-awareness, juxtaposed with a philosophically founded scepticism towards language, are the main themes of his work. Since the novel series »Sprickorna i muren« (t: The Cracks in the Wall), Gustafsson is regarded internationally as one of Scandinavia's best-known authors. Here the author uses crime motifs to present the fragility of a world view which relies on expressions such as »good« and »evil« and concepts of personal integrity. Yet the world is only out of joint for the hero of the first book »Historien med hunden« (1994; t: The Thing About the Dog). Lars Gustafsson is a master of the most varied literary forms. His most recent publications have been the poetry collection »En tid i Xanadu« (2002) and the novel »Dekanen« (2003).

Ein Vormittag in Schweden
Hanser
München, 1998
[Ü: Hans Magnus Enzensberger, Hanns Grössel, Verena Reichel]
Die Sache mit dem Hund
dtv
München, 1999
[Ü: Verena Reichel]
Der Tod eines Bienenzüchters
Fischer
Frankfurt am Main, 2001
[Ü: Verena Reichel]
Windy erzählt
dtv
München, 2003
[Ü: Verena Reichel]
Auszug aus Xanadu
Hanser
München, 2003
[Ü: Verena Reichel; Hans Magnus Enzensberger]
Der Dekan
Hanser
München, 2004
[Ü: Verena Reichel]

Blankhet

Den totala
perfekta spegelblankheten
som kunnat dödligt störas
av ett enda årtag

Och rädd att skada
denna vattenspegels sällsamt stora lugn
höll jag min åra svävande i luften.

Lars Gustafsson wurde 1936 in Västerås, Mittelschweden, geboren. Sein Studium der Philosophie an der Universität Uppsala und dem Magdelen College in Oxford schloss er mit einer Dissertation über drei »sprachphilosophische Extremisten« (Friedrich Nietzsche, Alexander Bryan Johnson und Fritz Mauthner) ab. Bereits mit 21 Jahren veröffentlichte Gustafsson mit »Wegesrast. Ein Mysterienspiel in Prosa« seinen ersten Roman. Sein »eigentliches Debüt« datiert der Schriftsteller selbst allerdings erst auf 1959, dem Erscheinungsjahr des Romans »Letzte Tage und Tod des Dichters Brumberg«.
Ab 1960 war Gustafsson Redakteur, von 1965 bis 1972 Chefredakteur der schwedischen Literaturzeitschrift »Bonniers Litterära Magasin«. Danach unternahm er ausgiebige Reisen. An verschiedenen Universitäten, u. a. auch in West-Deutschland, hatte er Gastdozenturen inne. 1972/73 führte ihn ein Stipendium des DAAD nach Berlin. Gustafsson hatte sich bereits international als Schriftsteller und Wissenschaftler einen Namen gemacht, als er 1982 beschloss, sich in einen völlig neuen Rahmen zu begeben: Er siedelte in die USA über, heiratete wieder und konvertierte zum Judentum. In Austin, Texas, unterrichtete der Autor als Adjunct Professor für Germanic Studies. Bereits 1983 nahm er die US-amerikanische Staatsbürgerschaft an. Für sein umfangreiches Werk erhielt der Autor unter anderem den europäischen Essay-Preis Charles Veillon (1983), den Bellman-Preis der Schwedischen Akademie (1990) und den schwedischen Pilot-Preis (1996). Seit 2000 ist er Mitglied der Akademie der Schönen Künste in München. In Deutschland wurde Gustafsson in den siebziger Jahren zuerst durch seine Lyrik bekannt. Sein Werk ist geprägt von der starken Wechselbeziehung zwischen Themen des Philosophen und Literaturwissenschaftlers Gustafsson und des Geschichtenerzählers bzw. Poeten. Die Suche nach Identität, das moralische Bewusstsein, die Beziehung zwischen persönlicher Erfahrung und Selbstreflexion sowie eine philosophisch untermauerte Sprachskepsis sind die Ausgangspunkte der Fragestellungen, die Gustafsson in seine Romane, Gedichte und Essays einbettet. Seit der Romanreihe »Die Risse in der Mauer« zählt Gustafsson international zu den bekanntesten Schriftstellern Skandinaviens. Der Autor benutzt hier Motive aus Kriminalromanen, um die Zerbrechlichkeit einer Weltanschauung darzustellen, die auf Ausdrücken wie »gut«, »böse« oder der Vorstellung von persönlicher Integrität basiert. So muss dem Helden des ersten Buches »Die Sache mit dem Hund« (1994) die Welt zwangsläufig aus den Fugen geraten. Lars Gustafsson ist ein Meister der verschiedensten literarischen Genres. In jüngster Zeit erschienen sein Lyrikband »En tid i Xanadu« (2002; dt. »Auszug aus Xanadu«, 2003) und sein Roman »Dekanen« (2003; dt. »Der Dekan«, 2004).

Blankheit

Das absolut
perfekte Spiegelblanke
tödlich störbar
durch einen einzigen Ruderschlag.

Und aus Angst
der seltsam großen Ruhe
des Wasserspiegels
zu schaden,
hielt ich mein Ruder
schwebend in der Luft.

[Übersetzung: Barbara M. Karlson]

christoph hein

biography

Christoph Hein was born in Heinzendorf, Silesa, in 1944. After the war he moved with his family to Bad Düben, near Leipzig. There, as son of an evangelical pastor, he was refused entrance to high school; he went to West Berlin in 1958, where he enrolled as a boarder at a humanistic comprehensive secondary school. Due to the construction of the Wall he had to leave school in 1961 without a diploma, but was able to complete his studies three years later at night school. Following that, he studied Philosophy and Logic from 1967-71. Among the numerous odd jobs that Hein undertook during this period were small acting roles and work as director's assistant. After completing his studies he worked as dramatic advisor under the guidance of Benno Besson at the Berlin Volksbühne, where he was house author from 1974. That year his play »Schlötel oder Was solls« (t: Schlötel or So what) debuted. In 1979 he left the theatre along with Besson and since then has been active as a freelance writer.

One of Hein's first big successes in both German states was the novella »Der fremde Freund« (1982; t: The alien friend), which came out in West Germany a year later under the title »Drachenblut« (t: Dragon blood). Written from the perspective of an East Berlin doctor, this life's confession – though lacking in true confessional nature – pitilessly balances coolness and alienation. In 1986 Hein managed to create a parable of the sinking GDR with his play »Die Ritter der Tafelrunde« (Eng. »Knights of the Round Table«). Its short-term approved debut in Dresden in 1989 and its publication in »Sinn und Form« represented a triumph over omnipresent censorship, against which Hein took a concrete stand. After the Cold War he issued numerous statements and essays in which he reflected on his role as an intellectual. The author, who often describes himself as a »chronicler without a message«, succeeds in his novels to chart social analyses of overwhelming concentration. By means of pithy dialogue and virtuoso use of character's speech, exemplary biographies are recounted in an almost restrained tone. Meanwhile, his characters shift between universality and determination through concrete historical circumstances. Christoph Hein's most recent novel, »Landnahme« (2004), praised by critics, redresses figures, setting and motifs from the novel »Horns Ende« (1985) and offers a chronicle covering over fifty years of German history.

Hein has received many literary awards, among them the Erich Fried Prize (1990), and the Schiller Gedächtnis Prize (2004), and is amongst the most widely read contemporary German authors. His work is translated into 35 languages. Hein lives in Berlin.

Willenbrock
Suhrkamp
Frankfurt am Main, 2001
Der fremde Freund / Drachenblut
Suhrkamp
Frankfurt am Main, 2002
Der Tangospieler
Suhrkamp
Frankfurt am Main, 2002
Aber der Narr will nicht
Suhrkamp
Frankfurt am Main, 2004
Als Kind habe ich Stalin gesehen
Suhrkamp
Frankfurt am Main, 2004
Landnahme
Suhrkamp
Frankfurt am Main, 2004
Nachtfahrt und früher Morgen
Suhrkamp
Frankfurt am Main, 2004
Öffentlich arbeiten
Suhrkamp
Frankfurt am Main, 2004

Christoph Hein wurde 1944 in Heinzendorf/Schlesien geboren. Nach Kriegsende zog die Familie nach Bad Düben, nahe Leipzig. Da ihm als Sohn eines evangelischen Pfarrers der Besuch der weiterführenden Schule verwehrt wurde, ging er 1958 nach Westberlin und wurde Internatsschüler eines humanistischen Gymnasiums. Wegen des Mauerbaus musste er die Schule 1961 ohne Abitur verlassen, das er erst drei Jahre später auf einer Abendschule nachholen konnte. Anschließend studierte er von 1967-71 Philosophie und Logik. Unter den zahlreichen Gelegenheitsarbeiten, die er in dieser Zeit übernahm, waren auch Engagements für kleinere Rollen und Tätigkeiten als Regieassistent. Nach dem Studium arbeitete er als Dramaturg unter der Leitung von Benno Besson an der Berliner Volksbühne, von der er ab 1974 als Hausautor verpflichtet wurde. Im gleichen Jahr wurde sein Stück »Schlötel oder Was solls« uraufgeführt. 1979 verließ er, gemeinsam mit Besson, das Theater und ist seither als freier Autor tätig.

Einen ersten großen Erfolg erzielte Hein in beiden deutschen Staaten mit der Novelle »Der fremde Freund« (1982), die in Westdeutschland ein Jahr später unter dem Titel »Drachenblut« veröffentlicht wurde. Diese Lebensbeichte ohne jeden Bekenntnischarakter, geschrieben aus der Perspektive einer Ostberliner Ärztin, bilanziert schonungslos Kälte und Entfremdung der zwischenmenschlichen Beziehungen. 1986 gelang ihm mit seinem Stück »Die Ritter der Tafelrunde« eine Parabel auf die untergehende DDR. Die kurzfristig genehmigte Uraufführung 1989 in Dresden und die Publikation in »Sinn und Form« waren ein Triumph über die allgegenwärtige Zensur, gegen die Hein stets klar Stellung bezog. Auch nach der Wende künden zahlreiche Stellungnahmen und Essays von seiner reflektierten Position als Intellektueller. Dem Autor, der sich selbst als »Chronist ohne Botschaft« bezeichnet, gelingt es in seinen Romanen, Gesellschaftsanalysen von großer Dichte zu zeichnen. In geradezu sprödem Ton, vermittels prägnanter Dialoge und virtuos eingesetzter Rollenprosa werden exemplarische Biographien erzählt. Dabei changieren seine Figuren zwischen Alltagswirklichkeit und Determiniertheit durch die konkreten historischen Umstände. Christoph Heins letzter Roman, »Landnahme« (2004), von der Kritik hoch gelobt, und in Schauplatz, Motiven und Figuren ein Rekurs auf den Roman »Horns Ende« (1985), bietet eine Chronik, die sich über fünfzig Jahre deutscher Geschichte erstreckt.

Auch international gehört der vielfach ausgezeichnete Autor (u. a. Erich Fried-Preis, 1990, Schiller-Gedächtnis-Preis, 2004) zu den meistgelesenen deutschen Gegenwartsautoren, seine Werke sind in 35 Sprachen übersetzt. Christoph Hein lebt in Berlin.

rolf hochhuth

biography

Rolf Hochhuth was born in Eschwege in Hessen 1931. After finishing his training as a retail bookseller, he worked in bookshops in Marburg, Kassel and Munich. In 1955 he took a job as editor at Bertelsmann-Lesering, at which he supervised various editions and anthologies. In 1963 he moved to the countryside around Basel, where he has lived ever since as a freelance writer.

In addition to his own prose pieces, Rolf Hochhuth has mainly written dramatic works, and he is considered the most important representative of German documentary theatre. His theatre pieces combine fictional dialogue with historical and incriminatory material, in which the artistic occasionally gives way to the factual. His flair for political as well as emotionally charged themes has made him one of the most successful and controversial artists in the country. As a consequence of his embracing social taboos, and his absolute insistence on the moral responsibility of the individual, Hochhuth has contributed to the development of the critical awareness in postwar Germany. He has been honoured many times for his multi-faceted work, most recently with the Jacob Grimme Prize, awarded for the first time in 2001.

Hochhuth's first literary work proved that writing can also change things politically. In 1963 the debuted documentary drama »Der Stellvertreter« raised the question of the complicity of Pope Pius XII in the crimes of the Third Reich; its overwhelming resonance throughout Europe forced the church to confront its disreputable past. Equally consequent was Hochhuth's short story »Eine Liebe in Deutschland« (1978), which, like the play »Juristen« (1979), dealt with the role of the former NS judges in Germany during the 1970's. The author attacked, among others, the then prime minister of Baden-Württemberg Hans Filbinger, who was forced to step down as a result of the revelations about his past as a naval judge during the Nazi period. Hochhuth has recently made headlines with »McKinsey kommt« (2003), a debate about unemployment and greed for profit in Germany ruled by capitalism since the end of the Cold War. The play, which asserted the inevitability of a future social revolution, became public even before its premier; Hochhuth was accused of advocating vigilantism and politically motivated murder; however the author did not let himself be deterred by this criticism; rather he wishes to continue making radical political theatre, because, »On stage things should be said like they are.«

Sommer 14
Rowohlt
Reinbek, 1992
Hitlers Dr. Faust
Rowohlt
Reinbek, 2000
Eine Liebe in Deutschland
Rowohlt
Reinbek, 2000
Wessis in Weimar
dtv
München, 2000
Die Geburt der Tragödie aus dem Krieg
Suhrkamp
Frankfurt am Main, 2001
Juristen
Rowohlt
Reinbek, 2001
Die Berliner Antigone
Rowohlt
Reinbek, 2002
Nietzsches Spazierstock
Rowohlt
Reinbek, 2003
McKinsey kommt
dtv
München, 2004
Der Stellvertreter
Rowohlt
Reinbek, 2004

Rolf Hochhuth wurde 1931 im hessischen Eschwege geboren. Nach Abschluss seiner Lehre als Sortimentsbuchhändler arbeitete er zunächst in Buchhandlungen in Marburg, Kassel und München. 1955 nahm er eine Tätigkeit als Lektor beim Bertelsmann-Lesering an, für den er verschiedene Werkausgaben und Anthologien betreute. 1963 zog es ihn ins Baseler Land, wo er seither als freier Schriftsteller lebt.
Rolf Hochhuth hat neben einzelnen Prosastücken vor allem dramatische Werke verfasst und gilt als wichtiger Vertreter des deutschen Dokumentarischen Theaters. Seine Bühnenstücke verknüpfen fiktive Dialoge mit historischen Beweis- und Belastungsmaterialien, wobei das Künstlerische bisweilen hinter das Faktische zurücktritt. Sein Gespür für politisch wie emotional stark aufgeladene Themen hat ihn zu einem der hierzulande erfolgreichsten, aber auch umstrittensten zeitgenössischen Dramatiker gemacht. Mit seinen Vorstößen in gesellschaftliche Tabuzonen und seiner unbedingten Forderung nach moralischer Verantwortung des Individuums hat Hochhuth zur Entwicklung eines kritischen Bewusstseins im Nachkriegsdeutschland beigetragen. Für sein Lebenswerk wurde der Autor vielfach ausgezeichnet, zuletzt mit dem Jacob-Grimme-Preis, der im Jahr 2001 erstmals vergeben wurde.
Schon Hochhuths literarischer Erstling bewies, dass das Schreiben auch politisch etwas bewegen kann. Das 1963 in Berlin uraufgeführte Dokumentardrama »Der Stellvertreter« stellte die Frage nach der Mitschuld von Papst Pius XII. an den Verbrechen des Dritten Reichs, und die überwältigende Resonanz in ganz Europa zwang die Kirche zur Auseinandersetzung mit ihrer unrühmlichen Geschichte. Ebenso folgenreich war Hochhuths 1978 erschienene Erzählung »Eine Liebe in Deutschland«, die wie das Stück »Juristen« (1979) in den Zusammenhang seiner Beschäftigung mit der Rolle ehemaliger NS-Richter im Deutschland der siebziger Jahre fällt. Der Autor griff darin unter anderem den zu jener Zeit amtierenden Ministerpräsidenten von Baden-Württemberg Hans Filbinger an, der sich in der Folge der Enthüllungen seiner Vergangenheit als Marinerichter im Nationalsozialismus zum Rücktritt gezwungen sah.
Zuletzt machte Hochhuth 2003 mit »McKinsey kommt« von sich reden, eine Auseinandersetzung mit Profitgier und Arbeitslosigkeit im vom Kapitalismus regierten Deutschland der Nachwendezeit. Das Stück, das die Unausweichlichkeit einer künftigen sozialen Revolution feststellt, entwickelte sich noch vor der Uraufführung zum Politikum: Hochhuth wurde die Befürwortung von Selbstjustiz und politisch motiviertem Mord vorgeworfen. Doch der Autor hat sich von dieser Kritik nicht beirren lassen; er will auch in Zukunft radikal politisches Theater machen, denn: »Auf der Bühne muss Klartext gesprochen werden.«

viktor jerofejew

biography

Viktor Erofeev was born in Moscow in 1947. As the son of a high ranking diplomat he spent some years of his childhood in Paris. This meant he had access early on to literature that was banned in the Soviet Union. The works of both Vladimir Nabokov and the Marquis de Sade greatly influenced him. At the end of the 1960's he studied literature in Moscow. He then worked for the Institute of World literature. In 1975 he completed his doctorate with a dissertation on »Dostoevsky and Existentialism«. As a literary critic he wrote some essays on the interpretation of the Marquis de Sade's writing and an article on the philosophy of Leo Shestov. The literary almanac »Metropol« (Eng. »Metropol«, 1982) first created a major scandal in 1979. It was a compilation of politically explosive texts, selected by Viktor Erofeev, Vassili Axionow, Andrei Bitov, Jevgeni Popov and Fasil Iskander, in which officially established writers were compared with renegade writers. The attempt to publish the almanac in the Soviet Union failed because it was judged to be ›pornography of the mind‹. The work was eventually published in the west. During this period his father, Vladimir Erofeev, a former interpreter for Stalin, was forced to resign and end his diplomatic career. From that time on Viktor Erofeev was considered a dissident, and his publications were banned. With the first signs of Glasnost and Perestroika Viktor Erofeev was able to publish again. In 1990 his first novel appeared, »Russkaia Krasavitsa« (Eng. »Russian Beauty«, 1992). With the story of the beautiful Irena, about a high-class prostitute in Moscow, the reader is transported into the world of the dark, grotesque aesthetics of sex, violence and death. With two essays, »Pominki po sovyetskoi literatur« (1990; t: An epitaph of Soviet literature) and »Russki svety sla« (1995; t: »Russia's Fleurs du mal«), Erofeev declared the literature of Socialist Realism dead. At the same time he declared a radical artistic manifesto for a new Literature of Evil. He was also the editor of the first Nabokov Russian edition, together with other anthologies of Russian literature. His story »Zhizn s idiotom« (Eng. »Life With an Idiot«, 1990) was adapted for opera by Alfred Schnittke. Erofeev writes regularly for »The New Yorker«, the »New York Review of Books«, as well as »Die Zeit« and the »Frankfurter Allgemeine Zeitung«. His latest publication is the autobiographical novel »Choroshi Stalin« (2004; t: The good Stalin). Viktor Erofeev lives in Moscow.

Die Moskauer Schönheit
Fischer
Frankfurt am Main, 1990
[Ü: Beate Rausch]

Leben mit einem Idioten
Fischer
Frankfurt am Main, 1991
[Ü: Beate Rausch und Rüdiger Wehling-Raspé]

Im Labyrinth der verfluchten Fragen
Fischer
Frankfurt am Main, 1993
[Ü: Beate Rausch]

Das jüngste Gericht
Berlin Verlag
Berlin, 1997
[Ü: Beate Rausch]

Männer
Kiepenheuer und Witsch
Köln, 2000
[Ü: Beate Rausch]

Der gute Stalin
Berlin Verlag
Berlin, 2004
[Ü: Beate Rausch]

Viktor Jerofejew wurde 1947 in Moskau geboren. Einige Jahre seiner Kindheit verbrachte der Sohn eines hochrangigen Diplomaten in Paris. Er hatte früh Zugang zu Literatur, die in der Sowjetunion verboten war. Insbesondere die Werke Vladimir Nabokovs und des Marquis de Sade beeinflussten ihn stark. Ende der sechziger Jahre studierte er Literaturwissenschaft in Moskau, arbeitete anschließend am Institut für Weltliteratur und erlangte 1975 seinen Doktortitel mit einer Dissertation über »Dostojewski und der französische Existentialismus«. Als Literaturkritiker schrieb er einige gewagte Aufsätze, darunter eine Interpretation der Schriften des Marquis de Sade und einen Artikel über den Philosophen Leo Schestow. Aber erst der Literaturalmanach »Metropol. Literaturnij almanach« (1979; engl. »Metropol. A Literary Almanac«, 1982) führte zum großen Skandal. Es handelte sich hierbei um eine politisch brisante Textsammlung – ausgewählt von Viktor Jerofejew, Wassili Axjonow, Andrej Bitow, Jewgeni Popow und Fasil Iskander –, die arrivierte und missliebige Autoren nebeneinanderstellte. Die Versuche, den Almanach in der Sowjetunion herauszubringen, scheiterten mit der Begründung, es handele sich um ›Pornografie des Geistes‹. Schließlich wurde das Werk im Westen veröffentlicht. Daraufhin erhielt Viktor Jerofejew Publikationsverbot, während sein Vater Wladimir Jerofejew, ehemaliger Dolmetscher Stalins und zu jener Zeit Botschafter in Wien, gezwungen wurde, seine diplomatische Karriere zu beenden. Erst im Zeichen von Glasnost und Perestroika durfte Viktor Jerofejew wieder publizieren. 1990 erschien sein erster Roman »Russkaja Krasawiza« (dt. »Die Moskauer Schönheit«, 1990). Die Geschichte der schönen Irina, einer Edelhure in Moskau, provozierte durch die dunkle, groteske Ästhetik von Sex, Gewalt und Tod. In den Essays »Pominki po sowjetskoij literatur« (1990; Ü: Nachruf auf die Sowjetliteratur) und »Russkie zwetij sla« (1993; engl. »Russia's Fleurs du mal«, 1995) erklärte er die Literatur des sozialistischen Realismus für tot und formulierte zugleich sein radikales künstlerisches Manifest für eine neue Literatur des Bösen. Er ist Herausgeber der ersten russischen Nabokov-Ausgabe sowie mehrerer Anthologien zur Neuen Russischen Literatur. Seine Erzählung »Schijsn s idiotom« (1991; dt. »Leben mit einem Idioten«, 1991) wurde von Alfred Schnittke für eine Oper adaptiert. Er schreibt regelmäßig für den »New Yorker«, die »New York Review of Books«, »Die Zeit« und die »Frankfurter Allgemeine Zeitung«. Zuletzt erschien sein autobiographischer Roman »Choroschi Stalin« (2004; dt. »Der gute Stalin«, 2004). Viktor Jerofejew lebt in Moskau.

navid kermani

biography

Navid Kermani was born in Siegen in 1967, the fourth son of Iranian parents. After studying Drama, Philosophy and Islamic Studies in Cologne, Cairo and Bonn, he taught at the University of Bonn and worked as a literary and artistic director at the Schauspielhaus in Frankfurt and the Theater an der Ruhr in Mülheim. His dissertation, an extensive analysis of the reception of the Koran, which he completed in 1997, was awarded the Ernst-Bloch-Förderpreis in 2000 and has already been reprinted in several editions.

His book entitled »Iran. Die Revolution der Kinder« (2001; t: Iran. The children's revolution) is the product of reports and essays which he published on the country as a writer for the »Frankfurter Allgemeine Zeitung« from 1995 onwards. In 2001 Kermani wrote »Ein Leben mit dem Islam« (t: A life with Islam), which is acclaimed for its sensitive treatment of a delicate subject. It is the life story of the Egyptian scholar Nasr Hamid Abu Zaid, whose modern interpretation of the Koran not only earned him a reputation as a heretic, but also brought about the spectacular forced divorce from his wife. The phenomenon of suicide bombers is the topic of »Dynamit des Geistes. Martyrium, Islam und Nihilismus« (2002; t: Dynamite of the Spirit. Martyrdom, Islam and Nihilism). »Schöner neuer Orient. Berichte von Städten und Kriegen« (2003; t: Beautiful new orient. Reports of cities and wars) is a collection of six reports on Muslim regions which, due to extremism and violent conflict, have become the subject of international debate. The thoroughly positive reviews were underscored by the Israeli sociologist Natan Sznaider – for him it is »one of the most important books on globalisation«.

With the intensity of his virtuoso literary style, which in making regular reference to his own encounters and experiences attests to the authenticity of his reports, Kermani has set standards for the art of reportage and historiography. A native Iranian and a German citizen, Kermani is considered to be one of Germany's leading scholars on Islam. He is at once an expert on, and critic of, the Islamic world and one of its most important mediators. Also he has made a name for himself as an author, essayist and literary critic. His book entitled »Das Buch der von Neil Young Getöteten« (2002; t: The book of those killed by Neil Young) is a homage to the Canadian musician, and at the same time a narrative about life and death, written for people who are unfamiliar with Neil Young. »Die Zeit« identified a possible motive: »In the end this beautiful, intelligent little book is a homage to playing – on the stage of life.« For three years Kermani held the post of Long-Term Fellow at the Berlin Wissenschaftskolleg (Institute for Advanced Study). Last year he returned to Cologne, where he lives as a freelance writer with his wife and daughter.

His latest book, »40 Leben« (2004; t: 40 Lives), was published this year and explores the mysticism of everyday life in the form of forty narratives.

Gott ist schön
Beck
München, 1999
Iran
Beck
München, 2001
Das Buch der von Neil Young Getöteten
Ammann
Zürich, 2002
Dynamit des Geistes
Wallstein
Göttingen, 2002
Schöner neuer Orient
Beck
München, 2003
40 Leben
Ammann
Zürich, 2004

Navid Kermani wurde 1967 als vierter Sohn iranischer Eltern in Siegen geboren. Nach dem Studium der Islamwissenschaft, Theaterwissenschaft und Philosophie in Köln, Kairo und Bonn lehrte er an der Universität Bonn und war als Dramaturg am Schauspielhaus Frankfurt sowie am Mülheimer Theater an der Ruhr tätig. Seine Dissertation aus dem Jahr 1997, eine umfangreiche Rezeptionsanalyse des Koran, wurde im Jahr 2000 mit dem Ernst-Bloch-Förderpreis ausgezeichnet und erreichte schon mehrere Auflagen.
Aus Berichten und Reportagen, die er seit 1995 als Autor der »Frankfurter Allgemeinen Zeitung« über das Land veröffentlichte, ging sein Buch »Iran. Die Revolution der Kinder« (2001) hervor. Im selben Jahr führte Kermani behutsam durch »Ein Leben mit dem Islam«. Es ist die Lebensgeschichte des ägyptischen Gelehrten Nasr Hamid Abu Zaid, dem die moderne Auslegung des Koran nicht nur den Ruf eines Ketzers einbrachte, sondern auch die spektakuläre Zwangsscheidung von seiner Frau. Das Phänomen der Selbstmordattentäter ist Thema von »Dynamit des Geistes. Martyrium, Islam und Nihilismus« (2002). »Schöner neuer Orient. Berichte von Städten und Kriegen« (2003) versammelt sechs Reportagen über muslimische Regionen, die durch Extremismus und gewaltsame Konflikte in den Fokus der Weltöffentlichkeit geraten sind. Der israelische Soziologe Natan Sznaider unterstrich die durchgehend positiven Rezensionen – er erklärte es sogar zu »einem der wichtigsten Bücher über Globalisierung«.
Mit seinem virtuos verdichtenden literarischen Stil hat Kermani, der immer wieder in Exkursen auf authentische Begegnungen und Selbst-Erlebtes zurückgreift, Maßstäbe für die Kunst der Reportage wie der Historiographie gesetzt. Kermani, iranischer und inzwischen auch deutscher Staatsbürger, gilt als einer der führenden Islamwissenschaftler Deutschlands. Als Kenner und Kritiker der islamischen Welt ist er zugleich einer ihrer wichtigsten Vermittler. Er ist zudem als Schriftsteller, Essayist und Literaturkritiker hervorgetreten. 2002 erschien »Das Buch der von Neil Young Getöteten« – eine Hommage auf den kanadischen Musiker und zugleich eine Erzählung über Leben und Tod im Allgemeinen. »Am Ende ist dieses schöne, kluge Büchlein ein großes Lob des Spielens - auf der Bühne und im Leben«, so »Die Zeit«.
In den vergangenen drei Jahren war Kermani Long Term Fellow am Berliner Wissenschaftskolleg. 2003 kehrte er nach Köln zurück, wo er mit Frau und Tochter als freier Autor lebt. Anfang des Jahres erschien sein Buch »40 Leben«, das in Form von 40 Erzählungen der Mystik des Alltags nachgeht.

nicole krauss

biography

Nicole Krauss was born in New York, USA, in 1974. She studied English Literature at Stanford University in California and at Oxford University in the UK, where she was a Marshall Scholar. She then went on to study at London's Courtauld Institute, where she wrote her Master's thesis on Rembrandt. From early on she admired the poetry of Zbigniew Herbert, Rainer Maria Rilke, and Joseph Brodsky, with whom she had a regular correspondence. During her studies she published poems in various British journals.
In 1999 she produced a radio portrait about Brodsky for the BBC. She founded and organised a series of readings at the New York restaurant »The Russian Samovar« in which numerous writers – among them John Ashbery, Susan Sontag, Derek Walcott, and Jonathan Franzen – took part.
The conflict of memory is of great importance in Krauss's work. Her Jewish grandparents left Europe in time before the war, while other family members perished in the Holocaust. Her debut novel, »Man Walks into a Room« (2002), also deals with identity, memory and its loss. Samson Greene, a thirty-six year old Literature professor, is found wandering disoriented through the Nevada desert. The removal of a small brain tumor saves his life, but his memories beyond the age of twelve are permanently lost. It is the story of an intelligent, sensitive man returned to a world in which everything is strange and new. At first he meets his condition with confusion, then, as a kind of liberation. When a charismatic scientist asks Samson to participate in a bold experiment, he agrees. In this novel, Nicole Krauss grapples with the emotional, scientific, historical, religious and literary facets of oblivion and remembrance. Critics were especially impressed by the conciseness of her literary images and the perspicacious representation of such complex themes.
Her first short story, »Future Emergencies«, was published in »Esquire« magazine in 2002, and collected in the anthology Best American Short Stories 2003. Her new novel, »The History of Love«, was excerpted in The New Yorker last February and will be published in German by Rowohlt in autumn of 2005. Nicole Krauss lives in New York.

Man Walks Into a Room
Nan A. Talese
New York, 2002

Nicole Krauss wurde 1974 in New York, USA, geboren. Sie studierte Englische Literatur an der kalifornischen Stanford University und als Marshall-Stipendiatin an der University of Oxford in Großbritannien. Weiterführende Studien am Londoner Courtauld Institute für Kunstgeschichte schloss sie mit einer Arbeit über Rembrandt ab. Früh begeisterte sie sich für die Lyrik von Zbigniew Herbert, Rainer Maria Rilke und Joseph Brodsky, mit dem sie in regem Briefkontakt stand. Während ihrer Studienzeit veröffentlichte sie einige Gedichte in verschiedenen britischen Zeitschriften. 1999 produzierte sie für die BBC ein Radioporträt über Brodsky. Im New Yorker Restaurant »Russian Samovar« initiierte und organisierte sie eine Reihe von Lesungen, an denen zahlreiche Autoren teilnahmen – darunter John Ashbery, Susan Sontag, Derek Walcott und Jonathan Franzen.

Die Auseinandersetzung mit Erinnerung ist für Nicole Krauss von besonderer Bedeutung. Ihre jüdischen Großeltern konnten Europa rechtzeitig vor dem Krieg verlassen, andere Familienangehörige kamen jedoch im Holocaust um. Auch in ihrem Debütroman »Man Walks Into a Room« (2002) geht es um Identität, Erinnerung und Gedächtnisverlust. Samson Greene, ein sechsunddreißigjähriger Literaturprofessor, wird orientierungslos in der Wüste von Nevada aufgefunden. Die Entfernung eines kleinen Gehirntumors rettet ihm das Leben, aber nach der Operation kehren nur die Erinnerungen bis zu Samsons zwölften Lebensjahr zurück. Es ist die Geschichte eines intelligenten, sensiblen Mannes, der in eine Welt zurückkehrt, in der alles fremd und neu für ihn ist. Er erlebt diesen Zustand erst als Irritation, dann als eine Art Befreiung. Als ein charismatischer Wissenschaftler ihn bittet, an einem gewagten Experiment teilzunehmen, willigt er ein. Nicole Krauss setzt sich in diesem Roman mit den emotionalen, wissenschaftlichen, historischen, religiösen und literarischen Aspekten des Vergessens und Erinnerns auseinander. Die Kritiker waren besonders von der Prägnanz ihrer sprachlichen Bilder und der klaren Darstellung solch komplexer Themen beeindruckt.

Ihre erste Kurzgeschichte, »Future Emergencies«, wurde 2002 im Magazin »Esquire« veröffentlicht und 2003 in die Anthologie »Best American Short Stories« aufgenommen. Ihr neuer Roman, »The History of Love«, wurde im Februar auszugsweise in der Zeitschrift »The New Yorker« veröffentlicht und wird in Deutschland im Herbst 2005 im Rowohlt Verlag erscheinen. Nicole Krauss lebt in New York.

antjie krog

biography

Antjie Krog was born on a farm in the Orange Free State, South Africa, in 1952. She completed her degree in Afrikaans, Philosophy and English at the University of the Orange Free State and obtained a Master's degree from the University of Pretoria and a teaching diploma from the University of South Africa. She has conducted workshops in rural areas for the South African Congress of Writers and has worked closely with the Poetry School in Bloemfontein and the Poetry Laboratory at the University of Stellenbosch. With her first volume of poetry in Afrikaans, »Dogter van Jefta« (1970), she provoked the literary public with her taboo-breaking style. Aside from poetry, Krog has published children's books, a novel, and a literary account of the hearings of the Truth and Reconciliation Commission. »Country of My Skull« (1998) is an attempt to reappraise the country's past since the collapse of the Apartheid regime without bringing anyone to trial. Krog sensitively describes the historically unique debate between victims and perpetrators, and aims at persuading them to apologise, forgive, and become reconciled with one another. The book brought her international acclaim and was awarded the prize of the Hiroshima Foundation for Peace and Culture 2000. It has been since made into a film starring Juliette Binoche.

In 1999 Krog was one of seven African poets who undertook a caravan trail along the former slave route from the coast of Africa to the legendary town of Timbuktu on the river Niger. »A Change of Tongue« (2003) takes stock of events in South Africa during the first ten years after Apartheid. Through a collage of eclectic material – reports and interviews, fragments from poems, children's rhymes, letters and newspaper articles – she offers a unique array of perspectives on the hopes and pains of radical change.

Antjie Krog's poetry, prose and non-fictional texts have won all the major awards in South Africa. She has been translated into five European languages, though as of yet, not German. Among the works Krog herself has translated into Afrikaans is Nelson Mandela's autobiography, »Long Walk to Freedom«. The author is married to the architect John Samuel, she has four children and lives in Cape Town. She is currently a professor extraordinary at the University of the Western Cape.

Dogter van Jefta
Human & Rousseau
Kapstadt, 1970
Januarie Suite
Human & Rousseau
Kapstadt,1972
Jerusalemgangers
Human & Rousseau
Kapstadt,1985
Lady Anne
Human & Rousseau
Kapstadt,1989
Country of My Skull
Random House
Johannesburg, 1998
Down to My Last Skin
Random House
Johannesburg, 2000
A Change of Tongue
Random House
Johannesburg, 2003

zwei jahre diesen monat

zwei jahre diesen monat
seit meinem letzten gedichtband
zwei jahre ohne eine zeile – dunkel
nicht mal ein gedanke, der ein gedicht werden könnte

genau so will ich mein leben (sage ich) dieses
atmen eines ungeschriebenen hauses: jedes kind
gebügelt, gefaltet, ausgehändigt – warm und brauchbar

sage ich und kritzele herum
in meinen ruinen düster und
deplaziert   wochenlang

vertage ich jede korrespondenz übersetzung
analyse und sitze schließlich
heute morgen vor dieser leeren seite
wie beginnt man ein gedicht?

spitz türkisch rot stift duftend radiergummi
ich spreize meine ohren nach innen
klopfe gegen die innenseiten empfangsbereit für jedes beben
verzweifelt schlage ich in jede wunde
doch bleibt sie innen abwartend verdickt dann

Antjie Krog wurde 1952 auf einer Farm im Oranjefreistaat, Südafrika, geboren. Sie studierte Afrikaans, Philosophie und Englisch an der University of the Orange Freestate und schloss ihre Ausbildung mit einem Master Titel an der University of Pretoria und einem Lehrerdiplom an der University of South Africa ab. Sie leitete Workshops in ländlichen Gegenden für den South African Congress of Writers und arbeitete eng mit der Poetry School in Bloemfontein und dem Poetry Laboratory an der University of Stellenbosch zusammen. Mit ihrem ersten Lyrikband »Dogter van Jefta« (1970) provozierte die in Afrikaans schreibende Autorin durch ihre tabubrechende Schreibweise die literarische Öffentlichkeit. Neben Gedichtbänden, Kinderbüchern und einem Roman verfasste sie einen literarischen Bericht über die Anhörungen der Wahrheitskommission, über die sie zuvor zwei Jahre lang als Radiojournalistin berichtet hatte. Mit »Country of My Skull«, einem Buch über die Truth and Reconciliation Commission, die nach dem Zusammenbruch des Apartheid-Regimes den Versuch unternahm, unter Verzicht auf juristische Verurteilung die Vergangenheit des Landes aufzuarbeiten, erlangte Antjie Krog 1998 internationale Anerkennung. In semifiktiven und dokumentarischen Passagen berichtet sie auf einfühlsame Weise über diese historisch einmalige Auseinandersetzung zwischen Opfern und Tätern, die sich Entschuldigung, Verzeihung und Versöhnung zum Ziel gesetzt hatte. Für dieses Buch, das inzwischen mit Juliette Binoche in der Hauptrolle verfilmt wurde, ehrte man sie u. a. mit dem Preis der Hiroshima Foundation for Peace and Culture 2000.

1999 nahm Antjie Krog gemeinsam mit sieben afrikanischen Autoren an der »Karawane der Dichter« teil, einer Reise, die entlang einer früheren Sklavenroute von der Küste Afrikas zur legendären Stadt Timbuktu am Niger führte. »A Change of Tongue« (2003) ist eine Bestandsaufnahme Südafrikas während der ersten zehn Jahre nach der Apartheid. Die Collage aus heterogenem Material – Berichte und Interviews, Fragmente aus Gedichten, Kinderreime, Briefe und Zeitungsartikel – eröffnet eine Vielzahl ungewöhnlicher Perspektiven auf die Hoffnungen und Schmerzen einer radikalen Veränderung. Antjie Krog wurde für ihre Lyrik und Prosa sowie für ihre dokumentarischen Texte mit den wichtigsten Literaturpreisen Südafrikas ausgezeichnet. Ihre Texte wurden in fünf europäische Sprachen – bisher jedoch noch nicht ins Deutsche – übersetzt. Nelson Mandelas Autobiographie »Long Walk to Freedom« befindet sich unter den Werken anderer Autoren, die sie ins Afrikaans übersetzte. Die Autorin ist mit dem Architekten John Samuel verheiratet, sie hat vier Kinder und lebt in Kapstadt. Derzeit übt sie eine außerordentliche Professur an der University of the Western Cape aus.

wirft sich aus irgendeinem grund plötzlich eine öffnung auf
etwas vibriert, mein atem verflacht sich
zu einem verhaltenen zittern ich warte

spitze des stiftes schwebt ab
der puls einer zeile erscheint
meine sinne drängen sich leicht aneinander

ein kind ruft von ferne / eine tür schlägt / schritte im flur

ich greif nach der öffnung - bitte auch ein spritzer wär genug
berge hastig den sich schließenden muskel
doch der tod beginnt an meinen füßen ich stehe
vor einem versperrten schlüpfrigen innen

vorsichtig betritt das kind das zimmer / mama arbeitest du? / seine
augen schmutzig grau

jonathan lethem

biography

Jonathan Lethem was born in New York, USA, in 1964. He spent the early years of his childhood in Kansas City. At the beginning of the 1970's his father, the avant-garde painter Richard Brown Lethem, moved with his family to the then still fully decrepit New York neighbourhood of Brooklyn, populated predominantly by blacks and Puerto Ricans. The experience of his adolescence on the Brooklyn streets, in which he belonged to a white minority, had a lasting effect on him. After finishing school he went to study Liberal Arts at Bennington College in Vermont, though he soon gave this up in favour of a career in writing. In 1984 he moved to Berkeley, on the West Coast, and for several years lived in San Francisco, where he worked in various antique shops and wrote short stories and his first novel.

He has published many short stories in publications such as »The Paris Review« and »Esquire«. In 1994 his first novel, »Gun, With Occasional Music«, came out. It is a fantastical genre cross-over which unfolds in a futuristic and surrealistic setting in the tradition of Raymond Chandler's »hardboiled« detective stories. Then followed the post-apocalyptic novel »Amnesia Moon« (1995) and »As She Climbed Across the Table« (1997), a grotesque love story between a female scientist and a vacuum which is the result of an experiment. Another work was »Girl in Landscape« (1998), a Western which takes place on Mars.

In 1996 Jonathan Lethem decided to return to Brooklyn, where he wrote his novel »Motherless Brooklyn« (1999), for which he won awards including the National Book Critics Circle Award. The protagonist of this unusual crime story is Lionel Essrog, who suffers from Tourette's Syndrome. His uncontrollable compulsion to repeat: obscene wordgames, abrupt movements, and other tics make him an outsider. When his friend and role model Frank Minna, a Brooklyn criminal with ties to the mafia and Zen monks, is stabbed to death, Lionel tries to solve the murder. Another novel: »The Fortress of Solitude« (2003), also takes place in Brooklyn. It is a semi-autobiographical story about growing up in Brooklyn. Dylan Ebdus, the protagonist, does not have an easy time of being the only young white kid in his neighbourhood. His black friend Mingus Rude shows him how one gets on in this world: comic superheroes, hip hop, graffiti, and drugs. »The Fortress of Solitude« was elected »Best Book of the Year 2003« by »The New York Times«. Jonathan Lethem lives in Brooklyn.

Gun, With Occasional Music
Harcourt Brace & Company
Orlando, 1994

Girl In Landscape
Doubleday
New York, 1998

Motherless Brooklyn
Tropen
Köln, 2001
[Ü: Michael Zöllner]

Als sie über den Tisch kletterte
Tropen
Köln, 2002
[Ü: Michael Zöllner]

Der kurze Schlaf
Tropen
Köln, 2003
[Ü: Biggi Winter, Michael Zöllner]

Die Festung der Einsamkeit
Tropen
Köln, 2004
[Ü: Michael Zöllner]

Men And Cartoons
Doubleday
New York, 2004

Jonathan Lethem wurde 1964 in New York, USA, geboren. Die frühen Jahre seiner Kindheit verbrachte er in Kansas City. Anfang der siebziger Jahre zog sein Vater, der Avantgarde-Maler Richard Brown Lethem, mit der Familie in den zu jener Zeit noch völlig heruntergekommenen New Yorker Stadtteil Brooklyn mit überwiegend schwarzer und puertoricanischer Bevölkerung. Die Erfahrung, als Jugendlicher auf den Straßen Brooklyns zur weißen Minderheit zu gehören, prägte ihn nachhaltig. Nach der Schule begann er am Bennington College in Vermont ein Studium der Freien Kunst, das er jedoch schon bald zugunsten des Schreibens aufgab. 1984 zog er nach Berkeley an die Westküste. Mehrere Jahre lebte er in San Francisco, wo er in verschiedenen Antiquariaten arbeitete und Kurzgeschichten sowie erste Romane verfasste.

Er veröffentlichte zahlreiche Kurzgeschichten, unter anderem in »The Paris Review« und »Esquire«. 1994 erschien sein erster Roman »Gun, With Occasional Music« (dt. »Der kurze Schlaf«, 2003), ein phantastisches Genre-Crossover mit futuristisch-surrealem Schauplatz in der Tradition von Raymond Chandlers ›Hard-boiled‹-Detektivgeschichten. Es folgten der postapokalyptische Roman »Amnesia Moon« (1995; Ü: Amnesie Mond), »As She Climbed Across the Table« (1997; dt. »Als sie über den Tisch kletterte«, 2002), eine groteske Liebesgeschichte zwischen einer Wissenschaftlerin und einem aus einem Experiment entstandenen Vakuum, sowie »Girl in Landscape« (1998; Ü: Mädchen in der Landschaft), ein Western, der auf dem Mars spielt.

1996 entschloss sich Jonathan Lethem zur Rückkehr nach Brooklyn. Dort schrieb er seinen Roman »Motherless Brooklyn« (1999; dt. »Motherless Brooklyn«, 2001), für den er unter anderem mit dem National Book Critics Circle Award ausgezeichnet wurde. Protagonist dieser ungewöhnlichen Kriminalgeschichte ist Lionel Essrog, der am Tourette-Syndrom leidet. Sein unkontrollierbarer Zwang zu Wiederholungen, obszönen Wortspielen, unvermittelten Berührungen und sonstigen Tics machen ihn zum Außenseiter. Als sein Freund und Vorbild Frank Minna, ein Brooklyner Krimineller mit Verbindungen zur Mafia und Zen-Mönchen, erstochen wird, versucht er, den Mord aufzuklären. Auch »The Fortress of Solitude« (2003; dt. » Die Festung der Einsamkeit«, 2004), eine Geschichte über das Erwachsenwerden mit autobiographischen Zügen, spielt in Brooklyn. Dylan Ebdus hat es als einziger weißer Junge in der Nachbarschaft nicht leicht. Sein schwarzer Freund Mingus Rude zeigt ihm, worauf es in dieser Welt ankommt: Comic-Superhelden, Hip-Hop, Graffities und Drogen. »The Fortress of Solitude« wurde von der New York Times zum »Besten Buch des Jahres 2003« gekürt.

Jonathan Lethem lebt in Brooklyn.

ma yuan
biography

Ma Yuan was born in the People's Republic of China in 1953. He studied Chinese at the Liaoning University in northeast China, and between 1982 and 1987 worked as a journalist in Tibet. In 1989 he returned to China, where he moved from city to city trying out jobs in diverse cultural sectors. During this peripatetic period emerged the collection of essays »Liangge Nanren« (t: Two men). Since 2000 he has taught Classical Literature and Creative Writing at Tongji University in Shanghai. His two volumes of essays, »Xuguo Zhi Dao« (1997; t: The knife of fabrication) and »Yuedu Dashi« (t: Reading the masters), offer an overview of his appreciation of literature and his approach towards Creative Writing. Ma Yuan is regarded as the most important pioneer of modern Chinese avant-garde literature. His stories about Tibetan culture, religion and mysticism, which he wrote during his residence there between 1984 and 1989, are among the most influential works of the new literary movement of the time. As opposed to the strict realism of modern Chinese literature which prevailed under the influence of Mao Zedong, the young avant-garde writers dared to experiment aesthetically with literary forms and narrative strategies, amongst other things, the result of the new availability of modern western literature in Chinese translation. The vital pulse therefore of Ma Yuan's short story »The Goddess of the River Llasa« (1984), with its labyrinthian construction, reminds one of Jorge Luis Borges. He also opens the story »The Wandering Spirit«, which takes place in Llasa, with a quote from Borges. By coincidence, the narrator named Ma Yuan discovers through an old Tibetan the existence of a few rare silver coins. He then becomes involved in a plan to steal the precious coins. In the complex multi-levelled structure of the story the author combines oral strategies, which every now and then abruptly interrupt the narrative flow with fantastic and fairy-tale like elements. The narrator's voice is conspicuously present in the narration of the allegedly autobiographical events. »After Ma all the taboos on fiction writing disappeared, and the search for an idiosyncratic style became the writer's legitimate pursuit.« A few of Ma Yuan's short stories have been translated into English, among them »Die zhiyao de sanzhong fangfa« (Eng. »More Ways Than One to Make a Kite«). Ma Yuan lives in Shanghai.

Ma Yuan wurde 1953 in der Volksrepublik China geboren. Er studierte Chinesisch an der Liaoning Universität im Nordosten Chinas. Von 1982 bis 1987 arbeitete er als Journalist in Tibet. 1989 kehrte er nach China zurück. Zunächst zog er dort von Stadt zu Stadt und betätigte sich in unterschiedlichen kulturellen Bereichen. Von dieser bewegten Zeit berichtet er in der Essaysammlung »Liangge Nanren« (Ü: Zwei Männer). Seit 2000 lehrt er Klassische Literatur und Kreatives Schreiben an der Tongji Universität in Shanghai. Mit den beiden Essaybänden »Xuguo Zhi Dao« (1997; Ü: Das Messer der Erfindung) und »Yuedu Dashi« (Ü: Die Meister lesen) gibt er einen Überblick über sein Verständnis von Literatur und seinen Ansatz des Kreativen Schreibens.

Ma Yuan gilt als wichtigster Pionier der modernen chinesischen Avantgarde-Literatur. Seine von der tibetischen Kultur, Religion und Mystik inspirierten Erzählungen, die er zwischen 1984 bis 1989 während seines Aufenthaltes in Tibet verfasste, zählen zu den einflussreichsten Werken der neuen Literaturbewegung jener Zeit. Im Gegensatz zum strikten Realismus der modernen chinesischen Literatur, der unter dem Einfluss von Mao Zedong vorherrschend war, wagten die jungen Avantgarde-Autoren – unter anderem auch, weil damals erstmals Werke der modernen westlichen Literatur in chinesischer Übersetzung zugänglich waren – ästhetische Experimente mit literarischen Formen und narrativen Strategien. Den entscheidenden Impuls dafür gab 1984 Ma Yuans Kurzgeschichte »The Goddess of the River Lhasa« aufgrund ihrer labyrinthischen Erzählkonstruktion, die an Jorge Luis Borges erinnert. Mit einem Zitat von Borges eröffnet er auch seine Kurzgeschichte »Youshen« (Ü: Ein umtriebiger Geist), die in Lhasa spielt. Durch Zufall erfährt der Erzähler namens Ma Yuan von Qimi, einem alten Tibeter, von der Existenz einiger seltener Silbermünzen. Daraufhin beteiligt er sich an dem Plan, die kostbaren Münzprägestempel zu entwenden. Der Autor kombiniert mündliche Erzählstrategien mit phantastischen und märchenhaften Elementen, die immer wieder den Erzählfluss abrupt unterbrechen. In der Schilderung der vermeintlich autobiographischen Begebenheiten ist die Stimme des Erzählers deutlich präsent. »Nach Ma verschwanden alle Tabus für das Verfassen von Prosa, und die Suche nach einem eigenen Stil wurde zum legitimen Ziel eines Schriftstellers.« Einige Kurzgeschichten von Ma Yuan wurden ins Englische übersetzt, darunter »Die zhiyao de sanzhong fangfa« (Ü: Mehr als eine Art, einen Drachen zu bauen). Ma Yuan lebt in Shanghai.

claudio magris

biography

Claudio Magris was born in Trieste, Italy, in 1939. He studied Literature and Philosophy in Turin. His dissertation »Il mito asburgico nella letteratura austriaca moderna« (1963; t: The Habsburg myth in modern Austrian literature), was published when he was twenty four, and formed the themes and theoretical sources for later publications. After an academic residency in Freiburg he taught at the University of Turin, before becoming Professor for New German Literature at the University of Trieste in 1978.
As a specialist in Middle European Literature, he has published numerous essays and critical studies on writers such as Wilhelm Heinse, E.T.A. Hoffmann and Joseph Roth. Since the late 1970's he has written regularly for a column in the newspaper »Corriere della Sera«. A selection of his texts, »Itaca e oltre« appeared in 1982. That same year a collaboration with the historian Angelo Ara was also published: »Trieste. Un'identita di frontiera«. On this cultural and literary foray through the city, in which James Joyce, Italo Svevo and other writers once lived, the authors ask questions regarding Trieste's identity with regard to the heterogenous influences of the empire and of Italian, Slovenian, German, Greek and Jewish culture. Four years later, in »Danubio« (1986), Claudio Magris set out to trace the diverse Habsburg realm. Following the course of the Danube, he offered in an essayistic-biographical travelogue consisting of myths, anecdotes, stories about men, cities and landscapes, as well as philosophical and literary meditations a detailed panorama of the cultural and literary area of this »only true European river«. Apart from his essays Magris wrote the novella »Illazioni su una sciabola« (1984), the play »Stadelmann« (1988) and the novel »Un altro mare« (1991). Claudio Magris has been honoured with many awards. In 1997 he received the most important literary prize in Italy: the Premio Strega, for »Microcosmi« (1996), as well as the 2004 Prince of Asturias Prize. Essays from 1974 to 1998 were collected in »Utopia e disincanto« (1999). His most recent work is the play »La Mostra« (2001). jClaudio Magris lives in Trieste.

Mutmaßungen über einen Säbel
Hanser
München, 1986
[Ü: Ragni Maria Gschwend]

Donau
Zsolnay
Wien, 1996
[Ü: Heinz-Georg Held]

Triest
zusammen mit Angelo Ara
Zsolnay
Wien, 1999
[Ü: Ragni Maria Gschwend]

Der habsburgische Mythos
Zsolnay
Wien, 2000
[Ü: Madeleine von Pasztory]

Utopie und Entzauberung
Hanser
München, 2002
[Ü: Ragni Maria Gschwend und Karin Krieger]

Die Ausstellung
Hanser
München, 2004
[Ü: Hanno Helbling]

Die Welt en gros und en détail
dtv
München, 2004
[Ü: Ragni Maria Gschwend]

Claudio Magris wurde 1939 in Triest, Italien, geboren. Er studierte Literatur und Philosophie in Turin. Seine Dissertation »Il mito asburgico nella letteratura austriaca moderna« (1963; dt. »Der Habsburgische Mythos in der österreichischen Literatur«, 1966/2000), die er im Alter von vierundzwanzig Jahren publizierte, bildet den thematischen und theoretischen Ausgangspunkt seiner späteren Publikationen. Nach einem Studienaufenthalt in Freiburg lehrte er zunächst an der Universität Turin, bevor er 1978 Professor für Neuere Deutsche Literatur an der Universtität Triest wurde.
Als Spezialist für mitteleuropäische Literatur publizierte er zahlreiche Essays und kritische Studien über Schriftsteller wie Wilhelm Heinse, E. T. A. Hoffmann und Joseph Roth. Seit den späten siebziger Jahren schrieb er regelmäßig für eine Kolumne der Zeitung »Corriere della Sera«. Eine Auswahl der Texte wurde 1982 in »Itaca e oltre« (Ü: Itaca und anderes) veröffentlicht. Im selben Jahr erschien in Zusammenarbeit mit dem Historiker Angelo Ara »Trieste. Un'identità di frontiera« (dt. »Triest. Eine literarische Hauptstadt in Mitteleuropa«, 1987). Auf dem kultur- und literaturwissenschaftlichen Streifzug durch die Stadt, in der einst James Joyce, Italo Svevo und andere Schriftsteller lebten, stellen die Autoren angesichts der heterogenen Einflüsse des k. u. k.-Imperiums und der italienischen, slowenischen, deutschen, griechischen und jüdischen Kulturen die Frage nach der Identität Triests.
Vier Jahre später begab sich Claudio Magris mit »Danubio« (1986; »Donau. Biographie eines Flusses«, 1988) auf Spurensuche nach der habsburgischen Vielvölkermonarchie. Während er dem Verlauf des ›einzig wahrhaft europäischen Flusses‹ folgt, zeichnet er in einem essayistisch-biographischen Reisebericht – bestehend aus Mythen, Anekdoten, Geschichten von den Menschen, Städten und Landschaften, philosophischen und literarischen Reflexionen – ein tailreiches Panorama des Kultur- und Literaturraumes Donau. Zu seinen nicht-essayistischen Texten zählen die Novelle »Illazioni su una sciabola« (1984; dt. »Mutmaßungen über einen Säbel«, 1986), das Theaterstück »Stadelmann« (1988) und der Roman »Un altro mare« (1991; dt. »Ein anderes Meer«, 1992). Claudio Magris wurde mit zahlreichen Preisen gewürdigt. 1997 erhielt er den wichtigsten italienischen Literaturpreis Premio Strega für »Microcosmi« (1996; dt. »Die Welt en gros und en détail«, 1999), sowie 2004 den Prinz-von-Asturien-Preis. Essays aus den Jahren 1974 bis 1998 sind in »Utopia e disincanto« (1999; dt. »Utopie und Entzauberung«, 2002) versammelt. Sein bisher letztes Werk ist das Drama »La Mostra« (2001; dt. »Die Ausstellung«, 2004). Claudio Magris lebt in Triest.

les murray

biography

Les Murray was born on a farm in Nabiac/New South Wales, Australia, in 1938. As an only child, he soon acquired autodidactic habits. Following family tradition – a relative in Scotland edited and wrote parts of the enormous Oxford English Dictionary – the young Murray turned out to be highly gifted in all language matters, though he was too dreamy and headstrong for an academic career. After his studies he worked as translator at the Australian National University in Canberra. In 1965, together with Geoffrey Lehmann, he published his first volume of poetry, »The Ilex Tree«, which won the Grace Leven Prize for Poetry. In the early 1970's Les Murray settled in Sydney as a freelance writer and literary critic. Between 1973 and 1980 he worked as an editor of »Poetry Australia«, and later became the literary editor of the magazine »Quadrant«. As an oft-awarded poet, Les Murray can look back on an extensive poetic oeuvre distinguished by an enormous diversity of themes, an extremely wide spectrum of poetic forms, and great linguistic virtuosity. He combines, for example, traditional lyrical forms of the western cultural area with the oral culture of the Aborigines. Inspired by their long narrative poems, he penned one hundred and forty sonnets for his first verse novel, »The Boys Who Stole a Funeral« (1979). For eight years, from 1988 to 1996, Murray suffered from severe depression. During this period, however, he produced some of his most important work: the unique animal and nature poems »Translations from the Natural World« (1992), »Subhuman Redneck Poems« (1993), a homage to simple people, and the epic novel in verse, »Fredy Neptune« (1998), which he describes as his »cryptic autobiography«.
Fredy Neptune is traumatised having been forced to witness an act of violence against Armenians. Since then insensitive to pain and therefore superhumanly strong, he has travelled around the world. About his relation to poetry, Murray says, »The poetic experience seems, at bottom, to be an experience of wholeness. If a poem is real, it is inexhaustible; it cannot be summarised or transposed into other words. It is marked by a strange simultaneity or stillness and racing excitement.« Les Murray lives in Bunyah/New South Wales.

The Boys Who Stole the Funeral
Angus & Robertson
Sydney, 1979
The Vernacular Republic
Angus & Robertson
Sydney, 1982
Ein ganz gewöhnlicher Regenbogen
Hanser
München, 1996
[Ü: Margitt Lehbert]
Subhuman Redneck Poems
Duffy & Snellgrove
Sydney, 1996
Conscious & Verbal
Duffy & Snellgrove
Sydney, 2000
Poems the Size of Photographs
Duffy & Snellgrove
Sydney, 2002
Learning Human
Duffy & Snellgrove
Sydney, 2003
New Collected Poems
Carcanet
Manchester, 2003
Fredy Neptune
Ammann
Zürich, 2004
[Ü: Thomas Eichhorn]

Les Murray wurde 1938 auf einer Farm in Nabiac/New South Wales, Australien, geboren. Als Einzelkind verfiel er bald autodidaktischen Gewohnheiten. Ganz in der Familientradition – ein Verwandter in Schottland hatte das riesige Oxford English Dictionary redigiert und teilweise geschrieben –, erwies sich der junge Murray als höchst sprachbegabt, allerdings für eine akademische Laufbahn als viel zu träumerisch und eigensinnig. Nach dem Studium arbeitete er als Übersetzer an der Australian National University in Canberra. 1965 brachte er zusammen mit Geoffrey Lehmann den ersten Gedichtband »The Ilex Tree« heraus, der mit dem Grace Leven Prize for Poetry ausgezeichnet wurde. Anfang der siebziger Jahre ließ sich Les Murray als freier Schriftsteller und Literaturkritiker in Sydney nieder. Von 1973 bis 1980 war er Herausgeber von »Poetry Australia«, später wurde er Literaturredakteur des Magazins »Quadrant«. Als mehrfach preisgekrönter Dichter kann Les Murray heute auf ein umfangreiches dichterisches Œuvre zurückblicken, das sich durch eine enorme Themenvielfalt, ein überaus breites Spektrum poetischer Formen und große sprachliche Virtuosität auszeichnet. So verbindet er beispielsweise traditionelle Lyrikformen des westlichen Kulturkreises mit poetischen Elementen aus der mündlichen Kultur der Aborigines. Inspiriert von deren langen narrativen Gedichten, verfasste er in hundertvierzig Sonetten seinen ersten Versroman »The Boys Who Stole a Funeral« (1979; Ü: Die Jungs, die ein Begräbnis stahlen). Acht Jahre lang, von 1988 bis 1996, litt er unter schweren Depressionen. Doch gerade in dieser Zeit schuf er einige seiner wichtigsten Werke: die einzigartigen Tier- und Naturgedichte »Translations from the Natural World« (1992), »Subhuman Redneck Poems« (1993), eine Hommage an die einfachen Leute, und den epischen Versroman »Fredy Neptune« (1998; dt. 2004), den er als seine »heimliche Autobiographie« bezeichnet.
Fredy Neptune ist durch eine Gewalttat an den Armeniern, die er hilflos mit ansehen musste, traumatisiert. Seither unfähig zur Schmerzempfindung und deshalb übermenschlich stark, reist er durch die Welt. Über seinen Zugang zur Poesie sagt Murray: »Die poetische Erfahrung scheint letztendlich eine Erfahrung der Ganzheit zu sein. Wenn ein Gedicht echt ist, ist es unerschöpflich; es lässt sich nicht zusammenfassen oder in andere Worte übertragen. Es ist gekennzeichnet durch eine merkwürdige Simultaneität von Stille und rasender Erregung.«
Les Murray lebt derzeit in Bunyah/New South Wales.

And how does one beguile a reluctant Muse? One simply arranges to do something businesslike in the big world, give a lecture, go on tour, write an article – and back she comes to assert her superior claim to your heart and your time. It's nearly infallible. Best wishes. Les Murray

oskar pastior

biography

Oskar Pastior was born in Sibiu in the Transylvanian region of Romania in 1927. A member of the minority ethnic German community, he spent five years in a Soviet forced-labour camp after the Second World War before being allowed to return home. From 1955 he studied German Language and Literature at the University of Bucharest, during which time he published his first poems. After graduating, he worked for the German language service of Romanian national radio. His first collection of poems, »Offne Worte«, was published in 1964. Despite winning literary awards in Romania, he felt confined by the »prefabricated and ideological language with its prescribed historical rules«. It was while studying in Vienna in 1968 that he emigrated to the west. He has since lived as a freelance writer and translator in Berlin. »Vom Sichersten ins Tausendste« (1969) was the first of his many books of poetry to be published in Germany.

In the poetically resonant parallel world of Pastior's writing, familiar language becomes alien and meaning is elevated to another dimension. The appeal of this surreal linguistic reality stems from a playful tendency to bend the rules. »He always perceived misconstruction, connotation, nonsense, wit and diversity as the true and genuine meaning of words«, Christoph Meckel once remarked about the linguistic pioneer. It comes as no surprise that Pastior is a member of OuLiPo (»Ouvroir de Littérature Potentielle«/»Workshop for Potential Literature«), a group that has worked with revived and original writing techniques since its foundation in 1960.

Oskar Pastior is a master of lyrical forms, ranging from conventional writing in »Gedichtgedichte« (1973) to the creation of »sonetburger« (1983), from rummaging around in »Höricht« (1975) to exploring the potential of the anagram in »Anagrammgedichte« (1985). He played with the palindrome in »Kopfnuß Januskopf« (1990), invented the vocalise (»Vokalisen & Gimpelstifte«, 1992) and founded »Das Hören des Genitivs« (1997). His »o du roher iasmin«, published in 2002, comprised 43 variations on Charles Baudelaire's poem »Harmonie du soir«.

Oskar Pastior has won numerous awards for his works, among them the Aachener Walter Hasenclever Prize (2000) and the Vienna Erich Fried Prize (2002). The second volume of his collected works, »Jetzt kann man schreiben was man will«, was published in 2003.

Lesungen mit Tinnitus
Hanser
München, 1986
Vokalisen & Gimpelstifte
Hanser
München, 1992
Das Unding an sich
Suhrkamp
Frankfurt am Main, 1994
Villanella & Pantum
Hanser
München, 2000
O du roher iasmin
Urs Engeler Editor
Basel/Weil am Rhein, 2002
Jetzt kann man schreiben was man will
Hanser
München, 2003
Mein Chlebnikov
Urs Engeler Editor
Basel/Weil am Rhein, 2003
Reread Another. A Play/Nochmal den Text ein anderer
Urs Engeler Editor
Basel/Weil am Rhein, 2004

Oskar Pastior wurde 1927 in Hermannstadt (Sibiu)/Siebenbürgen, Rumänien, geboren. Kurz vor Kriegsende wurde er als Angehöriger der deutschen Minderheit in sowjetische Arbeitslager deportiert. Erst nach fünf Jahren Zwangsarbeit konnte er in seine Heimat zurückkehren. Ab 1955 studierte er Deutsche Sprache und Literatur an der Universität Bukarest, nebenher veröffentlichte er seine ersten Gedichte. Nach dem Studium arbeitete er als Redakteur für deutschsprachige Inland-Sendungen beim Rumänischen Rundfunk. 1964 erschien sein erster Gedichtband »Offne Worte«. Obwohl er in Rumänien für seine Dichtung ausgezeichnet wurde, fühlte er sich von der »Fertigbauteil- und Ideologiesprache mit verordneten historischen Gesetzmäßigkeiten« eingeengt. So nutzte er 1968 einen Studienaufenthalt in Wien, um in den Westen überzusiedeln. Seither lebt Oskar Pastior als freier Schriftsteller und Übersetzer in Berlin. »Vom Sichersten ins Tausendste« (1969) war der erste seiner zahlreichen Gedichtbände, die in Deutschland veröffentlicht wurden.

In der lautpoetischen Wunderwelt von Pastiors Lyrik wird die vertraute Sprache fremd und der Sinn changiert in neuen Dimensionen. Der Reiz dieser surrealen Sprachrealität liegt im spielerischen Umgang mit den Regeln. »Falschsinn, Nebensinn, Unsinn, Witz und Vielfalt wörtlicher Bedeutungen sind ihm von jeher wahr und wirklich erschienen«, wie Christoph Meckel einmal über Pastior bemerkte. Es verwundert nicht, dass der Sprachkünstler Pastior der Gruppe OuLiPo (»Ouvroir de Littérature Potentielle«/»Werkstatt für potentielle Literatur«) angehört, die sich seit 1960 mit reanimierten wie mit neu erfundenen Literaturtechniken beschäftigt.

Oskar Pastior ist ein Meister der lyrischen Formen. Mal schrieb er »Gedichtgedichte« (1973), mal kreierte er »sonetburger« (1983). Er stöberte im »Höricht« (1975) und forschte nach den Möglichkeiten des Anagramms (»Anagrammgedichte«, 1985). Er spielte mit dem Palindrom in »Kopfnuß Januskopf« (1990), erfand die Vokalise (»Vokalisen & Gimpelstifte«, 1992) und ergründete »Das Hören des Genitivs« (1997). 2002 schuf er mit »o du roher iasmin« 43 Variationen von Charles Baudelaires Gedicht »Harmonie du soir«.

Oskar Pastior wurde für sein Schaffen mit zahlreichen Auszeichnungen gewürdigt, darunter mit dem Aachener Walter-Hasenclever-Preis (2000) und mit dem Wiener Erich-Fried-Preis (2002). Der zweite Band seiner Werkausgabe, »Jetzt kann man schreiben was man will«, erschien 2003.

Meine Muse liest in der Woche sich dreimal anders und viermal mich besonders auseinander, beziehungsweise beide uns auch zusammen, was dann etwa so aussieht:

So: Hagebuttenmusekstase
Mo: Apfelmuselektrolyse
Di: Quittenmusemailegende
Mi: Zwetschgenmusekunde
Do: Schmuseegrasmatratze
Fr: Pleonasmuseck con brio
Sa: Rhythmusesam Usedom

Mit pampelmusealgenoppten Grüßen -
Oskar Pastior

boualem sansal

biography

Boualem Sansal was born in Algeria in 1949 and started his career as a writer at the age of 50. Until that point the economist and engineer, who holds a doctoral degree, had worked as a high-ranking official in the Algerian ministry of industry. But the assassination of President Boudiaf (1992), the death of a friend, and the ordeal of persecution in a homeland burdened with civil war inspired him to write about his country, and in so doing enter into a state of inner exile. The outcome was his debut novel »Le serment des barbares«, which was published in France, where it was praised by the press and received the Prix du Premier Roman. »Le Nouvel Observateur« celebrated the book as a »masterpiece«.
The novel, now a film based on a screenplay by Jorge Semprúns, opens like a detective story: in the little Algerian city of Rouiba, two men of very different social standing – the wealthy and inviolable godfather of the region, Moh and the impoverished Bakour – are found murdered on the same day. When it becomes clear to the inspector in the Bakour case that the murders are related and that their background is politically charged, the story quickly turns into an examination of the state of affairs in the North African country. The inspector's investigations become a search for the roots of terrorist violence in present-day Algeria, amidst corruption, oppression and Islam.
In his novels Sansal draws the attention of Algerians, who have existed as a nation only since the independence of 1962, to potential ways to find their own identity. Indeed, this would seem to be the idea encapsulated in the title of the novel »L'enfant fou de l'arbre creux« (t: The mad child from the hollow tree), which was published in 2000 and won the Michel Dard Literature Prize the following year. Sansal explains how the child, tied up in the courtyard of a prison, stands for the Algerian people in »this giant prison of Algeria. A childish people, blinded, held captive by lies. These people have reached a point where they neither know who they are, where they come from, nor what they want.« In France, the former colonial power, Sansal is celebrated as a linguistic innovator because of his playful use of the French language. In Algeria on the other hand, due to the politically explosive topics of his satirical but poetic novels, he is perceived as a detriment to his country. Nevertheless he continues to reside with his wife and two adult daughters in his homeland and refuses to shield his identity by publishing under a pseudonym. The cheerfulness of Sansal's novels speaks for his faith in Algeria's future. His most recent work »Dis-moi le paradis« (2003; t: Tell me about paradise) represents a rough draft for such a future.

Das verrückte Kind aus dem hohlen Baum
Merlin
Gifkendorf, 2002
[Ü: Riek Walther]
Der Schwur der Barbaren
Merlin
Gifkendorf, 2002
[Ü: Regina Keil-Sagawe]
Erzähl mir vom Paradies
Merlin
Gifkendorf, 2004
[Ü: Regina Keil-Sagawe]

Der Algerier Boualem Sansal, geboren 1949, begann im Alter von fünfzig Jahren seine Karriere als Schriftsteller. Bis dahin hatte sich der promovierte Ökonom und Ingenieur auf seine Arbeit als hoher Beamter im algerischen Industrieministerium konzentriert. Das Attentat auf Präsident Boudiaf (1992), der Tod eines Freundes sowie die eigene Verfolgung in der bürgerkriegsbelasteten Heimat veranlassten ihn jedoch, sich in den neunziger Jahren mit dem Schreiben über sein Land ein inneres Exil zu schaffen. Sein Debüt »Le serment des barbares« (1999, dt. »Der Schwur der Barbaren«, 2003) erschien daher in Frankreich, wo es von der Presse gelobt und mit dem Prix du Premier Roman ausgezeichnet wurde. »Le Nouvel Observateur« feierte es als »Meisterwerk«. Der Roman, der mittlerweile nach einem Drehbuch Jorge Semprúns verfilmt wurde, beginnt zunächst wie ein Krimi. Im algerischen Städtchen Rouiba werden am selben Tag zwei Männer sehr unterschiedlichen Standes – der vermögende und unantastbare Pate der Region Moh sowie der mittellose Bakour – ermordet aufgefunden. Die Geschichte verwandelt sich allerdings schnell in eine Zustandsbeschreibung des nordafrikanischen Staates, als dem im Fall Bakour ermittelnden Kommissar klar wird, dass beide Morde zusammenhängen und einen politisch höchst brisanten Hintergrund haben. Seine Ermittlungen werden zur Suche nach den Wurzeln der terroristischen Gewalt im heutigen Algerien zwischen Korruption, Unterdrückung und Islamismus.
Sansal weist den Algeriern, die es als Nation erst seit der Unabhängigkeit von 1962 gibt, in seinen Romanen mögliche Wege zu einer eigenen Identität. Insbesondere der Titel des 2000 erschienenen Romans »L'enfant fou de l'arbre creux« (dt. »Das verrückte Kind aus dem hohlen Baum«, 2002), für den er 2001 den Michel-Dard-Literaturpreis erhielt, hat diesbezüglich symbolischen Charakter: Das Kind, das im Hof eines Zuchthauses angebunden ist, steht laut Sansal für das algerische Volk in »diesem riesigen Gefängnis Algerien. Ein infantilisiertes Volk, verblendet, durch Lügen gefesselt. Es ist an einem Punkt angekommen, an dem es weder weiß, wer es ist, woher es kommt, noch was es will.«
In Frankreich, der ehemaligen Kolonialmacht, wird Sansal wegen seines spielerischen Umgangs mit dem Französischen als Spracherneuerer gefeiert. Aufgrund der politisch explosiven Themen seiner satirischen und zugleich poetischen Romane gilt er in Algerien hingegen als Nestbeschmutzer. Dennoch bleibt er mit seiner Frau und den zwei erwachsenen Töchtern weiterhin in seiner Heimat und veröffentlicht ohne den Schutz eines Pseudonyms.
Trotz allem sprach die Heiterkeit seiner bisherigen Romane für Sansals Glauben an Algeriens Zukunft. Einen ersten Entwurf dafür stellt nun sein jüngstes Werk »Dis-moi le paradis« (2003; dt. »Erzähl mir vom Paradies«, 2004) dar.

marie-luise scherer

biography

Marie-Luise Scherer was born in Saarbrücken, Germany, in 1938. Between 1974 and 1998 she was a writer for the news magazine »Der Spiegel«, for which she meticulously researched and wrote brilliant linguistic reportages; texts which are not only extraordinary documentations, but also jewels of literary journalism. Marie-Luise Scherer has twice received the Egon-Erwin-Kirsch Prize: in 1978 for her reportage »Der Zustand, eine hilflose Person zu sein« (t: The condition of being a helpless person), and in 1980 for the family drama of a heroin addicted son »Auf Deutsch gesagt: gestrauchelt« (t: In plain language: derailed). Human beings and their destinies are registered under a »cold needlefine« gaze, which nevertheless remains committed to participation. At the same time, strikingly clear but partly terrifying panoramas emerge.
In 1988 a selection of Scherer's texts came out for the first time as a book, under the title »Ungeheurer Alltag« (t: Monstrous everyday life). Within the work one can find »Der unheimliche Ort Berlin« (t: That uncanny place Berlin), a place she enters as a »poetic commissar« (Hubert Winkels in »Die Zeit«). Her interest is always directed towards »the extreme rituals of quotidian coexistence«, »which ultimately turn extreme, just as they are grazed by Scherer's ›horrifying perception‹, wrote Angelika Overath in the »Neue Zürcher Zeitung«.
Gustav Seibt called Scherer's new book »Der Akkordeonspieler«, which appeared in 2004 in Hans Magnus Enzensberger's »Die Andere Bibliothek« series, »out-standing literature«. She chooses her subjects with ›equal attention‹: the mass murders in »Die Bestie von Paris« and the agony of the creature in the German-German »dogfrontiers« are treated with the same interest as the mundane milieu of the film and fashion world. Seibt's conclusion: »Marie-Luise Scherer can do anything«. Friedmar Appel sees her as a »physiognomist of the world of things... in the tradition of Walter Benjamin«. Arno Widmann called her »a master of clashing tendencies«, who has succeeded in »letting sentences full of the most sober reality sound as if they were from a fairy tale.« In 1994 Marie-Luise Scherer was awarded the Ludwig-Börne Prize in recognition of her distinguished performance in news reportage. The author lives in Damnatz on the Elbe.

Ungeheurer Alltag
Rowohlt
Reinbek, 1990
Der Akkordeonspieler
Eichborn
Frankfurt am Main, 2004

Marie-Luise Scherer wurde 1938 in Saarbrücken, Deutschland, geboren. Von 1974 bis 1998 war sie Autorin des Nachrichtenmagazins »Der Spiegel«, für den sie akribisch recherchierte und sprachlich brillante Reportagen schrieb; Texte, die nicht nur herausragende Dokumentationen, sondern auch Glanzstücke des literarischen Journalismus sind. Marie-Luise Scherer wurde zweimal mit dem Egon-Erwin-Kisch-Preis ausgezeichnet: 1978 für ihre Reportage »Der Zustand, eine hilflose Person zu sein«, 1980 für das Heroindrama in einer Familie »Auf deutsch gesagt: gestrauchelt«. Die Menschen und ihre Schicksale sind mit einem »kaltnadeligen« Blick erfasst, der dennoch der Anteilnahme verpflichtet bleibt. Dabei sind beeindruckend klare, teils erschreckende Panoramen entstanden.
Eine Auswahl ihrer Texte wurde 1988 unter dem Titel »Ungeheurer Alltag« erstmals als Buch veröffentlicht. Darin enthalten ist »Der unheimliche Ort Berlin«, den sie als »poetische Kommissarin« (Hubert Winkels in »Die Zeit«) betritt. Immer ist ihr »Interesse auf extreme Rituale im alltäglichen Miteinander gerichtet, die letztlich erst extrem werden, wenn Scherers ›schreckliche Wahrnehmungsfähigkeit‹ ... sie streift«, so Angelika Overath in der »Neuen Zürcher Zeitung«.
Für Gustav Seibt ist Scherers neues Buch »Der Akkordeonspieler«, 2004 in Hans Magnus Enzensbergers »Die Andere Bibliothek« erschienen, »bedeutende Literatur«. In ›gleichschwebender Aufmerksamkeit‹ wählt sie ihre Sujets: der Massenmörder in »Die Bestie von Paris«, das Leid der Kreatur an der deutsch-deutschen »Hundegrenze« sind von gleichem Interesse wie die mondänen Milieus der Film- und Modewelt. Seibts Resümee: »Marie-Luise Scherer kann alles«. Friedmar Apel sieht sie als »Physiognomikerin der Dingwelt ... in der Tradition Walter Benjamins«. Arno Widmann nannte sie »eine Meisterin der widerstrebenden Tendenzen«, der es gelungen sei »mit nüchternster Realität vollgestopfte Sätze klingen zu lassen, als stünden sie in einem Märchen«. 1994 erhielt Marie-Luise Scherer den Ludwig-Börne-Preis als Würdigung ihrer hervorragenden Leistungen im Bereich Reportage. Die Autorin lebt in Damnatz an der Elbe.

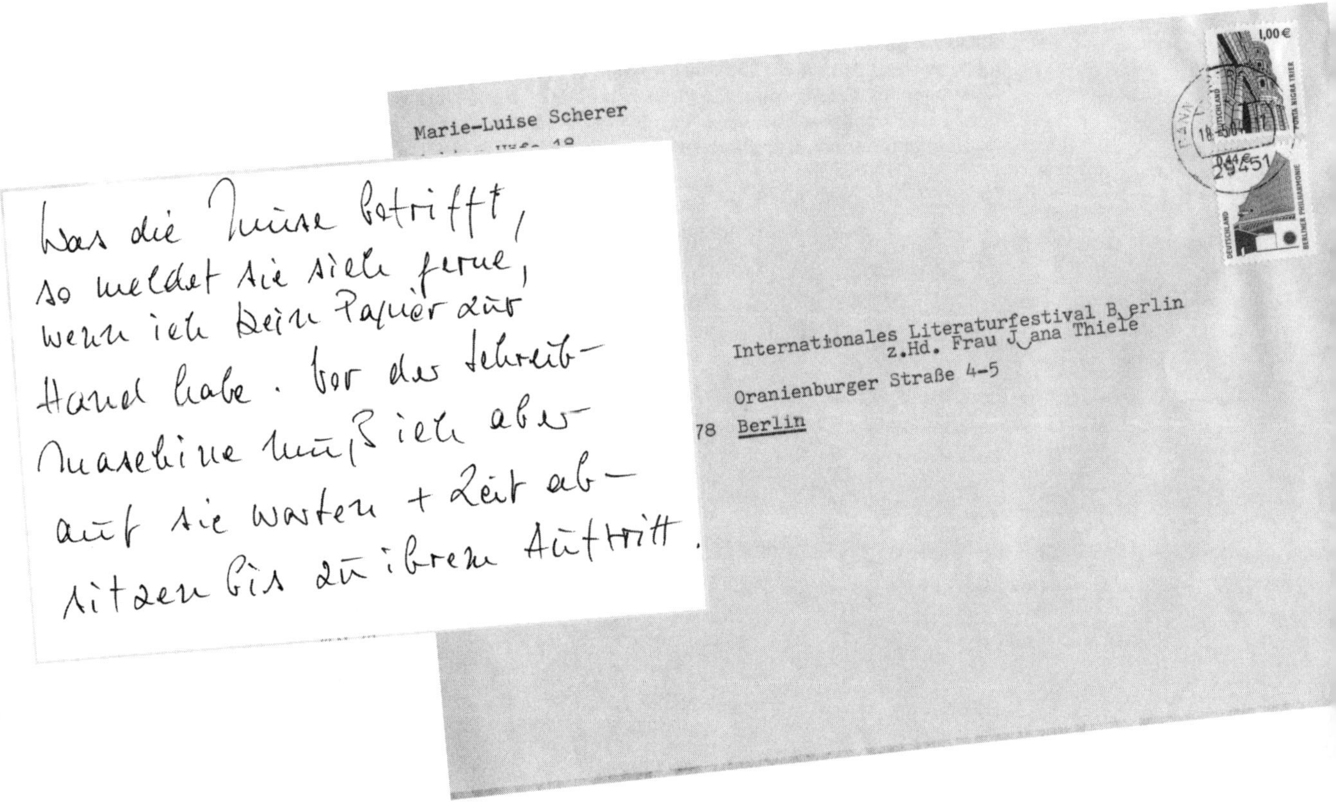
Was die Muse betrifft, so meldet sie sich gerne, wenn ich kein Papier zur Hand habe. Vor der Schreibmaschine muß ich aber auf sie warten + Zeit absitzen bis zu ihrem Auftritt.

Marie-Luise Scherer

Internationales Literaturfestival Berlin
z.Hd. Frau Jana Thiele
Oranienburger Straße 4-5
78 Berlin

alan sillitoe
biography

Alan Sillitoe was born in Nottingham in 1928. His father, a labourer, was unemployed throughout the economic depression of the 1930's, and as a child Sillitoe acquired books either by saving what pocket money he could get or borrowing them from the public library. He left school at fourteen, to work in various factories until 1946, when he joined the Royal Air Force and served as a wireless operator. After two years in Malaya he was diagnosed as having tuberculosis, and spent a year in an RAF hospital, at which time he embarked on reading the best of world literature, from Antiquity to the present day. Demobilised from the Air Force with a disability pension, he went to live in the south of France, and then Majorca, with the poet Ruth Fainlight, who later became his wife. During six years abroad he wrote half a dozen novels which failed to be published, though he was later glad that they were not. He then wrote »Saturday Night and Sunday Morning« (1958) which, after being rejected several times, appeared in 1958. The following year »The Loneliness of the Long-Distance Runner« came out. Both books received worldwide acclaim.

Never considering himself to be an »Angry Young Man«, he was nevertheless assumed to be part of the mainstream of the time, with such writers as John Osborne, Shelagh Delaney, John Braine, John Wain, Arnold Wesker and Kingsley Amis. Like these, Sillitoe introduced the realistic depiction of working people in the post-war period, though his heroes were not typical class warriors, but rather anarchic people who, regardless of so-called social standing, insisted on their own values and refused assimilation to any party or state. The problems of the individual were presented by Sillitoe with sympathy, understanding and imagination. The powerful tension reflected in his early work still stands as vintage Sillitoe. He has, however, written many more novels and short stories, half of which are set in Nottingham. The 1960's trilogy made up of: »The Death of William Posters« (1965), »A Tree on Fire« (1967) and »The Flame of Life« (1974), gave a view of the social and political currents of that controversial decade. In them the uncertain but searching protagonists turn away from the conventional family, yet eventually return to it, since they can find no better human arrangement fit to take its place.

Sillitoe is not only a novelist, having produced volumes of poetry, an autobiography (»Life Without Armour«, 1995), plays, essays, and children's books. His most recent novel »A Man of His Time«, about the life and tribulations of a Nottingham blacksmith and his family, was published this year. Alan Sillitoe lives and works in London, and has just finished another novel entitled: »Moggerhanger«.

Barbarians and Other Poems
Turret Books
London, 1973
Die Einsamkeit des Langstreckenläufers
Diogenes
Zürich, 1975
[Ü: Günther Klotz]
Samstagnacht und Sonntagmorgen
Diogenes
Zürich, 1976
[Ü: Gerda von Uslar]
The Saxon Shore Way
Hutchinson
London, 1983
Life without Armour
HarperCollins
London, 1995
Alligator Playground
Flamingo
London, 1998
Birthday
Flamingo
London, 2002
A Man of His Time
Flamingo
London, 2004

Alan Sillitoe wurde 1928 in Nottingham geboren. Sein Vater, ein Arbeiter, war während der Wirtschaftskrise in den dreißiger Jahren arbeitslos, und Sillitoe wandte sich den Büchern zu, die er sich von seinem ersparten Taschengeld kaufte oder aus der öffentlichen Bibliothek auslieh. Im Alter von vierzehn Jahren ging er von der Schule ab und arbeitete bis 1946 in verschiedenen Fabriken, später als Funker bei der Royal Air Force. Nach zwei Jahren in Malaya erkrankte er an Tuberkulose und verbrachte ein Jahr in einem Krankenhaus der RAF, währenddessen er sich dem Studium der Weltliteratur von der Antike bis zur Gegenwart widmete. Aus der Armee mit einer Versehrtenrente entlassen, lebte er mit der Schriftstellerin Ruth Fainlight, die später seine Frau wurde, in Südfrankreich und anschließend auf Mallorca. Während der sechs Jahre im Ausland schrieb Sillitoe mehrere Romane, die jedoch nicht veröffentlicht wurden, was er später für kein Unglück hielt. Dann verfasste er »Saturday Night and Sunday Morning« (dt. »Samstagnacht und Sonntagmorgen«, 1961): Das Werk erschien im Jahr 1958 – nachdem mehrere Verlage das Manuskript abgelehnt hatten. Ein Jahr später wurde »The Loneliness of the Long Distance Runner« (1959; dt. »Die Einsamkeit des Langstreckenläufers«, 1967) veröffentlicht. Beide Bücher erfuhren weltweit große Anerkennung.

Obwohl er sich selbst nie als »angry young man« sah, wurde er dennoch zur literarischen Strömung der damaligen Zeit um die Schriftsteller John Osborne, Shelagh Delaney, John Braine, John Wain, Arnold Wesker, Kingsley Amis und anderen gezählt. Wie sie führte Sillitoe die realistische Darstellung des Arbeitermilieus nach dem Krieg ein. Doch seine Helden sind keine typischen Klassenkämpfer, sondern anarchische Kraftprotze, die unabhängig von ihrem sogenannten sozialen Stand auf ihren eigenen Werten bestehen und jede Anpassung an Partei oder Staat verweigern. Die Probleme des Individuums sind bei Sillitoe mit Sympathie, Einfühlungsvermögen und Detailbewusstsein gezeichnet. Diese kraftvolle Spannung, die seine frühen Werke durchzieht, steht immer noch für den Autor Sillitoe – und doch hat er noch weitere Romane und Kurzgeschichten geschrieben, von denen die Hälfte in Nottingham spielt. So spiegelt die Trilogie »The Death of William Posters« (1965, dt. »Der Tod des William Posters«, 1969), »A Tree on Fire« (1967, dt. »Der brennende Baum«, 1975) und »The Flame of Life« (1974, dt. »Die Flamme des Lebens«, 1982) das kontroverse Jahrzehnt der sechziger Jahre mit ihren sozialen und politischen Strömungen. In diesen Werken wenden sich die unsicheren, suchenden Protagonisten von ihrem konventionellen Familienleben ab, um schließlich doch zu ihm zurückzukehren, weil sie keine bessere Form menschlichen Zusammenlebens finden können.

Sillitoe ist nicht nur Romancier; sein Werk umfasst auch Gedichtbände, die Autobiographie »Life Without Armour« (1995), Theaterstücke, Essays und Kinderbücher. Sein letzter Roman »A Man of His Time« behandelt Leben und Nöte eines Schmiedes in Nottingham und erschien dieses Jahr. Alan Sillitoe lebt und arbeitet in London. Kürzlich hat er einen neuen Roman mit dem Titel »Moggerhanger« fertiggestellt.

burkhard spinnen

biography

Burkhard Spinnen was born in Mönchengladbach, Germany, in 1956. He studied German Language and Literature, Journalism and Sociology at the University of Münster. After completing his Ph.D., he worked until 1995 as an academic assistant at the Institute of German Studies. His dissertation on the history of emblematic short prose with studies of Peter Altenberg and Karl Kraus was published in 1991 under the title »Schriftbilder« (t: Written images). His interest in short prose, however, extends beyond the purely scholarly. In the same year he made his literary debut with the publication of »Dicker Mann am Meer« (t: Fat man at sea). This volume of twelve short stories, about the abysms that lurk within seemingly normal everyday life, was awarded the aspekte-Literature Prize from ZDF in 1991. Alongside his academic, essayistic and literary texts, published in magazines such as »Freibeuter" and »Sprache im technischen Zeitalter«, Burkhard Spinnen writes reviews, for example for the »Frankfurter Allgemeine Zeitung«. He was visiting professor for Literary Aesthetics at the German Literary Institute in Leipzig from 1997 to 2000, and has been on the jury of the Klagenfurt Ingeborg Bachmann competition since 2000. Eight years before, Spinnen read his own story, »Der Pfeiler« (t: The pillar), to the jury and won the Kärtner Industrie prize. His stories show images of everyday life in the German provinces. He exposes his protagonists to small irritations through which the void of their lives of controlled torpor becomes visible. The author maintains an objective distance between himself and his characters. He describes their relation to their environment in detail and in a distinctively precise language, and as a result foregoes characterisation through psychological digressions of any kind. The second volume of stories, »Kalte Ente« (1994; t: Cold duck), followed the novel »Langer Samstag« (t: Long Saturday), in which the depiction of a failed relationship between a administrative lawyers and a business advisor allows, again and again, for small, quirky mind games and far flung anecdotes. Burkhard Spinnen's fascination with the short story form is also manifested in the sixty short stories of »Trost und Reserve« (1996; t: Comfort and reserve) and in his autobiographical prose miniatures, »Lego-Steine« (2004; t: Lego blocks). Alongside the distinction of having received the Konrad Adenauer grant in 1999, he has been awarded the Oldenburg Children and Youth's Literature Prize for the children's novel »Belgische Riesen« (2000) and the Herbert Quandt Media Prize for the exceptional biography of the Swabian enterpreneur Walter Lindenmaier, entitled »Der schwarze Grat« (2003; t: The black ridge). His most recent publication is »Der Reservetorwart« (2004; t: The reserve goalkeeper). Burkhard Spinnen lives in Münster.

Dicker Mann am Meer
FVA
Frankfurt am Main, 1991
Langer Samstag
Schöffling
Frankfurt am Main, 1995
Belgische Riesen
Schöffling
Frankfurt am Main, 2000
Kalte Ente
Goldmann
München, 2002
Schriftbilder
Schöffling
Frankfurt am Main, 2003
Der schwarze Grat
Schöffling
Frankfurt am Main, 2003
Lego-Steine
Schöffling
Frankfurt am Main, 2004
[Ill: Kai Voigtmann]
Der Reservetorwart
Schöffling
Frankfurt am Main, 2004

Burkhard Spinnen wurde 1956 in Mönchengladbach, Nordrhein-Westfalen, geboren. Er studierte Germanistik, Publizistik und Soziologie an der Universität Münster. Nach seiner Promotion war er dort bis 1995 wissenschaftlicher Assistent am Germanistischen Institut. Seine Dissertation über die Geschichte der emblematischen Kurzprosa mit Studien zu Peter Altenberg und Karl Kraus wurde 1991 unter dem Titel »Schriftbilder« publiziert. Seine Auseinandersetzung mit kurzen Prosatexten geht jedoch über ein rein wissenschaftliches Interesse hinaus. Im selben Jahr erschien mit »Dicker Mann am Meer« auch sein literarisches Debüt. Der Band mit zwölf Kurzgeschichten über die Abgründe des vermeintlich normalen Alltags wurde 1991 mit dem aspekte-Literaturpreis des ZDF ausgezeichnet. Neben wissenschaftlichen, essayistischen und literarischen Texten, die u. a. in Magazinen wie »Freibeuter« und »Sprache im technischen Zeitalter« veröffentlicht wurden, schreibt Burkhard Spinnen Rezensionen, beispielsweise für die »Frankfurter Allgemeine Zeitung«. Von 1997 bis 2000 war er Gastdozent für literarische Ästhetik am Deutschen Literaturinstitut in Leipzig. Seit 2000 ist er Juror beim Klagenfurter Ingeborg-Bachmann-Wettbewerb. Acht Jahre zuvor hatte er dort selbst als Autor vor der Jury seine Erzählung »Der Pfeiler« gelesen und den Preis der Kärntner Industrie erhalten. In seinen Geschichten zeichnet er Bilder des bundesdeutschen Provinzalltags. Er setzt seine Protagonisten kleinen Irritationen aus, durch die die Abgründe ihres bis zur Erstarrung geordneten Lebens sichtbar werden. Der Autor wahrt zu seinen Figuren nüchterne Distanz. Er beschreibt ihr Verhältnis zur Umwelt detailliert in einer unverwechselbar präzisen Sprache und verzichtet konsequent auf jegliche Charakterisierung durch psychologische Exkurse. Dem zweiten Erzählband »Kalte Ente« (1994) folgte 1995 der Roman »Langer Samstag«, der in der Schilderung einer missglückenden Beziehung zwischen einem Verwaltungsjuristen und einer Unternehmensberaterin immer wieder Raum für kleine verschrobene Gedankenspiele und abseitige Anekdoten lässt. Burkhard Spinnens Faszination für die erzählerische Kurzform zeigt sich u. a. in den sechzig Kürzestgeschichten von »Trost und Reserve« (1996) und in seinen autobiographischen Prosaminiaturen »Lego-Steine« (2004). Er erhielt neben den genannten Auszeichnungen den Literaturpreis der Konrad-Adenauer-Stiftung 1999, den Oldenburger Kinder- und Jugendliteraturpreis für den Kinderroman »Belgische Riesen« (2000) sowie 2003 den Herbert-Quandt-Medien-Preis für die ungewöhnliche Biographie des schwäbischen Unternehmers Walter Lindenmaier mit dem Titel »Der schwarze Grat« (2003). Zuletzt erschien »Der Reservetorwart« (2004). Burkhard Spinnen lebt in Münster.

peter truschner

biography

Peter Truschner was born in Klagenfurt in 1967 and grew up in Kärnten, Austria, in Maria Saal, the village already immortalised in literature by Thomas Bernhard and Peter Turrini. He studied communications, philosophy and politics at Salzburg University and from 1990 onwards his work was published in various cultural and literary magazines as a critic and author. In 1997 his play »Plexiglaswelten« was premiered in the TOI House Theatre in Salzburg, and in 1999 he was awarded the Austrian state grant for literature.
In addition to the narratives of Robert Musil, Truschner names in particular works of non-Austrian writers such as Harold Brodkey, Sylvia Plath and Vladimir Nabokov as »crucial readings« for his highly praised novel »Schlangenkind« (t: Snake child). For this novel, Truschner received the prize for literary debuts of the Austrian Chancellery (2001) as well as the yearly scholarship of the Austrian »Literatur-Mechana« 2002.
»One day life fell upon my grandfather like a drop of resin onto a fly. Whoever knew him swore that he moved in the resin as if nothing had happened.« Thus the brilliant start to one of the most highly regarded debut novels of 2001; »Schlangenkind« is a story which reconstructs, in poetic sobriety, memories of the good and evil spirits of a childhood in the country and a youth in the city: a coming of age tale. The chronicle starts in the village of Poppichl in Kärnten in the 1970's: the boy, born illegitimately, grows up on the dilapidated farm of his grandparents, under the roof of a lethargic and authoritarian grandfather yet enclosed by the warmth of his grandmother. With great precision, the first person narrator immerses himself in the sensory details of his childhood and here perceives his grandfather as an object, as a man who has »given up conscious life«. When the mother of the boy, who had run away many years before, returns and takes her child with her to the city, the false tranquillity of the coarse upbringing crumbles, and with it the life compromise of the grandmother. Robbed of the youth which surrounded her, she remains in paralised solitude. The son lives with his mother in Salzburg, but the closeness of the previously absent mother awakens rivalry and the need for boundaries rather than the happiness anticipated. »Tuschner tells of the pitiful, hopeless contacts of his human figures, of the joylessness of their relationships – but with special preciseness of the rare feelings of happiness which are actually only aroused through tender contact«, commented the dramaturg Hermann Beil on »Schlangenkind«, in which Peter Turrini also recognised the village of his youth: »Here is someone who lends his distinctive poetry to realism«. Peter Truschner has lived in Berlin since 1999.

Schlangenkind
Zsolnay, Wien, 2001

Dies wäre also mein
"Musen- und- Inspirations"-
Beitrag.
Herzliche Grüße
Peter Truschner

Peter Truschner, geboren 1967 in Klagenfurt, ist im österreichischen Kärnten aufgewachsen, in Maria Saal – dem Ort, der schon durch Thomas Bernhard und Peter Turrini literarisch verewigt wurde. Er studierte Kommunikationswissenschaften, Philosophie und Politikwissenschaft an der Universität Salzburg und veröffentlichte ab 1990 als Rezensent und Autor in diversen Kultur- und Literaturzeitschriften. 1997 wurde sein Stück »Plexiglaswelten« im TOI-Haus-Theater in Salzburg uraufgeführt; 1999 erhielt er das Österreichische Staatsstipendium für Literatur.
Als »entscheidende Lektüre« für seinen von der Kritik hoch gelobten Roman »Schlangenkind« vermerkt Truschner neben den Erzählungen Robert Musils vor allem Werke nicht-österreichischer Autoren wie Harold Brodkey, Sylvia Plath oder Vladimir Nabokov. Für diesen Roman erhielt er 2001 den für literarische Debüts vergebenen Preis des österreichischen Kanzleramtes sowie 2002 das Jahresstipendium der österreichischen »Literatur-Mechana«.
»Eines Tages war das Leben auf meinen Großvater herabgefallen wie ein Tropfen Harz auf eine Fliege. Wer ihn kannte, schwor, dass er sich im Harz bewegte, als wäre nichts weiter geschehen«, so der fulminante Auftakt zu einem der meistbeachteten Debütromane des Jahres 2001. »Schlangenkind« ist eine Geschichte, die in poetischer Lakonie Erinnerungen an die guten und bösen Geister einer Kindheit auf dem Lande und einer Jugend in der Stadt rekonstruiert: ein Entwicklungsroman. Die Chronik des Heranwachsens beginnt in dem Dorf Poppichl im Kärnten der siebziger Jahre: Der unehelich geborene Junge wächst auf dem heruntergekommenen großelterlichen Bauernhof auf, unter dem Dach eines trägen, autoritären Großvaters, umhüllt von der Wärme der Großmutter. Mit großer Präzision versenkt sich der Ich-Erzähler in die sinnlichen Details seiner Kindheit und nimmt darin den Großvater wie ein gegenständliches Phänomen war, als einen Mann, der »das bewusste Leben aufgegeben« hat. Als die Mutter des Jungen, die schon längst das Weite gesucht hatte, zurückkommt und ihr Kind zu sich in die Stadt holt, zerbricht die trügerische Beschaulichkeit der rauhbeinigen Erziehung, zerbröselt auch der Lebenskompromiss der Großmutter. Jeglicher Jugend in ihrer Umgebung beraubt, versinkt sie in lähmender Einsamkeit. Der Sohn lebt nun bei seiner Mutter in Salzburg, doch die Nähe der zuvor Vermissten weckt eher Rivalität und Bedürfnis nach Abgrenzung als erwartetes Glück. Truschner »erzählt von den armseligen, hoffnungslosen Berührungen seiner Menschenfiguren, von der Freudlosigkeit ihrer Berührungsbeziehungen – mit besonderer Genauigkeit aber von jenen seltenen Glücksgefühlen, die tatsächlich nur durch zärtliche Berührung entfacht werden«, bemerkt der Dramaturg Hermann Beil zu »Schlangenkind«, in dem auch Peter Turrini das Dorf seiner Jugend wiedererkennt: »Da ist einer, der dem Realismus seine unverwechselbare Poesie hinzufügt.« Seit 1999 lebt Peter Truschner in Berlin.

Velazquez' *Königin Maria Anna* hat kein Leben, sondern eine Funktion. Die Uniform ihrer Herkunft, ihres Ranges war von Beginn an über jenes Nackte, Unfaßliche gestülpt, das das Leben dieser Frau hätte sein können. Wohl nur selten hat eine Monarchin so unverhohlen zum Ausdruck gebracht, wie unwohl sie sich angesichts des höfischen Korsetts ihrer Haut fühlt. Wohl nie zuvor hat ein Maler des Hofs sich erst gar nicht bemüht, diesen Ausdruck zu kaschieren – im Gegenteil. Und anstatt wenigstens dem Widerstandsgeist seiner Herrscherin zu huldigen, hinterläßt sein Pinselstrich die Konturen von unspezifischem Unwillen und pubertärem Trotz auf dem Gesicht der Frau, die keine Kindheit hatte.
Was dieses Portrait für mich – immer wieder, wenn ich es betrachte – so inspirierend, ja, beglückend macht, ist, daß es (auch) davon erzählt, was in einer einzigen ‚Einstellung' – einer Pose, einer Mimik, einer Situation – einem Menschenleben an Geschichte(n) eingeschrieben werden kann. Weit über das Biographische hinaus gelingt es Velazquez in der Beiläufigkeit eines Portraits ein ganzes *System* zu imaginieren – sowie Wert und Schicksal des Einzelnen darin.
Wer kann solcherlei schon von sich und seiner Arbeit behaupten?

ayu utami

biography

Ayu Utami was born in Bogor near the Indonesian capital of Jakarta in 1968. She is one of the most prominent representatives of a new generation of Indonesian writers, who, even before the end of the Suharto regime, were already openly addressing the social and cultural conflicts of the island state, and today accompany the transition to democracy with a critical voice. While still studying Russian language and literature at the Universitas Indonesia in Jakarta, Utami began publishing reports and essays in various newspapers. As co-founder of a union of freelance journalists declared illegal by the government, she was banned from practising her occupation in 1994, and some of her colleagues were arrested. She continued her journalistic work underground, which included the anonymous publication of a black book on corruption in the Suharto regime.

With her debut novel »Saman« (1998) Ayu Utami achieved more than just her breakthrough as a writer – in her native country the book was reprinted many times and was celebrated as a literary sensation. »Saman« was published only a few weeks before General Suharto was removed from power, and its publication was a sign of the approaching political change. Utami treats social taboos in an open way, thereby breaking with Indonesian literature to date. She writes freely about love and sexuality and thematises the difficult relationship between Muslims and Christians – as well as the hatred towards the Chinese minority. Her novel focuses on the story of a Catholic priest, who through his advocacy work for oppressed small farmers, joins the Indonesian resistance, falls in love, gives up the priesthood and emigrates to New York. At the same time the story tells the fate of a group of young women, who self-confidently make decisions about their lives and renounce the traditional gender roles.

Utami's prose is lively and modern, and as such reflects the richness of Indonesian oral tradition. The author masterfully switches between various narrative perspectives, locations and time scales, links dream sequences and old myths with descriptions of the political and societal relations in Indonesia in the 1990's. »Saman« is the first in a cycle of novels, the second part of which was published in 2001 under the title »Larung.« Both of her novels have been published in Dutch. In 1998 »Saman« was awarded the prize for best Indonesian novel; in 2000 Ayu Utami received the renowned Prins Claus Prijs from the Dutch government. Today Ayu Utami lives in Jakarta, and since 1998 has been co-publisher of the culture magazine »Kalam«.

Saman
KPG
Jakarta, 2001
Larung
KPG
Jakarta, 2001
Larung
Breda
De Geus, 2001
[Ü: Maya Sutedja-Liem, Monique Soesman]
Saman missie
De Geus
Breda, 2001
[Ü: Maya Sutedja-Liem, Monique Soesman]
Si parasit lajang
GagasMedia
Jakarta, 2003

Ayu Utami wurde 1968 in Bogor, nahe der indonesischen Hauptstadt Jakarta, geboren. Sie gehört zu den prominentesten Vertretern einer neuen Generation indonesischer Schriftsteller, die sich schon vor dem Ende der Suharto-Herrschaft offen mit den sozialen und kulturellen Konflikten des Inselstaates auseinandersetzte und heute den Aufbruch in die Demokratie mit kritischer Stimme begleitet. Bereits während ihres Studiums der russischen Sprache und Literatur an der Universitas Indonesia in Jakarta begann Utami damit, Reportagen und Essays in verschiedenen Zeitschriften zu publizieren. Als Mitbegründerin einer Vereinigung unabhängiger Journalisten, die von der Regierung für illegal erklärt wurde, belegte man sie 1994 mit einem Berufsverbot und verhaftete einige ihrer Kollegen. Im Untergrund führte sie ihre journalistische Arbeit fort, unter anderem als anonyme Verfasserin eines Schwarzbuchs über die Korruption des Suharto-Regimes.

Mit ihrem Debütroman »Saman« (1998) gelang Ayu Utami nicht nur der Durchbruch als Schriftstellerin, vielmehr erreichte das Buch in ihrer Heimat sogar Höchstauflagen und wurde als literarische Sensation gefeiert. »Saman« erschien nur wenige Wochen vor der Entmachtung General Suhartos, gleichsam als Vorbote des politischen Wandels. Die Offenheit, mit der die junge Autorin gesellschaftliche Tabus behandelte, stellte einen Bruch mit der bisherigen indonesischen Literatur dar: Utami schrieb freizügig über Liebe und Sexualität, thematisierte das schwierige Verhältnis zwischen Muslimen und Christen sowie den Hass auf die chinesische Minderheit. Im Zentrum ihres Romans steht die Geschichte eines katholischen Priesters, der über sein Engagement für unterdrückte Kleinbauern zum indonesischen Widerstand stößt, sich dabei verliebt, sein Priesteramt aufgibt und nach New York emigriert. Gleichzeitig wird das Schicksal einer Gruppe junger Frauen erzählt, die selbstbewusst über ihr Leben bestimmen und sich den traditionellen Rollenzuweisungen verweigern.

Utami schreibt in einer lebendigen und modernen Prosa, in der sich auch die reiche indonesische Tradition der mündlichen Überlieferung widerspiegelt. Virtuos wechselt die Autorin zwischen verschiedenen Erzählperspektiven, Schauplätzen und Zeitebenen, verknüpft Traumsequenzen und alte Mythen mit Schilderungen der politischen und gesellschaftlichen Verhältnisse im Indonesien der neunziger Jahre. »Saman« bildet den Anfang eines Romanzyklus, dessen zweiter Teil 2001 unter dem Titel »Larung« erschien. Ihre beiden Romane erschienen in niederländischer Übersetzung. 1998 wurde »Saman« als bester indonesischer Roman ausgezeichnet, im Jahr 2000 erhielt Ayu Utami den renommierten Prins Claus Prijs der Niederländischen Regierung. Ayu Utami lebt heute in Jakarta und ist seit 1998 Mitherausgeberin des Kulturmagazins »Kalam«.

gore vidal

biography

Gore Vidal was born in Westpoint, New York, in 1925. His full name is Eugene Luther Gore Vidal, which refers back to his grandfather, Senator Thomas Pryor Gore, and thus, to his descent from one of the most politically influential families in the USA. He entered the army at eighteen and served 1945 as first mate on a transport ship in the Aleutian Islands near Alaska. During this time he wrote his first novel, »Williwaw«, a seafaring tale in the style of Melville and Hemingway, published in 1946. After its success he gave up the job at a publishing house that he had accepted upon his discharge. In 1946 he moved to Guatemala and worked as a freelance writer, and in 1948 embarked on extensive travels through Europe, during which he met literary greats including André Gide. That same year his novel »The City and the Pillar« was published, which caused a stir due to the appearance for the first time of a homosexual protagonist who was neither eccentric nor moved in a dubious milieu, but came rather from the petit-bourgeois middle class. Despite this first bestseller, Vidal failed to receive critical recognition in the years that followed. He turned to writing detective stories, scripts for film and television, as well as Broadway plays and essays.

In addition Vidal exhibited the political acumen that he had acquired through his familial ties to America's political elite. Since the mid 1950's his engagement in US politics has been highly visible. He ran for political office and belonged to John F. Kennedy's »inner circle«.

His minutely researched historical novels, in which ancient and American history and its ambivalent heroes such as Julian, Xerxes, Lincoln and Burr become characters, are a facet of his prolific and polymathic oeuvre. Another facet is the parodic, which finds expression in his play with travesty like in »Myra Breckinridge« (1968), or in »Messiah« (1954) and »Live from Golgotha« (1992), when questioning the Christian sanctimoniousness of society. His reputation as a biting and pertinent commentator on the political landscape of the United States is legendary. Current evidence for this lies in the volume of essays »Perpetual War for Perpetual Peace« (2002) and »Imperial America« (2004), in which he criticises above all US foreign policy. After many years in Italy, Gore Vidal once more lives mainly in the United States.

Hollywood
Goldmann
München, 1995
[Ü: Günter Panske]

Palimpsest
Goldmann
München, 1998
[Ü: Friedrich Griese]

Das goldene Zeitalter
Knaus
München, 2001
[Ü: Silvia Morawetz]

Ewiger Krieg für ewigen Frieden
eva
Hamburg, 2002
[Ü: Bernhard Jendricke, Barbara Steckhan]

Lincoln
Goldmann
München, 2002
[Ü: Christian Spiel, Rudolf Hermstein]

Bocksgesang
eva
Hamburg, 2003
[Ü: Bernhard Jendricke, Rita Seuß]

Die vergessliche Nation
eva
Hamburg, 2004
[Ü: ????????]

Gore Vidal wurde 1925 in Westpoint, New York, geboren. Sein vollständiger Taufname, Eugene Luther Gore Vidal, verweist auf seinen Großvater, den Senator Thomas Pryor Gore, und damit auf seine Herkunft aus einer der politisch einflußreichsten Familien der USA. Mit achtzehn Jahren trat er in die Armee ein und diente 1945 als Stabsobermaat auf einem Transportschiff in den Alëuten vor Alaska. Zu dieser Zeit entstand sein erster Roman »Williwaw«, eine an Hemingway und Melville orientierte Seefahrergeschichte, die er 1946 veröffentlichte. Nach diesem ersten Erfolg gab er seine Stellung bei einem Verlag, die er nach der Ausmusterung angenommen hatte, auf. Als freier Schriftsteller zog er 1946 nach Guatemala und brach 1948 zu einer ausgedehnten Europareise auf, in deren Verlauf er mit literarischen Größen wie z. B. André Gide persönlich bekannt wurde. Im gleichen Jahr wurde sein Roman »The City and the Pillar« (dt. »Geschlossener Kreis«, 1986) veröffentlicht, der die Öffentlichkeit schockierte, weil in ihm erstmals ein homosexueller Protagonist agierte, der weder exzentrisch war noch sich in einem zweifelhaften Milieu bewegte, sondern aus der kleinbürgerlichen Mitte der Gesellschaft stammte. Trotz dieses ersten Bestsellers blieb ihm die Anerkennung der Kritik in den Folgejahren verwehrt. Vidal wandte sich daraufhin Detektivgeschichten, Drehbüchern für Film und Fernsehen sowie Broadway-Stücken und Essays zu.

Nicht zuletzt durch die familiäre Nähe zu den Mächtigen des Landes entwickelte Vidal politisches Gespür. Seit Mitte der fünfziger Jahre war sein aktives Engagement in der Politik der Vereinigten Staaten unübersehbar, er kandidierte für politische Ämter und gehörte dem ›inner circle‹ von John F. Kennedy an.

Minutiös recherchierte historische Romane, in denen antike und amerikanische Geschichte und ihre ambivalenten Helden wie Julian, Xerxes, Lincoln und Burr charakterisiert werden, spiegeln eine Facette seines produktiven, in allen Sparten beheimateten Œvres. Eine andere ist die parodistische Komponente, die z. B. im Spiel mit der Travestie, wie in »Myra Breckinridge« (1968; dt. 1969), deutlich wird oder in »Messiah« (1954; dt. »Messias«, 1977) und »Live from Golgotha« (1992; dt. »Golgatha live«, 1993), wenn die christlich-scheinheiligen Fundamente der Gesellschaft infrage gestellt werden. Sein Ruf als bissiger und präziser Kommentator der politischen Verhältnisse in den USA ist legendär. Aktueller Beleg dafür sind seine auch in deutscher Übersetzung erschienenen Essaybände »Perpetual War for Perpetual Peace« (2002; dt. »Ewiger Krieg für ewigen Frieden«, 2002) und »Die vergessliche Nation« (2004), in denen er vor allem die amerikanische Außenpolitik kritisiert. Nach vielen Jahren in Italien lebt Gore Vidal nun hauptsächlich wieder in den USA.

eliot weinberger
biography

Eliot Weinberger was born in 1949 in New York City, where he still lives. At the age of 19, he published his first book, a translation of poetry by the later Nobel prizewinner Octavio Paz. Since 1970 Weinberger has translated numerous authors from the Spanish (including Octavio Paz, Jorge Luis Borges, and Vicente Huidobro) as well as from the Chinese (Bei Dao). He has edited anthologies of American and classical Chinese poetry, and in 1999 received the prize of the National Book Critics Circle for his edition of Borges' »Selected Non-Fictions«. In 1986, he published his first book of essays »Works on Paper«. Six of his books are now available in English, including »Karmic Traces« (2000) and a collection of recent political writings entitled »9/12« (2003). For the support he has given to Hispanic literature in the US, he was the first to receive the PEN/Kolovakos Award in 1992. In 2000 he was the first US writer to be honoured with the Order of the Aztec Eagle from the Mexican government. He is prominently featured in the »Visitor's Guide to Iceland«. His work has been translated into some twenty languages. In Germany, he regularly appears in »Lettre International« and a selection of his essays (»Kaskaden«) was published in 2003. »He has seemingly read, read about, or seen firsthand practically everything on planet Earth«, writes the »Multicultural Review« about Eliot Weinberger. And indeed there do not appear to be any limits to the essayist's subject matter – his texts are dedicated to the love life of guppies and naked mole rats, MTV and Icelandic sagas, saints and poets, precolonial India and the civil war in Rwanda. Even formally he uses the full scope of what he sees as the unlimited potential of the genre, and many of his texts, while strictly »non-fiction«, are closer to prose poetry or narrative than traditional essays. Although at first glance these texts appear very heterogeneous, there is nothing random about them. The political reality of our time together with literature are what constitute our world, which Weinberger discovers anew. There is one criteria that his essays must always fulfill: »I never make things up«, says Weinberger, referring to the verifiability of all of the seemingly fantastic details. »His work« writes the »Times Literary Supplement«, »makes you sit up in your seat.«

Bakers have days when they don't feel like making strudel,
but they don't see this as a metaphysical problem.
Writers, by their nature, imagine things,
and they enjoy pretending their lonely-typist
existence is an epic of struggle and an opera
of passion.
When a writer writes about writing, don't believe
a word, including this one.

Nineteen Ways of Looking at Wang Wei
Moyer Bell
Mount Kisco, 1987
The Collected Poems of Octavio Paz (Ed.)
New Directions
New York, 1987
Outside Stories
New Directions
New York, 1992
Karmic Traces
New Directions
New York, 2002
9/12: New York After
Prickly Paradigm Press
Chicago, 2003
Feldnotizen zur Dichtung
AltaQuito
Göttingen, 2003
[Ü: Ingrid und Reinhard Harbaum]
Kaskaden
Suhrkamp
Frankfurt a. M., 2003
[Ü: Peter Torberg]
The New Directions Anthology of Classical Chinese Poetry (Ed.)
New Directions
New York, 2003

Eliot Weinberger wurde 1949 in New York City geboren, wo er auch heute lebt. Bereits mit 19 Jahren veröffentlichte er seinen ersten Band mit Übersetzungen von Gedichten des späteren Nobelpreisträgers Octavio Paz. Seit 1970 folgten zahlreiche Übersetzungen aus dem Spanischen (u. a. Paz, Jorge Luis Borges, Vicente Huidobro) sowie aus dem Chinesischen (Bei Dao). Er edierte Anthologien amerikanischer und chinesischer Lyrik und wurde für seine Ausgabe der »Selected Non-Fictions« von Borges 1999 mit dem Preis des National Book Critics Circle ausgezeichnet. Mit »Works on Paper« erschien 1986 sein erster Band mit Essays. Inzwischen liegen auf Englisch sechs Bände vor, darunter »Karmic Traces« (2000) sowie unter dem Titel »9/12« (2003) eine Sammlung aktueller politischer Texte. Für seinen Beitrag zur Förderung hispanischer Literatur in den USA erhielt er 1992 als erster Preisträger den P.E.N./Kolovakos Award. 2000 zeichnete ihn die mexikanische Regierung als ersten US-amerikanischen Schriftsteller mit dem Order of the Aztec Eagle aus. Hervorgehoben wird er außerdem im »Visitor's Guide to Iceland«. Sein Werk wurde in rund zwanzig Sprachen übersetzt. In Deutschland schreibt er regelmäßig in »Lettre International«, eine Auswahl seiner Essays erschien 2003 unter dem Titel »Kaskaden«.
»Er hat ganz offenbar praktisch alles auf dem Planeten Erde gelesen, darüber gelesen oder mit eigenen Augen gesehen«, schreibt die »Multicultural Review« über Eliot Weinberger. Und tatsächlich scheint es für den Essayisten keine thematischen Grenzen zu geben – seine Texte widmen sich dem Liebesleben von Guppies und Nacktmullen, MTV und isländischen Sagen, Heiligen und Dichtern, dem präkolonialen Indien und dem bürgerkriegserschütterten Ruanda. Selbst formal nutzt er das in seinen Augen unbegrenzte Potential der Gattung in seiner ganzen Breite aus. So ähneln viele seiner Texte eher Prosagedichten oder Erzählungen als traditionellen Essays – auch wenn sie keineswegs fiktiv sind. Doch obgleich diese Texte auf den ersten Blick äußerst heterogen anmuten, wirken sie doch niemals beliebig. Immer stehen die politische Realität unserer Zeit und die Literatur hinter dieser Welt, die Weinberger neu entdeckt. Und immer müssen seine Essays einem Maßstab genügen: »Ich erfinde nie etwas«, behauptet Weinberger und verweist damit auf die Nachprüfbarkeit aller noch so phantastisch erscheinenden Details. »Sein Werk«, so das »Times Literary Supplement«, »verändert die Sicht auf die Dinge.«

Bäcker haben so Tage, an denen ihnen nicht danach ist, Strudel zu backen, aber sie betrachten das nicht als metaphysisches Problem.

Schriftsteller, ihrem Wesen entsprechend, stellen sich Dinge vor, und es macht ihnen Spaß, sich ihr Dasein eines einsamen Schreibers als Epos von Kämpfen und Oper von Leidenschaften auszumalen.

Schreibt ein Schriftsteller vom Schreiben, glaub ihm kein Wort, auch dieses nicht.

xi chuan

biography

Xi Chuan (real name Liu Jun) was born in Xuzhou, in the Jiangsu province of the People's Republic of China, in 1963. He studied English at the University of Peking from 1981 to 1985, and after his studies worked as an editor for the magazine »Huangqiu« (t: Globe), of the Chinese press agency Xinhua. He later taught English and Classical Chinese Literature at the Central Academy for Fine Arts in Beijing. Although his poems, in the style of the »New Poetry«, and his essays were not published until 1985, Xi Chuan has been since his student days a name on the literary scene. In 1988, together with friends, he founded the poetry journal »Qingxiang« (t: Tendency), which was, however, banned after three issues. Between 1990 and 1995 he worked as an editor for »Modern Han Poetry«, and in 1996 was elected to the board of directors of the Chinese Poets Organisation.

Xi Chuan is especially known for his long prose-poems. Among his most important works are »Zhijing« (1992; Eng. »Salute«, 1999) and »Ying de Huayu« (1999; t: What the eagle says), in which he reflects, in ninety-nine chapters, on things such as »the harmfulness and frightfulness of thinking«, »on solitude, that is, on unfulfilled wishes«, or »on false causality and real coincidence in dark rooms«. Xi Chuan has so far published four volumes of poetry, among them »Xugou de jiapu« (1997; t: A fictitious genealogy) and »Dayi ru ci« (1997; t: This is the idea), a play and three volumes of essays. He is furthermore featured in numerous national and international anthologies. In 1997 he edited the Collected Works of the writer Hai Zhi, who committed suicide in 1989. Xi Chuan also works as a translator, mainly of poetry. In addition to African and English poetry, he has translated works by Ezra Pound, Jorge Luis Borges and Czesław Miłosz into Chinese. His own poetry has been translated into several languages and has been awarded numerous prizes, among them the Modern Chinese Poetry Prize 1994 and the Anne-Kao-Prize 1995, as well as the national Luxun Prize. A series of grants enabled him long stays abroad, including in India, the United States and the artists residence Schloss Wiepersdorf in Germany. Xi Chuan lives in Beijing, where he works for the New China News Agency.

Dayi ru ci
Literature & Art Press
Hunan, 1997
Xugou de jiapu
Peace Press
Peking, 1997
Die Diskurse des Adlers
projekt
Bochum/Freiburg, 2004
[Ü: Brigitte Höhenrieder, Peter Hoffmann und Tübinger Arbeitskreis Chinesische Literatur]

Xi Chuan (eigentlich Liu Jun) wurde 1963 in Xuzhou, in der Provinz Jiangsu, Volksrepublik China, geboren. Von 1981 bis 1985 studierte er Englisch an der Universität in Peking. Nach dem Studium war er zunächst Redakteur für das Magazin »Huangqiu« (Ü: Globus) der chinesischen Presseagentur Xinhua. Später unterrichtete er englische und klassische chinesische Literatur an der Zentralakademie der Schönen Künste in Peking. Obwohl er seine Gedichte im Stil der »Neuen Poesie« und seine Essays erst nach 1985 veröffentlichte, hatte Xi Chuan schon zu Studienzeiten einen Namen in der literarischen Szene. 1988 gründete er mit Freunden das Lyrikmagazin »Qingxiang« (Ü: Tendenz), das jedoch nach nur drei Ausgaben verboten wurde. Von 1990 bis 1995 war er einer der Herausgeber von »Modern Han Poetry«. 1996 wurde er in den Vorstand des chinesischen Dichterverbandes gewählt.
Xi Chuan ist insbesondere für seine langen Prosa-Dichtungen bekannt. Zu seinen wichtigsten Texten zählen »Zhijing« (1992; Ü: Gruß) und »Ying de Huayu« (1999; dt. »Die Diskurse des Adlers«, 2004), mit dem er in neunundneunzig Abschnitten etwa »über die Schädlich- und Schrecklichkeit des Denkens«, »über die Einsamkeit, d. h. über unerfüllte Wünsche« oder »über falsche Kausalität und echten Zufall in dunklen Zimmern« sinniert. Bisher hat Xi Chuan vier Lyrikbände veröffentlicht, darunter »Xugou de jiapu« (1997; Ü: Ein fiktiver Stammbaum) und »Dayi ru ci« (1997; Ü: Dies ist die Idee), ein Theaterstück und drei Essaybände. Außerdem ist er in zahlreichen in- und ausländischen Anthologien vertreten. 1997 gab er die Gesammelten Werke des Schriftstellers Hai Zi heraus, der sich 1989 das Leben genommen hatte. Xi Chuan ist auch als Übersetzer, vor allem von Gedichten, tätig. Neben afrikanischer und englischer Lyrik übertrug er Werke von Ezra Pound, Jorge Luis Borges und Czesław Miłosz ins Chinesische. Seine eigenen Texte wurden in mehrere Sprachen übersetzt und mit zahlreichen renommierten Preisen ausgezeichnet, u. a. mit dem Modern Chinese Poetry Prize 1994, dem Anne-Kao-Preis 1995 sowie 2001 mit dem nationalen Luxun Preis. Mehrere Stipendien ermöglichten ihm längere Aufenthalte im Ausland, etwa in Indien, den USA und im Künstlerhaus Schloss Wiepersdorf in Deutschland. Xi Chuan lebt in Peking, wo er für die New China News Agency tätig ist.

internationale kinder- und jugendliteratur

maría teresa andruetto
azouz begag
martha brooks
melvin burgess
malika ferdjoukh
klaus hagerup
daniel hevier
louis jensen
michèle lemieux
per nilsson
anna onichimowska
mario ramos
nasrin siege
grégoire solotareff
jutta treiber
mohammad reza yousefi
kazumi yumoto

maría teresa andruetto
biography

María Teresa Andruetto was born in 1954 in Arroyo Cabral, in the Argentinian province of Córdoba where she still lives today. After studying Literature at the Universidad Nacional de Córdoba she specialised in Children's and Young Adults' Literature. She worked as editor at »Piedra Libre«, a literary magazine for children and adolescents, and played a part in the founding of a research centre for children's and youth literature, to whose board of directors she belonged for nine years. Since the end of the 1980's she has published scores of short stories, novels, poems and plays for adults, children and young adults.
Her novel »Stefano« (1997; German: »Stefanos weite Reise«, 2003) was her first novel for adolescents to appear in German. The book tells the story of Stefano, who in the 1940's migrated to Argentina to escape the miserable conditions of his life in the Italian Piemont. Following an adventurous crossover, Stefano initially eked out a living by simple jobs at a hotel for immigrants and at a cattle farm belonging to his friend Pino. He soon moved on however, and joined the circus as a saxophone player, before starting his own family in his new home.
Andruetto is a ›taciturn narrator‹, who nevertheless has much to say. Unsentimental and plain, she describes the long journey of a young man searching for his identity. By and by the fragmented memories and impressions of the first-person narrator fit together like pieces of a puzzle – ingeniously told from three perspectives. For the author, »Stefano« also represents a journey along her father's tracks. All the same, she does not narrate with biographical adherence, rather she relates his experience to the destiny of millions of immigrants who crossed over to Argentina between the end of the 19th century and the middle of the 20th. »If a book is a path towards knowledge, a way to grasp the world and search for our own place within it, then Stefano gave me the opportunity to re-experience the sensations of hunger, rootlessness and estrangement experienced by men and women who, like those who leave today, once arrived with the hope of a better life.«
María Teresa Andruetto has received many awards, among them one for the children's book »El anillo encantado« (1993) and »Huellas en la arena« (1997). Several of her works for children and young adults can be found in the »White Ravens« catalogue of the International Children's Library in Munich, such as the short story collection »La mujer vampiro« (2001), in which she borrows elements from old horror stories and weaves them into the everyday world of children in an exciting and humorous way. In addition to her literary work Andruetto teaches Creative Writing, trains mediators for children's literature and has taken up an editorial post at the publishing house Ediciones del Eclipse.

Caballito al viento
Aguilar
Buenos Aires, 1999
[Ill: Istvan Schritter]
¡Dale Campeón!
Sicornio
Córdoba, 1999
[Ill: Mayté Saine]
La mujer vampiro
(ab 10)
Sudamericana
Buenos Aires, 2001
[Ill: Lucas Nine]
El anillo encantado
Sudamericana
Buenos Aires, 2002
[Ill: Patricia Melgar]
Stefanos weite Reise
(ab 14)
Atlantis
Zürich, 2003
[Ü: Jochen Weber]
Benjamino
(ab 5)
Sudamericana
Buenos Aires, 2003
[Ill: Didi Grau]
El país de Juan
(ab 8)
Anaya
Madrid, 2003
[Ill: Gabriel Hernández]

María Teresa Andruetto wurde 1954 in Arroyo Cabral in der argentinischen Provinz Córdoba geboren, wo sie auch heute lebt. Nach ihrem Literaturstudium an der Universidad Nacional de Córdoba spezialisierte sie sich im Bereich Kinder- und Jugendliteratur. Sie arbeitete in der Redaktion des Kinder- und Jugendbuchmagazins »Piedra Libre« und wirkte an der Gründung eines Forschungszentrums für Kinder- und Jugendliteratur mit, dessen Direktorium sie neun Jahre angehörte. Seit Ende der achtziger Jahre sind zahlreiche Kurzgeschichten, Erzählungen, Romane, Gedichte und Theaterstücke für Erwachsene, Kinder und Jugendliche erschienen.

2003 wurde mit »Stefano« (1997; dt. »Stefanos weite Reise«) zum ersten Mal einer ihrer Jugendromane in deutscher Sprache publiziert. Darin erzählt sie die Geschichte Stefanos, der in den vierziger Jahren nach Argentinien auswandert, um den ärmlichen Verhältnissen im italienischen Piemont zu entfliehen. Nach einer abenteuerlichen Überfahrt in die Fremde schlägt sich Stefano zunächst mit einfachen Jobs im Immigrantenhotel und auf der Rinderfarm seines Freundes Pino durch. Doch schon bald zieht es ihn fort. Als Saxophonspieler kommt er zum Zirkus, bevor er in der neuen Heimat eine eigene Familie gründet. Andruetto erscheint wie eine ›schweigsame Erzählerin‹, die allerdings viel zu sagen hat. Unsentimental und schlicht beschreibt sie die lange Reise eines jungen Mannes zu sich selbst. Nach und nach fügen sich die bruchstückhaften Erinnerungen und Eindrücke des Ich-Erzählers wie Puzzlestücke zusammen – literarisch raffiniert aus drei Perspektiven erzählt. »Stefano« ist auch für die Autorin eine Reise zu den Spuren ihres eigenen Vaters. Dennoch erzählt sie nicht in biographischer Strenge. Vielmehr verknüpft sie seine Erlebnisse mit den Schicksalen von Millionen Einwanderern, die zwischen Ende des 19. und Mitte des 20. Jahrhunderts nach Argentinien kamen. »Wenn ein Buch ein Weg ist, die Welt zu begreifen und unseren Platz darin zu finden, dann hat mir ›Stefano‹ ermöglicht, die Erfahrungen von Hunger, Entwurzelung und Entfremdung nachzuempfinden, die Menschen auf der Suche nach einem besseren Leben damals wie heute immer wieder machen.«

María Teresa Andruetto wurde vielfach ausgezeichnet, unter anderem für die Kinderbücher »El anillo encantado« (1993) und »Huellas en la arena« (1997). Mehrere ihrer Kinder- und Jugendbücher fanden Eingang in den »White Ravens«-Katalog der Internationalen Jugendbibliothek München, darunter der Erzählband »La mujer vampiro« (2001; Ü: Die Vampir-Frau), in dem sie Elemente alter Gruselgeschichten aufgreift und diese spannend und humorvoll mit der heutigen Alltagswelt von Kindern verknüpft. Neben ihrer literarischen Tätigkeit unterrichtet die Autorin kreatives Schreiben, bildet Literaturvermittler im Kinder- und Jugendbuchbereich aus und arbeitet als Lektorin des Verlags Ediciones del Eclipse.

Lleva la letra de su madre

She carries her mother's handwriting

Extravío

Lleva un papel escrito
(en el hueco de la mano
lleva la letra de su madre).

Le han ordenado:
No te pierdas, y va mirándose
los pies, cuenta
los pasos.

Cree
(...pero es una intuición
oscura) que quien se mira
los pies no se extravía.

Cuenta los pasos
(y después las sílabas,
los cuentos, las monedas),
con los ojos fijos en los zapatos,
pero lo mismo se pierde
en el recuento.

Getting lost

She carries a written paper
(in the palm of her hand
she carries her mother´s handwriting)

They have ordered her
don´t get lost and she goes
looking at her feet, she counts
the steps.

She believes
(but it´s a dark
intuition) those who look at
the feet don´t get lost.

She counts the steps
(and then the syllables,
the stories, the coins)
with her eyes fixed on the shoes
but she gets lost all the same
in the recount.

azouz begag

biography

Azouz Begag, the son of an Algerian »guestworker«, was born in 1957 in Villeurbanne, near Lyon. He has a PhD in economics and is currently working as a sociologist in Paris and Lyon. Alongside his academic research, which focuses on the mobility and identity of immigrants, he has published highly acclaimed novels for children, young people and adults. His literary work has been well received by critics and the public in France and Germany, and is often an integral part of regional studies curricula used for French classes in schools.

In 1986 Begag became the best-known representative of »littérature beure« with the publication of his first, autobiographically inclined, novel, »Le gône du chaâba«, in which he describes a boy's childhood in a suburban slums of Lyon. In the eighties, literary texts, theatre plays and musical pieces written by »Beurs«, young people of North African origin who grew up in France, articulated the outlook on life shared by this second generation of immigrants, whose integration still poses a contentious problem in contemporary French society. Begag's first novel focuses on belonging to two cultures and the double identity that results from an affiliation to a distant, unknown homeland, and a new, unfamiliar country. The author colourfully depicts the »guestworker« child Azouz's efforts to be accepted in his own country. The adolescent Azouz has to fight against the isolation, which he experiences on the one hand on account of his intelligence, causing him to distance himself from the milieu of his illiterate parents and their Arabic family traditions, and on the other hand because his fellow pupils constantly make him aware of the stigma related to his North African origin. Begag by no means places emphasis »on pity and sentimentality, but rather on the subversive power of humour, by exposing comic and exact detail« (»Neue Zürcher Zeitung«). »Le gône du chaâba« was awarded many prizes including the French journalists' prize, Prix du meilleur roman in 1986. The film, directed by Christophe Ruggia, was shown at the Berlinale in 1998.

The politically active author views his writing, journalism and academic work as building blocks for a Franco-Maghrebian identity, and as a medium which can be used to mediate between the political elite in France and the reality in the immigrant quarters. In the sequel »Béni ou le paradis privé«, which was published in France in 1989, the emphasis is placed even more strongly on everyday racism in France, which begins long before the first steps to open violence are taken. The author lives in Paris.

Les voleurs d'écritures
(ab 10)
Seuil, Paris, 1990

Aber die Erde ist rund
(ab 8)
Beltz & Gelberg
Weinheim, 1993
[Ü: Ruth Subjetzki]

Azouz, der Junge vom Stadtrand
(ab 12)
Nagel & Kimche
Zürich, 1998
[Ü: Regina Keil]

Zenzela
(ab 6)
Picus, Basel, 1998
[Ü: Natalie Freud]

Fast überall
(ab 12)
Nagel & Kimche
Zürich, 2000
[Ü: Regina Keil]

Quand on est mort, c'est pour toute la vie
(ab 6)
Gallimard, Paris, 1994

Le théorème de Mamadou
(ab 8)
Seuil, Paris, 2002

Azouz Begag wurde 1957 als Sohn eines algerischen Gastarbeiters bei Lyon geboren. Er promovierte in Wirtschaftswissenschaften und arbeitet heute als Soziologe in Paris und Lyon. Neben wissenschaftlichen Studien, in denen sich Begag mit der Mobilität und Identität von Immigranten beschäftigt, hat er vielbeachtete Romane für Kinder, Jugendliche und Erwachsene veröffentlicht. Seine literarischen Werke fanden sowohl in Frankreich als auch in Deutschland große Resonanz bei Kritik und Publikum und sind oft Bestandteil von Landeskundedossiers für den Französisch-Unterricht in der Schule.

1986 avancierte Begag mit seinem ersten – autobiographisch gefärbten – Jugendroman »Le gône du chaâba« (dt. »Azouz, der Junge vom Stadtrand«, 1998), in dem er dessen Kindheit in einer »slumartigen« Lyoner Vorstadtsiedlung beschreibt, zum bekanntesten Vertreter der »littérature beure«. In literarischen Texten, Theater- und Musikstücken der in Frankreich aufgewachsenen Jugendlichen nordafrikanischer Herkunft, der »Beurs«, artikulierte sich in den achtziger Jahren das Lebensgefühl dieser zweiten Einwanderergeneration, deren Integration noch immer ein »brennendes« Problem der französischen Gesellschaft darstellt. Begag thematisiert die Zugehörigkeit zu zwei Kulturen und die doppelte Identität zwischen einer fernen, unbekannten Heimat und einem neuen, wenig vertrauten Land. Anschaulich schildert der Autor die Mühen des »Gastarbeiter«-Kindes Azouz, im eigenen Land anzukommen. Der heranwachsende Azouz hat mit der Isolation zu kämpfen, die er erleidet, weil er sich einerseits durch seine Intelligenz dem Milieu seiner Eltern, die Analphabeten sind, sowie den arabischen Familiensitten entfremdet und er andererseits durch seine Mitschüler immer wieder das Stigma seiner nordafrikanischen Abstammung zu spüren bekommt. Dabei setzt Begag »nicht auf Mitleid und Larmoyanz, sondern auf die subversive Kraft des Humors, auf entlarvende Komik und Detailtreue« (»Neue Zürcher Zeitung«). »Le gône du chaâba« wurde mit zahlreichen Preisen ausgezeichnet, u. a. 1986 mit dem französischen Journalistenpreis »Prix du meilleur roman«. Die Verfilmung des Regisseurs Christophe Ruggia wurde 1998 auf der Berlinale präsentiert.

Der politisch engagierte Autor versteht seine schriftstellerische, journalistische und wissenschaftliche Arbeit als Bausteine einer franko-maghrebinischen Identität und als Möglichkeit, zwischen den politischen Eliten in Frankreich und der Realität in den Immigrantenvierteln zu vermitteln. In seinem Fortsetzungsroman »Béni ou le paradis privé« (dt. »Fast überall«, 2000), der 1989 in Frankreich erschien, richtet er den Fokus noch stärker auf den alltäglichen Rassismus in Frankreich, der nicht erst beginnt, wenn offen gehetzt und zur Gewalt geschritten wird. Der Autor lebt in Paris.

martha brooks

biography

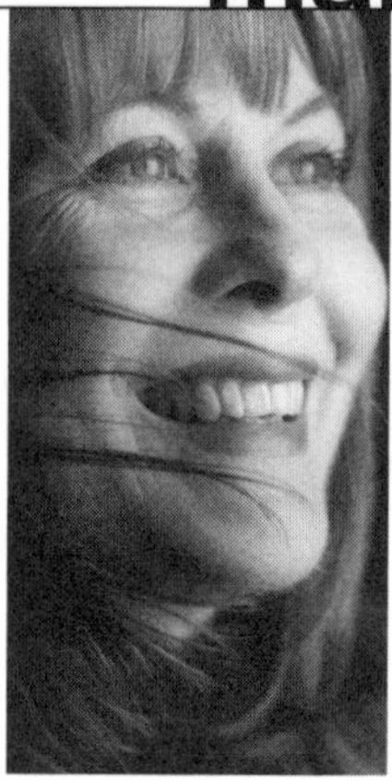

Martha Brooks was born in 1944 in Ninette, Manitoba and she is considered one of the most important authors for youthful readers. When asked about her personal style of narration, she says, »Each book takes me where I never expected to go. I don't plot. The energy is all in the internal workings of the character and the external workings of the place.« Her goal is to make stories authentic, and it is exactly this that distinguishes Martha Brooks' texts: strong, well defined characters who have reached a turning point in their lives. The stories are about love and grief, about goodbyes and new beginnings; and they always involve the courage to accept loss and to open up to new people and opportunities.

Brooks was first successful in 1988 with a collection of short stories, »Paradise Café and Other Stories«, which received numerous awards. In the following years, besides publishing further short stories and novels including »Bone Dance« (1997) and »Being with Henry« (1999) she also wrote dramas, including the prize-winning children's play »Andrew's Tree« (1996). Besides translations of her books into Italian, Japanese, French and Danish, two of her works, »Two Moons in August« (1991) and »Travelling into the Light« (1994) have been translated into German and were published in 2000.

Martha Brooks' most recent work, »True Confessions of a Heartless Girl«, published in 2002, is a novel for young adults and was awarded numerous prizes, including the Governor General's Award (2002). Refreshingly, lyrically and with illuminating irony she tells the story of Noreen's arrival in the small village of Pembina Lake; the seventeen year old arrives on a summer night in her boyfriend's truck, with a handful of stolen dollars, a baby in her womb, and a broken heart. At first she is rightfully regarded with scepticism, for the tense and insecure Noreen turns the lives of all those she encounters upside down. The author does not smooth the edges of her protagonist. She is the catalyst for the ›adult‹ characters in the book, each of whom carries their own secret. Brooks needs no unusual heroes and no sensational occurrences. She writes about ›everyday life‹ from the various perspectives of her characters and lets them learn from one another.

Martha Brooks is also a successful jazz singer. In 2001 she released the award winning CD »Change of Heart«. She has an adult daughter and lives with her husband Brian in Winnipeg.

AMUSE

My last muse was useless, ungracious. I shared her with my friend, the playwright Maureen Hunter. Our Muse frequently ditched us to take long vacations. Whenever she'd return – sullen, uncommunicative, refusing to remove her sunglasses – she'd go between our homes, chain-smoking and swilling scotch. Both Maureen and I are morning people. Our Muse could not be disturbed before two thirty in the afternoon. We finally released her from our tormented imaginations. Maureen acquired two entertaining cats, the regal Raj and la bella Luna. Into my life came a goofy play-crazed Airedale Terrier, named Drummer. Did I mention I'm also a jazz singer? Drummer, in touch with the heartbeat of the earth, speaks to both the writer and the singer in me. Now, whenever I'm stuck for inspiration I just look into her button bright eyes and laugh. The sacred clown is, of course, the wisest and the most magical muse of all.

Paradise Café and Other Stories
(ab 12)
Thistledown
Saskatoon, 1990
I Met a Bully on the Hill
Mit Maureen Hunter
J. Gordon Shillingford
Winnipeg, 1995
Bone Dance
(ab 13)
Orchard Books
New York, 1997
Der zweite Vollmond im August
(ab 13)
Middelhauve
München, 2000
[Ü: Tilmann Kleinau]
Being with Henry
(ab 11)
Groundwood Books
Toronto, 2000
Weiter ins Licht
(ab 13)
Middelhauve
München, 2002
[Ü: Wolfram Sadowski]
Wahre Geständnisse eines herzlosen Mädchens
(ab 13)
Dtv, München, 2004
[Ü: Birgitt Kollmann]

Martha Brooks wurde 1944 in Ninette, Manitoba, geboren und zählt zu den bedeutendsten Jugendbuchautorinnen Kanadas. Gefragt nach ihrem persönlichen Erzählstil sagt sie: »Jedes Buch führt mich an Orte, von denen ich niemals erwartet hätte, sie zu erreichen. Ich konstruiere keine Handlung. Die ganze Energie steckt im Innenleben der Charaktere und ihrer Umgebung.« Ihr Ziel ist es, Geschichten authentisch zu gestalten – und genau das zeichnet die Texte von Martha Brooks aus: starke, fein gezeichnete Charaktere, die an Wendepunkten ihres Lebens stehen. Dabei geht es um Liebe und Trauer, um Abschiede und Neuanfänge. Und immer wieder geht es um den Mut, Verluste zu akzeptieren und sich neuen Menschen und Möglichkeiten zu öffnen.
Ihren ersten großen Erfolg konnte Brooks 1988 mit der Kurzgeschichtensammlung »Paradise Café and Other Stories« feiern, die mehrfach ausgezeichnet wurde. In den folgenden Jahren erschienen neben weiteren Kurzgeschichten und Romanen wie »Bone Dance« (1997) und »Being with Henry« (1999) auch Dramen, darunter das preisgekrönte Kindertheaterstück »Andrew's Tree« (1996). Neben Übersetzungen ins Italienische, Japanische, Französische und Dänische wurden mit »Two Moons in August« (1991; dt. »Der zweite Vollmond im August«) und »Travelling on into the Light« (1994; dt. »Weiter ins Licht und andere Geschichten«) bereits im Jahr 2000 zwei ihrer Werke in deutscher Übersetzung veröffentlicht.
2002 erschien Martha Brooks' Roman für junge Erwachsene »True Confessions of A Heartless Girl« (dt. »Wahre Geständnisse eines herzlosen Mädchens«, 2004), u. a. mit dem Governor General's Award (2002) prämiert. Erfrischend, lyrisch und mit erhellender Ironie erzählt sie die Geschichte der siebzehnjährigen Noreen, die in einer Sommernacht das kleine Örtchen Pembina Lake erreicht – im Truck ihres Freundes, mit einer Hand voll gestohlener Dollar, einem Baby im Bauch und einem großen Schmerz im Herzen. Zunächst wird sie scheinbar zurecht skeptisch aufgenommen, denn die spröde und verunsicherte Noreen wirbelt das Leben all derer, die ihr begegnen, gehörig durcheinander. Die Autorin glättet ihre Protagonistin nicht. Sie ist der Katalysator für die ›erwachsenen‹ Charaktere des Buches, die allesamt ihr eigenes Geheimnis besitzen. Brooks braucht keine außergewöhnlichen Helden, keine sensationellen Ereignisse. Vielmehr schreibt sie aus den verschiedenen Perspektiven ihrer Figuren über das ›ganz normale Leben‹ und lässt sie voneinander lernen.
Martha Brooks ist auch als Jazzsängerin erfolgreich. 2001 erschien ihre preisgekrönte CD »Change of Heart«. Sie hat eine erwachsene Tochter und lebt mit ihrem Mann Brian in Winnipeg.

melvin burgess
biography

Melvin Burgess was born in London, Great Britain, in 1954. He is one of the most prolific and most widely discussed British authors of young people's fiction. He grew up in Sussex and Surrey, moved to Bristol after he had finished school and later to London and spent fifteen years experimenting with writing. He completed a training course in journalism and had numerous casual jobs before publishing his first book for young adults »The Cry of the Wolf« (1990), which was immediately nominated for the Carnegie Medal (1991).
Melvin Burgess writes challenging novels for young people. Honestly, relentlessly and humorously he tackles sensitive topics. His literature offers no easy answers but leaves his readers agitated. His style remains close to the adolescents about whom and for whom he writes. His gripping and fast tales are both entertainment and a warning, for example his socio-realistic novel for young adults »Junk« (1996) with which Burgess became known as a Brit-Pop author in Germany in 1999. In 1997, the remarkable story about homeless, drug-addicted youths in Bristol was awarded the Guardian Children's Fiction Award and the Carnegie Medal. In an open yet sensitive way, Burgess captures the way of life of Gemma and Tar who run away from home, become junkies, and nearly lose control of their lives.
While his books have won numerous awards, and are read eagerly by youths, critics and adult readers do not infrequently react to his openness with skeptisism. He himself points out that there is not enough literature for older youths which tackles their questions – questions that they find important and exciting. In his novel for teenagers »Lady. My life as a Bitch«, published in 2001, he tells the story of the phantasmagoric dual identity of a seventeen year-old who is turned into a dog and who starts to exploit her newly won freedom, while simultaneously reflecting self-critically on her previous life as a human. The offensive depiction of sexuality provided much food for discussion. Burgess views his novel as »a comic allegory about sex and life – and all the important, darker issues that some people can't handle teenagers reading about.«
Burgess' latest publication is his novel for young adults »Doing It« (2003) about six teenagers and their various experiences of sex. This »Burgess« also encourages us to reconsider the genre »youth literature«. »The Ghost behind the Wall« (2001) and »Billy Elliot« (2000), are two of his books for younger readers, and are just as warm-heartedly and vividly told as his novels for young adults. The author lives in Manchester.

Die letzten Wölfe
(ab 14)
Rowohlt
Reinbek, 1993

Junk
(ab 16)
Fischer
Frankfurt a.M., 1999
[Ü: Heike Brandt]

Schlachten
(ab 14)
Carlsen
Hamburg, 2000
[Ü: Heike Brandt]

Billy Elliot
(ab 11)
Ravensburger
Ravensburg, 2001
[Ü: Heike Brandt]

Das Geheimnis im Schacht
(ab 11)
Carlsen
Hamburg, 2003
[Ü: Heike Brandt]

Hundsfrau
(ab 14)
Carlsen
Hamburg, 2003
[Ü: Heike Brandt]

Doing it
(ab 14)
Carlsen
Hamburg, 2004
[Ü: Andreas Steinhöfel]

Melvin Burgess wurde 1954 in London, Großbritannien, geboren und ist einer der profiliertesten und meistdiskutierten britischen Jugendbuchautoren. Aufgewachsen in Sussex und Surrey, zog er nach seinem Schulabschluss nach Bristol, später nach London, und widmete sich fünfzehn Jahre lang auf experimentelle Weise dem Schreiben. Er absolvierte eine Journalistenausbildung und nahm Gelegenheitsjobs an, bevor 1990 mit »The Cry of the Wolf« (dt. »Die letzten Wölfe«, 1993) sein erstes Jugendbuch publiziert und sogleich für die Carnegie Medal (1991) nominiert wurde.
Melvin Burgess schreibt herausfordernde Romane für junge Menschen. Ehrlich, schonungslos und humorvoll greift er heikle Themen auf. Seine Literatur bietet keine einfachen Antworten und lässt seine Leser aufgewühlt zurück. In seinem Erzählstil bleibt Burgess den Heranwachsenden nahe, über die und für die er schreibt. Seine fesselnden und temporeichen Romane sind Unterhaltung und Warnung zugleich, so auch sein »sozialrealistischer« Jugendroman »Junk« (1996), mit dem Burgess 1999 als Brit-Pop-Autor in Deutschland bekannt wurde. Bereits 1997 wurde die bemerkenswerte Geschichte um drogenabhängige und heimatlose Jugendliche in Bristol mit dem Guardian Children's Fiction Award und der Carnegie Medal ausgezeichnet. Offen und sensibel fängt Burgess das Lebensgefühl von Gemma und Tar ein, die von Zuhause abhauen, zu Junkies werden und die Kontrolle über ihr Leben zu verlieren drohen.
Vielfach ausgezeichnet und von seinen jugendlichen Lesern begeistert gelesen, begegnen Kritik und erwachsene Leser Burgess' Offenheit nicht selten skeptisch. Er selbst weist darauf hin, dass es nicht genügend Literatur für ältere Jugendliche gebe, in der ihre Fragen aufgegriffen werden – Fragen, die für sie wichtig und aufregend sind. In seinem 2001 erschienenen Jugendroman »Lady. My Life as a Bitch« (dt. »Hundsfrau«, 2003) erzählt er von der phantastischen Doppelidentität einer Siebzehnjährigen, die in einen Hund verwandelt wird und ihre neu gewonnene Freiheit auszuleben beginnt, aber auch ihre Lebenssituation als Mensch selbstkritisch reflektiert. Die offensive Darstellung von Sexualität hat für Diskussionen gesorgt. Burgess sieht seinen Roman als »ein humorvolles Gleichnis über die Sexualität und das Leben – und all die wichtigen und schwierigen Aspekte des Lebens, über die sich viele Erwachsene mit ihren heranwachsenden Kindern nicht austauschen wollen«.
Zuletzt erschien Burgess' Jugendroman »Doing it« (2003; dt. »Doing it«, 2004) über sechs Jugendliche und ihre sehr unterschiedlichen sexuellen Erfahrungen. Auch dieser »Burgess« regt an, das Genre »Jugendbuch« neu zu überdenken. Mit »The Ghost behind the Wall« (2000; dt. »Das Geheimnis im Schacht«, 2003) und »Billy Elliot« (2001; dt. »Billy Elliot. I will dance«, 2001) legte er Bücher für jüngere Leser vor – ebenso warmherzig und plastisch erzählt wie seine Romane für junge Erwachsene. Der Autor lebt in Manchester.

When the muse her silence keeps,
I just lie down and have a sleep.
Or have a walk or drink a cup –
The wanton hussy won't shut up.

malika ferdjoukh

biography

Malika Ferdjoukh was born on the Mediterranean coast of Algeria in 1957 and has lived in Paris since childhood. After finishing school she studied Film and Literature, and then started working at a children's hospital and as a teacher. She says about herself: »I love everything that tells a story. Cinema as much as literature.« Since 1989 she has written children's books and novels for young adults, television scripts, and she has also published novels for adults under a pseudonym.

Ferdjoukh develops her stories elegantly and nimbly, as if with a smile. Frequently secrets, strange incidents and surprising discoveries become the young protagonists' field of action. She combines the cheerful tone of her texts with elements of suspense and a certain seriousness. Her playful, humorous handling of difficult themes such as love, divorce, unemployment and violence lends her books great complexity.

Thus a band of shrewd children defy a racist murderer in her thriller for adolescents, »Fais-moi peur« (1994; t: Frighten me!). The author tells the story of Monsieur N., who suffers from an ›illness‹ called xenophobia. While the Jewish siblings Mintz relish getting the creeps during »M – A City Searches for a Killer«, and take advantage of a Christmas eve without parents to make popcorn, a real murderer enters the setting. Ferdjoukh portrays familiar intimate gatherings between siblings with as much pleasure and authenticity as she does the different faces that evil can take – such as the too short Monsieur N., who was not always a murderer, or the SS-henchmen who still torment Grandma Mintz in her dreams. In 2004 Ferdjoukh's novel for adolescents »Sombres citrouilles« (1999; t: Black pumpkins) came out in German translation. When the twins Violette and Annette, and their siblings Colin, Hermès and Madeleine find a dead person in a pumpkin patch on the family property, a turbulent hunt for the murderer begins. Up until its exciting ending, the author produces a family portrait of great atmospheric density, behind which human abysses loom and children unmask the false world of adults. As in film, the writer utilises precise cuts and surprising shifts in perspective.

Malika Ferdjoukh won the Grand Prix du Roman Jeunesse for »Les joues roses« (1993; t: The reddened cheeks) and one year later the Prix Beaugency for the funniest children's book of the year. »Sombres citrouilles« was awarded the Prix Sorcières 2000. Her most recent works for young adults include the four-part »Quatre-Sœurs« series (2003).

La fiancé du fantome
(ab 9)
L'Ecole des loisirs
Paris, 1999

Mach mir Angst
Arena
Würzburg, 2001
[Ü: Uta Szyszkowitz]

Minuit-Cinq
(ab 9)
L'Ecole des loisirs
Paris, 2002

La fille d'en face
(ab 9)
Bayard Jeunesse
Montréal, 2002

L'assassin de papa
(ab 6)
Syros
Paris, 2003

Wie verliebt man seinen Vater?
(ab 10)
Fischer
Frankfurt a.M., 2004
[Ü: Hans Georg-Noack]

Schwarze Kürbisse
(ab 13)
Sauerländer
Düsseldorf, 2004
[Ü: Rosemarie Griebel-Kruip]

Malika Ferdjoukh wurde 1957 an der algerischen Mittelmeerküste geboren und lebt seit ihrer frühen Kindheit in Paris. Nach dem Abitur studierte sie Film- und Literaturwissenschaft, arbeitete zunächst in einem Kinderkrankenhaus und als Lehrerin. Über sich selbst sagt sie: »Ich liebe alles, was Geschichten erzählt. Das Kino ebenso wie die Literatur.« Seit 1989 schreibt sie Kinder- und Jugendromane, Fernsehdrehbücher und veröffentlicht Romane für Erwachsene unter Pseudonym.

Elegant, leichtfüßig und wie mit einem Lächeln auf den Lippen geschrieben, entwickelt Ferdjoukh ihre Geschichten, in denen häufig Geheimnisse, kuriose Vorfälle und überraschende Entdeckungen zum Aktionsfeld der jungen Protagonisten werden. Die heitere Grundmelodie ihrer Texte unterfüttert die Autorin mit Suspense-Elementen und zugleich einer gewissen Ernsthaftigkeit. Der spielerisch-humorvolle Umgang mit schwierigen Themen wie Liebe, Scheidung, Arbeitslosigkeit oder Gewalt verleiht ihren Büchern eine große Vielschichtigkeit. So trotzt in ihrem Jugendthriller »Fais-moi peur« (1994; dt. »Mach mir Angst!«, 2001) eine Schar gewitzter Kinder einem rassistischen Mörder. Die Autorin erzählt von Monsieur N., der an einer ›Krankheit‹ namens Fremdenhass leidet. Während sich die jüdischen Geschwister Mintz bei »M – eine Stadt sucht einen Mörder« lustvoll gruseln und den elternlosen Vorweihnachtsabend zum Popcornmachen nutzen, betritt ein wirklicher Mörder den Schauplatz. Ferdjoukh zeigt das familiär-vertraute Zusammensein unter Geschwistern ebenso vergnüglich und authentisch wie die verschiedenen Gesichter, die das Böse haben kann – das des zu klein geratenen Monsieur N., der nicht immer ein Mörder war, oder das der SS-Schergen, die Großmama Mintz noch heute in ihren Träumen peinigen. 2004 erschien Ferdjoukhs Jugendroman »Sombres citrouilles« (1999; dt. »Schwarze Kürbisse«) in deutscher Übersetzung. Als die Zwillinge Violette und Annette sowie Colin, Hermès und Madeleine an Halloween einen Toten im Kürbisbeet des Familienanwesens entdecken, entspinnt sich eine turbulente Mörderjagd. Bis zum spannenden Finale entwickelt die Autorin ein Familientableau von großer atmosphärischer Dichte, hinter dem sich menschliche Abgründe auftun und Kinder die verlogene Welt der Erwachsenen demaskieren. Wie im Film nutzt die Autorin dazu präzise Schnitte und überraschende Perspektivwechsel.

Für »Les joues roses« (1993; dt. »Wie verliebt man seinen Vater?«, 1996) erhielt Malika Ferdjoukh 1993 den Grand Prix du Roman Jeunesse und ein Jahr später den Prix Beaugency für das lustigste Kinderbuch des Jahres. »Sombres Citrouilles« wurde mit dem Prix Sorcières 2000 ausgezeichnet. Zu ihren zuletzt erschienenen Werken für Jugendliche gehört die vierteilige »Quatre Sœurs«-Serie (2003f.).

En relisant votre dernier fax, je me rends compte que je n'ai pas répondu à votre question "Make answer, muse!" – Probably I didn't have anything to say about it, except: Sorry, but there's no Muse – there's work, only work – Je ne sais pas si cette réponse suffira mais, vraiment, je ne sais pas quoi dire d'autre –

klaus hagerup
biography

Klaus Hagerup was born in Oslo, Norway in 1946 where he grew up in a family of authors. He decided to become an actor and partly funded his education with his poetry collection, »Silk tenker jeg på dere«, with which he made his debut in 1969. In the following years he worked as an actor, director, playwright and translator. In the eighties, writing increasingly took on a larger and larger role in his professional life. Today, Hagerup is considered one of the most important authors in Norway; he writes novels, theatre plays and radio plays, most of which target young adults. In a sensitive and humorous way, he writes about early puberty, finding oneself, friendship and the turbulent complexities of being in love for the first time. He does not write about the big leap into the well-defined world of adults, but about the many small, quaint and disproportionately more important developments. In doing so, he contrives to expose his protagonists to hysterically funny dialogues and hilarious scenes.

In his novel for young adults »Høyere en himmelen« (1990), the author tells the tale of twelve year-old Mari, who does not like herself very much and finds just about everything quite daft, until she meets the wacky yet impressive teacher: Miss Kjoer. The novel was awarded Sonja Hagemanns Barnebokpris (1990) and the IBBY-Certificate of Honour. Hagerup became hugely popular with the publication, in 1993, of the children's mystery »Bibbi Bokkens magiske bibliotek«, which he co-wrote with Jostein Gaarder, the author of »Sophie's World«. His international breakthrough came in 1994 with the publication of »Markus og Diana og lyset fra Sirius« (t: Marcus and Diana), the first book of several about the antihero, Markus Simonsen, who is afraid of everything, but most of all of girls. In an affectionate, charming, and yet always respectfully distant manner, Hagerup depicts the daily fears of a completely normal teenager and his first steps into the wide world of love, which are sometimes delightful and sometimes painful, but always instructive. His last book about Markus, »Markus og Karaokekongen« (t: Marcus and the Karaokeband) will be published in Norway in autumn 2004.

Klaus Hagerup's versatile work has been widely translated and has received numerous awards, among them the Norwegian Critics Price, the Culturaldepartments Price for Best Youth Book, and the Publishers Prize »Brageprisen«. In recent years, he has produced just as highly acclaimed books for adults, including »Herremannen« (2000). His work »Kaninen synger i mørket« (2001; t: Rabbits Sing in the Dark) which has been published in the German translation in 2004, proves that he has also remained faithful to his younger readers. In his version of the »Alice in Wonderland« motif, Else goes on a fantastical journey, where she meets rabbits in shorts and other curious creatures. Klaus Hagerup lives in Gressvik, Norway.

Tiefer als der Ozean
(ab 12)
Sauerländer
Frankfurt a. M., 1995
[Ü: Gabriele Haefs]

Markus und Diana
(ab 12)
Sauerländer
Frankfurt a.M., 1997
[Ü: Gabriele Haefs]

Küss mich - oder ich verlieb mich in dich!
(ab 12)
Carlsen
Hamburg, 2001
[Ü: Gabriele Haefs]

Verliebt zwischen Ecke und Elfmeter
(ab 12)
Sauerländer
Frankfurt a. M., 2001
[Ü: Gabriele Haefs]

Die Kaninchen singen in der Nacht
(ab 10)
Hanser
München, 2001
[Ü: Gabriele Haefs]

Markus og Karaokekongen
Aschehoug
Oslo, 2004

When I try to get her
the muse wants to be free.

Klaus Hagerup wurde 1946 in Oslo, Norwegen, geboren und wuchs in einer Literatenfamilie auf. Er entschied sich, Schauspieler zu werden, und finanzierte seine Ausbildung u. a. mit dem Gedichtband »Slik tenker jeg på dere«, mit dem er 1969 debütierte. In den Folgejahren arbeitete er als Bühnendarsteller, Regisseur, Dramatiker und Übersetzer. Mehr und mehr rückte in den achtziger Jahren das Schreiben in den Mittelpunkt seines beruflichen Schaffens. Heute gehört Hagerup zu den wichtigsten Literaten Norwegens und verfasst Romane, Theaterstücke und Hörspiele für ein größtenteils jugendliches Publikum. Empfindsam und humoristisch schreibt er über die frühe Phase der Pubertät, vom Sich-Finden, von Freundschaft und den turbulenten Verwicklungen der ersten Liebe. Er erzählt nicht vom großen Sprung in die abgeklärte Erwachsenenwelt, sondern von den vielen kleinen, wunderlichen und ungleich wichtigeren Entwicklungsschritten. Dabei versteht er es, seinen Helden urkomische Dialoge und wahnwitzige Szenen auf den Leib zu schreiben.
In seinem Jugendroman »Høyere enn himmelen« (dt. »Tiefer als der Ozean«, 1995) erzählt der Autor von der zwölfjährigen Mari, die sich selbst nicht besonders mag und alles irgendwie doof findet, bis sie die etwas schrullige und zugleich imponierende Lehrerin Fräulein Kjoer kennenlernt. Der Roman wurde mit dem Sonja-Hagemann-Preis (1990) und dem IBBY-Ehrendiplom prämiert. Große Popularität brachte Hagerup 1993 der Kinderkrimi »Bibbi Bokkens magiske bibliotek« (dt. »Bibbi Bokkens magische Bibliothek«, 2001), den er zusammen mit dem Autor von »Sofies Welt«, Jostein Gaarder, verfasste. Der internationale Durchbruch gelang ihm 1994 mit »Markus og Diana og lyset fra Sirius« (dt. »Markus und Diana«, 1997), dem ersten Band seiner mehrteiligen Buchserie um den Antihelden Markus Simonsen, der sich vor Gott und der Welt, vor allem aber vor den Mädchen fürchtet. Liebevoll, charmant und stets in respektvoller Distanz schildert Hagerup die Alltagsangst eines ganz normalen Teenagers und dessen erste Gehversuche im weiten Feld der Liebe, die manchmal schön und manchmal schmerzhaft, immer aber lehrreich sind. Der neueste »Markus«-Band, »Markus og Karaokekongen«, erscheint im Herbst 2004 in Norwegen.
Klaus Hagerups vielseitiges Werk wurde mehrfach übersetzt und ausgezeichnet, u. a. mit dem Norwegischen Kritikerpreis, dem Culturaldepartments-Preis für das beste Jugendbuch und dem Verlegerpreis »Brageprisen«. In den letzten Jahren hat er u. a. mit »Herremannen« (2000) auch vielbeachtete Romane für Erwachsene vorgelegt. Mit seinem Werk »Kaninene synger i mørket« (2001; dt. »Die Kaninchen singen in der Nacht«), das 2004 in deutscher Übersetzung erschien, ist er aber seinen jungen Lesern treu geblieben. In seiner Fassung des »Alice im Wunderland«-Motivs begibt sich Else auf eine phantastische Reise, auf der sie neben Kaninchen in kurzen Hosen allerhand anderen sonderbaren Gestalten begegnet. Klaus Hagerup lebt in Gressvik, Norwegen.

But when I run away from her
the muse runs after me.

daniel hevier

biography

Daniel Hevier was born in Bratislava, in the former Czechoslovakia, in 1955, and is considered one of the most popular children's book authors in Slovakia. He studied Slovakian Studies and Aesthetics at the Komenský University in Bratislava. Before founding his own publishing house HEVI in 1992, he worked as an editor for radio, and from 1989 to 1992 as the chief editor for the children's book publisher Mladé letá, and also as a freelance writer. Today Hevier is known as poet, short-story writer, songwriter, illustrator, publisher, playwright and screenwriter, and, as such, one of the most versatile writers in Slovakia. With his volumes of poetry from the 1970's and 1980's (among them »Motýlí kolotoč?«, 1974; t: The butterfly carousel; »Nonstop«, 1981; »Electrónkový klaun, 1983; t: The electronic clown), he invests Slovakian poetry with a spirit of lightness, rich metaphor and great humour.

In addition to his volumes of poetry for adults Hevier writes equally successful and original poetry and short prose for children. One finds similar traits in his books for children as in his early works for adults: the playful lyric, a masterful handling of word sounds, restrained humour, a childlike enthusiasm for games, and terse expression. With »Hovorníček?« (1992; t: The speaking book) he creates a book of rhymes for children of three years and up – an inspired source for a phonetic and semantic acquisition of language. Hevier's books often take place in the real world of children, yet at the same time are modelled on a boundless fantasy closer to science fiction. »Krajina AGORD« (2001; t: The land of GURD), which was awarded the IBBY certificate of honour, is a surreal fairytale in which Hevier gently introduces his young readers to the subject of drugs. The young Lucia is bored and all too readily accepts an invitation from some talking trees, who invite her to travel through space and time to the distant land of Gurd (›drug‹ spelt backwards) – yet without ever leaving behind real place or time. After some adventurous encounters with singing stones and other dazzling figures, she discovers, on the back of a medal, a sad youth who is slave to Gurd's magic flowers. She leaves the ambivalent fantasy world behind, but not without first conquering Evil.

Hevier was included in the IBBY Honour List for his collection of short stories »Kam chodia na zimu zmrzlinàri« (1986; t: What does the iceman do in winter?), which has been translated into various languages. He was awarded the Triple Rose for his literary oeuvre for children's.

Aprílový Hugo
Mladé Letá
Bratislava, 1985
[Ill: Blanka Šperková]

Was macht der Eismann im Winter
Werner Dausien Verlag
Hanau, 1986
[Ü: Eliška Jelinkova]
[Ill: L'uba Končeková-Veselá]

Aladár a Baltazár na kolotči
Mladé Letá
Bratislava, 1990
[Ill: Drahomir Trsčan]

Heviho ABC
Hevi
Bratislava, 1995

Volajú ma HEVI
Hevi
Bratislava, 1997

Krajina Agord
(ab 12)
Hevi
Bratislava, 2001

Futbal s papučou
Prvá kniha
Mladé Letá
Bratislava, 2004
[Ill: Martin Kellenberger]

Daniel Hevier wurde 1955 in Bratislava, der damaligen Tschechoslowakei, geboren und gehört zu den populärsten Kinderbuchautoren der Slowakei. Er studierte an der Komenský-Universität in Bratislava Slowakistik und Ästhetik. Bevor er 1992 seinen eigenen Verlag HEVI gründete, arbeitete er zunächst als Redakteur beim Rundfunk, von 1989 bis 1992 als Cheflektor des Kinderbuchverlags Mladé letá sowie als freischaffender Schriftsteller. Heute ist Hevier als Lyriker, Erzähler, Liedtexter, Illustrator, Verleger, Dramatiker und Drehbuchautor einer der vielseitigsten slowakischen Autoren. Mit seinen Gedichtbänden aus den siebziger und achtziger Jahren (u. a. »Motýlí kolotoč«, 1974; »Nonstop«, 1981; »Elektrónkový klaun«, 1983) bereicherte er die slowakische Lyrik mit dem Geist der Leichtigkeit, einer reichen Metaphorik und großem Witz.
Neben seinen Gedichtbänden für Erwachsene schreibt Hevier eine ebenso erfolgreiche und originelle Lyrik und Kurzprosa für Kinder. Schon seine frühen Arbeiten für Erwachsene weisen Merkmale auf, die auch für seine Kinderbücher charakteristisch bleiben: das spielerisch Lyrische, ein meisterhafter Umgang mit der Wortakustik, verhaltene Komik, kindliche Spielfreude und knapper Ausdruck. Mit »Hovorníček« (1992; Ü: Das Sprechbüchlein) kreierte Hevier ein Reimbuch für Kinder ab drei Jahren – eine inspirierende Quelle zum phonetischen und semantischen Spracherwerb.
Heviers Bücher spielen oft in der realen Lebenswelt von Kindern und sind zugleich von einer überbordenden Phantasie modelliert, die bis in die Science Fiction reicht. »Krajina AGORD« (2001; Ü: Das Land von GURD), mit dem IBBY-Ehrendiplom ausgezeichnet, ist ein surreales Märchen, mit dem Hevier seine jüngeren Leser behutsam an das Thema Drogen heranführt. Die junge Lucia langweilt sich und nimmt nur allzu gerne die Einladung sprechender Bäume an, durch Zeit und Raum ins ferne Land Gurd (engl. »drug« rückwärts buchstabiert) zu reisen – ohne jedoch ihren realen Ort und die wirkliche Zeit jemals zu verlassen. Nach abenteuerlichen Begegnungen mit singenden Steinen und anderen schillernden Gestalten entdeckt sie die Kehrseite der Medaille: einen traurigen Jungen, Sklave der magischen Blumen Gurd's. Sie verlässt die zwiespältige Phantasiewelt, nicht ohne vorher das Böse besiegt zu haben.
Mit seinem 1984 entstandenen Kurzgeschichtenband »Kam chodia na zimu zmrzlinàri« (dt. »Was macht der Eismann im Winter?«, 1986), in mehrere Sprachen übersetzt, wurde Hevier in die IBBY-Honour-List aufgenommen. Sein literarisches Gesamtwerk für Kinder und Jugendliche wurde zudem mit der Dreifachen Rose ausgezeichnet. Hevier lebt in Bratislava.

louis jensen

biography

Louis Jensen was born in Nibe, Denmark, in 1943. An architect and town planner by profession, Jensen has been working as a freelance writer of children's, youth and adult literature since 1993. He made his debut in children's and youth literature in 1983 with the short story »Insektmanden« (t: The insect man), which was published in the collection »Fantastiske Fortœllinger«. His four part book series, »Krystalmanden« (t: The crystal man) was published at the end of the 1980's. The first part tells the tale of a motorcycle trip through Denmark, of growing up and of homecoming. With this book Jensen proceeded to become one of Denmark's most highly regarded authors of children's and youth literature.

For readers as well as critics, Jensen is considered a »storyteller in a new guise«. He feels at home in the world of allegorical-phantasmagorical creatures as well as in that of the teenage video dealer. In his modern tales, stories and novels, Jensen uses understatement, humour and his secure grasp of young people's lived realities to roam the labyrinths of youthful consciousness. Sensitively and poetically, he tells of good and evil, light and darkness, love and suffering – occasionally sorrowful and serious, occasionally brave and witty, but always with a regard for the visible and invisible absurdities and magical moments in life.

Jensen's original profession as an architect is also reflected in his children's books. »Et hus er et ansigt« (1998; t: A house is a face) is an unconventional and striking architectural picture book for children consisting of a series of textual and photographic impressions of life, community, and change. Father and son roam their town, which is bathed in light and shadows, and contemplate roofs and niches, clouds and chimneys. Jensen's novel for young people »Skelettet på hjul« (1992; t: The skeleton on wheels), originally a play, belongs to the new classics of Danish children's and youth literature and tells the tale of Martin's search for the soul of his murdered dog. Jensen's ›magnum opus‹, a collection of 1001 short stories for children (among these »Hundrede firkande historier«, 2003, t: A Hundred squared stories) is in preparation. In this compendium of absurd, funny, serious and unbelievable stories one finds the sensitive tale of the love between a small loaf of rye bread and a French baguette, as well as stories about giants, rubber boots, hearts, star faces and dogs.

Louis Jensen has been awarded top literary awards for his work, including the Nordic Children's Book Prize (1996), Danmarks Skolebibliotekarforening (1998), and the prestigious Hans-Christian-Andersen-Stipend (1998). He was a member of the Danish Arts Foundation between 1994 and 1998. He lives near Århus.

Plus-Four og katten-skatten
Gyldendal
Kopenhagen, 1991

Et hus er et ansigt: en bog for børn om arkitektur
Gyldendal
Kopenhagen, 1998

Hundrede splinternye historier
Gyldendal
Kopenhagen, 2000
[Ill: Lilian Brøgger]

Den strandede mand
Høst & Søn
Kopenhagen, 2000

Den frygtelige hånd
Høst & Søn
Kopenhagen, 2001
[Ill: Cato Thau-Jensen]

Krystalmanden
Gyldendal
Kopenhagen, 2002

Hundrede firkantede historier
Gyldendal
Kopenhagen, 2003
[Ill: Lilian Brøgger]

Skelettet på hjul
Gyldendal
Kopenhagen, 2003

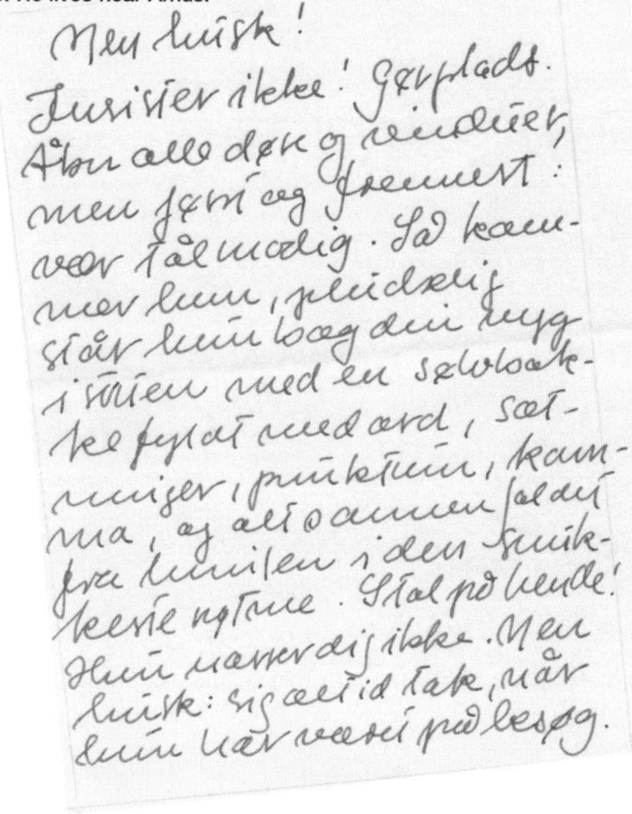

Men husk!
Insister ikke! Gør plads.
Åbn alle døre og vinduer,
men først og fremmest:
vær tålmodig. Så kom-
mer hun, pludselig
står hun bag din ryg
i stuen med en sølvbak-
ke fyldt med ord, sæt-
ninger, punktum, kom-
ma, og alt sammen faldet
fra himlen i den smuk-
keste rytme. Stol på hende!
Hun narrer dig ikke. Men
husk: sig altid tak, når
hun har været på besøg.

Louis Jensen, 1943 im dänischen Nibe geboren, Architekt und Stadtplaner, arbeitet seit 1993 als freier Schriftsteller und schreibt für Kinder, Jugendliche und Erwachsene. Als Kinder- und Jugendbuchautor debütierte er 1983 mit der Kurzgeschichte »Insektmanden« (Ü: Der Insektenmann), die in der Geschichtensammlung »Fantastiske Fortœllinger« veröffentlicht wurde. Mit seiner vierteiligen Buchserie »Krystalmanden« (1986f.; Ü: Der Kristallmann), die Ende der achtziger Jahre erschien und deren erster Teil von einer Motorradreise durch Dänemark, vom Erwachsenwerden und Heimkommen erzählt, avancierte er zu einem der meistverehrten Kinder- und Jugendbuchautoren Dänemarks.
Lesern wie Kritikern gilt Jensen als »Märchenerzähler im neuen Gewand«. Er ist in der Welt allegorisch-phantastischer Gestalten ebenso zuhause wie in der des Teenage-Videoverkäufers. Mit Understatement, Humor und sicherem Gespür für die Lebenswelt junger Menschen durchstreift Jensen in seinen modernen Märchen, Geschichten und Romanen die Labyrinthe kindlich-jugendlichen Bewusstseins. Berührend und poetisch erzählt er von Gut und Böse, Licht und Schatten, Liebe und Leid – mal traurig und ernst, mal mutig und schneidig, immer mit einem Blick für die sichtbaren und unsichtbaren Absurditäten und magischen Momente des Lebens.
Jensens ursprüngliche Profession als Architekt findet sich auch in seinen Kinderbüchern. »Et hus er et ansigt« (1998; Ü: Ein Haus ist ein Gesicht) ist ein unkonventionelles und bestechendes Architektur-Bilderbuch für Kinder, bestehend aus einer Serie von Text- und Fotoimpressionen über das Leben, über Gemeinschaft und Veränderung. Vater und Sohn durchstreifen ihre in Licht und Schatten getauchte Stadt, betrachten Dächer und Nischen, Wolken und Schornsteine. Jensens Jugendroman »Skelettet på hjul« (1992; Ü: Ein Skelett auf Rädern), ursprünglich ein Theaterstück für Kinder, gehört zu den neuen Klassikern der dänischen Kinder- und Jugendliteratur und erzählt von Martins Suche nach der Seele seines getöteten Hundes. Im Entstehen begriffen ist Jensens ›opus magnum‹, eine Sammlung von 1001 Kurzgeschichten für Kinder (u. a. »Hundrede firkantede historier«, 2003). In diesem Kompendium absurder, lustiger, ernster und unglaublicher Geschichten findet man das zarte Liebesband zwischen einem kleinen Roggenbrot und einem französischen Baguette ebenso wie Geschichten über Riesen, Gummistiefel, Herzen, Sternengesichter und Hunde.
Für sein Werk erhielt Louis Jensen die höchsten literarischen Auszeichnungen, darunter den Nordischen Kinderbuchpreis (1996), Danmarks Skolebibliotekarforening (1998) sowie das begehrte Hans-Christian-Andersen-Stipendium (1998). Von 1994 bis 1998 war er Mitglied der Danish Arts Foundation. Jensen lebt bei Århus.

But Remember

Don't insist. Make Room! Open all the doors and windows, but most importantly: be patient! Then she will come to you, suddenly standing behind you in the room bearing a silver platter filled with words, sentences, periods, commas, and all falling from heaven in the most beatiful rhythm. Trust her! She won't let you down. But remember: always give thanks when she has been on a visit.

michèle lemieux

biography

»This book is like a dialogue, an open door between our childhood world and the world of adults. I wanted to let the world be seen through the eyes of this young girl who wonders about a very simple experience: existence!« This is what Michèle Lemieux has to say about her picture book »Gewitternacht« (Eng. »Stormy Night«, 1999), which was published in Germany in 1996. The Canadian illustrator, author, lecturer and director was born in Québec. After finishing her degree in visual arts in Montreal, she lived in Germany for five years at the end of the 1970's. Since 1978 she has published fifteen books, which she both illustrated and wrote. They have been translated, filmed and put on stage in more than twenty languages.

In »Gewitternacht« Michèle Lemieux tells the story of a little girl who is unable to fall asleep during a stormy night and whose head is swarming with all kinds of thoughts: where does infinity end? Is there life on other stars? Do I exist only once in the world? Who is responsible for coincidence? And does dying hurt? In a silent dialogue with her dog Fido, she searches for answers to all her questions and ideas. The author's black and white ink drawings accompany the little girl's thoughts about being beautiful, being heroic and being scared. In 1997 Lemieux received the prestigious Bologna Ragazzi Award for »Gewitternacht«. This thoughtful picture book has been translated into more than ten languages, and the fourth edition has already been published in Germany. Lemieux's cinematic adaptation »Nuit d'orage« premiered in 2003 and was screened at the Children's Film Festival of the 54th Berlinale, where it was awarded the Crystal Bear for best animated short film.

Before »Gewitternacht« became a picture book it was a sketchbook, in which the author tried intuitively to grasp the simplicity and truthfulness of life. She loves authentic books that question the existential and that deal with universal themes. In her work Lemieux experiments with watercolours, gouache, acrylic, oils collages and pen and ink. Her drawings have a timeless-mystic quality that invites the viewer to dive into the picture and to become a part of the story. The author has illustrated a number of classical and modern texts including »Amahl and the Night Visitors« by Gian Carlo Menotti (1996) and »The Pied Piper of Hamelin« (1993). Her illustrations have been exhibited in New York, Mexico, Tokyo and Montreal to name but a few. Lemieux has been nominated for the Governor General's Award numerous times, and for the Hans Christian Andersen Award in 2001. After having spent many years abroad, she now lives in Canada. She devotes her time to illustrative work and has taught illustration at the Université du Quèbec since 1982.

Eveline Hasler
Im Winterland
Otto Maier
Ravensburg, 1984
[Ill: Michèle Lemieux]
Was hört der Bär?
Ravensburger,
Ravensburg, 1986
[Ü: Cris Baisch]
Gian Carlo Menotti
Amahl und die Könige aus dem Morgenland
Ravensburger,
Ravensburg, 1986
Sergei Prokofiev
Peter und der Wolf
Kids Can Press
Toronto, 1991
[Ill: Michèle Lemieux]
Der Rattenfänger von Hameln
(ab 4)
Ravensburger,
Ravensburg, 1994
Dorothee Kreusch-Jacob
Lieder von der Natur
Ravensburger,
Ravensburg, 1994
[Ill: Michèle Lemieux]
Gewitternacht
(ab 6)
Beltz & Gelberg
Weinheim, 2002

»Dieses Buch ist wie ein Dialog, eine offene Tür zwischen der Kinder- und der Erwachsenenwelt. Ich wollte die Welt aus den Augen dieses jungen Mädchens zeigen, das sich über eine ganz einfache Erfahrung wundert: das Dasein!« sagt Michèle Lemieux über ihr Bilderbuch »Gewitternacht«, das 1996 in Deutschland erschien. Geboren wurde die kanadische Illustratorin, Autorin, Dozentin und Regisseurin 1955 in Québec. Nach dem Studium der visuellen Kunst in Montréal lebte sie Ende der Siebziger fünf Jahre lang in Deutschland. Seit 1978 erschienen fünfzehn von ihr illustrierte und geschriebene Bücher, die in über zwanzig Sprachen übersetzt, verfilmt und inszeniert wurden.

In »Gewitternacht« zeichnet und erzählt Michèle Lemieux die Geschichte eines kleinen Mädchens, das in einer stürmischen Nacht keinen Schlaf findet und dem lauter Gedanken durch den Kopf schwirren: Wo endet die Unendlichkeit? Gibt es Leben auf anderen Sternen? Gibt es mich nur einmal auf der Welt? Und der Zufall, wer bestimmt den? Tut Sterben weh? In leisem Zwiegespräch mit ihrem Hund Fido versucht sie Antworten zu finden auf all' ihre Fragen und Einfälle. Mit schwarzweißen Federzeichnungen begleitet die Autorin die Gedanken des kleinen Mädchens über das Schön-Sein, Held-Sein und Angst-Haben. Für »Gewitternacht« erhielt Lemieux 1997 den bedeutenden Bologna Ragazzi Award. Das Gedanken-Bilder-Buch wurde in mehr als zehn Sprachen übersetzt und in Deutschland bereits in vierter Auflage publiziert. 2003 erschien Lemieux' filmische Adaption »Nuit d'orage«, die auf dem Kinderfilmfest der 54. Berlinale mit dem Gläsernen Bären als bester animierter Kurzfilm prämiert wurde.

Bevor »Gewitternacht« zu einem Bilderbuch wurde, war es ein Skizzenbuch, in dem die Autorin intuitiv die Einfachheit und Wahrhaftigkeit des Lebens festzuhalten versuchte. Sie liebt authentische Bücher, die Existentielles in Frage stellen und sich mit universellen Themen befassen. In ihren Werken experimentiert Lemieux mit Wasserfarbe, Gouache, Acryl, Öl und Collage, Feder und Tinte. Ihre Zeichnungen haben eine zeitlos-mystische Qualität, die den Betrachter einlädt, in das Bild einzutauchen und ein Teil der Geschichte zu werden. Die Autorin hat eine Vielzahl von klassischen und modernen Texten illustriert, darunter »Amahl and the Night Visitors« von Gian Carlo Menotti (1986) und »The Pied Piper of Hamelin« (1993). Ihre Illustrationen wurden u. a. in New York, Mexiko, Tokyo und Montréal ausgestellt. Lemieux war mehrfach für den Governor's General Award und 2001 für den Hans-Christian-Andersen-Award nominiert. Nach Jahren im Ausland lebt sie heute wieder in Kanada. Ihre Zeit widmet sie ihrer illustratorischen Arbeit und seit 1982 dem Unterrichten an der Université du Québec in Montréal im Fach Illustration.

per nilsson
biography

Per Nilsson was born in Malmö, Sweden in 1954 and is one of Sweden's leading authors of young people's literature. After finishing his degree, he began working as a mathematics and music teacher at a secondary school before making writing his only profession in 1999. Today he writes for all those young people who are thrown into the reality of life with heads full of dreams, fear and longing. »I think about my books as letters. I want to keep up a dialogue. About life and death, about hope and trust in the future, about the roles that we play, about the world we live in, and about love. Most of all I want to speak to somebody who is sixteen years old. Or thirteen or twenty.« In a mélange of classicalepic narrative, and cinematic storytelling structures, Nilsson's novels encompass the emotional lives of adolescents and pose the question of how a young adult can and should live today.
»Hjärtans fröjd« (1992; Eng. »Heart's Delight«, 2003), which was awarded the Deutscher Jugendliteraturpreis in 1997, and has been translated into numerous languages, is one of Nilsson's most important novels for young people. In possibly »the most beautiful and saddest, yet most comforting love story existing in modern youth literature« (Praxis Deutsch, 2000), he describes in hindsight the great tragedy of first love, with all its happy moments as well as its gnawing pain, and creates a novel of silent tones that uses the end as the beginning. As in many of his works for young adults, the characters in »du&du&du« (1998; t: You&You&You) are simultaneously eccentric outsiders, dreamers and loveable contemporaries, who protect their secrets vehemently and whose lives take a decisive turn within the course of a few hours. A pretty girl who contemplates the link between lust and love, a crazy boy who thinks his father is God, and a young man who allows himself to be buried alive in order to find out what life is all about – Nilsson has taken big themes and bundled them up to create a humorous, occasionally sad and not least erotically uninhibited novel. »Ett annat sätt att vara ung« (2000; t: A different way of being young) is an elegantly constructed and exciting novel. It realistically depicts eighteen year old Hannah, a curious and self-critical heroine, who questions how theory and practice are related in real life and how the soul, consciousness and the body can be reconciled.
Per Nilsson was honoured for his work with the Astrid Lindgren Prize in 1999, and has been nominated for the August Prize – the most important literature award in Sweden – four times already. He is married, has four children and lives in Sölvesborg, a small village on Sweden's Baltic coast.

Hej, Milena
(ab 8)
Oetinger,
Hamburg, 2000
[Ü: Brigitta Kicherer]
[Ill: Sabine Kraushaar]
Ett annat sätt att vara ung
Rabén & Sjögren
Stockholm, 2000
Sjutton
Rabén & Sjögren
Stockholm, 2002
Anarkai
(ab 12)
Carlsen
Hamburg, 2003
[Ü: Christel Hildebrandt]
Du & du & du
(ab 14)
Dtv
München, 2003
[Ü: Brigitta Kicherer]
Solprinsen
Rabén & Sjögren
Stockholm, 2004
So lonely
(ab 12)
Dtv
München, 2004
[Ü: Brigitta Kicherer]

Make answer, Muse!

All work and no play
makes Jack a dull boy
all work and no
play makes Jack a
dull boy all work and
no play makes Jack
a dull boy all
work and no play makes
Jack a dull
boy all work
and no play makes

Per Nilsson wurde 1954 in Malmö, Schweden, geboren und gehört zu den führenden Jugendbuchautoren Schwedens. Nach seinem Studium arbeitete er zunächst als Mathematik- und Musiklehrer an einem Gymnasium, bevor er das Schreiben 1999 ganz zu seinem Beruf machte. Heute schreibt er für all jene jungen Menschen, deren Köpfe voller Träume, Angst und Sehnsucht sind und die in die Realität des Lebens geworfen werden. »Ich sehe meine Bücher als Briefe. Ich möchte einen Dialog führen. Über das Leben und den Tod, über Hoffnung und Vertrauen in die Zukunft, über die Rollen, die wir spielen, über die Welt, in der wir leben, und über Liebe. Vor allem aber möchte ich jene ansprechen, die sechzehn Jahre alt sind, oder dreizehn oder zwanzig.« In einer Mischung aus klassisch-epischem Erzählen und filmischer Erzählstruktur kreisen Nilssons Romane um das Gefühlsleben von Heranwachsenden und fragen danach, wie man heute als junger Mensch leben kann oder soll.
1997 mit dem Deutschen Jugendliteraturpreis ausgezeichnet und in viele Sprachen übersetzt, gehört »Hjärtans fröjd« (1992; dt. »So lonely«, 1996) zu Nilssons wichtigsten Jugendromanen. In der vielleicht »schönsten, traurigsten und auch tröstlichsten Liebesgeschichte, die man in der neueren Jugendliteratur findet« (Praxis Deutsch, 2000), beschreibt er in Rückblenden die große Tragödie der ersten Liebe mit all ihrem Glück, aber auch ihrem nagenden Schmerz und kreiert einen Roman der leisen Töne, der das Ende zum Anfang nimmt. Wie in verschiedenen seiner Jugendromane sind auch die Figuren in »du&du&du« (1998; dt. »Du&du&du«, 1999) exzentrische Außenseiter, Träumer und liebenswerte Zeitgenossen zugleich, die ihre Geheimnisse mit aller Kraft verteidigen und deren Leben innerhalb weniger Stunden eine entscheidende Wendung nimmt. Ein schönes Mädchen, das sich Gedanken macht, wie Lust und Liebe zusammenpassen, ein verrückter Junge, der glaubt, sein Vater sei Gott und ein junger Mann, der sich lebendig begraben lässt, um zu begreifen, worum es im Leben geht – große Themen hat Nilsson hier zu einem humorvollen, mitunter traurigen und nicht zuletzt erotisch unverkrampften Roman verklammert. Elegant konstruiert, spannend und wahrhaftig zeigt Nilsson in »Ett annat sätt att vara ung« (2000) die achtzehnjährige Hannah, eine neugierige und selbstkritische Heldin, die sich fragt, wie Theorie und Lebenspraxis zueinander gehören und sich Seele, Bewusstsein und Körperlichkeit vereinbaren lassen.
Per Nilsson wurde 1999 für sein literarisches Werk mit dem Astrid-Lindgren-Preis geehrt, bereits viermal war er für den August-Preis nominiert, den bedeutendsten Literaturpreis Schwedens. Er ist verheiratet, hat vier Kinder und lebt in Sölvesborg, einem kleinen Ort an der schwedischen Ostseeküste.

... And since the picture of Jack Nicholson sitting in the library in the movie The Shining for some reason come up in my head I thought I might as well use it as an answer.

anna onichimowska

biography

Anna Onichimowska was born in Poland in 1952 and studied Polish Language and Literature. For several years she worked as a children's book publisher and editor and in 1980 brought out her own collection of poems, »Gdybym miał konia« (t: If I had a horse). Since then she has published over twenty books for children and adolescents of all ages, over forty plays for radio and theatre, and scripts for television. In her children's books, Anna Onichimowska advances the traditional form of the short story within the Polish tradition. In the spirit of Janucz Korczaks she looks to the everyday problems of her young readers, infusing them with sensitive humour and elements of the fantastic. Thus in her collection of stories »Najwyższa góra świata« (1996; t: The highest mountain in the world), the little protagonists live through arduous moments: illness and death in the family, separation of parents, exclusion and solitude, but also, experience from the point of view of adults, smaller existential problems such as the longing for a pet. As in many of her other works, there is no sharp distinction between reality and fantasy in her children's novel, »Koniec świata i poziomki« (1999; t: The end of the world and wild strawberries). Here the travel adventures of a family – which she relates by means of classical fairytale elements such as transformation, capture and discovery of treasure – seem to be a common game in which reality forms only a part of the great world of fantasy. »Dzieci zorzy polarnej« (1998; t: Children of the northern lights), a collection of short stories written with the Finnish author Tom Paxal, are inspired by Scandinavian myths. Here too magic, dream and sensations determine the experiences of the protagonists. In »Hera, moja miłość« (2003; t: Heroin, my love), Onichimowska depicts how easily young people can become junkies, and how drug addiction can lead to unintended and dramatic consequences. Her portrayal is honest and disturbing. She outspokenly describes adolescents as moody, and portrays adults in their frequently self-referential way of life. Her book brims with confidence, but also shows how love can cement what appeared to be broken for a long time.
Anna Onichimowska has won multiple awards both in Poland and abroad, among them the Kornel Makuszyński Literature Prize in 1997 and the IBBY Diploma in 2001. At the fourth European KIBUM in Saarbrücken, her illustrated book »Żółta zasypianka« (2000; t: Yellow Lullaby) came out in a German and French translation. Onichimowska is the director of the Świat Dziecka Foundation and second chairwoman of the Polish IBBY Section. She lives in Warsaw.

Gdybym miał konia
KAW
1980
[Ill: Janusz Stanny]
Dzieci zorzy polarnej
Mit Tom Paxal
Jacek Santorski
Warszawa, 1998
[Ill: Małgorzata Bieńkowska]
Dobry potwór nie jest zły
Edytorska Ezop
Warszawa, 2000
[Ill: Edyta Ćwiek]
Najwyższa góra świata
Świat Książki
Kraków, 2001
[Ill: Małgorzata Bieńkowska]
Hera moja miłość
Świat Książki
Kraków, 2003
Koniec świata i poziomki
Literatura
łódź, 2004
[Ill: Joanna Sedlaczek]
Eine gelbe Geschichte
Europäische Kinder-und Jugendbuchmesse e.V.
Saarbrücken, 2004
[Ü: Natalie Weber]
[Ill: Krystyna Lipka-Sztarbałło]

Anna Onichimowska wurde 1952 in Polen geboren und studierte polnische Sprache und Literatur. Mehrere Jahre war sie als Herausgeberin und Lektorin von Kinderbüchern tätig und debütierte 1980 mit der Gedichtsammlung »Gdybym miał konia« (Ü: Wenn ich ein Pferd hätte). Seither entstanden mehr als zwanzig Bücher für Kinder und Jugendliche aller Altersstufen, über vierzig Hörspiele und Theaterstücke sowie Fernsehdrehbücher.
In ihren Kinderbüchern entwickelte Anna Onichimowska die in der polnischen Literatur tradierte Form der Kurzerzählung für das junge Publikum weiter. Im Geiste Janucz Korczaks blickt sie auf die alltäglichen Probleme ihrer jungen Leser, stets von einfühlsamem Humor getragen und oft von phantastischen Elementen durchzogen. So in ihrer Erzählsammlung »Najwyższa góra świata« (1996; Ü: Der höchste Berg der Welt), deren kleine Helden schwierige Momente durchleben: Krankheit und Tod in der Familie, Trennung der Eltern, Ausgrenzung und Einsamkeit, aber auch aus der Sicht von Erwachsenen weniger existentielle Probleme wie der Wunsch nach einem Haustier. Wie in vielen ihrer Werke gibt es auch in ihrem Kinderroman »Koniec świata i poziomki« (1999; Ü: Das Ende der Welt und Walderdbeeren) keine scharfe Trennung zwischen Wirklichkeit und Phantasie. Die Reiseabenteuer einer Familie – erzählt mittels klassischer Märchenelemente wie Wanderung, Gefangennahme und Auffinden des Schatzes – scheinen ein gemeinsames Spiel zu sein, in dem die Realität nur ein Teil der großen Welt der Phantasie ist. Ihre zusammen mit dem finnischen Autor Tom Paxal geschriebenen Erzählungen »Dzieci zorzy polarnej« (1998ff.; Ü: Kinder des Polarlichts) sind inspiriert von skandinavischen Mythen. Auch hier bestimmen Magie, Traum und Gefühle die Erlebniswelt der Protagonisten. In »Hera, moja miłość« (2003; Ü: Heroin, meine Liebe) schildert Onichimowska, wie leicht junge Menschen zu Junkies werden können und Drogenabhängigkeit zu ungewollt dramatischen Konsequenzen führt. Ihre Darstellung ist aufwühlend und ehrlich. Jugendliche beschreibt sie unverblümt launisch, Erwachsene porträtiert sie in ihrer oft selbstbezogenen Lebensweise. Voller Zuversicht zeigt ihr Buch aber auch, was Familie ausmacht und wie sich mit Liebe kitten lässt, was lange zerbrochen scheint.
Anna Onichimowska wurde mit zahlreichen in- und ausländischen Preisen ausgezeichnet, so u. a. 1997 mit dem Kornel-Makuszyński-Literaturpreis und 2001 mit dem IBBY-Ehrendiplom. Auf der 4. Europäischen KIBUM in Saarbrücken hatte ihre Bilderbuch-Geschichte »Żółta zasypianka« (2000; dt. »Eine gelbe Geschichte«, 2004) in deutsch-französischer Übersetzung Premiere. Onichimowska ist Direktorin der Świat Dziecka Foundation und zweite Vorsitzende der polnischen IBBY-Sektion. Sie lebt in Warschau.

My muses fell down out of their prickly shells. I fill my pockets with them, put some under my pillow and out of the two prettiest ones I make a chesnut horse. I ride my little horse and trot away wherever either of us pleases. One can tame it and feed from a hand or let go and only watch it roam.
No need to follow, it comes back on its own.

mario ramos

biography

Mario Ramos was born the son of a Belgian mother and a Portuguese father in Brussels in 1958. He studied graphics and communication design at the local École Nationale Supérieure des Arts Visuels »La Cambre«. He then travelled Europe and from 1986 on worked as a freelance draughtsman, designer and poster artist. He decided to focus on illustrating and writing children's literature, which has since been published in the Netherlands, Germany, Denmark, Sweden, Spain, Italy, Korea, Japan and the US. Ramos' books feature a plain and clear symbolic language. He relies on the children's humour, intelligence, and imagination when presenting them with a startling finale. In his pictures and texts he tells of fear, power, otherness and tenderness. »As a starting point I take an idea coming by way of a memory, an incident or a conversation. It takes on a form and livens up all those important questions that I asked myself when a child, that all children ask and that still I ask often enough.«
Ramos' children's book »Le petit soldat qui cherchait la guerre« (t: The little soldier who was looking for the war) was published in German translation in 2000. A little soldier awakens all alone and left behind on a battlefield, and so takes to searching for the war. He meets victims of the war, loses his uniform, finally recognizes the absurdity of his quest, and discovers peace. In his most renowned illustrated book »C'est moi le plus fort« (t: I am the strongest), Ramos relates in a very humorous way using a colourful and effective language about being little and big. The young reader accompanies the »Big Bad Wolf« walking, boasting and bullying through the forest, and meets there well known figures from the world of fairy tales. A little rabbit, Red Riding Hood or the Seven Dwarves confirm to the wolf that he is the biggest and strongest. Only the small and cheeky toad, taunted as »Quabbelwabbel«, dares to contradict him, and by the end makes the wolf stop wanting to be the wickedest and wildest. Ramos' book »Le roi est occupé« (1998; t: The king is busy), published in German in August 2004, sends the reader in search of the king. Secret corridors, treasure chambers and dungeons lie hidden behind liftable flaps on the page, and after an exciting route through the castle the reader finds the king in a place where kings go all alone.
In 1993, Mario Ramos was awarded the Prix Versèle for his children's book »Djabibi« (1992) and in 1998 the Prix des Critiques en Belgique for his illustrated book »Quand j'étais petit« (1997). He lives with his family in Brussels.

Djabibi
Rascal
(ab 6)
L'Ecole des loisirs
Paris, 1992
Au lit, petit monstre!
L'Ecole des loisirs
Paris, 1998
Der kleine Soldat, der den Krieg wieder finden wollte
(ab 5)
Oetinger
Hamburg, 2000
[Ü: Alexandra Rak]
Nuno, der kleine König
(ab 3)
Moritz
Frankfurt a.M., 2001
[Ü: Tobias Scheffel]
La princesse grenouille
(ab 3)
L'Ecole des loisirs
Paris, 2003
Ich bin der Stärkste im ganzen Land!
(ab 3)
Moritz
Frankfurt a.M., 2003
[Ü: Markus Weber]
Der König hat zu tun
(ab 2)
Moritz
Frankfurt a.M., 2004
[Ü: Markus Weber]

Mario Ramos wurde 1958 als Sohn einer Belgierin und eines Portugiesen in Brüssel geboren und studierte an der dortigen Ecole Nationale Supérieure des Arts Visuels »La Cambre« Graphik- und Kommunikationsdesign. Nach seinem Studium bereiste er Europa und arbeitete ab 1986 als freier Zeichner, Graphiker und Plakatkünstler, bevor er Anfang der neunziger Jahre entschied, sich auf das Illustrieren und Schreiben von Kinderbüchern zu konzentrieren, die seither in den Niederlanden, Deutschland, Dänemark, Schweden, Spanien, Italien, Korea, Japan und den USA erschienen. Ramos' Bücher zeichnen sich durch eine einfache und klare Bildsprache aus. Er setzt auf den Humor, die Intelligenz und die Vorstellungskraft von Kindern, wenn er ihnen ein verblüffendes Finale präsentiert. In seinen Bildern und Texten erzählt er von Angst, Macht, Anderssein und Zärtlichkeit. »Ausgangspunkt ist eine Idee, die mir durch eine Erinnerung, Begebenheit oder Unterhaltung kommt. Sie nimmt Gestalt an und lässt all jene wichtigen Fragen wieder aufleben, die ich mir als Kind gestellt habe, die sich alle Kinder stellen und die ich mir immer noch oft genug stelle.«
Im Jahr 2000 erschien Ramos' Kinderbuch »Le petit soldat qui cherchait la guerre« (1999; dt. »Der kleine Soldat, der den Krieg wieder finden wollte«) in deutscher Sprache. Ein kleiner Soldat erwacht allein, zurückgelassen auf dem Schlachtfeld, und begibt sich auf die Suche nach dem Krieg. Er begegnet den Kriegsopfern, verliert seine Uniform, erkennt schließlich die Absurdität seiner Suche und entdeckt den Frieden. In seinem bekannten Bilderbuch »C'est moi le plus fort« (2001; dt. »Ich bin der Stärkste im ganzen Land«, 2003) erzählt Ramos mit viel Witz und kräftigen Farbakzenten vom Groß- und Kleinsein. Der junge Leser begleitet den großen bösen Wolf auf seinem ›Egotrip‹ durch den Wald und begegnet dabei alten Bekannten aus der Märchenwelt. So bestätigen ein Häschen, Rotkäppchen oder die Sieben Zwerge dem Wolf, dass er der Größte und Stärkste ist. Nur ein kleiner vorwitziger Kröterich, verhöhnt als »Quabbelwabbel«, wagt es, ihm zu widersprechen und sorgt dafür, dass der Wolf am Ende nicht mehr der Böseste und Wildeste sein will. Im August 2004 erschien Ramos' »Le roi est occupé« (1998; dt. »Der König hat viel zu tun«) in deutscher Übersetzung, in dem er seine Leser auf die Suche nach dem König schickt. Hinter Papp-Klappen verbergen sich geheime Gänge, Schatzkammern und Verliese, und nach einem spannenden Gang durch die Burg findet der Leser den König dort, wo auch ein König nur allein hingeht.
Mario Ramos erhielt 1993 den Prix Versèle für sein Kinderbuch »Djabibi« (1992), und sein Bilderbuch »Quand j'étais petit« (1997) wurde 1998 mit dem Prix des Critiques en Belgique prämiert. Er lebt mit seiner Familie in Brüssel.

nasrin siege

biography

Nasrin Siege was born in Iran in 1950 and came to Germany when she was nine years old. She grew up in Hamburg and Flensburg, studied Psychology and Pedagogics in Kiel and worked as a psychotherapist in a hospital for drug addicts in Friedrichdorf, Taunus. Since 1983 Nasrin Siege has lived for extensive periods of time in Africa with her husband, a German development worker. She works as a freelance writer, is engaged in traditional healing methods, collects fairly tales and is interested in African art. She is involved in several projects with street children in Tanzania, and is a counseller in the children's remand prison of Dar-Es-Salaam.

Nasrin Siege's texts deal with prejudices towards other cultures. They dismantle clichés and look into the circumstances of children in diverse cultures. »As a child, I was often angry about the representation of other cultures in young people's books either as »exotic«, as scenery for the white heroes, or as object of ridicule. I missed books for children in which there were girls like me with problems similar to mine.« Her first children's book »Sombo, das Mädchen vom Fluss« (t: Sombo, the girl from the river) was published in 1990. With great empathy it tells the story of a girl growing up in Zambia. The author describes farming, fishing and hunting of the Luvale people in a stirring and colourful manner. She tells of Sombo's initiation in the Mukanda, the girls' bush school, where she is prepared for her life as a woman, as well as of her dream of achieving more than the village women. The book about Sombo is frequently used in classes and was awarded the Children's Literature Award of the Berlin Senate's Commissioner for Foreigners, alongside the novel »Wie der Fluss in meinem Dorf« (1994, t: Like the river in my village). Nasrin Siege's books very often reflect her own life, as in her novel »Shirin« (1996). Eleven year old Shirin moves from Iran to Germany with her parents in 1960. While her difficulties finding friends become more and more irrelevant, she at the same time becomes estranged from her parents.

Nasrin Siege's role as a mediator between cultures is evident in her fairy tales. In »Kalulu und andere afrikanische Märchen« (1993, t: Kalulu and other african fairy tales) she follows the track of the rabbit Kalulu. The tales tell of fighting and submission, love and hatred; they surprise by sudden turns, African wisdom and European influences. Siege's latest young people's book »Hyänen im hohen Gras. Spuren in der Serengeti« (t: Hyaenas in the grass. Tracks in the serengeti) appeared this August. The author currently lives in Germany again.

„Make answer, Muse!"

Wenn ich dich nicht spüre
Spüre ich dir nach
In mir
Horche blind in das Dunkel
Versuche dich zu locken:
Mit Mozart, Beethoven,
Schumann, den Beatles,
Persischen Liedern
Kann ich dich manchmal erreichen.
Und mich glücklich daran preisen
Doch nicht immer läßt du mit Musik
dich gnädig stimmen:
Dann:

Eingesperrter Löwe. Hungriger, der um den Schreibtisch streift. Der nichts zum Fressen findet. Du, Muse, schweigst – der Löwe brüllt – gegen den Hunger. Manchmal hilft nur Warten. Manchmal habe ich Glück und du kommst zurück – besänftigst den Löwen mit neuen Geschichten!

Doch wenn du nicht kommst, verhungere ich!

– Nasrin Siege – 2004

Sombo, das Mädchen vom Fluss
(ab 10)
Beltz & Gelberg
Weinheim, 1990

Kalulu und andere afrikanische Märchen
Brandes & Apsel
Frankfurt a.M., 1993
[Ill: Barbara Rieder]

Wie der Fluss in meinem Dorf
(ab 12)
Beltz & Gelberg
Weinheim, 1994

Shirin
(ab 11)
Beltz & Gelberg
Weinheim, 1996

Juma, ein Strassenkind aus Tansania
(ab 11)
Beltz & Gelberg
Weinheim, 1998

Als die Elefanten kamen
(ab 11)
Beltz & Gelberg
Weinheim, 2001

Hyänen im hohen Gras. Spuren in der Serengeti
Brandes & Apsel
Frankfurt a.M., 2004

Nasrin Siege wurde 1950 im Iran geboren und kam als Neunjährige in die Bundesrepublik. Sie wuchs in Hamburg und Flensburg auf, studierte Psychologie und Pädagogik in Kiel und arbeitete als Psychotherapeutin in einer Suchtklinik in Friedrichsdorf im Taunus. Seit 1983 hält sich Nasrin Siege mit ihrem Ehemann, einem deutschen Entwicklungshelfer, immer wieder für längere Zeit in Afrika auf. Sie arbeitet als freischaffende Schriftstellerin, beschäftigt sich mit traditionellen Heilmethoden, sammelt Märchen und befasst sich mit afrikanischer Kunst. In Tansania engagierte sie sich in verschiedenen Straßenkinderprojekten und als Beraterin im Kinderuntersuchungsgefängnis von Dar-Es-Salaam.
Nasrin Sieges Texte bringen Vorurteile gegenüber fremden Kulturen zur Sprache, brechen Rollenklischees auf und setzen sich mit der Lebenssituation von Kindern in unterschiedlichen Kulturen auseinander. »Als Kind habe ich mich oft darüber geärgert, dass fremde Kulturen in Jugendbüchern entweder als ›exotisch‹ dargestellt wurden, als Kulisse für die weißen Helden dienten oder ganz einfach lächerlich gemacht wurden. Und ich habe Kinderbücher vermisst, in denen Mädchen wie ich vorkamen, die ähnliche Probleme hatten wie ich.« 1990 erschien mit »Sombo, das Mädchen vom Fluss« ihr erstes Kinderbuch. In einfühlsamen Worten erzählt sie die Geschichte eines heranwachsenden Mädchens in Sambia. Spannend und anschaulich beschreibt sie Landwirtschaft, Fischfang und Jagd bei den Luvale. Sie berichtet von Sombos Initiation im Mukanda, der Mädchen-Buschschule, wo sie auf ihr Leben als Frau vorbereitet wird, und von ihrem Wunsch, einmal mehr erreichen zu können als die Frauen in ihrem Dorf. Das »Sombo«-Buch wird häufig als Unterrichtslektüre verwendet und wurde zusammen mit »Wie der Fluss in meinem Dorf« (1994) mit dem Kinderbuch-Preis der Ausländerbeauftragten des Berliner Senats ausgezeichnet. Oft sind Nasrin Sieges Bücher Spiegel ihres eigenen Lebenswegs, was ihr Roman »Shirin« (1996) zeigt. Die elfjährige Shirin kommt 1960 mit ihren Eltern aus dem Iran nach Deutschland, und während die anfänglichen Schwierigkeiten, Freunde zu finden, nach und nach unbedeutender werden, entfremdet sie sich zunehmend von ihren Eltern.
Nasrin Sieges Rolle als ›Vermittlerin‹ wird auch in ihren Märchen deutlich. In »Kalulu und andere afrikanische Märchen« (1993) folgt sie der Spur des Hasen Kalulu. Die Märchen erzählen von Kampf und Unterwerfung, Liebe und Hass, und überraschen mit plötzlichen Wendungen und witzigen Bildern, afrikanischen Weisheiten und europäischen Einflüssen. Im August 2004 ist Sieges neuestes Jugendbuch »Hyänen im hohen Gras. Spuren in der Serengeti« erschienen. Die Autorin lebt derzeit wieder in Deutschland.

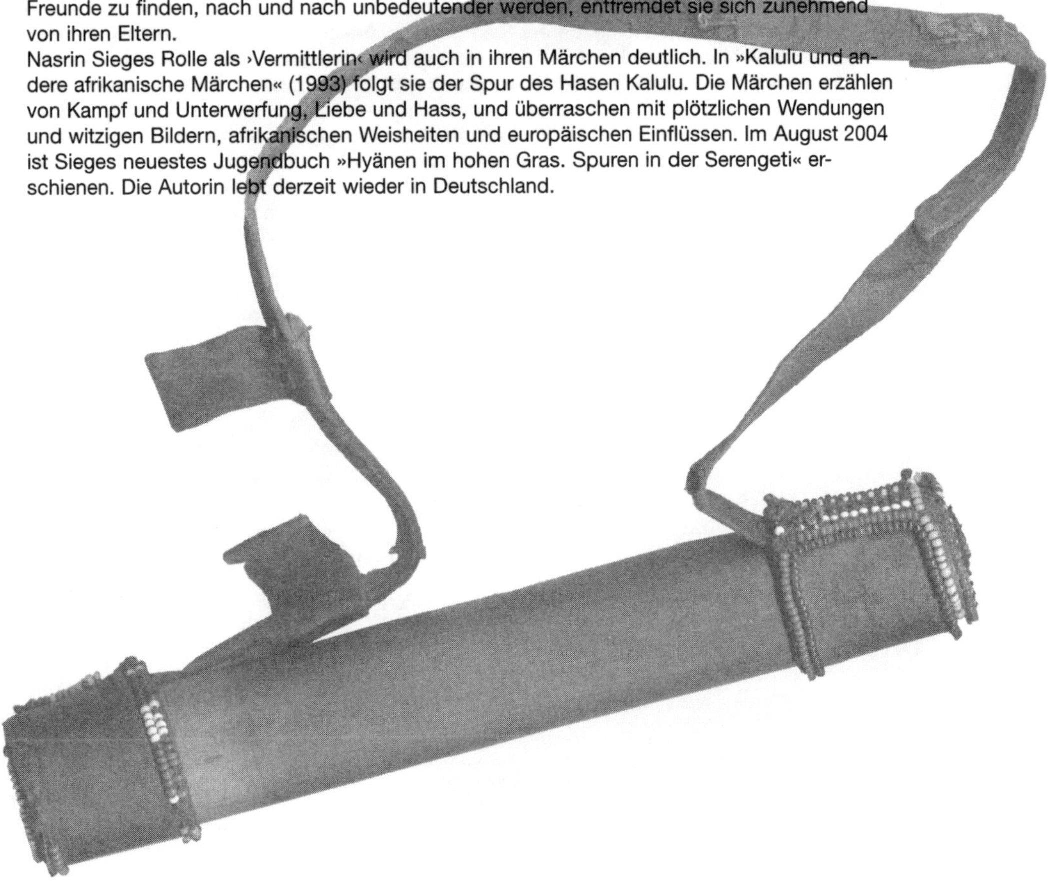

grégoire solotareff
biography

»When one makes children's books, one actually makes them first and foremost for oneself, for the child that one was and, wishfully, still is.« Grégoire Solotareff is a child of various cultures. He was born in 1953 in Alexandria, Egypt, the son of the Lebanese doctor Henri El-Kayem, and the Russian emigrant and artist Olga Solotareff. Political disturbances, revolutions and civil war forced the family from Egypt to Lebanon at the end of the 1950's, and finally to France. Children in Solotareff's family did not attend school. Instead, learning, storytelling and drawing took place at home. His immense familiarity with sketch books and books stems from this time. Like his father, who was once the medical attendant to the Egyptian crowned prince, Solotareff studied medicine and worked as a doctor for five years. As time went by he began drawing again and he formed impression he was regaining contact with something long forgotten, something which goes by the name of ›childhood‹. Today Solotareff is one of the most important European illustrators and authors. More than 120 books have been created since the middle of the 1980's, which have been translated, exhibited and staged around the world. The spectrum of his work is huge: fit-for-the-bathtub plastic fold-out books for the littlest ones, innumerable picture books and stories, a novel for children and a few books that Olga Lecaye and his sister Nadja have illustrated. In 2003, »Loulou et autres loups« hit the French cinemas, a series of five animated short films based on Solotareff's picture book »Loulou« (1989) about a young wolf who chooses to become friends with, of all animals, a hare.
Solotareff has brought a new hue to children's literature. Insubordinate, fresh and with black humour, in a fairytale and secretive manner, but never harmlessly comforting, he tells the story of friendship and love – always in his clear, reduced handwriting and in the primary colours red, yellow and blue. Solotareff depicts animals that for him are »caricatures of humans«. His pictures give human attributes to dreamy hares, lonely wolves, Italian mice, career-tired gnomes, freezing crocodiles and frogs in love. In his much applauded picture book »Toi grand et moi petit« (1996; t: You big and me small), which was awarded the Deutscher Jugendliteraturpreis in 1997, an elephant in need of protection forms a friendship with the powerful lion king; the friendship becomes unhinged with time as the little elephant grows bigger than his royal friend. Solotareff illuminates the ancient story of father and son, of power and powerlessness with exciting and intense pictures. The flatly applied, pure and bright colours with their black contours join the simplified, but never simple forms into a harmonious unit. »In my pictures, as in my soul, I attempt to reconcile both sides – the striving for softness, for happiness, for intense and strong things on the one hand, and simultaneously the quest for things that awaken the senses of humour and wickedness.«
Grégoire Solotareff has been honoured with the most important awards in France and a number of international prizes, including the Prix de Montreuil (1992) and the Bologna Ragazzi Award (1993). In 2004 he was a finalist in the Hans Christian Andersen Awards. He lives and draws in Paris.

Wer hat Angst vor einem Hasen
Moritz
Frankfurt a.M., 1994
Maximilian
Moritz
Frankfurt a.M., 1995
[Ü: Erika & Karl A. Klewer]
Théo et Balthazar au royaume des lutins
(ab 6)
Hatier
Paris, 1998
Rollstiefelchen
(ab 5)
Moritz
Frankfurt a.M., 2000
[Ü: Erika & Karl A. Klewer]
Du groß, und ich klein
Moritz
Frankfurt a.M., 2000
[Ü: Erika & Karl A. Klewer]
Wenn der Wolf kommt
Beltz & Gelberg
Weinheim, 2003
[Ü: Erika & Karl A. Klewer]
Sommergeschichten
(ab 6)
Dtv
München, 2004
[Ü: Werner Leonhard]

Vous m'avez demandé de vous envoyer une image de ma Muse. Je suppose que vous attendiez un dessin. J'en ai deux et voici leurs portraits. Vous voyez, elles sont réelles et ce ne sont pas des lapins G. Solotareff

»Wenn man Kinderbücher macht, dann macht man sie eigentlich immer vor allem für sich, für das Kind, das man war und das man im Innern – hoffentlich – immer noch ist.« Grégoire Solotareff ist ein Kind verschiedener Kulturen. Er wurde 1953 in Alexandria, Ägypten, als Sohn des libanesischen Arztes Henri El-Kayem und der russischen Emigrantin und Künstlerin Olga Solotareff geboren. Politische Wirren, Umstürze und Bürgerkriege führten die Familie Ende der fünfziger Jahre von Ägypten in den Libanon und schließlich nach Frankreich. In Solotareffs Familie ging man nicht zur Schule, statt dessen wurde zuhause gelernt, gezeichnet und erzählt. Aus dieser Zeit stammt seine große Vertrautheit mit Malblock und Büchern. Wie sein Vater, einst Leibarzt des ägyptischen Kronprinzen, studierte Solotareff Medizin und arbeitete fünf Jahre lang als Arzt. Im Laufe der Zeit begann er wieder zu zeichnen und hatte den Eindruck, damit an etwas lange Verschüttetes anzuknüpfen, das den Namen ›Kindheit‹ trägt. Heute gehört Solotareff zu den bedeutendsten europäischen Illustratoren und Autoren. Seit Mitte der achtziger Jahre entstanden mehr als 120 Bücher, die weltweit übersetzt, ausgestellt und inszeniert wurden. Das Spektrum seines Werks ist groß: badewannentaugliche Plastik-Leporellos für die Kleinsten, unzählige Bilderbücher und Geschichten, ein Roman für Kinder und einige Bücher, die Olga Lecaye und seine Schwester Nadja illustriert haben. Im Jahr 2003 kam »Loulou et autres loups« in die französischen Kinos, fünf animierte Kurzfilme, basierend auf Solotareffs Bilderbuch »Loulou« (1989; dt. »Wer hat Angst vor einem Hasen«, 1994) über einen jungen Wolf, der sich ausgerechnet mit einem Hasen anfreundet.
Solotareff hat einen neuen Farb-Ton in die Kinderliteratur gebracht. Aufmüpfig, frech, mit boshaftem Humor, märchenhaft und geheimnisvoll, aber nie harmlos, erzählt er von Freundschaft und Liebe – stets in seiner klaren, reduzierten Handschrift und in den Grundfarben Rot, Gelb und Blau. Solotareff zeigt Tiere, die für ihn »Karikaturen der Menschen« sind. Seine Bilder werden bevölkert von verträumten Hasen, einsamen Wölfen, italienischen Mäusen, berufsmüden Kobolden, frierenden Krokodilen und verliebten Fröschen. In seinem gefeierten Bilderbuch »Toi grand et moi petit« (1996; dt. »Du groß, und ich klein«, 1996) – 1997 mit dem Deutschen Jugendliteraturpreis ausgezeichnet – schließt ein schutzbedürftiger Elefant Freundschaft mit dem mächtigen Löwenkönig, die ins Wanken gerät, als der kleine Elefant mit der Zeit über seinen königlichen Freund hinauswächst. Die uralte Geschichte von Vater und Sohn, von Macht und Ohnmacht, leuchtet Solotareff in aufregend intensiven Bildern aus. Die flächig aufgetragenen, reinen und lichtvollen Farben und ihre schwarze Kontur fügen die vereinfachten, aber nie einfachen Formen zu einer harmonischen Einheit. »Ich suche in meinen Bildern wie in meiner Seele beide Seiten zu vereinen – das Streben nach Sanftheit, nach Glück, nach intensiven und starken Dingen einerseits und gleichzeitig nach Dingen, die aufwecken, nach Humor und Boshaftigkeit.«
Für sein Werk wurde Grégoire Solotareff mit den bedeutendsten Auszeichnungen Frankreichs und einer Vielzahl internationaler Ehrungen bedacht, u. a. mit dem Prix de Montreuil (1992) und dem Bologna Ragazzi Award (1993). 2004 war er Finalist des Hans-Christian-Andersen-Awards. Er lebt und zeichnet in Paris.

jutta treiber

biography

Jutta Treiber was born in Oberpullendorf, Austria, near the Hungarian border, in 1949. After studying German and English at the University of Vienna she worked at a secondary school in her hometown. In addition she ran the local cinema owned by her family for more than twenty years. At the age of eight she first experienced writing and the therapeutic power of art, after the birth of her disabled brother. At that time she also became familiar with fiction and fantasy by means of the cinema that her grandfather had founded. On the fascination of writing she comments: »On the one hand it means coming to terms with past events and experiences, on the other hand it is an obsession. I have to write, cannot live without writing.« The author from the Burgenland debuted in 1979 with a volume of short stories entitled »Ich will eine Geschichte schreiben« (t: I want to write a story). Since 1988 when she published her young adults' novel »Popcorn zum Frühstück« (t: Popcorn for breakfast), she has worked as a freelance writer. Her oeuvre comprises illustrated books and children's books, poetry, short prose, novels for young people, cabaret programmes, radio plays and short films.
In an empathic and humorous way Jutta Treiber depicts children and young people who must make important decisions and face big changes. Avoiding soft-focussing, she chooses as central themes taboos and emotional devastations which are often hushed up and which threaten to break young people. The writer offers her readers ways of identifying with what is not talked about. At the same time she shows that one is not alone with one's efforts to regain wholeness and dignity after loss, harm or fear. Her stories always end with the power of hope and the will to continue living despite everything.
In the book series about »children-in-between« (among other in »Dazwischenkinder sind wir alle«, 1999; t: We all are children-in-between) she describes the often ignored difficulties of the middle siblings. Her latest young people's novel »Julia spielt Julia« (t: Julia plays julia) describes the dreams, fears and passions of young adults as seen from the perspective of a young lady who wants to become a theatre star. Equally multi-facetted is Treiber's psychological portrayal of seventeen year old Franka, who becomes a rape victim and almost breaks down in the aftermath (»Vergewaltigt«, 2003, t: Raped). The author manages to look sensitively into the complex world of a grieving child's soul, as well as to humorously describe first love, the everyday war between parents, or a grumpy father convinced by his family to have a laugh pacemaker implanted (»Lachschrittmacher«, 2001, t: Laugh pacemaker).
Jutta Treiber has given more than 1600 readings in fourteen European countries. She has received the City of Vienna's Award for Children's and Young People's Literature, the Austrian Young People's Literature Award and the Libraries' Readers' Voices Award. Jutta Treiber lives in Oberpullendorf – above the cinema.

O Muse, hast du jemals mich geküsst
nicht nur gestreift, berührt, vielleicht gekitzelt
geärgert gar, ins Auge mir geblickt
jedoch geküsst, fürwahr, ich glaub es nicht
müsst ich's nicht wissen?

O Muse, oft hast du mich schon genarrt
gelächelt, deine Lippen keck gespitzt
mich angelacht und – als ich näher kam
gegrinst mit breitem Mund
von Kuss schon keine Spur mehr.

Du hast mir zart die Finger
auf den Arm gelegt
dein Atem wehte leicht an meiner Stirn
aber ein Kuss, ein saftig dicker Kuss
aus dem ein ganzes Werk geflossen wär – nein:

Dass ich nicht lache, Mjuz
den Dichtkunst Stachel hast du
mir ins Fleisch getrieben
gepaart mit Unzulänglichkeit.

Der Rest ist Schweiß und Ausdauer, Geduld
und Zittern, Bangen, Hadern
und große Bogen gehen um
ein plärrend Schreibgerät.

Der Rest ist Schreiben

Dazwischenkinder sind wir alle
(ab 8)
Dachs, Wien, 1999
[Ill: Reinhold Prandl]

Felsen küssen mit der Nase
(ab 12)
Dachs
Wien, 2000

Die Blumen der Engel
(ab 6)
Betz
Wien, 2001
[Ill: Maria Blazejovky]

Maxeline Regenschirm
(ab 4)
Dachs, Wien, 2003
[Ill: Birgit Antoni]

Solange die Zikaden schlafen
(ab 12)
Carlsen
Hamburg, 2004

Vergewaltigt
(ab 14)
Carlsen
Hamburg, 2003

Julia spielt Julia
(ab 12)
G&G Wien, 2004

Jutta Treiber wurde 1949 im österreichischen Oberpullendorf nahe der ungarischen Grenze geboren. Nach dem Germanistik- und Anglistikstudium an der Universität Wien arbeitete sie als Lehrerin am Gymnasium ihrer Heimatstadt. Mehr als zwanzig Jahre betrieb sie dort das familieneigene Kino. Erste Schreiberfahrungen machte sie mit acht Jahren, als sie nach der Geburt ihres behinderten Bruders die therapeutische Kraft der Kunst entdeckte. Schon damals machte das Kino, das ihr Großvater gegründet hatte, sie mit Phantasie und Fiktion vertraut. Über die Faszination des Schreibens sagt sie: »Einerseits ist es die Bewältigung eigener Erlebnisse und Erfahrungen, andererseits eine Besessenheit: Ich muss schreiben, kann ohne Schreiben nicht leben.« 1979 debütierte die Burgenländerin mit dem Kurzgeschichtenband »Ich will eine Geschichte schreiben« und lebt seit 1988, seit der Veröffentlichung des Jugendromans »Popcorn zum Frühstück«, als freie Schriftstellerin. Ihr Werk umfasst Bilder- und Kinderbücher, Lyrik, Kurzprosa und Romane für Jugendliche und Erwachsene, Kabarettprogramme, Hörspiele und Kurzfilme.

Mit großer Einfühlsamkeit und viel Humor zeigt Jutta Treiber Kinder und Jugendliche, die vor großen Entscheidungen oder Veränderungen stehen. Ohne Weichzeichner thematisiert sie auch Tabus und emotionale Verwüstungen, die oft totgeschwiegen werden und an denen junge Persönlichkeiten zu zerbrechen drohen. Die Autorin schenkt ihren Lesern Identifikationsmöglichkeiten für das Unausgesprochene. Dabei zeigt sie auch, dass man nicht allein ist im Bemühen, nach Verlust, Verletzung oder Angst seine Ganzheit und Würde zurückzuerlangen. Am Ende ihrer Geschichten steht immer das ›weiterleben, trotz allem‹ und die Kraft der Hoffnung.

So schildert sie in ihrer Buchreihe über die ›Dazwischenkinder‹ (u. a. »Dazwischenkinder sind wir alle«, 1999) die oft ignorierten Schwierigkeiten mittlerer Geschwister. Ihr aktueller Jugendroman »Julia spielt Julia« zeigt aus dem Blickwinkel einer jungen Frau, die Theaterstar werden möchte, die Träume, Ängste und Leidenschaften von Jugendlichen. Ebenso facettenreich ist Treibers psychologische Darstellung der siebzehnjährigen Franka, die Opfer einer Vergewaltigung wird und an den Folgen fast zerbricht (»Vergewaltigt«, 2003). Der Autorin gelingt der sensible Blick in die komplexe Welt einer trauernden Kinderseele genauso wie die humorvolle Beschreibung der ersten Liebe, des Alltagskriegs zwischen Eltern oder eines grantigen Vaters, der von seiner Familie überredet wird, sich einen Lachschrittmacher einpflanzen zu lassen (»Lachschrittmacher«, 2001).

Jutta Treiber hat mehr als 1.600 Lesungen in vierzehn Ländern Europas gehalten. Für ihr Werk erhielt sie u. a. den Kinder- und Jugendbuchpreis der Stadt Wien, den Österreichischen Jugendbuchpreis sowie den Leserstimmenpreis der Bibliotheken. Jutta Treiber lebt in Oberpullendorf – über dem Kino.

Make answer, Muse

O, Muse, hast du jemals mich geküsst,
nicht nur gestreift, berührt, vielleicht gekitzelt
geärgert gar, ins Auge mir geblickt,
jedoch geküsst, fürwahr, ich glaub es nicht,
müsst ich's nicht wissen?

O, Muse, oft hast du mich schon genarrt,
gelächelt, deine Lippen keck gespitzt,
mich angelacht und – als ich näher kam
mich angegrinst mit breitem Mund
von Kuss schon keine Spur mehr.

Du hast mir zart die Finger
auf den Arm gelegt
dein Atem wehte licht an meiner Stirn,
aber ein Kuss, ein saftig dicker Kuss
aus dem ein ganzes Werk geflossen wäre – nein!

Dass ich nicht lache, Mju:z,
der Dichtkunst Stachel hast du
mir ins Fleisch getrieben
gepaart mit Unzulänglichkeit.

Der Rest ist Schweiß und Ausdauer, Geduld
und Zittern, Bangen, Hadern
und große Bogen gehen um
ein glotzend Schreibgerät.

Der Rest ist Schreiben.

mohammad reza yousefi

biography

Mohammad Reza Yousefi was born in Hamadan, Iran, in 1953. With over one hundred and fifty titles to his name, he is one of the most prolific authors of children's and young adult books in Iran. His childhood in a large family of herdsmen and cattle breeders living on the fringes of the Zagros mountains led to a profound knowledge of the nomadic everyday life of an traditional tribal community, as well as of nature and its dangers, and the mythical traditions of the country. After studying History and Literature in Teheran, Yousefi worked as a teacher and appeared as an actor and director in street theatres around the entire country. This peripatetic lifestyle brought him closer to the realities of life in Iran's diversely populated society: »I have lived with all the children of Iran: with the child of the desert, of the forests and mountains; the child that goes fishing at night in the turbulent waters of the Persian Gulf, the Turkmen Child who rides untamed horses; the Turkish child who cherishes grandfather's musical instrument as a holy souvenir, and the Kurdish child with his love for horses and wrestling.« Yousefi has worked as a freelance author since 1978 and writes in Farsi.

For over twenty years a large spectrum of works has been published, among them adaptations of folkloric tales, interpretations of classical legends, modern fairytales and everyday stories from present-day Iran, whose focus is the fantasy and lives of children and adolescents. In his stories, distant times and cultures acquire a new timeliness for his readers. He skilfully describes human differences and reveals the apparent imperfections of his characters to be in fact strengths and human greatness. In his much noted keywork, the symbolic novella »Dokhtarane Khorshidi« (1999; t: The sunlike girls), the inhabitants of the drought stricken pottery city of Meybod search for the »sunlike girl«. Their master Mehraban informs them that her sacrifice, based on an old myth, will bring the hoped-for rain. When no girl from the village passes the master's test, the desired girl appears to his student Merhad in a dream. As soon as he realises that each of the girls inherits a part of the divine quality, it starts to rain and Merhad becomes the new master.

Mohammad Reza Yousefi has received many prizes and a number of his texts have been adapted for children's and young people's theatre. His play »Khaleh tanha, Khaleh ba ma« premiered at the Hamadan Theatre Festival in 1998. He has twice received the IBBY Diploma, and in 2000 was nominated for the Hans Christian Andersen Award. Yousefi lives with his family in Tehran.

Hassani be maktab nemiraft
Ghadyani-Banafsheh
Tehran, 1994
[Ill: K. Tabai]

Dareyeh Ahouan
Soroush
Tehran, 1995
[Ill: Heydarzadeh]

Setarehi be name goul
Ghadyani-Banafsheh
Tehran, 1996

Darse anar
Paydayesh
Tehran, 1997
[Ill: F. Shafii]

Yek vajab az aseman
Kanoun
Tehran,1997

Dokhtarane Khorshidi
Paydayesh
Tehran, 1999
[Ill: M. Zamani]

Arezooye Piran
Shabaviz
Tehran, 2002
[Ill: Sara Iravani]

Sari Keh Bi-kolah Mand
Shabaviz
Tehran, 2004
[Ill: Rashin Khyrieh]

She is the Mother of All Stories

Since I was a little boy I have been in love with a cherub called Elham (Inspiration). This happened with the first stories that I heard from old tellers of tales. Elham pulled me everywhere.
But one day, when I called her there was no answer. I knew that on that day I could not write. I searched for her frantically in the streets and in the alleys. I knew that she would be among the people. She might be anywhere, at a bus station, in a cinema queue, in virgin forests, on the ocean waves, in the mountains, behind closed windows, or in any classroom. She is in fact everywhere and yet nowhere.
I finally found her by the Azadi (Freedom) Tower in Tehran. Lost in the crowd, she was pointing to the top of the tower. "That man", she said, "Wants to throw himself down, write about him!"
I always listen to her with great care. I stared at the man for a long time. Then I jumped into a taxi. She came with me. Next to us was a mother with her child. I was afraid to forget the details of the scene: his distant cry, his hopes, his eyes... Elham was staring at me. I asked the child if she had anything to write with. She searched her mother's bag and gave me a pencil that had a thick black tip. It seemed that even the little girl wanted me to write something about the man.
Later I discovered that I was scribbling with an eyebrow pencil! Elham was laughing, but I was taking notes of that man's cry.
Although I wanted to go home, I found myself at the cemetery. Last night I dreamt of my mother. I owe all my writings to her. She and Elham are old friends. When I can no longer cope with all that Elham (Inspiration) heaps on me, I run to her. On her grave there is a

Mohammad Reza Yousefi wurde 1953 in Hamadan, Iran, geboren und ist mit mehr als 150 Werken einer der produktivsten Kinder- und Jugendbuchautoren des Iran. Aus seiner Kindheit in einer Großfamilie von Hirten und Viehzüchtern am Rande des Zagrosgebirges schöpft er sein tiefes Wissen über den nomadischen Lebensalltag einer festgefügten Stammesgesellschaft, über die Natur mit ihren Gefahren und die Mythentraditionen seines Landes. Nach seinem Geschichts- und Literaturstudium in Teheran arbeitete Yousefi als Lehrer und trat als Schauspieler und Regisseur bei Straßentheatern im ganzen Land auf. Dieses Wanderleben brachte ihm die Lebenswirklichkeiten im Vielvölkerstaat Iran nahe: »Ich habe mit allen Kindern des Iran gelebt; mit den Kindern der Wüste, der Wälder und der Berge; dem Kind, das nachts in den unruhigen Gewässern des Persischen Golfs fischt, dem turkmenischen Kind, das ungezähmte Pferde reitet, dem türkischen Kind, das das Musikinstrument seines Großvaters als heiliges Andenken pflegt, und mit dem kurdischen Kind und seiner Liebe für Pferde und Ringkämpfe.« Yousefi lebt seit 1978 als freier Schriftsteller und schreibt in Farsi.
Seit mehr als zwanzig Jahren hat er eine große Bandbreite von Werken veröffentlicht, darunter Adaptionen folkloristischer Erzählungen, Interpretationen klassischer Legenden, moderne Märchen und Alltagsgeschichten aus dem heutigen Iran, in denen die Phantasie und das Leben von Kindern und Jugendlichen im Zentrum stehen. Ferne Zeiten und Kulturen gewinnen in seinen Geschichten für die Leser eine ganz neue Aktualität. Kunstvoll beschreibt er menschliche Unterschiede und offenbart die scheinbare Unvollkommenheit seiner Figuren als ihre eigentliche Stärke und menschliche Größe. In seinem viel beachteten Schlüsselwerk, der symbolischen Novelle »Dokhtarane Khorshidi« (1999; Ü: Das Sonnenmädchen), suchen die Bewohner der von Dürre und Missernten geplagten Töpfer-Stadt Meybod das ›sonnengleiche Mädchen‹. Ihr Meister Mehraban berichtet ihnen, dass dessen Opferung nach einem alten Mythos den erhofften Regen bringt. Als keines der Mädchen aus dem Dorf die Prüfung des Meisters besteht, erscheint seinem Schüler Merhad die Gesuchte im Traum. Sobald er erkennt, dass jedem der Mädchen ein Stück der Göttlichen innewohnt, beginnt es zu regnen und Merhad wird der neue Meister.
Mohammad Reza Yousefi wurde vielfach ausgezeichnet, viele seiner Texte wurden für das Kinder- und Jugendtheater adaptiert. Sein Theaterstück »Khaleh tanha, Khaleh ba ma« wurde 1998 auf dem Hamadan Theatre Festival prämiert. Bereits zweimal erhielt er das IBBY-Ehrendiplom, im Jahr 2000 war er für den Hans-Christian-Andersen-Award nominiert. Yousefi lebt mit seiner Familie in Teheran.

geranium pot. She loves this flower. She stares at the coming coffin and says, "Mohammad, dying is easy; it is living that is difficult." The man standing at the top of the Freedom Tower was lying in the coffin. A crowd of women and men were moving it towards an empty grave. My mother cried out, "Why did you kill that man? Jesus resurrected the dead!"
She then handed me a pencil and paper, the same way she had done on my first day at school, and said, "Write!" I started writing with great speed. Not only did I have to write about his life, but I also had to rescue him from death. It is always the same scene. Inspiration was combing my mother's hair and they were both staring at me. I heard the man crying and weeping seemingly from the bottom of the grave.
I don't know how many nights and days I spent on my mother's grave. She kept watering the geranium plant, with Elham at her side till I finished that man's story. The ending was happening in a fantasy world. The Freedom Towers' giant legs were folding, like an old man, and his back was bending down, and his forehead was touching the ground. The man jumped onto the grass and started laughing. Joy was everywhere. When those men who were carrying the coffin to the cemetery saw that it was empty, they screamed and fled from the scene. Mother, Elham and I were laughing.
I am happy that Elham is always kind to me, that I get my pen from children, and that I have a mother, who is a storyteller. The mother of all stories.

kazumi yumoto

biography

Kazumi Yumoto was born in Tokyo, Japan, in 1959 and got into literature via music. She studied composition at Tokyo College of Music and during this time wrote opera libretti and plays for radio and television. Her first novel »Natsu no niwa« (Eng. »The Friends«, 1996) appeared in 1992 to international acclaim. In a direct and warmhearted style it tells the story of three adolescents in contemporary Japan who want to learn more about death and decide to spy on an old man whom they assume will die soon, but things develop in an unexpected manner. A fragile friendship grows between Kiyama, Yamashita and Kawabe, in which they learn a lot about life, tolerance and the dignity of getting old. Yumoto approaches the frightening and fascinating ›event‹ of death in a vital and uninhibited way. What does a dead body look like? How many times have we taken breath? What happens afterwards? The book is narrated in a clear and quiet fashion. Other issues, such as the mother's alcoholicism or the troubling war memories of the old man, are also discreetly incorporated. In this way, a children's novel is built up which excludes nothing, which touches on the horrible without dramatising it, which treats a delicate issue lightly but never frivolously« (Neue Züricher) and which quietly brings a strange culture closer. »Natsu no niwa« received the Boston Globe-Horn Award (1997) and was nominated for the German Juvenile's Literature Prize (1996); it was made into a film by Shinji Somai (1996). Again and again Yumoto takes up the difficult experiences of growing up and the conflicts that for children can be associated with it. In doing so she never avoids serious questions such as illness, death, suicide and religion, as in the book for young adults, »Popura no aki« (1997; Eng. »The Letters«, 2002), her third novel that was translated into German. Chiaki, a young woman, remembers how she moved into the »Poplar-House« with her mother when she was six years old. There the eccentric yet loveable landlady Mrs Yanagi helped her to fight her anxieties – which above all had to do with the to her incomprehensible fact of her father's death. When the old lady tells her that she will convey letters to the dead when dying, Chiaki starts writing letters to her father dealing with her pain and her questions. Very often in Yumoto's novels old people play a fundamental role. »I believe that there is a kind of relationship with children that is only feasible for adults who at the same time are not the parents, and that such a relationship can strongly influence a child's course in a certain part of its life.« Kazumi Yumoto lives in Tokyo.

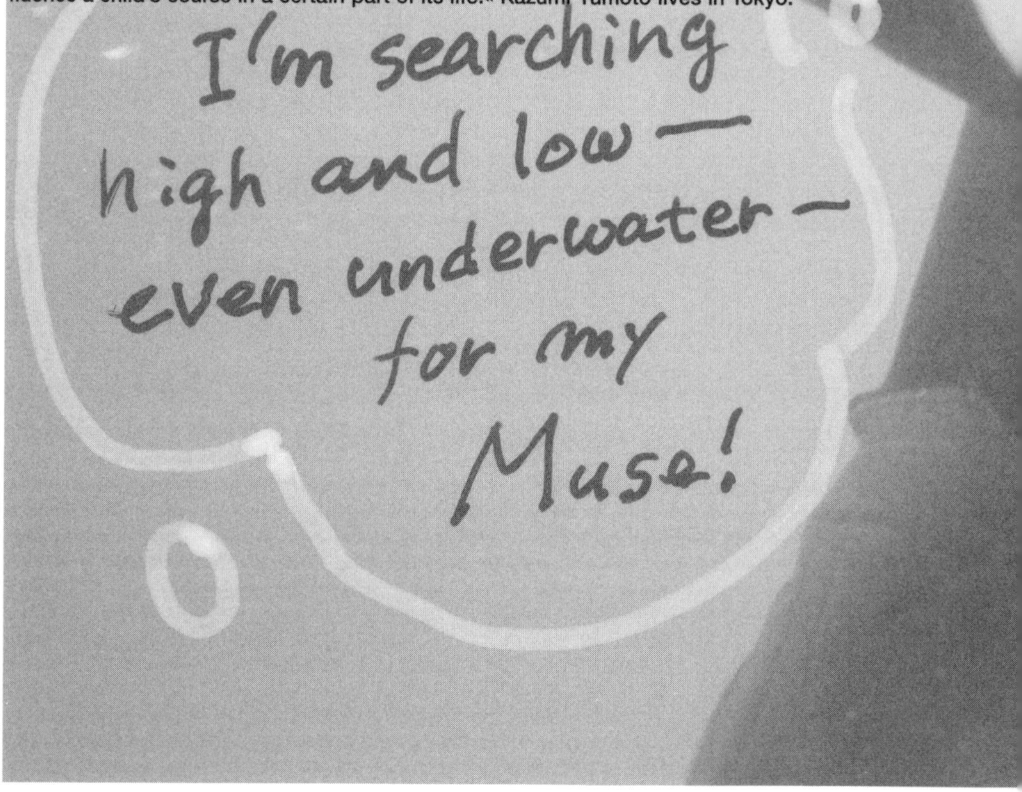

Kitsune no Suketo
Tokuma Shoten
Tokyo, 1998
Gespensterschatten
(ab 12)
Beltz & Gelberg
Weinheim, 1999
[Ü: Yoko Koyama-Siebert]
Kumatte Iinioi
Tokuma Shoten
Tokyo, 2000
Tomomis Traum
(ab 12)
Nagel & Kimche
Zürich, 2001
[Ü: Ulli und Herbert Günther]
Nishibi no Machi
Bungei Shunju
Tokyo, 2002
Kame no Henry
Fukuinkan Shoten
Tokyo, 2003
[Ill: Rimako Horikawa]
Eine Schublade voller Briefe
(ab 13)
Sauerländer
Düsseldorf, 2003
[Ü: Gabriele Haefs]

Kazumi Yumoto wurde 1959 in Tokio, Japan, geboren und kam über die Musik zur Literatur. Sie studierte Komposition am Tokyo College und schrieb bereits während ihres Studiums Opernlibretti und verfasste Hörspiele und Drehbücher für Radio und Fernsehen. Ihr erster Roman »Natsu no niwa« (dt. »Gespensterschatten«, 1995) erschien 1992 und fand internationale Beachtung. Direkt und warmherzig erzählt sie von drei Jugendlichen im heutigen Japan, die mehr über den ›Tod‹ erfahren möchten und beschließen, einen alten Mann, von dem sie annehmen, dass er bald sterben müsse, auszuspionieren. Doch die Dinge entwickeln sich anders. Eine fragile Freundschaft entsteht, in der Kiyama, Yamashita und Kawabe viel über das Leben, Toleranz und die Würde des Alters lernen. Lebendig und unbefangen nähert sich Yumoto dem beängstigenden und faszinierenden Ereignis ›Tod‹: Wie sieht eine Leiche aus? Wie viele Male haben wir schon geatmet? Was geschieht danach? Dabei fließen in ihre klare und ruhige Erzählweise dezent auch andere problematische Aspekte der Protagonisten ein, wie z. B. die Alkoholkrankheit der Mutter oder die bestürzende Kriegserinnerung des alten Mannes. So entsteht ein Kinderroman, »der nichts ausgrenzt, der Schreckliches streift, ohne es zu dramatisieren, der das heikle Thema leicht, aber nicht leichtfertig behandelt« (Neue Zürcher Zeitung) und der leise eine fremde Kultur nahebringt. »Gespensterschatten« wurde u. a. mit dem Boston Globe-Horn Book Award (1997) ausgezeichnet, für den Deutschen Jugendliteraturpreis (1996) nominiert und von Shinji Somai verfilmt.
Immer wieder greift Yumoto die schwierigen Erfahrungen des Erwachsenwerdens und die Konflikte auf, die für Kinder damit verbunden sein können. Dabei scheut sie ernste Themen wie Krankheit, Tod, Selbsttötung und Religiöses nicht. So in ihrem Jugendbuch »Popura no aki« (1997; dt. »Eine Schublade voller Briefe«, 2003), dem dritten ihrer Romane, der in deutscher Übersetzung vorliegt. Chiaki, eine junge Frau, erinnert sich, wie sie als Sechsjährige mit ihrer Mutter in das ›Pappelhaus‹ zog und die kauzig-liebenswerte Vermieterin Frau Yanagi ihr half, gegen ihre Ängste anzukämpfen – Ängste, die vor allem mit dem Tod ihres Vaters zusammenhingen, den sie nicht verstehen konnte. Als die alte Frau ihr erzählt, dass sie Briefe an die Toten übermitteln wird, sobald sie einmal stirbt, beginnt Chiaki, an ihren Vater zu schreiben und sich mit ihrem Schmerz und ihren Fragen auseinanderzusetzen. Alte Menschen spielen sehr häufig in Yumotos Romanen eine tragende Rolle. »Ich glaube, dass es auch eine Art von Beziehungen zu Kindern gibt, die nur Erwachsenen, die nicht gleichzeitig auch die Eltern sind, möglich ist, und dass eine solche Beziehung den Weg eines Kindes in einem bestimmten Lebensabschnitt stark beeinflussen kann.« Kazumi Yumoto lebt in Tokio.

gäste des DAAD berlin

daniel bănulescu
petr borkovec
gianni celati
feng li
amanda michalopoulou
asher reich
ottó tolnai

daniel bănulescu

biography

Daniel Bănulescu was born in Bucharest, Romania, in 1960. After studying engineering he worked as a copy editor, reporter, and night watchman. In 1981, »Amfiteatru« was the first magazine to publish his poetry. From the beginning, Bănulescu has aimed to be provocative in his poetry, which revels in insanity, obscenity, and images of death. In its aggressive combination of sexuality and religion it is reminiscent of the aesthetics of Georges Bataille, François Villon or Charles Baudelaire. The first poetry collection »Ziua în care am fost publicat« (t: The day I was published) appeared in 1987 as an insert in the magazine »Convingeri Comuniste«. The »poet of the explosive and not the conceptual«, as he was called by Mircea Martin, the Bucharest patron of literature, was permitted to publish the forceful title poem; the censors, however, balked at his other texts with their eloquent torrents of sexuality. Only half of the original number of poems were printed. After the end of Ceausescu's dictatorship the missing poems were published in a second volume entitled »Te voi iubi pân' la sfârşitul patului« (1993; t: I will love you till the end of bed). The first novel »Te pup in fund, conducător iubit!« (1994; t: I kiss your ass, beloved leader) reinforced Bănulescu's reputation as the controversial enfant terrible of contemporary Romanian literature and won him the prize of the Romanian writers' Union. In addition to his second novel »Cei şapte regi ai oraşului Bucureşti« (1998; t: The seven kings of Bucharest), he published the poetry volumes »Balada lui Daniel Bănulescu« (t: Daniel Bănulescu's ballad) in 1997, and »Republica federăla Daniel Bănulescu« (t: Federal republic of Daniel Bănulescu) in 2000, as well as »Daniel, al rugaciunii« (t: The prayer of Daniel) in 2002. A selection of his poetry, entitled »Schrumpeln wirst du wirst eine exotische Frucht sein« (t: You'll shrivel you'll be an exotic fruit) was published in German translation in 2003. The megalomaniac lyrical voice seeks, with lecherous bragging, to go beyond societal as well as poetic limits; at times, however, more sensitive tones are struck. The author prefaces the volume with a note in which he, again, provokes his critics: »Although he knows hundreds of colleagues who are more talented than himself, the modest and tight-lipped author can detect only three major chances for Romanian literature: the poet Daniel Bănulescu, the novelist Daniel Bănulescu, and the dramatist Daniel Bănulescu.« Daniel Bănulescu lives in Bucharest. In 2004/2005 he holds a scholarship of the DAAD in Berlin.

Ziua în care am fost publicat
Cartea cea mica
Bukarest, 1987
Te pup in fund, conducător iubit!
Editura Nemira
Bukarest, 1994
Instrument Erinnerung
Neue Literatur
Bukarest/
Frankfurt am Main, 1995
Balada lui Daniel Bănulescu
Cartea Românească
Bukarest, 1997
Cei şapte regi ai oraşului Bucureşti
Editura Nemira
Bukarest, 1998
Republica federăla Daniel Bănulescu
Editura Vinea
Bukarest, 2000
Daniel, al rugaciunii
Editura Muzeul Literaturii Române
Bukarest, 2002
Schrumpeln wirst du wirst eine exotische Frucht sein
edition per procura
Wien/Lana, 2003
[Ü: Ernest Wichner]

Daniel Bănulescu wurde 1960 in Bukarest, Rumänien, geboren. Nach einem Ingenieursstudium arbeitete er u. a. als Korrektor, Reporter und Nachtwächter. 1981 wurden in der Zeitschrift »Amfiteatru« erstmals einige seiner Gedichte publiziert. Von Anfang an wollte Bănulescu mit einer Lyrik provozieren, die in Wahnsinn, Obszönität und Todesbildern schwelgt und in ihrer provokanten Verknüpfung von Sexualität und Religion an die Ästhetik Georges Batailles, François Villons oder Charles Baudelaires erinnert. Der erste Gedichtband »Ziua în care am fost publicat« (Ü: Der Tag, an dem ich publiziert wurde) konnte 1987 als Beilage der Zeitschrift »Convingeri Comuniste« (Ü: Kommunistische Überzeugungen) erscheinen. Der »Dichter der Explosion und nicht des Konzeptes«, wie ihn der Bukarester Literaturförderer Mircea Martin nannte, durfte das forsche Titelgedicht publizieren, die Zensur zeigte sich jedoch angesichts der sexuellen Wortgewaltigkeit seiner Texte irritiert. Nur die Hälfte von ursprünglich fünfzehn Gedichten ging in den Druck. Die fehlenden Gedichte wurden nach dem Ende der Diktatur Ceausescus im zweiten Gedichtband »Te voi iubi pân' la sfârşitul patului« (1993; Ü: Ich werde dich lieben bis zum Ende des Bettes) veröffentlicht. Den Ruf des umstrittenen enfant terrible der rumänischen Gegenwartsliteratur zementierte er mit seinem ersten Roman »Te pup in fund, conducător iubit!« (1994; Ü: Ich küsse dir den Hintern, geliebter Führer!), für den er den Preis der Vereinigung Rumänischer Schriftsteller erhielt. Neben einem zweiten Roman »Cei şapte regi ai oraşului Bucureşti« (1998; Ü: Die sieben Könige der Stadt Bukarest) liegen mit »Balada lui Daniel Bănulescu« (1997; Ü: Die Ballade des Daniel Bănulescu), »Republica federăla Daniel Bănulescu« (2000; Ü: Bundesrepublik Daniel Bănulescu) und »Daniel, al rugaciunii« (2002; Ü: Daniel, des Gebets) weitere Gedichtbände vor. Eine Auswahl seiner Gedichte ist unter dem Titel »Schrumpeln wirst du wirst eine exotische Frucht sein« (2003) in deutscher Übersetzung erschienen. Mit lüsterner Prahlerei sucht das selbstherrliche lyrische Ich die Grenzüberschreitung gesellschaftlicher wie poetischer Regeln, zuweilen klingen jedoch auch zartere Töne an. Dem Band hat der Dichter eine Notiz vorangestellt, mit dem er seine Kritiker aufs Neue herausfordert: »Obwohl er Hunderte Kollegen kennt, die talentierter sind als er selbst, kann der bescheidene und wortkarge Autor lediglich drei große Chancen für die rumänische Literatur erkennen: den Dichter Daniel Bănulescu, den Romancier Daniel Bănulescu und den Dramatiker Daniel Bănulescu.« Daniel Bănulescu lebt in Bukarest. 2004/2005 ist er DAAD-Stipendiat in Berlin.

Die Ballade des Daniel Bănulescu
(Fragment)

In mein Gebet habe ich auch die Hände und Füße mit einbezogen

Meine Stirne habe ich ans kühle Fenster meiner Gebete gelehnt
Und mich erinnert:
»Jeder der Gottes Namen anruft Wird erlöst«
Also rief ich Jehowas Namen an und wartete

Vom ersten Stock des Wohnblocks in dem ich bete
Entweicht mein Gebet durchs Fenster
Zerschneidet die Ankerschnur die den Wohnblock
mit der Erde verbindet
Und das Haus beginnt sich in die Luft zu erheben
Gefolgt von meiner Seele

Fern bleiben die Tage zurück
An denen mein Leben Mist auf dem Rücken trug
Und beobachten verwundert wie mein Gebet
Sich fragwürdige Vertraulichkeiten mit den Engeln erlaubt
Und bis in den neunzehnten Himmel dringt
Wo der Tod an Kraft verliert
Und seine Stimme sich mit der Stimme meiner Gebete vereint

petr borkovec

biography

Petr Borkovec was born in Louňovice, central Bohemia, in 1970. Since 1992 the poet and arts editor has worked for the arts magazine »Souvislosti« (t: Connections) and since 2000 with the literature journal »Literární noviny«. As a translator, his interests have been predominantly in Russian poetry (for example, Vladimir Nabokov, Vladislav Chodasevic, Jevgenij Rejn, and Jurij Odarcenko) but together with philologists he has also translated Ancient drama and Korean poetry. Critics testify that he masters the traditional techniques of poetry writing to a standard no other Czech writer of his generation can equal, and that he was able very early on to develop his own distinctive language. Since 1990 Borkovec has published six volumes of poems, among which are »Prostírání do tichého« and »Mezi oknem, stolem a postelí«. For his collection entitled »Ochoz« he was awarded the »Jiří Orten Poetry Prize« in 1995. A selection from the original volumes have been collected in four Czech-German books, e. g. »Feldarbeit« (2001; »Polní práce«, 1998), and »Nadelbuch« (2004; »Needle-Book«, 2003).
Borkovec's poems document the period of upheaval in Czecholovakia, in Prague and its surrounding towns. Quietly, concisely with precise observation and apparently by simple means, he sharpens the reader's eye for moments and situations in everyday life: a provincial railway station in some provincial area, or a house in some desolate villa suburb reveal their strangeness. The writer says of this town in which he still lives with his wife and three children: »Sunday evening, from the car, when we approach the southern town, this terrible estate where the number of filling stations is increasing – this is my town. And where I now live, in Černošice, I experience that continually: from there you can see the town, and it looks like Jerusalem when the lights begin to flicker on different levels. That is my Prague.« The view from afar determines the quietness and precise nature of the description, which distinguishes his language. »His elaborately rhyming poems – often sonnets – resemble still lives, precarious momentary shots in which inside and outside come into contact«, wrote Ilma Rakusa about the poet. »In this way the world of tangible objects develops a strange, sometimes metaphysical and moribund magic. Melamine and concrete, balconies, curtains and fences come together there, the aspens seem ›as if of alpaca‹, the polystyrene crib desolate, the typewriter – ›an altar for ashes‹.« »Vakats« is what Borkovec calls a cycle of poems, as if he wanted to declare invalid what was written; but the words assert themselves through their concentrated terseness.

Ochoz
Mladá fronta
Praha, 1994
Aus drei Büchern
Thanhäuser
Ottensheim, 1996
[Ü: Christa Rothmeier]
Überfuhr/Prívoz
Thanhäuser
Ottensheim, 1997
[Ü: Christa Rothmeier]
Feldarbeit/Polní práce
Edition Korrespondenzen
Wien, 2001
[Ü: Christa Rothmeier]
A.B.A.F.
Opus
Praha, 2002
Nadelbuch/Needle-Book
Edition Korrespondenzen
Wien, 2004
[Ü: Christa Rothmeier]

Petr Borkovec wurde 1970 in Louňovice, Mittelböhmen, geboren. Der Dichter und Kulturredakteur arbeitet seit 1992 für das Kulturmagazin »Souvislosti« (Ü: Zusammenhänge) und seit 2000 bei der Literaturzeitschrift »Literární noviny«. Als Übersetzer übertrug er vorwiegend russische Poesie (u. a. von Vladimir Nabokov, Wladislaw Chodassewitsch, Jewgenij Rein, Juri Odarcenko), in Zusammenarbeit mit Philologen aber auch antike Dramen und koreanische Lyrik ins Tschechische. Kritiker bescheinigen ihm, er beherrsche die tradierten dichterischen Mittel so souverän wie kein anderer tschechischer Autor seiner Generation und habe es daher vermocht, frühzeitig eine eigene, markante Stimme zu entwickeln. Seit 1990 sind sechs Gedichtbände des Lyrikers erschienen, darunter »Prostíraní do tichého« (Ü: Entfaltung in die Stille) und »Mezi oknem, stolem a postelí« (Ü: Zwischen Fenster, Tisch und Bett). Für den Band »Ochoz« (Ü: Der Rundgang) wurde er 1995 mit dem Jiří-Orten-Lyrikpreis ausgezeichnet. Aus den Lyrikbänden Borkovecs wurden bislang vier tschechisch-deutsche Auswahlbände zusammengestellt, u. a. »Feldarbeit« (»Polní práce«, 1998) und 2004 »Nadelbuch« (»Needle-Book«, 2003).
Borkovecs Gedichte dokumentieren die Zeit des Umbruchs in der Tschechoslowakei, in Prag und seinen Vorstädten. Präzise beobachtend, leise, lakonisch und mit scheinbar einfachen Mitteln schärft er den Blick des Lesers für Momente und Situationen des Alltags: Orte wie ein Bahnhof in der Provinz oder ein Haus in einem desolaten Villenvorort enthüllen ihre Morbidität. Von der Stadt, in welcher der Autor noch heute mit seiner Frau und seinen drei Kindern lebt, sagt er: »Sonntagabend, aus dem Auto, wenn wir uns der Südstadt nähern, dieser schrecklichen Siedlung, wo sich die Tankstellen häufen – das ist meine Stadt. Auch wo ich jetzt lebe, in Černošice, habe ich das ständig: Von dort sieht man die Stadt, und sie sieht aus wie Jerusalem, wenn die Lichter beginnen auf verschiedenen Ebenen zu blinken. Das ist mein Prag.« Der distanzierte Blick prägt seine Sprache, die sich durch Ruhe und Genauigkeit auszeichnet. »Seine kunstvoll gereimten Gedichte – häufig Sonette – gleichen Stillleben, prekären Momentaufnahmen, in denen sich Außen und Innen kurzschließen«, schrieb Ilma Rakusa über den Dichter. »Dabei entfaltet die Dingwelt einen seltsamen, mitunter metaphysisch-morbiden Zauber. Resopal und Beton, Altane, Gardinen und Zäune geben sich ein Stelldichein, die Espen sind ›wie aus Alpaka‹, die Styroporkrippe trostlos, die Schreibmaschine – ›ein Aschenaltar‹.« »Vakats« nennt Borkovec einen Gedichtzyklus, als wollte er das Geschriebene für nichtig erklären. Doch die Worte behaupten sich mit Kraft und Lakonie.

EUTERPÉ

M.C.

Kampf grüner Massen.
Ein Donner poltert durch die Geschosse.
Die kleinen Geräuschsorten flüchten
in ihre Löcher. Ein an der Türkante
verbogenes Blatt zischt wie eine Schlange.
Weisse Nachtfalter gleiten aus dem Gras,
Miniaturen von Vogelgerippen.
Wir stehen vorerst im Kreis des Vergleichens,
bewachen einander.
Nachts ein Traum vom Unkrautjäten:
Die tauben Senken der Kletten, Platten
zottiger Bleche. Ich trenne den Stoff auf,
zerreisse die Polsterung voller Wasser.

gianni celati
biography

Gianni Celati was born in Sondrino, Italy, in 1937. He earned his PhD from Bologna University with a dissertation on James Joyce. In 1966, one of his short stories attracted the attention of Italo Calvino, who was chief editor of the Einaudi publishing house, which in 1970 published Celati's first book »Comiche«. The following novels »Le Avventure do Guizzardi« (1973), »La Banda die Sospiri« (1976) and »Lunario del Paradiso« (1979) established Celati as an author of the neo-avant-garde group, along with Umberto Eco and Italo Calvino. From 1973 to the early 1980's he was professor of English and American literature at the University of Bologna, where he worked on his studies of literary aesthetics. After leaving academia, he devoted himself to writing and film making. He produced several experimental documentaries, including »Visioni di casa che crollano« (»Crumbling Houses«) – a critical meditation on the decay of deserted houses in the plains area of the River Po. The prize-winning volume of short stories »Narratori delle pianure« (1985; Engl. »Voices from the Plains«, 1991) marks the beginning of Celati's experimentation with new methods of minimalist narration. Oscillating between fiction and documentary, his extraordinary tales are supposed to have taken place in the everyday lives of existing people. Celati invents a chronicler who not only narrates, but also plays with the idea of narrative.

On the subjects of irony and the grotesque in his short stories, of the cinematographic element in literature, and of the writing process itself, Celati has said: »I had been working on these stories for over twenty years; then, over a long period of time, I rewrote them, partly to keep myself busy and partly to see what was happening to them. When you write stories or read them, you see landscapes and figures and you hear voices: in other words, you have a sort of natural cinema going on in your head, and you don't need to watch Hollywood films any more.«

Seeing, perceiving and observing are also the preeminent issues of »Avventure in Africa« (1998; Eng. »Adventures in Africa«, 2000). In 1999, Celati was awarded the New York University Prize for Italian Fiction for this unusual travelogue, which is both a documentary on his unsuccessful film project about the Dogon people of West Africa, and also a record of his own experiences as a tourist. Apart from his work as an author he πhas been a visiting lecturer at several universities. In addition, he has translated the works of numerous writers into Italian, including Jonathan Swift, Mark Twain, Céline, Stendhal, Samuel Beckett, Joseph Conrad and Roland Barthes. Gianni Celati lives in Brighton, UK.

Der wahre Schein
Wagenbach
Berlin, 1988
[Ü: Marianne Schneider]
Landauswärts
Suhrkamp
Frankfurt am Main, 1993
[Ü: Marianne Schneider]
Erzähler der Ebenen
Wagenbach
Berlin, 1997
[Ü: Marianne Schneider]
Avventure in Africa
Feltrinelli
Mailand, 1998
Mondphasen im Paradies
Suhrkamp
Frankfurt am Main, 1999
[Ü: Marianne Schneider]
Cinema naturale
Wagenbach
Berlin, 2001
[Ü: Marianne Schneider]

Gianni Celati wurde 1937 in Sondrio, Italien, geboren. An der Universität Bologna promovierte er mit einer Dissertation über James Joyce. 1966 wurde Italo Calvino, der damals Leiter des Einaudi Verlags war, durch eine Kurzgeschichte auf ihn aufmerksam. Gianni Celatis erstes Buch »Comiche« (Ü: Stummfilmsketch) erschien 1970, gefolgt von den Romanen »Le Avven-ture di Guizzardi« (1973; Ü: Guizzardis Abenteuer), »La Banda dei Sospiri« (1976; Ü: Die Seufzer-Clique) und »Lunario del Paradiso« (1979; dt. »Mondphasen im Paradies«, 1999), die seine Position als Autor der literarischen Neo-Avantgarde neben Umberto Eco und Italo Calvino festigten. 1973 wurde er Professor für Englische und Amerikanische Literatur an der Universität Bologna. In jener Zeit entstanden auch einige seiner literaturwissenschaftlichen Essays. Anfang der achtziger Jahre unterbrach er seine akademische Laufbahn zugunsten des Schreibens und des Filmemachens. Er drehte mehrere experimentelle Dokumentarfilme, darunter »Visioni di case che crollano« (engl. »Crumbling Houses«), eine kritische Meditation über den Zerfall verlassener Häuser in der Po-Ebene. Mit dem preisgekrönten Erzählband »Narratori delle pianure« (1985; dt. »Erzähler der Ebenen«, 1997) begab er sich auf die Suche nach neuen Möglichkeiten des minimalistischen Erzählens. An der Grenze zwischen Fiktion und Dokumentation konstruierte er den erzählenden und zugleich mit der Idee des Erzählens spielenden Chronisten von außergewöhnlichen Geschichten, die sich – angeblich – im Alltag dritter Personen zugetragen haben.
Über seine ironisch-grotesken Kurzgeschichten von »Cinema Naturale« (2001; dt. »Cinema Naturale«, 2001), das kinematographische Moment in der Literatur und den Prozess des Schreibens an sich sagt Gianni Celati: »An diesen Erzählungen habe ich über zwanzig Jahre geschrieben, dann habe ich sie lange Zeit neu geschrieben, um eine Beschäftigung zu haben und zu sehen, was sich unterdessen tut. Denn wenn man Erzählungen schreibt oder liest, sieht man Landschaften, sieht man Gestalten, hört man Stimmen: Man hat ein natürliches Kino im Kopf und braucht sich keine Hollywoodfilme mehr anzusehen.«
Ums Sehen, Wahrnehmen und Beobachten geht es auch in »Avventure in Africa« (1998; engl. »Adventures in Africa«, 2000). Für den außergewöhnlichen Reisebericht, in dem er das Scheitern eines Filmprojekts über das westafrikanische Dogon-Volk sowie seine Erfahrungen als Tourist dokumentiert, erhielt er 1999 den New York University Prize for the Italian Fiction. Neben seiner Tätigkeit als Schriftsteller war er Gastdozent an verschiedenen Universitäten und übersetzte Werke u. a. von Jonathan Swift, Mark Twain, Céline, Stendhal, Samuel Beckett, Joseph Conrad sowie Roland Barthes. Gianni Celati lebt in Brighton, Großbritannien.

For Jana Thiele and Co. of The Literaturfestival Berlin, here's another sonnet about a truant Muse, with my regards. G. C. June 2004

Another sonnet about a truant Muse
(after Shakespeare's sonnet no.101)

My old mop-headed Muse she doesn't answer
I sent her thousands letters, no reply.
She ran away with that bohemian dancer;
For her I was too normal, that is why.

Since then she has inspired ten best-sellers,
Worked for a school of writing, Tennessee,
Married two American storytellers,
And run a new publishing company.

But how can I go on without my Muse?
Poor clown in a sea of business tricks,
I invoke her help to lure or to amuse
My reader out of his anxiety fix.

Answer me, Muse, by letter or by dream:
you spasm, whiff, down-to-the-mothers gleam.

feng li
biography

Feng Li was born in Shenyang, in the northeast of the People's Republic of China, in 1963. She studied Chinese Literature at Liaoning University in Shenyang. From 1985 to 1990 she worked as a journalist for the Lhasa evening paper in Tibet. After her return to China she worked for seven years at the Liaoning Research Institute for Art as an academic associate with a focus on drama theory. In addition, she worked between 1995 and 1998 as director for the women's program »Half the Sky« for the TV channel CCTV (Chinese Central Television) and produced several documentary portraits about women. After that she spent two years as editor and translator at the Chunfeng Literature Publishing House. During this time she translated from German ten children's books by Janosch, among them »Oh, wie schön ist Panama« (Eng. »The trip to Panama«, 1978) and »Ich sag, du bist ein Bär« (t: I say you are a bear). These appeared in Chinese translation in 1999.

Feng Li has also had success as a writer herself (with seven books published), yet none have been translated into western languages. She began to write in the 1980's, and her first story came out in 1987 during her stay in Tibet. Feng Li publishes her stories and novels under the pseudonym Pipi, named after Astrid Lindgren's children's hero Pippi Longstocking. She depicts everyday life in China with distinctive style and light irony, from the individual search for happiness, to problematic relationships, to the difficulties of finding a flat – yet without joining the current trend of other young writers in the so-called ›westernisation‹ of Chinese literature. Admittedly, influences from that period of change are noticeable in her prose, from a time when China strengthened its ambition to transform the country through economic and cultural aperture.

Two of her short story collections are especially popular, »Quan Shijie Don Ba Sui« (2000; t: We are all eight years old) and »Weixian De Richang Shenghuo« (2000; t: Dangerous everyday life). In 1999 her novel »Kewang« (1998; t: Thirst for passion) was distinguished as an »outstanding national book«. The orderly life of a middle-aged married couple goes off the rails when the husband falls in love with another woman. A tragedy is played out against the backdrop of a quest for self-realisation and fulfilment in love, at whose centre are posed questions of togetherness and the value of family. The prose pieces »Chumai Yangguang« (2003; t: Sunshine on sale) and her memoirs »Bu Xiang Zhangda« (2003; t: I don't want to grow up) were published last year. Feng Li lives in Beijing but is currently a guest of the DAAD in Berlin.

Kewang Jiqing
Chunfeng Wenyi
Shenyang, 1998
Quan Shijie Don Ba Sui
Nanhai Chuban Gongsi
Hainan, 2000
Weixian De Richang Shenghuo
Shidai Wenyi
Changchun, 2000
Chumai Yangguang
Zuojia
Beijing, 2003
Bu Xiang Zhangda
Nanhai Chuban Gongsi
Hainan, 2000

Feng Li wurde 1963 in Shenyang, im Nordosten der Volksrepublik China, geboren. Sie studierte Chinesische Literaturwissenschaft an der Liaoning Universität in Shenyang. Von 1985 bis 1990 arbeitete sie als Journalistin für die Lhasa-Abendzeitung in Tibet. Nach der Rückkehr nach China war sie sieben Jahre lang wissenschaftliche Mitarbeiterin mit dem Schwerpunkt Theatertheorie am Liaoning Forschungsinstitut für Kunst. Außerdem produzierte sie zwischen 1995 und 1998 als Regisseurin für das Frauenprogramm »Half The Sky« beim CCTV (Chinese Central Television) dokumentarische Porträts über Frauen. Anschließend war sie zwei Jahre lang als Lektorin und Übersetzerin für das Chunfeng Literature Publishing House tätig. In diesem Zeitraum übersetzte sie aus dem Deutschen zehn Kinderbücher von Janosch, darunter »Oh, wie schön ist Panama« und »Ich sag, du bist ein Bär«. 1999 erschienen sie in der chinesischen Übersetzung.
Als Schriftstellerin hat sie selbst mit großem Erfolg sieben Bücher veröffentlicht, die bisher nicht in westliche Sprachen übersetzt worden sind. Mit dem Schreiben begann sie in den achtziger Jahren. Ihre erste Erzählung entstand 1987 während ihres Aufenthaltes in Tibet. Feng Li publiziert ihre Erzählungen und Romane unter dem Pseudonym Pipi, nach Astrid Lindgrens Kinderheldin Pipi Langstrumpf. Mit unverkennbarem Stil und mit leiser Ironie erzählt sie vom Alltag in China – von der individuellen Suche nach dem Glück, von problematischen Beziehungen oder von den Schwierigkeiten bei der Wohnungsvergabe –, ohne sich dem derzeit unter jungen Schriftstellern populären Trend zur sogenannten ›Verwestlichung‹ in der chinesischen Literatur anzuschließen. In ihrer Prosa sind allerdings Einflüsse aus jener Zeit des Wandels spürbar, in der sich China verstärkt dem Ziel einer wirtschaftlichen und kulturellen Öffnung des Landes zuwandte.
Besonders erfolgreich waren die beiden Erzählbände »Quan Shijie Don Ba Sui« (2000; Ü: Wir sind alle acht Jahre alt) und »Weixian De Richang Shenghuo« (2000; Ü: Gefährlicher Alltag). 1999 wurde ihr Roman »Kewang Jiqing« (1998; Ü: Durst nach Leidenschaft) als ›national herausragendes Buch‹ ausgezeichnet. Das geordnete Leben eines Ehepaars im mittleren Alter gerät aus der Bahn, als sich der Mann in eine andere Frau verliebt. Vor dem Hintergrund des Strebens nach Selbstverwirklichung und Erfüllung in der Liebe entspinnt sich eine Tragödie, in deren Zentrum die Frage nach Zusammengehörigkeit und dem Stellenwert der Familie gestellt wird. Im letzten Jahr erschienen Prosastücke unter dem Titel »Chumai Yangguang« (2003; Ü: Sonnenschein zu verkaufen) und ihre Memoiren »Bu Xiang Zhangda« (2003; Ü: Ich möchte nicht erwachsen werden). Feng Li lebt in Beijing. Sie ist derzeit Stipendiatin des DAAD in Berlin.

amanda michalopoulou

biography

Amanda Michalopoulou was born in Athens, Greece, in 1966. She studied French Literature in Athens, and journalism in Paris. Since 1990 she has been working as a columnist for the newspaper »I Kathimerini«. The literary magazine »Revmata« awarded her the first prize for the best short story in its literary contest. Shortly afterwards, she published her first book, »Éxo i zoi ine políchromi« (1994; t: Life is colourful outside), which is a collection of five short stories. Michalopoulou's keen eye detects the unusual in everyday situations, poignantly depicted in the surrealistic endings of the stories. Fantastic and alienating tones are prevalent in her subsequent publications too, which were often inspired by her visits to Germany, France, the USA and Switzerland – where she held scholarships. Far from the familiar conventions of home, life abroad becomes a source of inspiration to her. Her creativity is spurred by the feeling of speechlessness in a foreign language and of confrontation with her identity reflected in unfamiliar surroundings. »Living in a foreign country allows me to invent varying identities – but nonetheless, I cannot escape myself. This mixture is an ideal breeding ground for the imagination.«

She refers to her three novels, »Jándes« (1996; t: Wishbone memories), »Osses forés antéxis« (1998; t: As often as you can bear it) and »Paliókeros« (2001) as a self-referential trilogy about the writing of the first novel. Her protagonists are writers, translators and or editors who, during the course of the narration, set out on their journeys in order to search for their true lives, histories and selves. Michalopoulou's debut novel, »Jándes«, is a family saga which was awarded the prestigious prize of the literary magazine »Diavazo«. In »Osses forés antéxis«, the female Greek first-person narrator is pursuing her Czech lover through several European cities. The lover looks like Franz Kafka, and even calls her »my little bug«. This postmodern odyssey is sprinkled with eighty quotations from Kafka and numerous allusions to Kafka's life. Amanda Michalopoulou is also the author of a successful series of children's books, published in 2000: »Jatí jeníthika« (t: Why I was born), »Dyo spítia« (t: Two houses) and »T'agapiména mu sawatokyriaka« (t: My favorite weekend) which combine art with family life. Her latest novel, »Giati skotosa tin kaliteri mou fili« (2003 t: Why did I kill my best friend?), is about the politics of friendship. For 2004/2005 Amanda Michalopoulou has been granted a scholarship by the DAAD and she currently lives in Berlin.

Oktopusgarten
Rotbuch
Hamburg, 1999
[Ü: Birgit Hildebrand]
Dyo spítia
Patakis
Athen, 2000
Jatí jeníthika
Patakis
Athen, 2000
T'agapiména mu sawatokyriaka
Patakis
Athen, 2000
So ist das Leben
Rotbuch
Hamburg, 2001
[Ü: Birgit Hildebrand]
Ich mach euch den Garaus
Edition Solitude
Stuttgart, 2002
[Ü: Birgit Hildebrand]
Giati skotosa tin kaliteri mou fili
Kastaniotis
Athen, 2003

Amanda Michalopoulou wurde 1966 in Athen, Griechenland, geboren. Sie studierte Französische Philologie in Athen und Journalismus in Paris. Seit 1990 arbeitet sie als Kritikerin und Kolumnistin für die Tageszeitung »I Kathimerini«. Bei einem Literaturwettbewerb der Zeitschrift »Revmata« erhielt sie 1993 den ersten Preis für die beste Kurzgeschichte. Bald darauf erschien ihr erstes Buch »Éxo i zoi ine políchromi« (1994; Ü: Draußen ist das Leben bunt), ein Sammelband, bestehend aus fünf Erzählungen. Mit scharfem Blick fürs Detail schildert sie alltägliche Situationen, deren Ausgang oft surrealistisch pointiert ist. Das phantastische und befremdliche Element findet sich auch in ihren weiteren Veröffentlichungen, die vorwiegend während ihrer Aufenthalte als Stipendiatin in Deutschland, Frankreich, den USA und in der Schweiz entstanden. Fern von den vertrauten Konventionen der Heimat sieht sie das Leben im Ausland, das Moment der Sprachlosigkeit in einer fremden Sprache, die Konfrontation mit der eigenen Identität im Spiegel einer fremden Umgebung als Motor für ihre Kreativität. »Die Fremde gibt mir die Freiheit, wie eine Schauspielerin andere Identitäten zu erfinden – und doch kann ich meiner griechischen Identität nicht entkommen. Diese Mischung ist ein idealer Nährboden für die Phantasie.«
Ihre komplexen Romane »Jándes« (1996; dt. »Oktopusgarten«, 1999), »Osses forés antéxis« (1998; dt. »So ist das Leben«, 2001), und »Paliókeros« (2001, Ü: Sauwetter) bezeichnet sie als »Trilogie des Selbstbezogenseins«. Oft sind ihre Hauptfiguren Schriftsteller, Übersetzer oder Verleger, die der Welt des Wortes und der Literatur angehören und die sich im Verlauf der Erzählung auf Reisen begeben, auf die Suche nach dem wahren Leben, ihrer Geschichte und Identität. Der Debütroman »Oktopusgarten«, der mit dem renommierten Kritikerpreis der Literaturzeitschrift »Diavazo« ausgezeichnet wurde, erzählt eine Familiengeschichte. In »So ist das Leben« sucht die griechische Ich-Erzählerin in verschiedenen europäischen Städten nach ihrem tschechischen Geliebten, der sie zärtlich »mein Käferchen« nennt und wie Franz Kafka aussieht. Amanda Michalopoulou erzählt diese postmoderne Odyssee unter Verwendung von achtzig Kafka-Zitaten und unzähligen Anspielungen auf sein Leben. Sie ist außerdem Autorin einer Kinderbuchserie (2000; »Jatí jeníthika«, Ü: Warum ich geboren wurde; »Dyo spítia«, Ü: Zwei Häuser; »T'agapiména mu sawatokyriaka«, Ü: Meine Lieblingswochenenden). Auf deutsch liegt der Erzählband »Ich mach euch den Garaus« (2002) vor. Ihr jüngster Roman »Giati skotosa tin kaliteri mou fili« (Ü: Warum ich meine beste Freundin umbrachte) erschien 2003. Amanda Michalopoulou lebt 2004/2005 als DAAD-Stipendiatin in Berlin.

asher reich

biography

Asher Reich was born in Jerusalem in 1937, when the city was still within Palestine, and under the British Protectorate. He grew up isolated from modern life in Jerusalem's Jewish Orthodox quarter Mea Sharim. He had a strict and purely orthodox upbringing and education, and his schooling was based exclusively on the scriptures. At 18 he took the radical step of leaving the quarter, which was like taking »a leap in time onto another planet«. After his military service he studied Hebrew literature and philosophy at the Hebrew University in Jerusalem. He worked in Tel Aviv as a journalist and editor for several newspapers, as well as teaching Creative Writing at the Be'er Sheva University. Between 1980 and 2002 he was the chief editor of »Moznain«, the literary publication of the Israeli Authors' Association. His first poetry volume »Ha-Shana Ha-Svi'it Le-Nedudai« (t: In the seventh year) was published in 1961, and won the Anne Frank Award from the American Israeli Cultural Foundation. To date thirteen poetry volumes have been published, among them »Zrihat Layla« (1972; t: Night rise), »Avodot Al Nyar« (1988; t: Work on paper) and »Musikat Horef« (1996; t: Winter music). The intensity of his poems, and the poetic sensuality of his images are mingled with quotes from the Talmud and the Bible. This aspect of Reich's work originates from the contradictory influences of the poet's disparate environments. Christopher Meckel wrote in the epilogue of the German translation of »Avodot Al Nyar«, »The scribe had to learn to incorporate the different dialects of the modern world: the jargon and tone of our profane times, the political propaganda and technical vocabulary of the modern state, the secret languages of love, the body, the soul, slang and colloquial language, academic and literary hypertrophies.« Asher Reich describes his childhood influences thus: »I was fortunate enough that, even before I was three, I was transported, through the words of the Tora into an enchanted universe of words, sounds, and prayers; a world which took me away from the desert of my childhood.« His »Tel Aviver Ungeduld« (2002; t: Tel Aviv impatience) is another collection of poetry published in German. Together with his poetry publications, radio plays and stories, he has also published the autobiographical novel »Zichronot Shel Holeh Schiheha« (1993; t: Memoirs of a forgetful person). The latter was written while in Berlin receiving a DAAD grant. He has received a string of awards for his work, including the Israeli Presidential Prize for Literature in 2000. Asher Reich lives in Tel Aviv.

Ha-Shana Ha-Shvi'it Le-Nedudai
Ekked
Tel Aviv, 1961
Mar'eh Makom
Massada
Givàtayim, 1978
Hafisah Hadashah
Am Oved
Tel Aviv, 1983
Seder Shirim
Sifriat Poàlim
Tel Aviv, 1986
Arbeiten auf Papier
Rowohlt
Reinbek, 1992
[Ü: Judith Brüll, Jehuda Eren, Efrat Gal-Ed, Gila Lustiger, Christoph Meckel, Andrea Schatz]
Erinnerungen eines Vergesslichen
Bleicher
Gerlingen, 2000
[Ü: Ruth Achlama]
Tel Aviver Ungeduld
Axel Dielmann
Frankfurt am Main, 2000
[Ü: Lydia Böhmer, Paulus Böhmer, Werner Söllner]

Die Muse im Krieg

Sie ist wohlgeformt, mythologisch aber fragil, inspirierend, so romantisch, besitzt eine klassische Schönheit, eine Göttin, eigentlich neun Geschwistergöttinnen, die in einem Elfenbeinturm in Griechenland geboren wurden und die als Erlösung in der Seele des Künstlers erscheinen, der sich ununterbrochen nach ihnen sehnt. Die Muse: Sie ist eine wunderschöne junge Frau und der Krieg ist ein Monstrum, das sie vergewaltigen möchte.

Auch ist die Muse die einzige Waffe des Künstlers in schwierigen Zeiten wie in diesen Tagen, wie in unserer Vergangenheit voller Kriege und Spannungen, bei denen nur die Muse kommen und uns unter ihre Fittiche nehmen kann, damit wir in Ruhe unsere Arbeit tun können. Aber wer kann überhaupt in schweren Stunden wenn in unseren Städten das Blut Reiner und Unschuldiger fließt, an Rückzug mit der Muse denken? In solchen Zeiten ändert die Muse ihr fragiles Aussehen, setzt eine harte Miene auf und wechselt ihre virtuellen Knöpfe und verwandelt sich sowohl in eine Art Verteidigungs- als auch Angriffswaffe, die dem Künstler zur Verfügung steht, um gegen den Krieg zu kämpfen, mit anderen Mitteln, geistigeren. Das heißt: sich bewusst zu sein, dass unser geistiges Leben auch dann weitergeht, wenn sich Menschen offenlegen und das Tier in sich entdecken.

Die Muse ist das einzige Gegenmittel, das der Privatkünstler besitzt, sie ist die Impfung, das Antibiotikum, mit dessen Hilfe man die Stimme erheben kann, in einem Schrei Schreiben und Protest ausdrücken kann, weil die Muse die Stimme des menschlichen Herzen ist, Echo des klaren Verstandes.

Kalliope ist die Muse des Heldenepos und Erato ist die Muse der Lyrik und der Elegie in der griechischen Mythologie und diese beiden sind unsere passive Widerstandswaffe.

Das Schwert und die Feder sind niemals zur gleichen Zeit zur Welt hinab gekommen. Beide sind sich naturgemäß nicht grün, sind einander

Asher Reich wurde 1937 in Jerusalem, im damals unter britischem Protektorat stehenden Palästina, geboren. Er wuchs isoliert vom modernen Leben in Mea Shearim auf, dem orthodoxen Stadtviertel Jerusalems. Die streng religiöse Erziehung durch die Eltern setzte sich in der Schule fort, wo der Unterricht ausschließlich auf dem Studium heiliger Schriften basierte. Als Achtzehnjähriger verließ er das Viertel – ein radikaler Schritt, den er einmal als »Sprung über die Zeit, auf einen anderen Planeten« bezeichnete. Nach dem Militärdienst studierte er Hebräische Literatur und Philosophie an der Hebrew University in Jerusalem. In Tel Aviv arbeitete er als Journalist und Redakteur für verschiedene Zeitungen und unterrichtete kreatives Schreiben an der Universität in Be'er Sheva. Von 1980 bis 2002 war er Chefredakteur von »Moznaim«, der Literaturzeitschrift des israelischen Schriftstellerverbandes. Sein erster Lyrikband »Ha-Shana Ha-Svi'it Le-Nedudai« (Ü: Im siebten Jahr) wurde 1961 veröffentlicht und mit dem Anne-Frank-Preis der American Israel Cultural Foundation ausgezeichnet. Bis heute sind dreizehn Gedichtbände erschienen, darunter »Zrihat Layla« (1972; engl. Ü: Night rise), »Avodot Al Nyar« (1988; dt. »Arbeiten auf Papier«, 1992) und »Musikat Horef« (1996; Ü: Wintermusik). Die Intensität seiner Lyrik, die sinnlich-poetische Bilder mit Zitaten aus Talmud und Bibel verbindet, entspringt aus den gegensätzlichen Einflüssen der konträren Lebenswelten des Dichters. Christoph Meckel schreibt im Nachwort zu »Arbeiten auf Papier«: »Der Schriftkundige hatte die Sprachen der Welt zu lernen, Jargon und Tonarten der profanen Zeit, politisches und technisches Vokabular des modernen Staates und seiner Propaganda, die Geheimsprachen der Liebe, des Körpers, der Seele, Dialekte des täglichen Lebens und der Straße, akademische, literarische Hypertrophien.« Asher Reich hingegen betont den Einfluss seiner Kindheit: »Andererseits war es mir vergönnt, noch bevor ich drei Jahre alt war, zu den Worten und Klängen der Gebete und der Thora zu schreiten. In diesem Schreiten verbrachte ich die Wüste meiner Kindheit und lebte halb in einer verzauberten, verbalen Welt.« Mit »Tel Aviver Ungeduld« (2000) liegt eine weitere Gedichtsammlung in deutscher Übersetzung vor. Neben Lyrik veröffentlichte er Hörspiele, Erzählungen und den autobiographischen Roman »Zichronot Shel Holeh Shichehah« (1993; dt. »Erinnerungen eines Vergesslichen«, 2000), der 1990 während eines DAAD-Stipendiums in Berlin entstand. Für seine Werke erhielt er eine Reihe von Auszeichnungen, u. a. 2000 den Präsidentenpreis für Literatur in Israel. Asher Reich lebt in Tel Aviv.

feindselig. Das Schwert rostet bedauerlicherweise niemals. Aber auch die Feder im metaphorischen Sinne besteht und existiert. Und die Muse oder wenigstens einer ihrer Schatten steht in der Mitte und versucht einen Funken des allmählich erlöschenden Lichts zu retten. Es schmerzt zu wissen, dass bis heute das Schwert noch flammend ist und das nicht nur in den Toren des Paradieses sondern auch in den Toren unseres Landes und in vielen anderen Ländern.

Wie bedauerlich ist es, dass der Mensch immer noch der Verführung erliegt, von der verbotenen Frucht des Baumes der Erkenntnis zu essen. Aber die Erkenntnis macht ihn nicht so klug, um sein Ende zu verhindern. Der Mensch ist das einzige Wesen auf dieser Erde, das seine eigene Art mit vielfältigen Mitteln zerstört. Auch jetzt, in diesem ureigenen Augenblick, in dem ich zu Ihnen rede, ereignen sich kleine und große Kriege in Afrika, in Asien und im Nahen Osten.

Die kognitive Muse vertritt den Charakter und das Verhalten eines Künstlers in Kriegszeiten. Die Menschen gewöhnen sich ja gelegentlich an das Böse wie sie sich an das Gute gewöhnen. Und solange die Muse existiert und uns zur Seite steht, haben wir, die Autoren, eine persönliche Waffe, um gegen Kriege zu kämpfen und gegen deren Verursacher. Gegen Diskriminierungen und menschliches Unrecht, das in unserer Gesellschaft besteht. Die Muse, die häufig in unserer Reichweite ist, macht es erforderlich, von ihr keinen konventionellen Gebrauch zu machen.

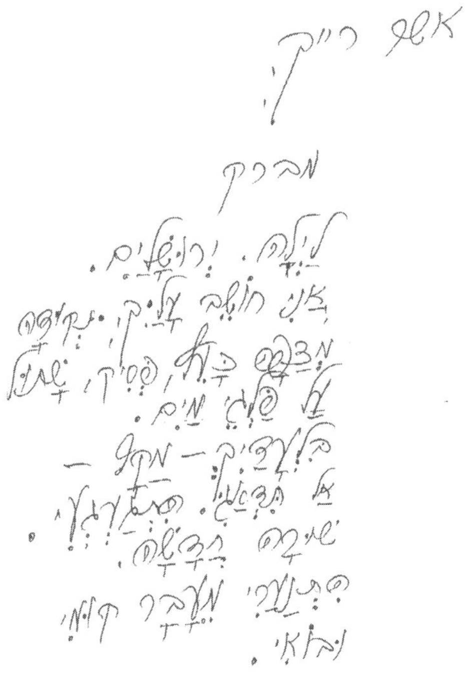

ottó tolnai

biography

Ottó Tolnai was born in Kanjiza in the Hungarian speaking region Vojvodina, now a part of Serbia, in 1940. He studied Hungarian Literature, Linguistics and Philosophy in Novi Sad and Zagreb. In 1956 Tolnai's first contributions to journals and magazines were published. His first volume of poetry, »Homorú versek« (t: Hollow verse), which consists of free verse, was published in 1963. In 1965 he began writing texts for the literary magazine »Új Symposion« (t: New symposium) – an important forum for literature and politics, in which the Hungarian avant-garde was able to express itself freely until its prohibition in 1972 – of which he would later become editor-in-chief. In 1968 he published a book of poetry called »Valóban mi lesz velünk« (t: What will become of us?) jointly with István Domonkos, in which he experimented with both concrete and visual poetry. This was followed in 1969 by »Rovarház« (t: Insect house), a seemingly autobiographical debut novel, in which linear narrative conventions are breached by the superimposition of collage-like constructions. From the early 1970's until the mid-90's, Ottó Tolnai was cultural editor of the Hungarian-speaking programme of Radio Novi Sad. As well as writing plays, novels and poetry he also published essays and art reviews in the magazine »Jelenkor«. Since 1993 he has been chief editor of »Ex Symposion«. His poems, prose and drama, which have been published in an edition consisting of around thirty volumes in both Hungary and former Yugoslavia, have earned him numerous prizes, including the Attila József prize in 1991. »Ich kritzelte das Akazienwäldchen in mein Heft« (2002; t: I scribbled the acacia wood into my notebook) is his first prose volume translated into German. In this collection of four short stories, all loosely related to one another through inter-textual indices, the protagonists' inner monologues are filled with memories. Actual experiences and fiction are evoked equally, surreal anecdotes are mingled with the mundane. The author's style is articulate and lucent, yet poetic; his non-linear narration is amplified by repetition and gains structure through the use of leitmotifs and recurring metaphors. The literary critic Ilma Rakusa has stated »Tolnai does not intone lament, but rather lets his characters speak of the everyday-uncanny s... With exquisite use of suggestion Ottó Tolnai creates a world whose archaic elements border on violence, but without renouncing the last remainders of poetry.« Ottó Tolnai lives in Palics. He is residing in Berlin throughout 2004/ 2005 as a beneficiary of the DAAD.

Rovarház
Forum
Novi Sad, 1969
Vidéki Orfeusz
Magvető
Budapest, 1983
Versek könyve
Széphalom
Budapest, 1992
Kékítőgolyó
Széphalom
Budapest, 1994
Balkáni babér
Jelenkor
Pécs, 2001
Ich kritzelte das Akazienwäldchen in mein Heft
Edition per procura
Wien, 2002
[Ü: György Buda, Géza Deréky]

Ottó Tolnai wurde 1940 in Kanjiza in der ungarischsprachigen Region Vojvodina im heutigen Serbien geboren. Er studierte Hungarologie und Philosophie an den Universitäten in Novi Sad und Zagreb. 1956 veröffentlichte er seine ersten Beiträge in Zeitschriften. 1963 erschien sein erster Gedichtband »Homorú versek« (Ü: Hohle Gedichte), eine Sammlung freier Verse. 1965 begann er mit dem Schreiben von Texten für die Literaturzeitschrift »Új Symposion« (Ü: Neues Symposium), deren Chefredakteur er später wurde. Es handelte sich hierbei um ein wichtiges literarisches und politisches Forum, in dem sich die ungarische Avantgarde bis zum Verbot der Zeitschrift 1972 frei äußern konnte. Gemeinsam mit István Domonkos publizierte er den Gedichtband »Valóban mi lesz velünk« (1968; Ü: Was wird denn mit uns), in dem er mit konkreter und visueller Poesie experimentierte. 1969 folgte der nur scheinbar autobiographische Debütroman »Rovarház« (Ü: Insektenhaus), der durch seine formale Konstruktion als Collage erstmals die bis dahin vorherrschenden linearen Erzählkonventionen in der ungarischen Gegenwartsliteratur durchbrach. Anfang der siebziger bis Mitte der neunziger Jahre arbeitete Ottó Tolnai als Kulturredakteur des ungarischsprachigen Programms von Radio Novi Sad. Neben Dramen, Romanen und Gedichten schrieb er Artikel und Kunstkritiken für die Zeitschrift »Jelenkor«. Seit 1993 ist er Chefredakteur der Zeitschrift »Ex Symposion«. Für seine Lyrik, Prosa, Theaterstücke und Essays, die in rund dreißig Bänden sowohl in Ungarn als auch im ehemaligen Jugoslawien veröffentlicht wurden, erhielt er zahlreiche Auszeichnungen, darunter 1991 den Attila József Preis. Mit »Ich kritzelte das Akazienwäldchen in mein Heft« (2002) liegt erstmals ein Prosaband in deutscher Übersetzung vor. In vier Erzählungen, die durch kleine Verweise lose miteinander verbunden sind, lässt Ottó Tolnai seine Protagonisten auf ihr Leben zurückblicken. In ihren inneren Monologen wuchern Erinnerungen, stehen Fiktives und Erlebtes gleichwertig nebeneinander, und skurril-surreale Anekdoten vermischen sich mit Beschreibungen eines ländlichen Alltags. Der Autor verwendet eine klare, dennoch poetische Sprache und verleiht seiner nichtlinearen Erzählweise durch Wiederholungen und leitmotivisch wiederkehrende Metaphern Struktur. Die Literaturkritikerin Ilma Rakusa urteilte: »Tolnai intoniert keine Klage, sondern legt das Alltäglich-Ungeheuerliche seinen Figuren in den Mund... Ungemein suggestiv entwirft Ottó Tolnai eine Welt, deren elementare Archaik ans Gewalttätige grenzt, ohne einen Rest von Poesie zu verleugnen.« Ottó Tolnai lebt in Palics. 2004/2005 ist er auf Einladung des DAAD Stipendiat in Berlin.

ingeborg arvola
valeria parrella
owen sheers
gernot wolfram

ingeborg arvola

biography | biographie

Ingeborg Arvola was born in Nordkapp county, Norway, in 1974. She grew up in Tromsø, but has lived in Oslo in recent years. She is working on her MA in literature, and is married to the illustrator Vidar Høyvang. Ingeborg Arvola made her literary debut with the novel »Korellhuset« (1999; t: The house of Coral), which has since been translated into German. In 2000 the author published the short story collection »Livet i et skillepaddeskall og andre historier« (t: Life in a tortoiseshell and other stories), as well as the children's book »Blod, snørr og tårer« (t: Blood, snot and tears) which has been translated into Danish and Dutch. In 2003 she published the novel »Straffe« (t: Punishment), and in 2004 the novel »Forsiktig glass« (t: Glass! Handle with care!).

Blod, snørr og tårer
Cappelen, Oslo, 2000
Livet i et skilpaddeskal og andre historier
Cappelen, Oslo, 2000
Am Ende der Sehnsucht
dtv, München, 2002
Straffe
Cappelen, Oslo, 2003
Forsiktig glass
Cappelen, Oslo, 2004

Ingeborg Arvola wurde 1974 in der Gemeinde Nordkapp, Norwegen, geboren. Sie wuchs in Tromsø auf, lebt aber seit einigen Jahren in Oslo. Sie studiert Literaturwissenschaft und ist mit dem Illustrator Vidar Høyvang verheiratet. 1999 veröffentlichte Ingeborg Arvola ihr erstes Buch, den Roman »Korellhuset«, der unter dem Titel »Am Ende der Sehnsucht« (2000) auch in deutscher Übersetzung vorliegt. 2000 erschien ein Band mit Erzählungen unter dem Titel »Livet i et skilpaddeskal og andre historier« (Ü: Das Leben in einem Schildkrötenpanzer und andere Geschichten) sowie das Kinderbuch »Blod, snørr og tårer« (Ü: Blut, Rotz und Tränen), das ins Dänische und Niederländische übersetzt wurde. 2003 erschien der Roman »Straffe« (Ü: Strafe) und 2004 der Roman »Forsiktig glass« (Ü: Vorsicht, Glas!).

valeria parrella

biography | biographie

Valeria Parrella was born in Torre del Greco, Italy, in 1974. She lives in Naples. Having graduated in Classics and as interpreter for the Lingua Italiana Segni, she now works for the Ente Nazionale Sordomuti, a Neapolitan institute for the deaf and dumb. She is a contributor to the Naples edition of »La Repubblica« and to »Marie Claire«. In 2003 Minimumfax published her short story collection »Mosca più balena«, and her stories have been selected for various anthologies, including: »Pensa alla salute« (2003), »Bloody Europe« (2004) and »La qualità dell'aria« (2004). Her writings have appeared in the literary magazines: »Nuovi Argomenti«, »Origine«, and »Accattone«.

Mosca più balena
minimum fax, Rom, 2003

Valeria Parrella wurde 1974 in Torre del Greco, Italien, geboren und lebt in Neapel. Nach einem Studium der Klassischen Philologie und einer Ausbildung zur Gebärdensprachdolmetscherin arbeitet sie beim Nationalen Taubstummenverband in Neapel. Sie ist Mitarbeiterin der neapolitanischen Redaktion der Tageszeitung »La Repubblica« sowie des Magazins »Marie Claire«. 2003 veröffentlichte sie den Erzählband »Mosca più balena« (Ü: Mücke plus Walfisch) und einzelne Erzählungen in diversen Anthologien, u. a. in »Pensa alla salute« (2003), »Bloody Europe« (2004) und »La qualità dell'aria« (2004). Texte von ihr sind in den Zeitschriften »Nuovi Argomenti«, »Origine« und »Accattone« erschienen.

owen sheers

biography | biographie

Owen Sheers was born in Fiji in 1974. A winner of an Eric Gregory Award and the 1999 »Vogue« Young Writers Award, his debut collection of poetry, »The Blue Book« (2000), was shortlisted for the Forward Prize Best 1st Collection and the Welsh Book of the Year 2001. His debut prose work, »The Dust Diaries« (2004), is creative non-fiction set in Southern Rhodesia and Zimbabwe. Chosen by »The Independent on Sunday« as one of the top thirty young British writers, he was also identified by Andrew Motion in the January 1st 2000 »Times« as a poet to watch in the new millennium. He is currently the writer in residence at The Wordsworth Trust in the Lake District.

The Blue Book
Seren, Bridgend, 2000
The Dust Diaries
Faber and Faber
London, 2004

Owen Sheers wurde 1974 auf den Fidschiinseln geboren. 1999 gewann er den Eric Gregory- sowie den Young Writers Award der »Vogue«, 2001 wurde seine erste Gedichtsammlung »The Blue Book« (2000) für den Forward Prize Best 1st Collection und das Welsh Book of the Year nominiert. Seine erste Prosaarbeit, »The Dust Diaries« (2004), ist ein Dokuroman über Südrhodesien und Simbabwe. »The Independent on Sunday´s« kürte Owen Sheers zu den Top Thirty der britischen Schriftsteller, und Andrew Morton schrieb in der »Times« vom 1. Januar 2000 über ihn, er gehöre zu den Dichtern, die es im neuen Jahrtausend zu beachten gelte. Gegenwärtig ist er Writer in Residence im Wordsworth Trust im Lake District.

gernot wolfram

biography | biographie

Gernot Wolfram was born in Zittau, Saxony, in 1975 and studied German and Communication Studies at the FU Berlin. He lives and works as a writer and journalist in Berlin. He has written short stories and poems for various magazines and has published numerous articles and essays in the »Frankfurter Allgemeine Zeitung«, »Die Welt« and the »Süddeutsche Zeitung«. In 2001 he wrote a concert collage entitled »Flucht auf der Einbahnstraße« for the actress Eva-Maria Hagen, and in 2002 he won the Walter-Serner-Preis. His book »Der Fremdländer« was published in 2003. At the beginning of the year critics placed it on the prestigious Südwestfunk list of best books. At the moment Gernot Wolfram is working as a lecturer in Inter-Cultural Communication at the University of Wrocław in Poland. In the autumn of 2004 his novel »Samuels Reise«, a literary road-movie, is due to be published. Aside from writing, Gernot Wolfram is interested in the cultural implications of the European unification process, especially in eastern Europe, and in the concerns of minorities in this context.

Freundschaft mit Sisyphos
Ars essentia,
Tübingen, 1999
Der Fremdländer
DVA, München, 2003
Samuels Reise
DVA, München, 2004

Gernot Wolfram, geboren 1975 in Zittau/Sachsen, studierte Germanistik und Kommunikationswissenschaften an der FU Berlin. Er lebt als Autor und Journalist in Berlin. Er schrieb Erzählungen und Gedichte für Zeitschriften und publizierte eine Vielzahl von Artikeln und Essays in der »Frankfurter Allgemeinen Zeitung«, der »Welt« und der »Süddeutschen Zeitung«. 2001 schrieb er die Konzertcollage »Flucht auf der Einbahnstraße« für die Schauspielerin Eva-Maria Hagen, 2002 gewann er den Walter-Serner-Preis. Sein Buch »Der Fremdländer« wurde 2003 veröffentlicht. Zu Jahresbeginn wurde es von Kritikern in die renommierte Bestenliste des Südwestfunks gewählt. Im Moment arbeitet Gernot Wolfram als Dozent für Interkulturelle Kommunikation an der Universität Wrocław in Polen. Im Herbst 2004 wird sein Roman »Samuels Reise«, ein literarisches Roadmovie, erscheinen. Neben dem Schreiben interessiert sich Gernot Wolfram für die kulturellen Aspekte des europäischen Einigungsprozesses, vor allem in Osteuropa, und für die Belange von Minderheiten in diesem Kontext.

»Make answer, muse!«

Ingeborg Arvola (far left)
Valeria Parrella (left)
Gernot Wolfram (right)

mihran dabag
roméo dallaire
carla del ponte
alexander demandt
peter eigen
michel friedman
jörg friedrich
hannes heer
hans-peter kaul
thomas macho
salah negm
rupert neudeck
john prendergast
hazem saghieh
karl schlögel
hani shukrallah
natan sznaider
christian tomuschat
michael warschawski
ian williams

born in 1944, studied philosophy, history, sociology and political science in Bonn and Bochum and did his Phd in philosophy of history. He is director of the Institute for the research in diaspora and genozide at the Ruhr-Universität in Bochum and co-editor of numerous books about gobalisation, violence, genozide and colonialism, as well as of the magazine for the research in genozide. Dabag received the Franz Werfel Human Rights Prize in 2003.

Mihran Dabag

geboren 1944, studierte Philosophie, Geschichte, Soziologie und Politikwissenschaften in Bonn und Bochum und promovierte im Bereich Geschichtsphilosophie. Er ist Direktor des Instituts für Diaspora- und Genozidforschung an der Ruhr-Universität Bochum und Mitherausgeber zahlreicher Bücher über die Globalisierung, Gewalt, Genozid und Kolonialismus sowie der Zeitschrift für Genozidforschung. Dabag ist Träger des Franz-Werfel-Menschenrechtspreises 2003.

was born in Denekamp, the Netherlands, in 1946. The retired lieutenant general spent thirty-six years serving in the Canadian army. As commander of the UN Blue Helmets in Rwanda in 1993 and 1994 he called in vain for a military UN mandate to stop the genocide. In 2003 he published »Shake Hands with the Devil«, a critical account of genocide.

Roméo Dallaire

wurde 1946 in Denekamp, Niederlande, geboren. Der pensionierte Generalleutnant diente 36 Jahre lang in der kanadischen Armee. Als Kommandeur der UN-Blauhelme in Ruanda 1993 bis 1994 forderte er vergeblich ein militärisches UN-Mandat zur Verhinderung des Völkermordes. 2003 veröffentlichte er »Shake Hands With the Devil«, eine kritische Chronik des Genozids.

Mihran Dabag

Roméo Dallaire

Alexander Demandt

Carla Del Ponte

Ponte is chief prosecutor in The Hague for the International War Crimes Tribunal for former Yugoslavia and Rwanda. She was born in Lugano in 1947 and opened her own law and notary firm in 1975, three years after competing her studies of law. In 1981 she became an examining magistrate, and four years later a public prosecutor. In 1994 she was named the highest criminal prosecutor in Switzerland. In 1999 she was called upon her current position.

Carla Del Ponte

ist Chefanklägerin des Internationalen Kriegsverbrechertribunals für das frühere Jugoslawien und Ruanda in Den Haag. Sie wurde 1947 in Lugano geboren und eröffnete drei Jahre nach ihrem Jura-Studium ihre eigene Anwalts- und Notariatskanzlei. 1981 wurde sie Untersuchungsrichterin, vier Jahre später Staatsanwältin. 1994 wurde sie zur obersten Strafverfolgerin der Schweiz ernannt, 1999 erfolgte ihre Berufung nach Den Haag.

was born in 1937 in Marburg, Germany. Since 1974 he has been professor for Ancient History at the Free University Berlin, with Antiquity, Philososophy of History and History of Science as his main focuses. Recent publications are the historical-philosophical essays »Zeit und Unzeit« (2002) and »Kleine Weltgeschichte2 (2003). 2003 he was awarded the Ausonius-Prize of the University of Trier.

Alexander Demandt

wurde 1937 in Marburg geboren. Seit 1974 ist er Professor für Alte Geschichte an der Freien Universität Berlin mit den Schwerpunkten Spätantike, Geschichtsphilosophie sowie Wissenschaftsgeschichte. Jüngste Publikationen sind die geschichtsphilophischen Essays »Zeit und Unzeit« (2002) und »Kleine Weltgeschichte« (2003). 2003 wurde ihm der Ausonius-Preis der Universität Trier verliehen.

was born in Augsburg, Germany, in 1938. The lawyer has worked for the World Bank in South America and Africa since 1968, most recently as the Director of the World Bank in East Africa. In 1993 he founded »Transparency International«, an NGO, campaigning against corruption in ninety countries. His book »Das Netz der Korruption«, about the work and goals of the organisation, was published in 2003.

Peter Eigen

wurde 1938 in Augsburg geboren. Der promovierte Jurist war seit 1968 für die Weltbank in Südamerika und Afrika tätig, zuletzt als Weltbankdirektor in Ostafrika. 1993 gründete er »Transparency International«, eine NGO, die mittlerweile in 90 Ländern gegen Korruption aktiv ist. Sein Buch »Das Netz der Korruption« über das Arbeitsfeld und die Ziele der Organisation erschien 2003.

was born in Paris in 1956 and moved with his family to Mainz, where he studied Law. He got involved in politics and in public life, among others in the Federal Executive Board of the Christdemocrats and as vice-president of the Central Council of Jews in Germany. He was a board member of several foundations and editor of the newspaper »Jüdische Wochenzeitung«. At present Friedman works as editor at the publishing house Aufbau-Verlag and as TV moderator.

Michel Friedman

wurde 1956 in Paris geboren und siedelte mit seiner Familie 1965 nach Mainz über, wo er Jura studierte. Er engagierte sich in Politik und Öffentlichkeit, u. a. im Bundesvorstand der CDU und als Vizepräsident des Zentralrats der Juden. Er war Vorstandsmitglied mehrerer Stiftungen und Herausgeber der »Jüdischen Wochenzeitung«. Zurzeit arbeitet Friedman u. a. als Herausgeber beim Aufbau-Verlag und als Fernsehmoderator.

Peter Eigen

Jörg Friedrich

Hannes Heer

was born in 1944. Since the seventies he deals critically with the martial law, the refurbishment and the inadequate juristic prosecution of the NS-crimes. With the contro versial publications »Der Brand« (2002) and »Brandstätten« (2003) he focused on and documented the air raids of the allies and their disastrous impacts on the german civil population.

Jörg Friedrich

wurde 1944 geboren. Seit den siebziger Jahren setzt er sich kritisch mit dem Kriegsrecht, der Aufarbeitung und der unzureichenden juristischen Verfolgung der NS-Verbrechen auseinander. Mit den kontroversen Publikationen »Der Brand« (2002) und »Brandstätten« (2003) thematisierte und dokumentierte er die Bombardements der Allierten und ihre verheerenden Auswirkungen auf die deutsche Zivilbevölkerung.

was born in Wissen/Sieg, Germany, in 1941. He studied Literature and History in Bonn. A journalist and film director, he was awarded the Carl-von-Ossietzky-Medal in 1997. Until 1999 he was the director of the exhibition »Vernichtungskrieg. Verbrechen der Wehrmacht 1941 bis 1944«. He recently published the book »Vom Verschwinden der Täter« (2004).

Hannes Heer

wurde 1941 in Wissen/Sieg geboren. Er studierte Literaturwissenschaft und Geschichte in Bonn. Der Historiker, Journalist und Filmregisseur wurde 1997 mit der Carl-von-Ossietzky-Medaille ausgezeichnet. Bis 1999 war er der Leiter der Ausstellung »Vernichtungskrieg. Verbrechen der Wehrmacht 1941 bis 1944«. Zuletzt veröffentlichte er das Buch »Vom Verschwinden der Täter« (2004).

born in 1943, studied law after serving in the army for four years. Her worked in the Foreign Service, e. g. as a consul to Norway, as a spokesman of the German embassy in in Israel and as the director of the Department of International Law in Berlin. Kaul campaigned decisively for the creation of an International Criminal Court where he was sworn in as a judge in March 2004.

Hans-Peter Kaul

geboren 1943, studierte nach vierjährigem Militärdienst Jura. Er arbeitete im diplomatischen Dienst, u. a. als Konsul in Norwegen, als Sprecher der deutschen Botschaft in Israel und als Leiter des Völkerrechtsreferats in Berlin. Kaul setzte sich maßgeblich für die Schaffung eines internationalen Strafgerichtshofs ein und wurde dort im März 2004 als Richter vereidigt.

was born in Vienna, Austria, in 1952. He studied Philosophy, Music and Pedagogy. A Professor of Cultural Studies at the Humboldt University in Berlin, he is also co-founder of the Hermann von Helmholtz Centre for Cultural Sciences, established at the Humboldt University in 1999. In 2001 he won the Prize of the Aby-Warbung-Stiftung, and most recently has published »Tiere-Menschen-Maschinen. Zur Kritik der Anthropologie«.

Thomas Macho

wurde 1952 in Wien geboren. Er studierte Philosophie, Musikwissenschaft und Pädagogik. Der Professor für Kulturwissenschaften an der Humboldt Universität zu Berlin ist Mitbegründer des 1999 eröffneten Hermann von Helmholtz-Zentrums für Kulturtechnik an der HU. 2001 war er Preisträger der Aby-Warburg-Stiftung. Zuletzt publizierte er »Tiere – Menschen – Maschinen. Zur Kritik der Anthropologie«.

Thomas Macho

Rupert Neudeck

has been editor-in-chief of the Arabic broadcast station »Al Arabiya« in Dubai since 2002. Until 2001, he worked for the competing broadcast station »Al Jazeera« based in Qatar. He took a significant part in its build-up since 1996. Before, he was newsreader at Radio Cairo, editor at Radio Netherlands International and programme director at the BBC Arabic Television.

Salah Negm

Salah Negm ist seit 2002 Chefredakteur des arabischen Nachrichtensenders »Al Arabiya« in Dubai. Bis 2001 arbeitete er für den in Qatar ansässigen Konkurrenzsender »Al Jazeera«, an dessen Aufbau er seit 1996 maßgeblich beteiligt war. Zuvor war er u. a. Nachrichten sprecher bei Radio Cairo, Redakteur bei Radio Netherlands International und Programmchef beim arabischen Fernsehen der BBC.

was born in Gdańsk in 1939. He made his PhD in Theology in 1972. Since 1976 Neudeck has worked as a freelance journalist, among others for the Deutschlandfunk in Cologne. Together with Heinrich Böll he founded the Cap Anamur/ German Emergency Physicians. Since 1998 he is official spokesman of the organisation, and in 2003 he became chairperson of the Grünhelme e. V. Neudeck received numerous awards.

Rupert Neudeck

wurde 1939 in Danzig geboren. 1972 promovierte er in Theologie. Seit 1976 ist Neudeck als freier Journalist tätig und arbeitet u. a. für den Deutschlandfunk in Köln. Zusammen mit Heinrich Böll gründet er 1982 das Komitee »Cap Anamur/Deutsche Notärzte e. V.« Seit 1998 ist er offizieller Sprecher der Organisation und seit 2003 Vorsitzender von Grünhelme e.V. Neudeck erhielt zahlreiche Auszeichnungen.

lives in Washington. For several years he has worked in Africa with human rights organisations. He was special advisor to the U. S. State Department on conflict resolution and served as director of African Affairs at the National Security Council. Prendergast is the author of numerous books on Africa, and is currently working as special advisor for the International Crisis Group, for which he visited Sudan in July 2004.

John Prendergast

lebt in Washington. Jahrelang arbeitete er in Afrika mit Menschenrechtsorganisationen zusammen. Er war Sonderberater des U. S. State Department für Konfliktlösung und Direktor für afrikanische Angelegenheiten im Nationalen Sicherheitsrat. Prendergast ist Autor zahlreicher Bücher über Afrika und arbeitet als Sonderberater der International Crisis Group, für die er im Juli 2004 den Sudan besuchte.

was born in Lebanon. He is columnist and editor of the political weekly supplement »Tayyarat« of the daily newspaper »Al-Hayat« in London. Especially in the western world, he is esteemed for his commentaries regarding the current political situation in the Near and Middle East. He published several books in Arabic, at last in 2003 a book about the history of the Iraqi Baath party.

Hazem Saghieh

wurde im Libanon geboren. Er ist Kolumnist und Redakteur des wöchentlichen Politikdossiers »Tayyarat« der Tageszeitung »Al-Hayat« in London. Für seine Kommentare zur aktuellen politischen Situation im Nahen und Mittleren Osten wird er insbesondere auch im Westen geschätzt. Auf Arabisch veröffentlichte er mehrere Bücher, zuletzt 2003 ein Buch über die Geschichte der irakischen Baath-Partei.

John Prendergast

Hazem Saghieh

Karl Schlögel

Hani Shukrallah

was born in Hawangen/Allgäu, Germany, in 1948. He is Professor of Eastern European History at the Europa Universität Viadrina in Frankfurt/Oder. He has published a series of groundbreaking essays on the history and presence of Eastern Europe, as well as on Europe in transition in view of the Eastern expansion of the EU. His latest publication is a collection of essays, »Im Raume lesen wir die Zeit« (2003).

Karl Schlögel

wurde 1948 in Hawangen/Allgäu, Deutschland, geboren. Er ist Professor für Osteuropäische Geschichte an der Europa Universität Viadrina in Frankfurt/Oder. Er veröffentlichte eine Reihe von wegweisenden Essays zur Geschichte und Gegenwart Osteuropas sowie über Europa im Übergang angesichts der EU-Osterweiterung. Zuletzt erschien die Essaysammlung »Im Raume lesen wir die Zeit« (2003).

was born in Egypt in 1950. He studied Political Science. Since 1993 he has worked for »Al-Ahram Weekly«, since 2003 as editor-in-chief. In his column »Reflections« he writes about Egyptian state and political society, political Islam, the Palestinian-Israeli conflict, »the War on Terror« and Iraq. He is a member of the Egyptian Organisation for Human Rights (EOHR), the NGO »Arabs Against Discrimination«, and the Centre for Arab and African Research.

Hani Shukrallah

wurde 1950 in Ägypten geboren und studierte Politische Wissenschaften. Seit 1993 arbeitet er bei der »Al-Ahram Weekly« und ist seit 2003 deren Chefredakteur. In seiner Kolumne »Reflections« schreibt er u. a. über ägyptische Verhältnisse, den politischen Islam, den palästinensisch-israelischen Konflikt, den »Krieg gegen den Terror« und den Irak. Er ist Mitglied der Egyptian Organisation for Human Rights (EOHR), der NGO Arabs Against Discrimination, und des Zentrums für Arabische und Afrikanische Studien.

was born near Mannheim, Germany, in 1954, and has lived in Israel since 1974. He is Professor of Sociology at the Academic College in Tel Aviv-Jaffa. In »Erinnerung im globalen Zeitalter: Der Holocaust« (2001) he pursues the question, together with the sociologist Daniel Levy, as to what extent the Holocaust has changed from a national to a global memory.

Natan Sznaider

wurde 1954 in der Nähe von Mannheim geboren. Seit 1974 lebt er in Israel. Er ist Professor für Soziologie am Academic College in Tel Aviv-Jaffa. In »Erinnerung im globalen Zeitalter: Der Holocaust« (2001) ging er zusammen mit dem Soziologen Daniel Levy der Frage nach, inwiefern sich der Holocaust von einer nationalen zu einer globalen Erinnerung gewandelt hat.

was born in Szczecin in 1936. From 1985 to 1996 he was a member of the Human Rights Commission of the UN, and since then has been an independent advisor to various other international boards. He is Professor at the Humboldt University Berlin and Director of the Institute for European and International Law. His publications include »The United Nations at Age Fifty: A Legal Perspective« (1995).

Christian Tomuschat

wurde 1936 in Stettin geboren. Von 1985 bis 1996 war er Mitglied der Völkerrechtskommission der UNO, seither ist er unabhängiger Berater verschiedener internationaler Gremien. Er ist Professor an der Humboldt-Universität zu Berlin und Direktor des Instituts für Europa- und Völkerrecht. Er veröffentlichte u. a. »The United Nations at Age Fifty: A Legal Perspektive« (1995).

Michael Warschwaski

was born in Strasbourg, France, in 1949. Since 1965 he has lived in Israel. In 1984 he founded the Israeli-Palestinian Alternative Information Centre (AIC), which campaigns for freedom in the Near East. He was director of the AIC until 1999. Since 2001 he has represented the centre at the International Council of the World Social Forum. In his book »An der Grenze« (2004) he discusses the Israeli-Palestine conflict.

Michael Warschwaski

wurde 1949 in Strasbourg, Frankreich, geboren. Seit 1965 lebt er in Israel. 1984 gründete er das Alternative Information Center (AIC), das sich für Frieden im Nahen Osten einsetzt. Bis 1999 war er Direktor des AIC, seit 2001 vertritt er es im International Council of the World Social Forum. In seinem neuen Buch »An der Grenze« (2004) thematisiert er den israelisch-palästinensischen Konflikt.

was born in Liverpool in 1949. Before he moved to New York in 1989, where he lives today, he wrote for numerous English newspapers. Williams was repeatedly president of the UN Correspondents Association. His third book »The Deserter. Bush' s War on Military Families, Veterans and His Past« was published in 2004. He works for various international newspapers and for radio and television.

Ian Williams

wurde 1949 in Liverpool geboren. Der Journalist schrieb für zahlreiche englische Zeitungen, bevor er 1989 nach New York zog, wo heute lebt. Williams war wiederholt Präsident der Vereinigung der Korrespondenten der UN. Sein drittes Buch »The Deserter. Bush's War on Military Families, Veterans and His Past« erschien 2004. Neben seiner journalistischen Tätigkeit für verschiedene internationale Zeitungen arbeitet er auch für Funk und Fernsehen.

Pressestimmen 2003

«Zuerst gibt es einmal sehr viel Literatur für Kinder. Das ist das Erfreulichste.»
rbb Radio Kultur

«Schön für Berlin: Das Internationale Literaturfestival ist im dritten Jahr seines Bestehens zur Institution geworden – ein Großereignis, nicht nur, was das Format und die globale Herkunft der Autoren betrifft, sondern auch hinsichtlich der Besucherzahl.»
FAZ

«Ulrich Schreiber ist der vielleicht einzige Architekt der Welt, den beim Anblick von baulichem Verfall keine Abriss- und Wiederaufbaupläne umtreiben, sondern der ganz im Gegenteil die Ruine als einen Ort höchster Erbaulichkeit schätzt – nämlich als Schauplatz des Internationalen Literaturfestivals Berlin, eines der grössten seiner Art, dessen Leiter er ist und dessen dritte Ausgabe sich erneut mit grossen Namen schmücken konnte.»
NZZ

«Das Literaturfestival verführt – ohne jede aristokratische Attitüde – durch Überfluss.»
Der Tagesspiegel

«So entließ das charmante Festival sein Publikum mit dem schönen Gefühl, dass man sich um die Zukunft der Poesie wenig Sorgen machen muss.»
Stuttgarter Zeitung

«Unter der Regie des Begründers Ulrich Schreiber hat sich das Festival in nur drei Jahren zu einem der weltweit wichtigsten Treffpunkte etablierter Schriftsteller mit neu entdeckten Literaten und einem Leckerbissen für Bücherwürmer gemausert.»
Fränkischer Tag

«Wahrer und schöner und besser als Frankfurt, denn hier werden keine Geschäfte gemacht, da ist nur die Literatur. Pur.»
Die Zeit

«Die überbordende Fülle des Festivals ließ ein breites Panorama entstehen.»
Süddeutsche Zeitung

«Mit seinem breiten wie ambitionierten Programm wird sich das Internationale Literaturfestival Berlin fest etablieren.»
Neues Deutschland

«Niemals sonst im Jahr hat man die Gelegenheit, so viele literarische Stimmen kennen zu lernen, wieder zu hören und Leseeindrücke im Gespräch zu vertiefen, wie an diesen zwölf Tagen im September.»
Berliner Zeitung

«So könnte das Paradies für passionierte Leser aussehen. Die Begegnung etablierter Schriftsteller mit neu entdeckten Literaten dürfte in dieser Zahl weltweit einmalig sein.»
Gießener Allgemeine

«Allein schon mit wedelnden Nerven mitten am Tag durch sie Stadt zu radeln, atemlos von Lesung zu Lesung zu hechten: dieses herrlich hysterische Festivalgefühl.»
taz

«Höhepunkt des 3. Internationalen Literaturfestivals dürfte für Cineasten die Veranstaltungsreihe ‚Literatur auf Celluloid' sein.»
Berliner Morgenpost

«Das Berliner Literaturfestival findet das dritte Jahr in Folge statt und ist dabei, einen Stellenwert unter den führenden Literaturfesten der Welt zu erringen.»
Die Jüdische

«Schön am internationalen Literaturfestival ist, dass es seinem Namen durch und durch gerecht wird. Es ist richtig international. Und es ist ein echtes Festival. Fast wie zur Berlinale ist man versucht, sich ein paar Tage freizuhalten und durch die verschiedenen Programmsparten zu stöbern. Bei diesem Festival kann man auf verschiedenste Arten glücklich und auch ein bißchen klüger werden, Letzteres liegt daran, wie fundiert hier Internationalität buchstabiert wird, jenseits von Verlagstrends.»
zitty

«Das 3. Internationale Literaturfestival Berlin, das mittlerweile zu den größten Literaturfestivals der Welt zählt, leistet damit einen Beitrag zur Weltoffenheit und Gastfreundschaft der Hauptstadt.»
Berliner Wirtschaft

«Liebe Lehrer und Eltern, das Angebot richtet sich an Schüler aller Klassenstufen! Es lohnt sich!»
tip

4. internationales literaturfestival berlin

21. September bis 2. Oktober 2004
www.literaturfestival.com

Das internationale literaturfestival berlin ist eine Veranstaltung der Peter-Weiss-Stiftung für Kunst und Politik e.V. und der Berliner Festspiele unter der Schirmherrschaft der Deutschen UNESCO-Kommission.
Es wird wesentlich ermöglicht aus Mitteln des Hauptstadtkulturfonds.

UNESCO Berliner Festspiele HAUPT STADT KULTUR FONDS

candance allen
martin amanshauser
apti bisultanov
henning boëtius
arne dahl
sophie dannenberg
lászló földényi
günter herburger
josé luis de juan
bertram job
wolfgang kubin
allan levine
henning mankell
poni micharvegas
birgit müller-wieland
marilene phipps
frank schätzing
tilman spengler
gerald uhlig
stefan ludmilla wieszner
wolf wondratschek

was born in Boston, USA, in 1950. She studied in Harvard and New York and worked in the Hollywood film industry. After several screenplays she wrote her first novel »Valaida« (2004), which is the biography of the Afro-American jazz trumpeter Valaida Snow. The author lives in London.

Candace Allen

wurde 1950 in Boston, USA, geboren. Sie studierte in Harvard und New York und arbeitete in der Filmindustrie Hollywoods. Nach mehreren Drehbüchern verfasste sie ihren ersten Roman »Valaida« (2004). Darin entwirft sie die Biographie der afro-amerikanischen Jazz-Trompeterin Valaida Snow. Die Autorin lebt in London.

born in Salzburg in 1968, lives in Vienna. The author, journalist and translator was awarded several times. His poems »Hunderttausend verkaufte Exemplare« was very successful (e. g. at the ilb SLAM! Revue 2002). He published also »in der todesstunde von alfons alfred schmidt« (2000), »Chicken Christl« (2004).

Martin Amanshauser

1968 in Salzburg geboren, lebt in Wien. Der Autor, Journalist und Übersetzer wurde mehrfach ausgezeichnet. Mit seinem Gedichtband »Hunderttausend verkaufte Exemplare« war er sehr erfolgreich (u. a. bei der ilb-SLAM!-Revue 2002). Er veröffentlichte u. a. »in der todesstunde von alfons alfred schmidt« (2000) und »Chicken Christl« (2004).

Candace Allen

Martin Amanshauser

Apti Bisultanov

Henning Boëtius

was born in 1959 in Goichu/Chechnya. He studied philology and worked as a lecturer, editor, publisher, minister and partisan. In 1992, he received the Chechen National Award for his poem »Written in Chaibach«. Since 2002 he has been living in Berlin. He received the award of the Poets of All Nations Foundation in 2003. In 2004, his collection of poems »Schatten eines Blitzes« appeared.

Apti Bisultanov

wurde 1959 in Goitschu/Tschetschenien geboren und studierte Philologie. Er arbeitete als Dozent, Redakteur, Herausgeber, Minister und Partisan. Für sein Poem »In Chaibach verfasst« erhielt er 1992 den tschetschenischen Nationalpreis. Seit 2002 lebt er in Berlin. 2003 erhielt er den Poets of All Nations-Preis. Sein zweisprachiger Gedichtband »Schatten eines Blitzes« erschien 2004.

born in 1939, studied German. He was editor-in-chief of the critical edition of Brentano's works. He wrote books of juveniles' literature and radio plays. Boëtius published novelistic biographies, for example about Georg Christoph Lichtenberg and Rimbaud, and the bestseller »Phönix aus Asche« (2000) as well as five detective stories featuring superintendent Piet Hieronymus. The author lives in Berlin.

Henning Boëtius

geboren 1939, studierte Germanistik. Er war Redaktionsleiter der kritischen Brentano-Ausgabe und arbeitete als Wissenschaftsjournalist, Jugendbuch- und Hörfunkautor. Boëtius verfasste Roman-Biografien, z. B. über Georg Christoph Lichtenberg und Rimbaud, den Bestseller »Phönix aus Asche« (2000) und bislang fünf Kriminalromane um den Kommissar Piet Hieronymus. Der Autor lebt in Berlin.

Dahl is the pseudonym of Swedish author Jan Arnald, who was born in 1963. He received the Palle Rosenkrantz Award for his crime novels featuring Stockholm inspector Paul Hjelm. The author works also as a publisher of the magazines »Artes« and »Aiolos«, critic for the »Göteborgs Posten«, and for the Swedish Academy, that awards the annual Noble Prize.

Arne Dahl

ist das Pseudonym des 1963 geborenen schwedischen Autors Jan Arnald. Für seine Kriminalromane um den Stockholmer Inspektor Paul Hjelm wurde er 2004 mit dem Palle Rosencrantz Preis ausgezeichnet. Der Autor ist außerdem Herausgeber der Zeitschriften »Artes« und »Aiolos«, Kritiker bei der »Göteborgs Posten« und arbeitet für die Schwedische Akademie, die jährlich die Nobelpreise vergibt.

was born in 1971. She studied literature and philosophy in Dublin, New Albany and in Capri. Her first novel »Das bleiche Herz der Revolution« (t: The pale heart of revolution), a sardonic satire about the generation of '68 from the point of view of their children, was published in 2004. Sophie Dannenberg lives in Berlin.

Sophie Dannenberg

wurde 1971 geboren. Sie studierte Literaturwissenschaft und Philosophie mit Studienaufenthalten in Dublin, New Albany und auf Capri. Ihr Romandebüt »Das bleiche Herz der Revolution«, eine bissige Satire auf die 68er-Generation aus der Sicht ihrer Kinder, erschien 2004. Sophie Dannenberg lebt in Berlin.

Arne Dahl

Sophie Dannenberg

László Földényi

Günter Herburger

was born in 1952. He is an art historian, literary scholar and essayist. He worked as a dramatic advisor and translated numerous contemporary dramatists. He is co-editor of the Hungarian Kleist edition. His essays »Heinrich von Kleist. Im Netz der Wörter« (1999) was enthusiastically reviewed by the critics. In 2002, he received the Blauer Salon award of the Frankfurt Literaturhaus.

László Földényi

geboren 1952, ist Kunsttheoretiker, Literaturwissenschaftler und Essayist. Er arbeitete als Dramaturg und übersetzte zahlreiche zeitgenössische Dramatiker. Er ist Mitherausgeber der ungarischen Kleist-Ausgabe. Seine Essays »Heinrich von Kleist. Im Netz der Wörter« (1999) wurden von der Kritik begeistert aufgenommen. 2002 erhielt er den Blauen-Salon-Preis des Literaturhauses Frankfurt.

was born in Isny, Bavaria, in 1932 and lives in München. He studied theatre, philosophy and Sanskrit in Munich and Paris and for several years tramped through North Africa, Spain and France. In 1992 he was awarded the Peter Huchel Prize. He has published screenplays, radio plays, children's books, novels, stories and poems. Most recently »Schlaf und Strecke« (2004; t: Sleep and distance) appeared.

Günter Herburger

wurde 1932 in Isny/Allgäu geboren und lebt in München. Er studierte Theaterwissenschaften, Philosophie und Sanskrit in München und Paris und vagabundierte mehrere Jahre durch Nordafrika, Spanien und Frankreich. Der Autor erhielt 1992 den Peter-Huchel-Preis und schrieb Drehbücher und Hörspiele, Kinderbücher, Romane, Erzählungen sowie Gedichte. Zuletzt veröffentlichte er »Schlaf und Strecke« (2004).

was born in Palma in 1956. At the age of 17 he wrote an award-winning novella about Hemingway. Later he studied Law and Information Science in Barcelona and worked as a lawyer, before starting to write again. For his novels as »El apicultor de Bonaparte« (1996; t: Bonaparte's bee-keeper) he received various Spanish literature awards. The author and writer of book reviews lives in Mallorca.

José Luis de Juan

wurde 1956 in Palma geboren. Mit 17 Jahren schrieb er eine preisgekrönte Erzählung über Hemingway. Später studierte er Jura und Informationswissenschaft in Barcelona und arbeitete als Rechtsanwalt, bevor er wieder zu schreiben begann. Für seine Romane wie »El apicultor de Bonaparte« (1996) erhielt er zahlreiche spanische Literaturpreise. Der Autor und Verfasser von Buchrezensionen lebt auf Mallorca.

born in 1959, writes for various newspapers and magazines, and has established himself as one of the most profound experts in boxing. For severals years he worked as a media advisor for Axel Schulz and Henry Maske, with whom he edited a dictionary of boxing. In April 2003 he published the illustrated book »Boxen«, which is considered as »a standard work of international format.«

Bertram Job

geboren 1959, schreibt für verschieden Zeitungen und Magazine und hat sich als einer der profiliertesten Kenner des Boxsports etabliert. Mehrere Jahre lang arbeitete er als Medienberater für Axel Schulz und Henry Maske, mit dem er 1995 ein Boxlexikon veröffentlichte. Im April 2003 gab er den Text- und Bildband »Boxen« heraus, der als »Standardwerk von internationalem Format« gilt.

José Luis de Juan

Bertram Job

Allan Levine

was born in 1945. The professor of Sinology, translator and author lives in Bonn and Vienna. He writes poems, essays and stories. He was given various awards for his translations; for his volume of poetry »Narrentürme« he was awarded the Literature Prize 2003 of the Readers' Society. »Die Geschichte eines Kusses« is his first volume of prose. His third volume of poetry »Schattentänzer« is to be published soon.

Wolfgang Kubin

wurde 1945 geboren. Der Sinologe, Übersetzer und Schriftsteller lebt in Bonn und Wien. Er schreibt Lyrik, Essays und Erzählungen. Für seine Übersetzungen erhielt er mehrere Auszeichnungen, für den Gedichtband »Narrentürme« den Literaturpreis 2003 der Lesegesellschaft. »Die Geschichte eines Kusses« ist sein erster Erzählband. Sein dritter Gedichtband »Schattentänzer« erscheint in Kürze.

was born in Winnipeg, Canada. In 1999, he was awarded for »Fugitives of the Forest« the Yad Vashem Award. For the first volume of his crime trilogy featuring the Jewish detective Sam Klein, »The Blood Libel«, he received the Margaret McWilliams award. The second volume, »The Sins of the Suffragettes« was published in Germany in 2004. Levine teaches History at the St. John's Ravenscourt School in Winnipeg.

Allan Levine

wurde in Winnipeg, Kanada, geboren. Der Historiker erhielt 1999 für »Fugitives of the Forest« den Yad Vashem Preis. Der erste Band seiner Krimitrilogie um den jüdischen Detektiv Sam Klein, »The Blood Libel« (dt. »Mit falscher Zunge«, 2001) wurde mit dem Margaret McWilliams Award ausgezeichnet. Der zweite Band, »Die Sünden der Suffragetten«, erschien 2004. Levine unterrichtet Geschichte an der St. John's Ravenscourt School in Winnipeg.

was born in Stockholm, in 1948. Since 1968 he worked as a writer and director. In 1979 his first novel, »Fångvårdskolonin som försvann«, was published. In the 1980's, then he worked as a director and theatre manager, and he published in the 1990's his novells featuring inspector Wallander. In 1996 he directed the »Teatro Avenida« in Maputo, Mozambique. His children's books and novels were translated into numerous languages.

Henning Mankell

wurde 1948 in Stockholm geboren. Seit 1968 Tätigkeit als Autor und Theaterregisseur. 1979 erschien sein erster Roman: »Das Gefangenenlager, das verschwand«. In den Achtzigern arbeitete er auch als Regisseur und Intendant, in den Neunzigern entstanden seine Wallander-Romane. 1996 leitete er das »Teatro Avenida« in Maputo, Mosambik. Er schrieb Kinderbücher, die wie seine Romane in viele Sprachen übersetzt wurden.

was born in San Fernando, near Buenos Aires, in 1953. He studied Medicine and worked as a physician, he published poems and other texts, was educated in psychoanalysis, was involved in the work of various theatre groups and went on lecture and concert tours in Argentina. After the military coup of 1976, he emigrated via Brazil to Madrid, where he continued his numerous literary and musical activities.

Poni Micharvegas

was born in San Fernando, near Buenos Aires, in 1953. He studied Medicine and worked as a physician, he published poems and other texts, was educated in psychoanalysis, was involved in the work of various theatre groups and went on lecture and concert tours in Argentina. After the military coup of 1976, he emigrated via Brazil to Madrid, where he continued his numerous literary and musical activities.

Henning Mankell

Birgit Müller-Wieland

Marilene Phipps

was born in Schwanenstadt, Austria, in 1962. She studied German and Psychology and wrote a PhD on »The Aesthetics of Resistance« by Peter Weiss. She has published poems, prose, essays and stories for children in literary magazines, anthologies and on the radio, and has received several prizes. Her first collection of poems »Ruhig Blut« t: Calm blood) appeared in 2002. She has lived in Berlin since 1996.

Birgit Müller-Wieland

wurde 1962 in Schwanenstadt, Österreich, geboren. Sie studierte Germanistik und Psychologie und promovierte über »Die Ästhetik des Widerstands« von Peter Weiss. Sie veröffentlichte u. a. Lyrik, Prosa, Essays und Kindergeschichten in Literaturzeitschriften, Anthologien und im Rundfunk. Für ihre Arbeiten erhielt sie zahlreiche Auszeichnungen. Ihr erster Gedichtband »Ruhig Blut« erschien 2002. Seit 1996 arbeitet sie als freie Schriftstellerin in Berlin.

was born in Haiti. The artist and poet studied Anthropology and Art in the USA, where she lives today. Her artistic and poetic work is greatly inspired by the culture, nature and religion of Haiti. She is known internationally for her paintings. For the volume of poetry, »Crossroads and Unholy Water« (2000), she received the Crab Orchard Review Poetry Prize.

Marilene Phipps

wurde in Haiti geboren. Die Künstlerin und Dichterin studierte Anthropologie und Kunst in den USA, wo sie heute lebt. Sowohl ihre künstlerischen als auch ihre poetischen Werke sind stark von der Kultur, Natur und Religion Haitis inspiriert. Sie ist für ihre Malerei international bekannt. Für den Lyrikband »Crossroads and Unholy Water« (2000) erhielt sie den Crab Orchard Review Poetry Prize.

was born in Cologne in 1957. His first book, the historical novel »Tod und Teufel« was published in 1995. This was followed by »Mordshunger«, the short stories »Keine Angst« and the thriller »Die dunkle Seite« in 1999. His political thriller »Lautlos« appeared in 2000. Frank Schätzing is creative director of an advertising agency. His ecothriller »Der Schwarm« ranks currently top of the German bestseller list.

Frank Schätzing

wurde 1957 in Köln geboren. 1995 erschien sein erstes Buch, der historische Roman »Tod und Teufel«. Es folgten »Mordshunger« und 1999 die Kurzgeschichten »Keine Angst« sowie der Thriller »Die dunkle Seite«. 2000 erschien der Politthriller »Lautlos«. Frank Schätzing ist kreativer Geschäftsführer einer Kölner Werbeagentur. Sein Ökothriller »Der Schwarm« rangiert derzeit ganz oben auf den deutschen Bestsellerliste.

was born in Oberhausen in 1947. He studied Sinology, Political Science and Modern History in Heidelberg, Taipeh and Munich. Since 1980 he has been co-publisher of the »Kursbuch«. His first novel, »Lenins Hirn« (1991; Eng. »Lenin's Brain«, 1993), has been translated into 21 languages. He received the Ernst-Hoferichter-Preis in 2003 for his work. A freelance journalist and writer, he lives in Ambach and in Berlin.

Tilman Spengler

wurde 1947 in Oberhausen geboren. In Heidelberg, Taipeh und München studierte er Sinologie, Politologie und Neuere Geschichte. Seit 1980 ist er Mitherausgeber des »Kursbuch«. »Lenins Hirn« (1991), sein erster Roman, wurde in 21 Sprachen übersetzt. 2003 wurde er mit dem Ernst-Hoferichter-Preis für sein Schaffen ausgezeichnet. Er lebt als freier Journalist und Schriftsteller in Ambach und in Berlin.

Frank Schätzing

Gerald Uhlig

born in Heidelberg in 1953, worked after his studies of Music and Perfoming Arts in Vienna as a director and actor at several German-speaking theatres. As libretto writer and director he staged from 1992 to 1994 three musicals about Otto Dix, Pablo Picasso and George Grosz. With Yoko Ono he staged in 1996 the German premiere of »New York Story«. In 1996 he founded the »Cafe Einstein Unter den Linden«, including a gallery.

Gerald Uhlig

geboren 1953 in Heidelberg, studierte Musik und Schauspiel in Wien. Er arbeitete als Regisseur und Schauspieler an zahlreichen deutschsprachigen Theatern. 1992-1994 realisierte er als Librettist und Regisseur drei Musiktheaterprojekte über Otto Dix, Pablo Picasso und George Grosz. Mit Yoko Ono inszenierte er 1996 die deutsche Erstaufführung des Musicals »New York Story«. 1996 gründete er das »Cafe Einstein Unter den Linden« und dazugehörige Galerie.

geboren 1964 an der Nordsee, studierte Philosophie, Theaterwissenschaft und Vergleichende Literaturwissenschaft in München, Wien und Berlin. Der Autor zahlreicher Theaterstücke war als Dramaturg und Regieassistent u. a. am L' Odéon Théâtre Paris, sowie am Deutschen Theater Berlin tätig. 2002 erschien sein Gedichtzyklus »Südlich von Hagi«, 2004 »Labyrinth & Vermächtnis«. Er lebt in Berlin und Paris.

Stefan Ludmilla Wieszner

born on the German coast of the North Sea in 1964, studied philosophy, drama and comparative literature in Munich, Vienna and Berlin. He wrote numerous plays and worked as a dramatic advisor and assistant director at L'Odéon Théâtre, Paris, and at the Deutsches Theater, Berlin. His poems »Südlich von Hagi« was published in 2002, his volume of poetry »Labyrinth & Vermächtnis« in 2004. He lives in Berlin and Paris.

was born in Rudolstadt, Thuringia, in 1943 and grew up in Karlsruhe. He studied literature, philosophy and sociology. He advancing to a classic writer of contemporary German poetry as a »rock poet« in the 1970's. In 1971, he was awarded the Prize of the Blind Veterans of War for radio drama. In 1987 he followed up his fascination for boxing with »People Places Wrists«. The writer lives in Munich and Vienna.

Wolf Wondratschek

wurde 1943 in Rudolstadt/Thüringen geboren und wuchs in Karlsruhe auf. Er studierte Literaturwissenschaft, Philosophie und Soziologie. In den Siebzigern avancierte der »Rock Poet« zum Klassiker zeitgenössischer Lyrik. 1971 erhielt er den Hörspielpreis der Kriegsblinden. 1987 ging er mit »Menschen Orte Fäuste« seiner Faszination für den Boxsport nach. Der Autor lebt in München und Wien.

Wolf Wondratschek

hayden chisholm
rebecca horn
hartwig klappert
jens komossa
jakob mattner
birgitta wollenweber

rebecca horn

biography I biographie

Born in 1944. Teaching since 1989 at the HdK (UdK) Berlin. Performance, installation, film, drawing and painting on photographs. In 1992 Kaiserring from the town Goslar and Medienkunstpreis Karlsruhe. Solo exhibitions e.g., in the Guggenheim Museum New York, the Neue Nationalgalerie Berlin, the Tate Gallery London and in 2001 at the Irish Museum of Modern Art, Dublin. The artist lives in Berlin and Paris.

Geb. 1944. Seit 1989 Lehrtätigkeit an der HdK (UdK) Berlin. Performances, Installationen, Filme, Zeichnungen und Fotoübermalungen. 1992 Kaiserring der Stadt Goslar und Medienkunstpreis Karlsruhe. Einzelausstellungen unter anderem im Guggenheim Museum New York, in der Neuen Nationalgalerie Berlin, in der Tate Gallery London, 2001 im Irish Museum of Modern Art, Dublin. Die Künstlerin lebt in Berlin and Paris.

hartwig klappert

biography I biographie

Born in Siegen, Germany in 1947 and studied graphic design at the HdK (UdK) Berlin. After working as art director for the advertising agency Gruppe 96, he became a freelance photo designer in 1975. He held a guest professorship at the Hochschule für Bildende Künste in Braunschweig from 1994-97. He lives in Berlin.

Geb. 1947 in Siegen. Nach dem Abitur Grafik-Design-Studium an der HdK (UdK) Berlin. Nach Tätigkeit als Art-Director in der Werbeagentur Gruppe 96 machte er sich 1975 als Foto-Designer selbstständig. 1994-97 hatte er eine Gastprofessur an der Hochschule für Bildende Künste in Braunschweig inne. Er wohnt in Berlin.

jens komossa

biography | biographie

When the stage of daily life is abandoned by its actors, Jens Komossa reaches for his camera. His enigmatic, revery-filled »night photos«, taken through hour-long light exposure, have already been seen on the ilb's poster series in 2003. After finishing his studies at the Folkwang School in Essen, followed by a working residency in Paris, Komossa came to Berlin in 1994 to devote his work to the facets of night. It originated from »Berliner Zimmer«, a series of views out a window, which focuses on the junction of public and private space, staged theatre, and is free from the clichés which a more intimate portrait of Berlin would impart. After his series »Berlinchen«, »Juist« and »Berlin Nacht«, he recently compiled a series of »television rooms« in Berlin and New York, soon to appear as a book with accompanying texts by German and American authors. At present Jens Komossa is developing the series »Wandbilder«, in which constellations of space are challenged and turned into the stage of the beholder's imagination. Komossa, who is represented by the Cologn-based gallery Sabine Schmidt, has meanwhile been featured at international art fairs such as Art Cologne or Paris Photo. Since 2003 he has been Deputy Professor of Photography at FH Mainz. Further information on the work of Jens Komossa is available at www.komossa.net.

Wenn die tagsüber bespielte Bühne von ihren Akteuren zurückgelassen wird, greift Jens Komossa zu seiner Fotokamera. Seine rätselhaft entrückten »Nachtaufnahmen«, die durch stundenlange Belichtungszeit entstehen, schmückten bereits 2003 die Plakatserie des ilb. Nach Abschluss seines Studiums an der Folkwangschule in Essen und Arbeitsaufenthalten in Paris kam Komossa 1994 nach Berlin, um hier seine Arbeit den Facetten der Nacht zu widmen. Es entstanden die »Berliner Zimmer«, eine Serie von Fensterausblicken, die das Aufeinandertreffen von öffentlichem Raum und privat inszenierter Bühne thematisiert und jenseits von Klischees ein intimes Berlin-Bild vermittelt. Nach Serien wie »Berlinchen«, »Juist« und »Berlin Nacht« erarbeitete er zuletzt eine Serie von »Fernsehzimmern« in Berlin und New York, die in Kombination mit Texten deutscher und amerikanischer Autoren demnächst als Buch erscheinen soll. Aktuell entwickelt Jens Komossa die Reihe »Wandbilder«, in der Raumkonstellationen hinterfragt und zur Bühne der Imaginationen des Betrachters werden. Der von der Kölner Galeristin Sabine Schmidt vertretene Künstler wird mittlerweile auf internationalen Kunstmessen wie der Art Cologne oder Paris Photo gezeigt. Seit 2003 ist er Vertretungs-Professor für Fotografie an der FH Mainz. Weitere Informationen zu den Arbeiten von Jens Komossa unter www.komossa.net.

hayden chisholm

biography | biographie

Born in Auckland, New Zealand in 1975. He studied composition and saxophone in Switzerland, Greece, India, Yugoslavia, Japan and Cologne. Since 1995 concert tours of India, Europe, Africa, Latin America. Numerous collaborations with artists and musicians, e. g. since 2002 with Rebecca Horn.

Geb. 1975 in Auckland, Neuseeland. Der Komponist und Saxophonist studierte in der Schweiz, Griechenland, Indien, Jugoslawien, Japan und in Köln. Seit 1995 Konzerttourneen durch Indien, Europa, Afrika, Südamerika. Zahlreiche Kooperationen mit Musikern und Künstlern, darunter seit 2002 mit Rebecca Horn.

jakob mattner

biography I biographie

Jakob Mattner, born 1946 in Lübeck, studied at the Hochschule der Künste in Berlin until 1972. A scholarship awarded by the Berliner Akademie der Künste took him to the Villa Serpentara in Olevano. He spent 1973 to 1974 in Rome on a DAAD scholarship. Assisted by the German Interior Ministry, he spent the next year in the Cité des Arts in Paris. In 1981 he was awarded an arts scholarship by the Kunstfonds in Bonn. He received the Villa Romana Prize from Florence in 1977 and the arts award of the Heitland Foundation, Celle in 1994.
Jakob Mattner's image compositions and installations have already been exhibited in numerous cities at home and abroad, including Munich, Berlin, Geneva, Paris, Barcelona, Moscow and New York. In 1996 the artist designed a »light curtain« for the Hebbel Theater in Berlin. Other »curtains« have been on display since 1999 at the Hessische Landesbank, Frankfurt/Main. He has exhibited works from his series »Zwielicht« (Twilight), compositions of light and shadow, at the Hamburger Bahnhof in Berlin. At EXPO 2000 in Hanover he arranged the stage for »Wörter:Welt« and »Lied:Strahl« at the theatre in the German pavilion. Since, 2001 Mattner has been stage designer at the Berlin Literature Festival. In 2002 the Moritzburg, Halle/Saale, presented his exhibition »Camera Lucida«. At the Salzburg Festival Mattner was stage and costume designer for the performance of »Musiquette Poétique« which was directed by Robert Gernhardt and Martin Mosebach. Mattner lives in Berlin.

Jakob Mattner wurde 1946 in Lübeck geboren. Er studierte bis 1972 an der Hochschule der Künste in Berlin. Danach führte ihn ein Stipendium der Berliner Akademie der Künste in die Villa Serpentara nach Olevano. 1973/74 hielt er sich als DAAD-Stipendiat in Rom auf. Unterstützt vom Bundesministerium des Inneren, residierte er im Jahr darauf in der Cité des Arts, Paris. 1981 war er Stipendiat des Kunstfond, Bonn. Er erhielt 1977 den Villa-Romana-Preis, Florenz, und 1994 den Kunstpreis der Heitland Foundation, Celle.
Jakob Mattners Bildkompositionen und Installationen wurden bereits in zahlreichen Städten des In- und Auslands ausgestellt, unter anderem in München, Berlin, Genf, Paris, Barcelona, Moskau und New York. 1996 gestaltete der Künstler einen »Lichtvorhang« für das Hebbel-Theater Berlin. Weitere »Vorhänge« sind seit 1999 in der Hessischen Landesbank, Frankfurt a. M., zu sehen. Mit Werken aus der Reihe »Zwielicht«, Kompositionen aus Licht und Schatten, trat er im Hamburger Bahnhof, Berlin auf. Für die EXPO 2000 in Hannover stattete er die Bühne für »Wörter:Welt« und »Lied:Strahl« im Theater des Deutschen Pavillons aus. Für das internationale literaturfestival berlin gestaltet er seit 2001 die Bühne. 2002 präsentierte die Moritzburg, Halle/Saale, seine Ausstellung »Camera Lucida«. Für die Aufführung »Musiquette Poétique« bei den Salzburger Festspielen, die Robert Gernhardt und Martin Mosebach ausrichteten, gestaltete Mattner die Bühne und die Kostüme. Jakob Mattner lebt in Berlin.

birgitta wollenweber

biography | biographie

Birgitta Wollenweber was born near Cologne. She studied at the College of Music in Detmold, being a student of Prof. Renate Kretschmar-Fischer, and at the Royal College of Music in London. Brigitta Wollenweber gives concerts internationally as a soloist and as a member of chamber music ensembles. Her repertoire contains works of all eras. Radio and television stations hold numerous musical productions and recordings featuring her playing. Her discography contains, among others, many rediscovered composers. She teaches as a professor for piano at the »Hanns Eisler« College of Music in Berlin.

Birgitta Wollenweber wurde in der Nähe von Köln geboren. Sie studierte an der Hochschule für Musik in Detmold bei Prof. Renate Kretschmar-Fischer und am Royal College of Music in London. Birgitta Wollenweber konzertiert international als Solistin und Kammermusikpartnerin. Ihr Repertoire umfasst Werke sämtlicher Epochen. Es liegen zahlreiche Produktionen und Mitschnitte bei Funk und Fernsehen mit ihr vor. Ihre Diskographie beinhaltet u.a. viele wiederentdeckte Komponisten. Sie unterrichtet als Professorin für Klavier an der Hochschule für Musik »Hanns Eisler« Berlin.

berlińska polska

festa della letteratura

henryk bereska
aleksandra david
agnieszka dębska
brigitta helbig-mischewski
magdalena liskowski
anna krenz
lopez mausere
krzysztof niewrzęda
piotr olszówka
leszek oświęcimski
isabella potrykus
krzysztof pukański
michał szalonek
katarzyna weintraub

teodora ansaldo
sebastian baur
... e la luna?
roberto giardina
alessandro pirovano
fabrizia ramodino
franco sepe

Born in 1926 in Katowice-Szopienice (Upper Silesia, PL). Translator and publisher of Polish literature between Renaissance and contemporary. Poet and aphorist. He lives in Berlin.

Henryk Bereska

Geboren 1926 in Katowice-Szopienice (Oberschlesien/PL). Übersetzer und Herausgeber polnischer Literatur zwischen Renaissance und Gegenwart. Lyriker und Aphoristiker. Lebt in Berlin.

Born 1956 in Gdańsk; study of Polish Philology. Poet. First published in: »Ich bin der, der angekommen ist«. Since 2002 she is working for the website www.foreigner.de. She lives in Berlin.

Aleksandra David

Geboren 1956 in Gdańsk. Studierte Polonistik. Dichterin. Erstveröffentlichung im Buch »Ich bin der, der angekommen ist«. Seit 2002 arbeitet sie für die website www.foreigner.de. Sie wohnt in Berlin.

Henryk Bereska

Aleksandra David

Brigitta Helbig-Mischewski

Born in 1978 in Olsztyn, has lived in Germany since 1989. She works and studies in Berlin. Poet and translator. She has published in »Hamburger Ziegel«, »kursywa«, »WIR«, »Zeichen und Wunder«.

Agnieszka Dębska

Geboren 1978 in Olsztyn, lebt seit 1989 in Deutschland, arbeitet und studiert in Berlin. Dichterin, Übersetzerin. Veröffentlichungen in »Hamburger Ziegel«, »kursywa«, »WIR«, »Zeichen und Wunder«.

Born in 1963 in Szczecin, she studied Polish Philology in Szczecin and Slavic and German Philology in Bochum. She has published in: »Znakolog«, »Zeitschrift für Slawistik«, »Teksty drugie«, »Twórczość«, »Fa-Art«, »Polen und wir«, »Język a kultura« and »b1«. Her published books: »New-Age-Diskurs« (1995), »Jasmin-Gedichte« (1997), »Pałówa« (2000). Since 1983 in Germany, now in Berlin, where she teaches at the Humboldt University.

Brigitta Helbig-Mischewski

Geboren 1963 in Szczecin, studierte Polonistik in Szczecin sowie Slawistik und Germanistik in Bochum. Veröffentlichungen in: »Znakolog«, »Zeitschrift für Slawistik«, »Teksty drugie«, »Twórczość«, »Fa-Art«, »Polen und wir«, »Język a kultura« und »b1« u. a. Eigene Bücher: »New-Age-Diskurs« (1995), »Jasmin-Gedichte« (1997), »Pałówa« (2000). Seit 1983 lebt sie in Deutschland, zur Zeit in Berlin, wo sie an der Humboldt-Universität lehrt.

Born in 1971 in Gdańsk, studied Polish Philology and education science at the Humboldt University, is currently writing her thesis. Poet, translator and organiser of the international literary competition »Ich bin der, der angekommen ist«.

Magdalena Liskowski

Geboren 1971 in Gdańsk, studiert Polonistik und Pädagogik an der Humboldt Universität, schreibt in diesem Jahr ihre Diplomarbeit. Dichterin, Übersetzerin und Organisatorin des internationalen Literaturwettbewerbs »Ich bin der, der angekommen ist«.

Born in 1976 in Poznań. Studied architecture in Poznań and London. Painter, draughtswoman and journalist. Lives in Berlin since 2003 and since then she has already had seven exhibitions. In 2003 along with Jacek Slaski, she has co-founded Galerie Zero in Berlin-Kreuzberg.

Anna Krenz

Geboren 1976 in Poznań, studierte Architektur in Poznań und in London. Malerin, Zeichnerin, Journalistin. Wohnt seit 2003 in Berlin und hatte in dieser Zeit bereits sieben Ausstellungen. 2003 eröffnete sie mit Jacek Slaski die Galerie Zero in Kreuzberg.

Anna Krenz

Krzystof Niewrzęda

Born 1965 in Gdańsk. Poet, prose writer, playwrights for film and TV. Published in: »bruLion«, »b1«, »Tygodnik Literacki« and anthologies »Xerofeeria«, »Overground«, »Macie swych poetów«, »Geschrieben in Deutschland«. A book published by »Lampa i Iskra Boża«. Lives in Berlin.

Lopez Mausere

Geboren 1965 in Gdańsk. Dichter, Prosaist, Dramatiker. Er publizierte in Zeitschriften »bruLion«, »b1«, »Tygodnik Literacki«, in Anthologien »Xerofeeria«, »Overground«, »Macie swych poetów«, »Geschrieben in Deutschland«. Buchdebüt im Verlag »Lampa i Iskra Boża«. Er lebt in Berlin.

Born in 1964 in Szczecin. Poet, writer and playwright. Won the »Silver Pegas« in »European Competition of the Polish Poem of Emigration 97«. He published in periodicals »Akant«, »Arkusz«, »b1«, »Kolano«, »Pogranicza«, »Suplement«, »Twórczość« and also three volumes of poetry (1998, 1999, 2000) and a novel »w poszukiwaniu całości« (1999). Since 2001 has lived in Berlin.

Krzysztof Niewrzęda

Geboren 1964 in Szczecin. Dichter, Prosaist und Dramatiker. Ausgezeichnet mit dem »Silbernen Pegasus« im »Europäischen Wettbewerb des Polnischen Emigrationsgedichts 97«. Veröffentlichungen in Zeitschriften »Akant«, »Arkusz«, »b1«, »Kolano«, »Pogranicza«, »Suplement«, »Twórczość« sowie drei Gedichtbände (1998, 1999, 2000) und einen Roman »w poszukiwaniu całości« (1999). Lebt seit 2001 in Berlin.

Born in 1956 in Katowice, studied philosophy, religion science and art. 1989-1993 he worked for »taz«, afterwards for »Gazeta Wyborcza«. As Wiktor Winogradski he published a volumen of prose »Moabit Hilton« (1997) and »Herbapol czyli zielnik polski« (1998). Performs with the band »Don't Shelest«. He lives in Berlin.

Piotr Olszówka

Geboren 1956 in Katowice, studierte Philosophie, Religionswissenschaft und Kunst. 1989 bis 1993 Kolumnist bei der »taz«, dann Korrespondent der »Gazeta Wyborcza«. Unter dem Künstlernamen Wiktor Winogradski hat er 1997 ein Prosabändchen »Moabit Hilton« und 1998 »Herbapol czyli zielnik polski« veröffentlicht und tritt auch mit dem Trio »Don't Shelest« auf. Lebt in Berlin.

Born in 1959 in Koszalin, studied Polish language and literature in Gdańsk. Poet, publicist, co-founder of the periodical »Kolano«. Since 1998 has lived in Berlin. In 2004 his novel »Klub der polnischen Wurstmenschen« (t: Club of Polish sausage people) was published in German.

Leszek Oświęcimski

Geboren 1959 in Koszalin, studierte Polonistik in Gdańsk. Dichter, Publizist, einer der Gründer der Literaturzeitschrift »Kolano«. Seit 1998 lebt er in Berlin. 2002 erschien sein Roman »Klub der polnischen Wurstmenschen« (auf Deutsch 2004).

Piotr Olszówka

Isabella Potrykus

Krzysztof Pukański

Born in 1973 in Kartuzy, since 1989 in Germany. Poet (publications in anthologies and periodicals, one volume of poetry), organiser of the international literary competition »Ich bin der, der angekommen ist«.

Isabella Potrykus

Geboren 1973 in Kartuzy, lebt seit 1989 in Deutschland. Dichterin (Veröffentlichungen in Anthologien und Literaturzeitschriften, ein Gedichtband), Organisatorin des internationalen Literaturwettbewerbs »Ich bin der, der angekommen ist«.

Born in 1971 in Szczawnica. Interpreter, translator, concert manager and photographic artist. Lives and works in Berlin.

Krzysztof Pukański

Geboren 1971 in Szczawnica, Diplom-Dolmetscher, Übersetzer, Konzertmanager, Photokünstler. Lebt und arbeitet in Berlin.

Born in 1966. Has lived in Berlin since 1975. Prose writer and translator. He co-founded »Der Club der Polnischen Versager« (t: The Club of Polish loosers) in Berlin. Laureate of the Deutsche Welle Literary Contest in 2003.

Michał Szalonek

Geboren 1966. Lebt in Berlin seit 1975. Autor und Übersetzer. Mitbegründer des »Clubs der Polnischen Versager«. Erster Preis bei dem Literarischen Wettbewerb der Deutsche Welle 2003.

Born in 1947. A freelance journalist working for rbb, WDR, Deutsche Welle and the Polish-German magazine »Dialog«. She lives in Berlin.

Katarzyna Weintraub

Geboren 1947, ist freie Journalistin und arbeitet unter anderem für den rbb, den WDR, die Deutsche Welle und die deutsch-polnische Zeitschrift »Dialog«. Sie lebt in Berlin.

Born in Genoa in 1956. Former lawyer with the European Court of Justice in Luxembourg. Has been living in Berlin since 1990, working as an author and movie director for social and cultural documentaries addressing the problems of women living as political refugees in Berlin (»Avventura voce« about Giovanna Marini and »La mia terra promessa«). Also writes for the theatre.

Teodora Ansaldo

Geb. 1956 in Genua. Arbeitete als Rechtsanwältin beim Europäischen Gerichtshof. Seit 1990 in Berlin, wo sie als Autorin und Regisseurin für soziale und kulturelle Dokumentarfilme (»Avventura voce«, ein Film über Giovanna Marini und »La mia terra promessa«) über die Probleme der Frauen als politische Flüchtlinge in Berlin arbeitet. Schreibt auch fürs Theater.

Born in Toblach in 1950, trained as an actor in Vienna, Paris, and New York. Performed in numerous international theatre and television productions. Studied Linguistics, English Literature, Romance Languages, and Philosophy in Salzburg, Paris, and Berlin. Translates Italian (»Porci con le ali«), French (Jarry, Derrida, Vian), English, and Jiddish texts into German. Author, performer, and lecturer at the TU and FU Berlin.

Sebastian Baur

Geb. 1950 in Toblach. Schauspielausbildung in Wien, Paris und New York. Darsteller in zahlreichen internationalen Theater- und Fernsehproduktionen. Studium der Linguistik, Anglistik, Romanistik und Philosophie in Salzburg, Paris und Berlin. Übersetzer aus dem Italienischen (»Porci con le ali«), Französischen (Jarry, Derrida, Vian), Englischen und Jiddischen. Autor, Rezitator sowie Dozent an der TU und FU Berlin.

... e la luna?

Teodora Ansaldo

Roberto Giardina

An Italian singer (Eva Spagna) plays with a German guitarist (Holger Schliestedt). The singer also happens to know a cellist (Martin Klenk) and sings one of Mina's songs for the two of them – and before you know it they're off doing other things together, grooving as a trio; Italian music light as a warm summer afternoon comes into being ...

... e la luna?

Eine italienische Sängerin (Eva Spagna) macht mit einem deutschen Gitarristen Musik (Holger Schliestedt), kennt da auch noch einen Cellisten (Martin Klenk), singt ihnen ein Stück von Mina vor – und schnell ist man dabei, ein bisschen mehr zusammen zu machen, es groovt zu dritt, es entstehen italienische Stücke mit der Leichtigkeit eines warmen Sommernachmittages ...

Born in Palermo in 1940, moved to Germany (first to Bonn, then to Berlin) in 1986, where he has since been working as a foreign correspondent for »La Nazione« and »Il Resto del Carlino.« Writes novels and essays which have been translated into various languages, such as »Anleitung die Deutschen zu lieben« (»The Guide to Loving Germans«).

Roberto Giardina

Geb. 1940 in Palermo. Lebt in Deutschland seit 1986, zuerst in Bonn, dann in Berlin als Auslandskorrespondent für »La Nazione« und »Il Resto del Carlino«. Schriftsteller und Journalist, Autor von Romanen und Essays, die in diverse Sprachen übersetzt worden sind – u. a. »Anleitung die Deutschen zu lieben«.

Born in Milan in 1956, studied Law in Milan and Journalism in Berlin. Lived in London and a host of other European cities until finally settling in Berlin in 1981. Published his first book, »Berlino,« in 1987; his second book came out in 1991 bearing the same title. A freelance journalist from 1989 to 1994, he currently works as a translator and freelance author.

Alessandro Pirovano

Geb. 1956 in Mailand. Studierte Jura an der Universität Mailand und Journalismus in Berlin. Wohnte in London und verschiedenen anderen europäischen Städte und ließ sich ab 1981 in Berlin nieder. 1987 wurde sein Buch »Berlino« bei dem mailändischen Clup Verlag veröffentlicht und 1991 ein anderes Buch mit gleichem Titel bei Citta' Studi, Mailand. Von 1989 bis 1994 hat er als freier Journalist gearbeitet und ist heute Übersetzer und freier Autor.

Born in Naples in 1936, studied Literature and Romance Languages. Teacher. New Left activist in the sixties. Now lives as a freelance author and literary critic in Itri

Fabrizia Ramodino

Geb. 1936 in Neapel. Studium der Literaturwissenschaften und Romanistik. Lehrerin. In den sechziger Jahren in der Neuen Linken aktiv. Lebt als freie Schriftstellerin und Literaturkritikerin in Itri bei Neapel.

Fabrizia Ramondino

Franco Sepe

Born in Fondi, Italy, in 1955. Studied psychology and philosophy, lectured at the Institute for Psychology of the University of Rome. Received a research grant from the Consiglio Nazionale delle Ricerche (1979-80) to investigate the theoretical aspects of German Psychology at the Institute for Psychology at the FU Berlin. Assistant professor at the Institute for Romance Language and Literature at the FU from 1984 to 1995. Italian lector at the University of Potsdam since 1995. Also works as an author, correspondent for Italian newspapers, and freelance contributor to Italian and German periodicals.

Franco Sepe

Geb. 1955 in Fondi, Italien. Studium der Psychologie und Philosophie, wissenschaftliche Mitarbeit am Institut für Psychologie der Universität Rom. 1979-80 Forschungsstipendium der Consiglio Nazionale delle Ricerche zu wissenschaftstheoretischen Aspekten der deutschen Psychologie am Psychologischen Institut der Freien Universität Berlin. 1984 bis 1995 Lehrbeauftragter am Institut für Romanische Philologie der FU Berlin. Seit 1995 italienischer Lektor an der Universität Potsdam. Autor, Kulturkorrespondent für italienische Zeitungen und freier Mitarbeiter für italienische und deutsche Zeitschriften.

hiphop

slam ! revue

crauss
fuat
justus
krämerladen
taktlo$$
v-räter

gaby bila-günther
maroula blades
fiva
nora-eugenie gomringer
ulrich herlyn
emil jensen
maciej kaczka
stan lafleur
tracy splinter
ricardo peredo wende

Crauss

born in 1971, is a poet and member of literary circles, editor and publishes his works in several magazines und anthologies. He was awarded scholarships and prizes. His latest work »Crausstrophobie. Texte & Remixes« was published in the Lyrikedition 2000.

geb. 1971, ist Lyriker, Mitglied mehrerer Literaturgruppen, Redakteur und veröffentlicht seine Werke in verschiedenen Zeitschriften und Anthologien. Er wurde mit Stipendien und Preisen ausgezeichnet. Zuletzt erschien »Crausstrophobie. Texte & Remixes«.

Fuat

was born in Berlin in 1972, lived in Turkey and has now returned to Kreuzberg. His Turkish raps are stamped by his own life circumstances and political conditions in Turkey. Besides his »Hassikdir« tapes, he released the album »Rapüstad« (with Killa Hakan).

geb. 1972 in Berlin, lebte in der Türkei und nun in Kreuzberg. Seine türkischen Raps sind u. a. geprägt von eigenen Lebensumständen und den politischen Zuständen in der Türkei. Neben seinen »Hassikdir« tapes erschien das Album »Rapüstad« (mit Killa Hakan).

Crauss

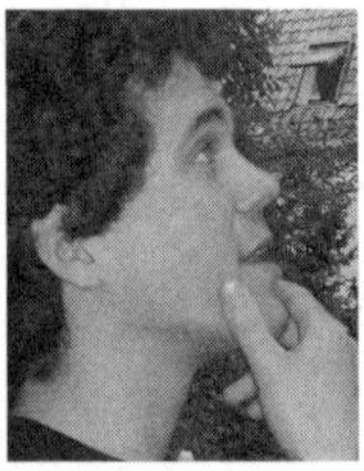
Justus

Krämerladen

Justus

geb. 1977, war Mitglied der Gruppe »M.O.R.«, nahm das Tape »Neue Wahrheit« und die LP »Zeichen und Muster« auf. Er bestritt zahllose Auftritte in Clubs, Discos und Jugendzentren. Exklusiv für das ilb gibt er einen seiner mittlerweile raren Auftritte.

was born in 1977. He was a member of the »M.O.R.« group, recorded the tape »Neue Wahrheit« and the LP »Zeichen und Muster« and did numerous gigs in clubs, discotheques and youth centers. He will be making one of his rare appearances exclusively for the ilb.

Krämerladen

formed together in 2000. They consist of Cris Colombo, El.dari and Monomo. They interface spoken word, contemporary Electro and HipHop and published their first EP »Inventur«; in spring 2004 they founded the online-label »Kwatro.com«.

gibt es seit 2000 und besteht aus Cris Colombo, El.dari und Monomo. Sie verbinden Spoken Word, aktuellen Electro und HipHop. 2003 veröffentlichten die Mitglieder ihre erste EP »Inventur« und gründeten im Frühjahr 2004 das Online-Label »Kwatro.com«.

whose name reflects his programme, was born in 1975 and a member of »West-Berlin Maskulin«. Having released nine albums (the latest was »BRP56«.) and founding his label »Fick die Biaaatch Recordz«, he must be ranked among the classics in German rap.

Taktlo$$

geb. 1975, dessen Name Programm ist, war bis 2000 Mitglied von »Westberlin Maskulin«. Mit Veröffentlichungen und der Gründung des Labels »Fick die Biaaatch Recordz« zählt er zu den Klassikern des deutschen Raps. Sein letztes Album heißt »BRP56«.

Martin is V-räter with »Sichtbeton«, beat programmer and interfaces rap and poetry. With his mixed tapes he crosses genre borders: Electro meets abstract HipHop and Soul. By night a member of »Funkviertel«, he works the turntables for Marcello and V-mann.

V-räter

Martin ist V-räter bei »Sichtbeton«, Beatprogrammierer und verbindet Rap und Lyrik. Mit seinen Mixtapes überschreitet er Genregrenzen: Electro trifft HipHop und Soul. Abends steht er für Marcello und V-mann als Teil des Künstlerkollektivs »Funkviertel« an den Plattenspielern.

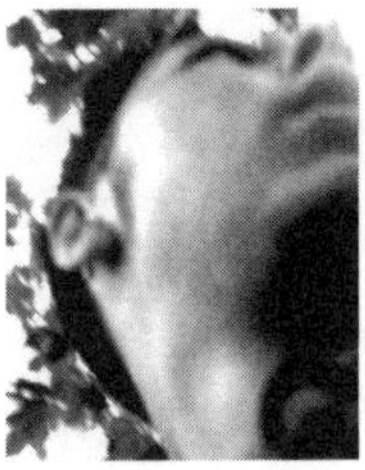
V-räter

born in Romania. Lived in Australia from 1995 to 2000, where she took a degree in »Professional Writing and Editing«. Her poetry and short stories have been published in Australia, Germany and Britain. She is one of the founders of »Flush«, a group of artists who perform spontaneously in public places.

Gaby Bila-Günther

kommt ursprünglich aus Rumänien. 1995 bis 2000 Australien, Abschluss in »Professional Writing and Editing« in Melbourne. Gedichte, Kurzgeschichten wurden u. a. in Australien, Deutschland und Großbritannien veröffentlicht. Mitbegründerin der Künstlergruppe »Flush«, die spontan an öffentlichen Plätzen auftritt.

born in Southhampton, UK, in 1964, professional singer and poet. Has been living in Berlin since 1992. Performs in locations such as Berlin's only English language theatre »Friends of the Italian Opera«. Successful participant in various competitions; several times winner of the International Poetry Competition in Scotland.

Maroula Blades

wurde 1964 in Southhampton, Großbritannien, geboren, ausgebildete Sängerin und Poetin. Seit 1992 in Berlin, performt u. a. im einzigen englischsprachigen Theater »Friends of the Italian Opera«. In zahlreichen Wettbewerben erfolgreich, mehrfache Gewinnerin des International Poetry Competition in Schottland.

Maroula Blades

Fiva

Ulrich Herlyn

started performing together with rapper Radrum in 1999. 2001 they signed with the Hamburg record label Buback. Despite having been trained as bookseller and publisher and studying at the university of Munich, music is her main occupation.

Fiva

tat sich 1999 mit dem Rapper Radrum zusammen. 2001 unterschrieben sie einen Vertrag bei dem Hamburger Label Buback. Trotz ihrer Ausbildung zur Verlagskauffrau und dem Studium an der Uni in München ist die Musik für Fiva der wichtigste Lebensinhalt.

born in Neunkirchen / Saar in 1980, student of English and German studies. Lived abroad in Los Angeles, New York and elsewhere. Organiser of poetry slams and founder of the bego publishing house. First collection of poems published in 2000, received Hattinger literary award in 2003.

Nora-Eugenie Gomringer

geboren 1980 in Neunkirchen / Saar, studiert Germanistik und Anglistik, zahlreiche Auslandsaufenthalte u. a. Los Angeles und New York. Sie organisiert Poetry Slams, ist Gründerin des bego-Verlags. 2000 erster Lyrikband, 2003 erhielt sie den Hattinger Literaturpreis.

born in 1966, lives in Greifswald. Received a wood carvers training at Oberammergau; studied as a sculptor at the State Acadamy of Art and Design Stuttgart. Received a Waldorf school teacher training and has been teaching at the free Waldorf school in Greifswald since 2001. Winner of Greifswald's first Poetry Slam in 2003.

Ulrich Herlyn

geboren 1966, lebt in Greifswald. Ausbildung zum Herrgottsschnitzer in Oberammergau; Studium der freien Bildhauerei an der Kunstakademie zu Stuttgart. Später Studium zum Waldorflehrer; seit 2001 an der Freien Waldorfschule in Greifswald tätig. 2003 Gewinner des ersten Greifswalder Poetry Slams.

born in Sweden in 1974, poet, dramatist and musician. His performances are a mixture of lyric, spoken word, theatre and music. Recently signed with the Swedish record label Adrian Recordings. Swedish SLAM Champion of 2003.

Emil Jensen

1974 in Schweden geboren, Poet, Dramatiker und Musiker. Seine Performances sind eine Mischung aus Lyrik, Spoken Word, Theater und Musik. Seit kurzem beim schwedischen Label Adrian Recordings unter Vertrag. 2003 wurde er schwedischer SLAM-Champion.

born in 1966, lives in Krakow. He is a slam poet, singer-songwriter and comedian. His actual job is as a travel agent; he is a patron of pub-frequenting young writers.

Maciej Kaczka

geboren 1966, lebt in Krakau. Er ist Slam-Dichter, Liedermacher, Hobbysänger, Kabarettist. Von Beruf Reiseveranstalter, unterstützt er als Mäzen das Kneipenleben junger Schriftsteller.

born in Karlsruhe in 1968, lives in Cologne. 1994-1998 publisher of the magazine »elektro-pansen«, founder of a »Speaker's Corner« in the city garden of Cologne. Winner of several poetry slams, received Rolf Dieter Brinkmann grant in 2001 and the literary award of the state of North Rhein-Westphalia in 2002.

Stan Lafleur

1968 geboren in Karlsruhe, lebt in Köln. 1994 bis 1998 Herausgeber der Zeitschrift »elektropansen«. Gründete die Kölner »Sprechecke« im Stadtgarten. Gewann Poetry Slams und erhielt u. a. 2001 das Rolf Dieter Brinkmann-Stipendium und 2002 den Literaturpreis des Landes Nordrhein-Westfalen für Lyrik.

Emil Jensen

Stan Lafleur

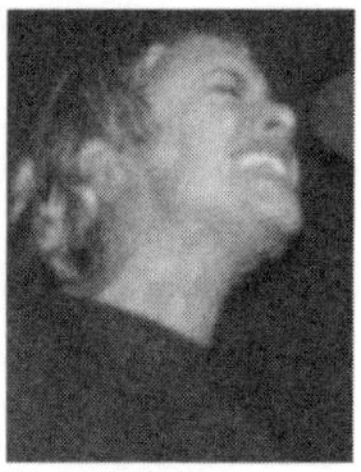
Tracy Splinter

born in Cape Town, South Africa, in 1971, lives in Hamburg. Well known as a performer in Berlin, Munich and Rotterdam, with the series »Wired On Words« and other spoken word readings. Won the poetry competition of the Hamburg Literature House in 2000, did her first poetry clip for MTV Europe in Berlin the same year. Released her debut album »Verbalize« with Ariel publishers.

Tracy Splinter

geboren 1971 in Kapstadt, Südafrika, lebt heute Hamburg. Performerin, bekannt in der Hamburger, Berliner, Münchner und Rotterdamer Szene u. a. mit »Wired On Words«, einer »spoken poetry« Lesungsreihe. 2000 gewann sie den Lyrikwettbewerb des Literaturhauses Hamburg; im selben Jahr der erste Poetry Clip für MTV Europe in Berlin. Ihre Debut-CD »Verbalize« ist im Ariel-Verlag erschienen.

born in La Paz, Bolivia, in 1962, musician, painter, performer and film maker. Degree in »Audiovisual Media«, senior pupil of Nam June Paik at the art acadamy in Düsseldorf. Participant of festivals such as the New York Video and New Media Festival and the Berlin International Film Festival. Exhibitions in Paris, Berlin, Venice, São Paulo and elsewhere.

Ricardo Peredo Wende

1962 in La Paz, Bolivien, geboren. Musiker, Maler, Performer und Filmemacher. Studierte »Audiovisuelle Medien« in Köln, war Meisterschüler von Nam June Paik an der Kunstakademie Düsseldorf. Teilnehmer u. a. des New York Video and New Media Festival und der Internationalen Filmfestspiele Berlin. Seine Werke wurden u. a. in Paris, Berlin, Venedig und São Paulo ausgestellt.

Andersen, U. I 140
Aufbau Verlag I S. 205
Barba Lopez, Andrés I S. 20
Bertini, Jean Luc / Opale I S. 54
Biermann, Pamela I S. 84
bloomsbury I S. 56
Brandt, Renate I S. 102
Buchkultur / Manfred Riegleder I S. 184
Caillot, Richard I S. 52
Derlath, Volker / A1 Verlag I S. 213
Deus, Lothar I S. 96, 104
Dreissinger, Sepp I S. 217
Dürer, Jenia I S. 110
edition nautilus I S. 208
Europa Universität Viadrina Frankfurt/O. I S. 207
Felbert, Peter von I S. 213
Fischer Verlag I S. 90
Fricke, Thomas I S. 152
Gelberg, Alexa I S. 172
Grupello Verlag I S. 68
Hagen, Eva-Maria I S. 201
Hanser Verlag I S. 215
Hattori, Shoichiro I S. 180
Hauser, Tony I S. 44
Hein, Christa I S. 212
Hermann, M. I S. 205
Hohhman, Adina I S. 94
Hubbard, Sally I S. 12
Hyman, David I S. 204
Iglesias, Carlos I S. 26
Karr, Timothy I S. 36
Klähn, Andreas I S. 108
Klappert, Hartwig / ilb I S. 150
Krogvold, Morten 1996 I S. 158
Lex, Sonja / Verein der Bücherwürmer I S. 196
Luján, Juana I S. 148
Maetzl, Julia / Jutta Treiber I S. 176
McCarter, Graham I S. 124
Medlicott, Charlotte I S. 201
Mehdizadeh, Omid I S. 178
Melis, Roger I S. 86
Mordzinski, Daniel I S. 28
Munk, Karin I S. 162
Ohlbaum, Isolde I S. 80, 126
Olofsson, Tommy / Grupp Fem I S. 166
Paustian, Sven / Suhrkamp I S. 106
Perrey, Ute I S. 220
Plachy, Silvia I S. 118
privat I S. 14, 18, 22, 24, 30, 32, 34, 38, 40, 42, 46, 50, 62, 64, 66, 72, 74, 78, 88, 98, 114, 116, 120, 144, 154, 156, 160, 164, 170, 174, 188, 190, 194, 200, 204, 205, 206, 207, 208, 212, 213, 214, 215, 220, 221, 222, 223, 226, 232, 234
Rival, André I S. 216
Rock, Sheila I S. 212
Rowohlt Verlag I S. 82
Sassier, J. I S. 128
Schindler, Barbara I S. 122
Schleyer, Susanne I S. 60
Schmitz, Paul I S. 216
Schröder, Harald H. I S. 92
Sillitoe, David I S. 48
Soesman, Monique I S. 138
spielboden 2004 I S. 100
Stieler, Helmut I S. 212
Stiens, Peter I S. 134
Subin, Nina I S. 16, 70
Subin, Nina / Suhrkamp I S. 142
SUM I S. 213
Tappe, Horst I S. 132
Transparency Organization I S. 205
Tsoublekas, Dimitris I S. 192
Týlzanowska, Hanna I S. 168
van der Hulst, Wim I S. 58
Vennemann, Gerd I S. 130
Wäldele, Martina I S. 136
Zöllner, Rolf I S. 112

Sonstige Biographen

Chloe Aridjis
Andrés Barba, Alonso Cueto, Álvaro Enrigue
Hanno Depner
Wolf Biermann, Alan Sillitoe
Beatrice Faßbender
Eliot Weinberger
Babette Jonas
Ayu Utami
Alexandra Kleihues
Bora Ćosić, Lars Gustafsson
Miriam Gabriela Möllers
mit Anna Holthaus, Hendrik Peeters, Karl-Sebastian Schulte
sämtliche Biographien
»Internationale Kinder- und Jugendliteratur«
Juliane Schmidt-Wellenburg
Rolf Hochhuth, Adrian Mitchell
Anne-Kathrin Schulz
Peter Truschner
Ute Stollreiter
Boualem Sansal
Jana Thiele
Christoph Hein, Gore Vidal

Ein ganz besonderer Dank gilt den Praktikanten des Lektorats:
Birthe Grabowsky, Juliane Helbig, Christoph Janke, Virginia Maiorino, Jana Obermüller

Das internationale literaturfestival berlin ist eine Veranstaltung der Peter-Weiss-Stiftung für Kunst und Politik e.V. und der Berliner Festspiele unter der Schirmherrschaft der Deutschen UNESCO-Kommission. Es wird ermöglicht aus Mitteln des Hauptstadtkulturfonds.

Förderer
argonauten360 gmbh, MIM Multi International Media GmbH, Hayn/ Willemeit Media GmbH, Vöslauer Mineralwasser AG, illy cafe, Berliner Kindl Brauerei AG (Sponsor des Musikprogramms), Zapf Umzüge GmbH, DER SPIEGEL, Škoda Auto Deutschland GmbH (Hauptsponsor des Programms »Internationale Kinder- und Jugendliteratur«), Dresdner Bank AG, Hotel Brandenburger Hof, Weinhandlung Foradori.

Unterstützer
Berliner Ensemble, Berliner Flughafen GmbH, C. Bechstein Pianofortefabrik AG Berlin, C.H. Beck, Copy Clara Goethestraße, Deuticke Verlag, Deutsche Bahn/ICE, Dinamix Werbemedien GmbH, Evangelische Jeremia Kirchengemeinde Spandau, Flughafen GmbHs in Frankfurt, Nürnberg, Düsseldorf, Stuttgart und Dortmund, Friedrich-Ebert-Stiftung, G.M.X.Y., Hebbel am Ufer (HAU 1-3), Heinrich-Böll-Stiftung, Hessischer Rundfunk/Kanal 4, JSB GmbH, Kalkscheune, Literaturhaus Berlin, LiteraTurm - 2. Literaturfest der Stadt Frankfurt am Main, Makarov-Stiftung, Merlin Verlag, Minhoff GmbH, Myllykoski Sales GmbH, Nautilus Verlag, Osteria Nr. 1, Pegasus Hostel, primeline.werbemedien gmbh, Robert Bosch Stiftung, Sale e Tabbacchi, Sony Center Entertainment Berlin, Stiftung Starke, TNT.

Medienpartner
Lettre International, Radio Eins, Kulturradio, RBB Fernsehen, Berliner Zeitung, The Guardian, tip, Perlentaucher Medien GmbH.

Botschaften und Kulturinstitute
Australian Embassy, British Council, Bureau du Livre de Jeunesse, Canada Council, Collegium Hungaricum Berlin, Botschaft von Frankreich, Generalkommissariat für internationale Beziehungen der Gemeinschaft Wallonie-Bruxelles und der Delegation Wallonie-Bruxelles in Berlin, Goethe Institut Berlin, Indische Botschaft, Botschaft der Republik Indonesien, Institut Français - Bureau de Cinéma, Instituto Cervantes, Italienische Botschaft/Italienisches Kulturinstitut, The Japan Foundation, Botschaft von Kanada, Botschaft der Republik Lettland, Literature Centre Kopenhagen, Botschaft des Königreichs der Niederlande, NLPVF/Stiftung für die Produktion und Übersetzung niederländischer Literatur, NORLA - Norwegian Literature Abroad, Königlich Norwegische Botschaft, Botschaft der Republik Polen, Polnisches Institut in Berlin, Schwedische Botschaft, Slowakisches Institut, Botschaft von Spanien/Kulturabteilung, Botschaft der Republik Südafrika, Tschechisches Zentrum, Botschaft der Vereinigten Staaten von Amerika.

Hotels
ABACUS Tierpark Hotel, Angleterre Hotel, Hotel Bogotá, Hotel Brandenburger Hof, Citadines Apart Hotel Berlin, Dietrich-Bonhoeffer-Haus, East Side City Hotel Berlin, Estrel Berlin, Hotel Gendarm, Hotel Hansablick Garni, Hecker's Hotel Berlin, Hotel Heidelberg Garni, Hilton Berlin, Holiday Inn Berlin City Centre East, Hostel am Tierpark, Hotel Morgenland, Hotel an der Oper, Künstlerheim Luise, Mercure Hotel Berlin Mitte, relexa hotel Stuttgarter Hof, Hotel Riehmers Hofgarten, Hotel Savoy, Sorat Hotel Spree-Bogen Berlin, Hotel Villa Kastania.

Restaurants
Cassambalis, Cibo Matto, Hackescher Hof, Oxymoron, Paris Bar, Rosmini Pastamanufaktur, Schwarzenraben, Trattoria la Grotta Azzurra, ZUCCA.

Kooperationspartner in Berlin und Brandenburg
Agentur Gesichter, ALPHABET, ART FORUM BERLIN, Berliner Filmkunsthaus Babylon, Berliner Märchentage, Besucher-Dienste der Staatlichen Museen zu Berlin PK, Brandenburgische Universitätsdruckerei, Broadway, Cabuwazi e.V., Café Einstein unter den Linden, Café Littéraire/TU Berlin, carrousel Theater an der Parkaue, Columbia TriStar Germany, Gäste des Berliner Künstlerprogramms des DAAD, Deutsches Herzzentrum, Deutsches Historisches Museum, Deutsches Theater, Die gelbe Villa Kreativ- und Freizeitzentrum für Kinder und Jugendliche, Dorotheenstädischer Friedhof, Evas Arche, Facharbeitskreis Kinder- und Jugendbibliothek Berlin, Filmtheater am Friedrichshain, Freunde der Deutschen Kinemathek, Friedrich-Bödecker-Kreis in Brandenburg e.V., Georg Klein (bild. Künstler), GRIPS Theater, Guardini Stiftung, Hastings Music GmbH, hentschel SCHAUSPIEL Theaterverlag, Ibero-Amerikanisches Institut, International Womens Club Berlin, JugendKulturService gGmbH, JVA Lichtenberg, JVA Moabit, JVA Tegel, Kaisersaal, Kiek Mal Die Berliner Kinderzeitung, Karstadt, Konken Studios, Kurvenstar, Kulturjahr der Zehn Mai 04 – Mai 05, LE MATOU, LesArt Berliner Zentrum für Kinder- und Jugendliteratur, Le Monde diplomatique, LISUM Berlin, LISUM Brandenburg, Literaturforum im Brechthaus, Lokalrunde im Café Moskau, Master School Drehbuch, MD Berlin, Middle East Media Research Institute, Ministerium für Bildung, Jugend und Sport Brandenburg, Mori Ogai Gedenkstätte, Museum für Kommunikation Berlin, Ö Filmproduktion GmbH, Partner für Berlin GmbH, Pfefferberg, Popkomm, Potsdamer Platz Arkaden, Quartier 205, Rosemarie Köhler (Autorin), SCC-RUNNING (real,- BERLIN-MARATHON), Schreibstudio, Schrumpfende Städte//Shrinking Cities, Schwartzkopffbuchwerke Hamburg & Berlin, Scriptforum Conference 2004, Senatsverwaltung für Bildung, Jugend und Sport, Berlin, Societa Dante Aligheri, Stiftung Brandenburger Tor, Studio Babelsberg GmbH, Tacheles e.V., Theater o.N., trasa (Kunstprojekt), Trick Wilk, TU Berlin, unesco-projekt-schulen, Unsicht Bar, uniRadio Berlin-Brandenburg, Universität der Künste Berlin, Weinmeisterhaus, Werkstatt der Kulturen, Whisky and Cigars, WIR – polnischer Literaturverein Berlin, Yorck Kino GmbH, vis-à-vis Film, Zentrale Landesbank Berlin, Zentral- und Landesbibliothek Berlin.

Kooperationspartner in Deutschland
Concorde Film, Deutsches Nationaltheater Weimar, Ficom Design, Kinderfilm GmbH, Phoenix, Westdeutscher Rundfunk WDR, »Sendung mit der Maus«, ZDF Nachtstudio.

Kooperationspartner international
Alte Schmiede, Wien, BAOBAB Kinderbuchfonds, Basel, Christina Olofson/CO.FILM, Estonian Film Foundation, Film Polski, Hollandfilm, International Board on Books for Young People (IBBY), Basel, International Festival of Festivals, Sankt Petersburg, Internationales Literaturfestival Leukerbad, Festivaletteratura Mantova, The Guardian Hay Festival, Bjørnsonfestivalen Molde og Nesset, Les Films des Tournelles, Lithuania Film Studio, National Film Centre Latvia, Norwegian Film Institute, Office National du Film du Canada, Portman Film, Prima Linea Productions, Robert-Musil-Institut der Universität Klagenfurt, Slovak Film Institute, Slovenian Film Fund, Swedish Film Institute, Yomiuri TV Co.

VON POLITTHRILLER BIS WIRTSCHAFTSKRIMI